U.S. Fish & Wildlife Service

Oxbow National Wildlife Refuge

Final Comprehensive Conservation Plan

January 2005

I0500451

This goose, designed by J.N. "Ding" Darling, has become the symbol of the National Wildlife Refuge System

The U.S. Fish and Wildlife Service is the principle federal agency for conserving, protecting, and enhancing fish and wildlife in their habitats for the continuing benefit of the American people. The Service manages the 96-million acre National Wildlife Refuge System comprised of 544 national wildlife refuges and thousands of waterfowl production areas. It also operates 65 national fish hatcheries and 78 ecological services field stations. The agency enforces federal wildlife laws, manages migratory bird populations, restores significant fisheries, conserves and restores wildlife habitat such as wetlands, administers the Endangered Species Act, and helps foreign governments with their conservation efforts. It also oversees the Federal Aid program which distributes hundreds of millions of dollars in excise taxes on fishing and hunting equipment to state wildlife agencies.

Comprehensive Conservation Plans provide long term guidance for management decisions; set forth goals, objectives, and strategies needed to accomplish refuge purposes; and, identify the Service's best estimate of future needs. These plans detail program planning levels that are sometimes substantially above current budget allocations and, as such, are primarily for Service strategic planning and program prioritization purposes. The plans do not constitute a commitment for staffing increases, operational and maintenance increases, or funding for future land acquisition.

Cover photo: Northern Flickers © Bruce Flaig

Comprehensive Conservation Plan Approval
for Oxbow National Wildlife Refuge

Submitted by:

_____   12/7/04
Elizabeth A. Herland   Date
Project Leader,
Eastern Massachusetts National
Wildlife Refuge Complex

Approved by:

_____   12/8/04
Richard W. Dyer   Date
Refuge Supervisor, North
National Wildlife Refuge System

Approved by:

_____   12/8/04
Anthony D. Léger   Date
Northeast Regional Chief,
National Wildlife Refuge System

Final Approval:

_____   1-5-05
Marvin E. Moriarty   Date
Regional Director, Region 5
U.S. Fish and Wildlife Service

Finding of No Significant Impact
Assabet River, Great Meadows, and Oxbow National Wildlife Refuges
Comprehensive Conservation Plans

The Draft Comprehensive Conservation Plan and Environmental Assessment (Draft CCP/EA) of July 2003 for Assabet River, Great Meadows, and Oxbow National Wildlife Refuges (NWRs) evaluated three management alternatives, carefully considering their impacts on the environment, and their potential contribution to the mission of the National Wildlife Refuge System, and each refuge's purposes and goals. A brief summary of the three alternatives follows.

Alternative A: This was the No Action Alternative in the Draft CCP/EA required by the Council of Environmental Quality's regulations on implementing the National Environmental Policy Act. Under this alternative, there would be no change from our current resource management programs on refuge lands. The refuges continue programs they currently have in place. No new efforts are undertaken, and land acquisition occurs only for those parcels already within the approved refuge boundaries.

Alternative B: This alternative was the Service's Proposed Action in the Draft CCP/EA. Land acquisition occurs only within the refuge boundaries. This alternative emphasizes inventorying and monitoring refuge resources. It includes increased opportunities for habitat management. This alternative also offers more wildlife observation, photography, environmental education, and interpretation opportunities as well as new hunting and fishing opportunities on all three refuges. Under this alternative dog walking is eliminated as an activity on the refuges.

Alternative C: Alternative C is similar to Alternative A, but places emphasis on a less intrusive management style. Inventory and monitoring of refuge resources would occur, but would be limited. The refuges would support similar programs as existing now, but not expand habitat management programs as Alternative B does. This alternative is also distinguished from others with less expansion of the priority public use opportunities and active management programs.

The draft CCP/EA was distributed for a 45 day public review and comment period from July 20th to September 3rd, 2003. After consideration of all public comments, I determined that this Environmental Assessment was sufficient to support my findings.

After careful review of the proposed management actions, and based on the analysis provided in the EA and the comments received during the review period, I have selected Alternative B (the Service's Proposed Action in the Draft CCP/EA) for implementation, with the following modifications:

- Alternative B proposed continuing to allow jogging on Great Meadows and Oxbow NWRs. We have completed a Compatibility Determination (CD) which concludes that jogging is compatible with refuge purposes. However, a study of the impacts of jogging on wildlife will be initiated and results evaluated to evaluate site specific impacts to wildlife. The CD will be reviewed and any appropriate changes will be made using the site specific data in 5 years.

- Alternative B proposed to eliminate all picnicking from the refuges. We have clarified our rules, such that no picnic tables will be provided nor will large gatherings or events involving food be permitted. Eating snacks on refuge benches and trails is allowed.

- Alternative B proposed a variety of hunting opportunities on all 3 refuges. We proposed creating hunting opportunities on Assabet River and Great Meadows NWRs and expanding hunting opportunities on Oxbow NWR. We have modified our hunting proposal:

  - We modified our original hunting proposal based upon additional analysis of state mandated safety zones, our ability to effectively administer the hunt program, and to balance the needs of the different wildlife-dependent recreationists.

  - We clarified that the waterfowl hunting areas along the Concord and Sudbury Rivers at Great Meadows and the Nashua River at Oxbow areas include the main stems of the rivers as well as adjacent wetlands and pools.

  - We adjusted the proposed waterfowl hunting areas to remove areas near concentrations of houses, playing fields, and high numbers of additional users.

  - The total acreage that we are proposing for waterfowl hunting is 1,192 acres.

  - We revised the deer hunting program to archery hunting only in areas of specific safety concern.

- We have revised the proposed fee program to be consistent with other Region 5 refuges and to encourage purchase of the "local" annual pass. Fees would be required at Assabet River, Oxbow (south of Route 2), and the Concord impoundments of Great Meadows. Visitors would be able to use a duck stamp in lieu of the refuge access fee. All access fees are per car or per group for pedestrians.

- We have not modified our proposal to eliminate dog-walking on Great Meadows and Oxbow NWRs. Assabet River NWR is not yet open to the public. When it opens, dog-walking will not be allowed.

I have selected Alternative B, with the modifications noted above, because it helps fulfill the mission of the National Wildlife Refuge System; best achieves each refuge's purposes, vision, and goals; maintains and, where appropriate, restores the ecological integrity of both refuges; addresses the significant issues identified during the planning process; and is consistent with principles of sound fish and wildlife management.

I find that the implementation of modified Alternative B will not have a significant impact on the quality of the human environment in accordance with Section 102 (2) (c) of the National Environmental Policy Act. It adheres to all legal mandates and Service policies. As such, I have concluded that an Environmental Impact Statement is not required, and this Finding of No Significant Impact is appropriate and warranted.

1-5-05

Marvin Moriarty
Regional Director
U.S. Fish and Wildlife Service
Hadley, Massachusetts

Date

Table of Contents

List of Figures

Chapter 1: Introduction and Background

This Final Comprehensive Conservation Plan (CCP) has been prepared for the Oxbow National Wildlife Refuge (NWR), which is one of eight refuges of the Eastern Massachusetts NWR Complex (Complex) (see Map 1-1). Concurrently, we are releasing the Final CCPs for Great Meadows (Concord and Sudbury Divisions), and Assabet River NWRs.

We will prepare a separate CCP and Environmental Impact Statement (CCP/EIS) for Monomoy and Nomans Land Island NWRs beginning later in 2004. We propose to begin the CCP process for Massasoit NWR in 2005 and Nantucket and Mashpee NWRs in 2006.

This CCP is the culmination of a planning process that began in January 1999. Numerous meetings with the public, the state, and conservation partners were held to identify and evaluate management alternatives. A draft CCP and Environmental Assessment (CCP/EA) was distributed in July 2003. This CCP presents the management goals, objectives, and strategies that we believe will best achieve our vision for the refuge, contribute to the National Wildlife Refuge System (Refuge System) Mission, achieve refuge purposes and legal mandates, and serve the American public.

Refuge Overview

The refuge is located in north-central Massachusetts, approximately 35 miles northwest of Boston, MA. The refuge lies within the towns of Ayer and Shirley in Middlesex County and the towns of Harvard and Lancaster in Worcester County. The refuge consists of approximately 1,667 acres of upland, southern New England floodplain forest and wetland communities along nearly 8 miles of the Nashua River corridor.

Oxbow NWR: USFWS photo

The refuge is a long, narrow parcel with a north/south orientation. Roadways running east/west divide the parcel into three sections. The northern end of the refuge abuts the former Fort Devens, Moore Army Airfield just south of Massachusetts Route 2A. Shirley Road/West Main Street in Ayer separates the northern and middle portions of the refuge. Massachusetts Route 2 bisects the middle and southern parcels. The refuge's southern boundary is at Still River Depot Road in Harvard, MA.

The refuge was formed by three land transfers from the former U.S. Army, Fort Devens Military Installation, and a recent purchase of private land in Harvard, MA. Two of the transfers from

Map 1-1: Eastern Massachusetts National Wildlife Refuge Complex

Eastern Massachusetts National Wildlife Refuge Complex
Massachusetts

Oxbow NWR

Concord Division

Assabet River NWR

Great Meadows NWR

Sudbury Division

Boston

ATLANTIC OCEAN

MA

Plymouth

Massasoit NWR

Cape Cod Bay

Providence

RI

Mashpee NWR

Chatham

Falmouth

Monomoy NWR

Newport

Nantucket Sound

Nantucket NWR

Martha's Vineyard

Nantucket Isl.

Nomans Land Island NWR

ATLANTIC OCEAN

Data Sources:
USFWS refuge boundaries

Map prepared for Oxbow National Wildlife
Refuge Comprehensive Conservation Plan,
August 2004. This map is for planning purposes only.

0   10   20   30   Miles

0   10   20   30   40 Kilometers

N

Oxbow National Wildlife Refuge

the Army (May, 1974 and February, 1988) formed the original 711.03 acre portion of the refuge located south of Massachusetts Route 2. The third Army transfer occurred in May of 1999, and added the 836.3 acre portion of the refuge that is located north of Route 2. Finally, approximately 120 acres was added to the refuge in April, 2001, with the acquisition of the former Watt Farm property along Still River Depot Road in Harvard.

The primary purpose for which the refuge was created is its "...particular value in carrying out the National Migratory Bird Management Program" (16 U.S.C. 667B, An Act Authorizing the Transfer of Certain Real Property for Wildlife, or Other Purposes, as amended). The refuge's interspersion of wetland, forested upland and old field habitats is ideally suited for this purpose. The refuge supports a diverse mix of migratory birds including waterfowl, wading birds, raptors, shorebirds, passerines, as well as resident mammals, reptiles, amphibians, fish and invertebrates. The extensive and regionally significant wetlands occurring on and adjacent to the refuge, including their associated tributary drainages and headwaters, have been listed as a priority for protection under both the North American Waterfowl Management Plan (NAWMP) and the Emergency Wetlands Resources Act of 1986.

The portion of the refuge south of Route 2 lies within the 12,900 acre Central Nashua River Valley Area of Critical Environmental Concern (ACEC) designated by the Massachusetts Secretary of Environmental Affairs due to its unique environmental characteristics and values (MADEP 1998). The refuge's geographic position, accessibility to the local and regional communities, and its diverse biological resources also makes it highly attractive for natural resource educational or interpretive programs, and compatible wildlife dependent recreational uses. An estimated 70,000 people visited the refuge in 2003. All of this use occurred within the older portion of the refuge, south of Route 2.

Purpose and Need for a CCP

The purpose of a CCP is to provide managers and other interested partners guidance and direction for each refuge over the next 15 years, thus achieving refuge purposes and contributing to the mission of the Refuge System. The plan identifies what role the refuges play, consistent with sound principles of fish and wildlife conservation, in the protection, enhancement and restoration of trust resources.

This plan is also needed to:
- provide a clear statement of desired future conditions for habitat, wildlife, visitors and facilities;
- provide refuge neighbors, visitors, and partners with a clear understanding of the reasons for management actions;
- ensure management reflects the policies and goals of the Refuge System and legal mandates;

- ensure the compatibility of current and future uses;
- review current boundaries of the refuges, and evaluate the need to revise boundaries to better achieve refuge purposes;
- provide long-term continuity and direction for refuge management; and,
- provide a basis for staffing and operations, maintenance, and the development of budget requests.

Currently, there is no management plan in place for the refuge that establishes priorities or provides consistent direction for managing fish, wildlife, habitats, and public uses on these refuges. This plan will help to resolve issues related to control of nuisance and invasive species, public uses in conflict with wildlife needs, lack of opportunities for wildlife dependent recreation, and the needs of our federal trust wildlife species.

U.S. Fish and Wildlife Service Mission

The Refuge System is managed by the U.S. Fish and Wildlife Service (Service) under the Department of Interior. The mission of the Service is:

"...working with others to conserve, protect, and enhance fish, wildlife, and plants and their habitats for the continuing benefit of the American people."

The Service manages NWRs, waterfowl protection areas, and National Fish Hatcheries. By law, Congress entrusts the following federal trust resources to the Service for conservation and protection: migratory birds and fish, endangered species, interjurisdictional fish, and certain marine mammals. The Service also enforces federal wildlife laws and international treaties on importing and exporting wildlife, assists with state fish and wildlife programs, and helps other countries develop wildlife conservation programs.

"To administer a national network of lands and waters for the conservation, management, and where appropriate, restoration of the fish, wildlife, and plant resources and their habitats within the United States for the benefit of present and future generations of Americans." (Refuge Improvement Act; Public Law 105-57)–*Mission of the Refuge System.*

National Wildlife Refuge System Mission

The Refuge System is the world's largest collection of lands and waters set aside specifically for the conservation of wildlife and ecosystem protection. The Refuge System consists of 544 national wildlife refuges that provide important habitat for native plants and many species of mammals, birds, fish, invertebrates, and threatened and endangered species, encompassing over 95 million acres. Refuges offer a wide variety of recreational opportunities, and many have visitor centers, wildlife trails, and environmental education programs. Nationwide, over 34 million visitors annually hunt, fish, observe and photograph wildlife, or participate in interpretive activities on NWRs.

In 1997, the National Wildlife Refuge Improvement Act (Refuge Improvement Act) established a unifying mission for the Refuge System, a new process for determining compatible public uses, and the requirement to prepare a CCP for each refuge. The new law states that the Refuge System must focus on wildlife conservation. It further states that the National mission, coupled with the purpose(s) for which each refuge was established, will provide the principal management direction for each refuge.

Laws

While the Refuge System mission and each refuge's purpose provide the foundation for management, NWRs are also governed by other federal laws, executive orders, treaties, interstate compacts, and regulations pertaining to the conservation and protection of natural and cultural resources (see appendix A for a more complete list of guiding laws).

A primary law affecting refuge management is the National Wildlife Refuge System Administration Act of 1966 (Administration Act) which authorizes the Secretary of the Interior to permit any uses of a refuge "...whenever it is determined that such uses are compatible with the major purposes for which such areas were established." The Administration Act was amended by the Refuge Improvement Act. It is also the key legislation on managing public uses, and protecting the Refuge System from incompatible or harmful human activities to insure that Americans can enjoy Refuge System lands and waters.

Beaver activity: Photo by Marijke Holtrop

Additionally, it is Service policy to address how each refuge, with an approved CCP, can help achieve the goals of the National Wilderness Preservation system. Thus, concurrent with the CCP process, we have incorporated a summary of a wilderness assessment into this document (see Wilderness Assessment section).

The Refuge Recreation Act of 1962 requires that any recreational use of refuge lands be compatible with the primary purposes for which a refuge was established and not inconsistent with other previously authorized operations.

The National Historic Preservation act of 1966 provides for the management of historic and archaeological resources that occur on any refuge. Other legislation, such as the Endangered Species Act, the North American Wetlands Conservation Act (NAWCA), the Wilderness Act of 1964 and particularly the National Environmental Policy Act (NEPA) all provide guidance for the conservation of fish and wildlife and their habitats.

National and Regional Conservation Plans and Initiatives Guiding this CCP

Gulf of Maine - Ecosystem Priorities

There are 52 ecosystem teams across the country. The refuge is located in the Gulf of Maine ecosystem (see Map 1-2). The ecosystem priorities that are applicable to the refuge are:

- Recover populations and habitats of endangered and threatened species.
- Protect, enhance, and restore coastal habitats for trust resources of concern.
- Protect, enhance, and restore populations of migratory bird species of special concern and their habitats.
- Manage Service lands to protect, enhance and restore habitats to maintain biodiversity.

North American Waterfowl Management Plan

The NAWMP documents the strategy between the United States, Canada and Mexico to restore waterfowl populations through habitat protection, restoration, and enhancement. Implementation of the plan is at the regional level. Ten regional habitat "joint ventures" are partnerships involving federal, state, provincial, tribal nations, local businesses, conservation organizations, and individual citizens. Units of the Complex are contained within the Atlantic Coast Joint Venture.

Wood Duck: Photo by Bruce Flaig

The Atlantic Coast Joint Venture Program identifies seven focus areas in Massachusetts. One of these focus areas includes the inland rivers of the Blackstone, Nashua, and the Sudbury-Assabet-Concord Rivers. Oxbow NWR is part of this focus area, with nationally significant wetlands that support migrating waterfowl. The Program is developing a focus area report that identifies important waterfowl resources, threats, and conservation recommendations.

A draft updated NAWMP document is at: http://birdhabitat.fws.gov/NAWMP/2003nawmpdraft.htm. In the Implementation Framework section of this document species priorities are listed for each region. Table 1-1 includes species identified in the NAWMP that occur at Oxbow NWR.

Table 1-1: NAWMP Species Occurring at Oxbow NWR

Species	Continental Priority	Breeding Importance	Breeding Need	Nonbreeding Importance	Nonbreeding Need
American Black Duck	High	Mod. High	High	High	Highest
Mallard	High	Mod. Low	Moderate	Mod. High	High
Green-winged Teal	Moderate			Mod. Low	Mod. Low
Wood Duck	Moderate	Mod. Low	Mod. Low	Mod. Low	Mod. Low

Oxbow National Wildlife Refuge

Map 1-2: Gulf of Maine Rivers Ecosystem

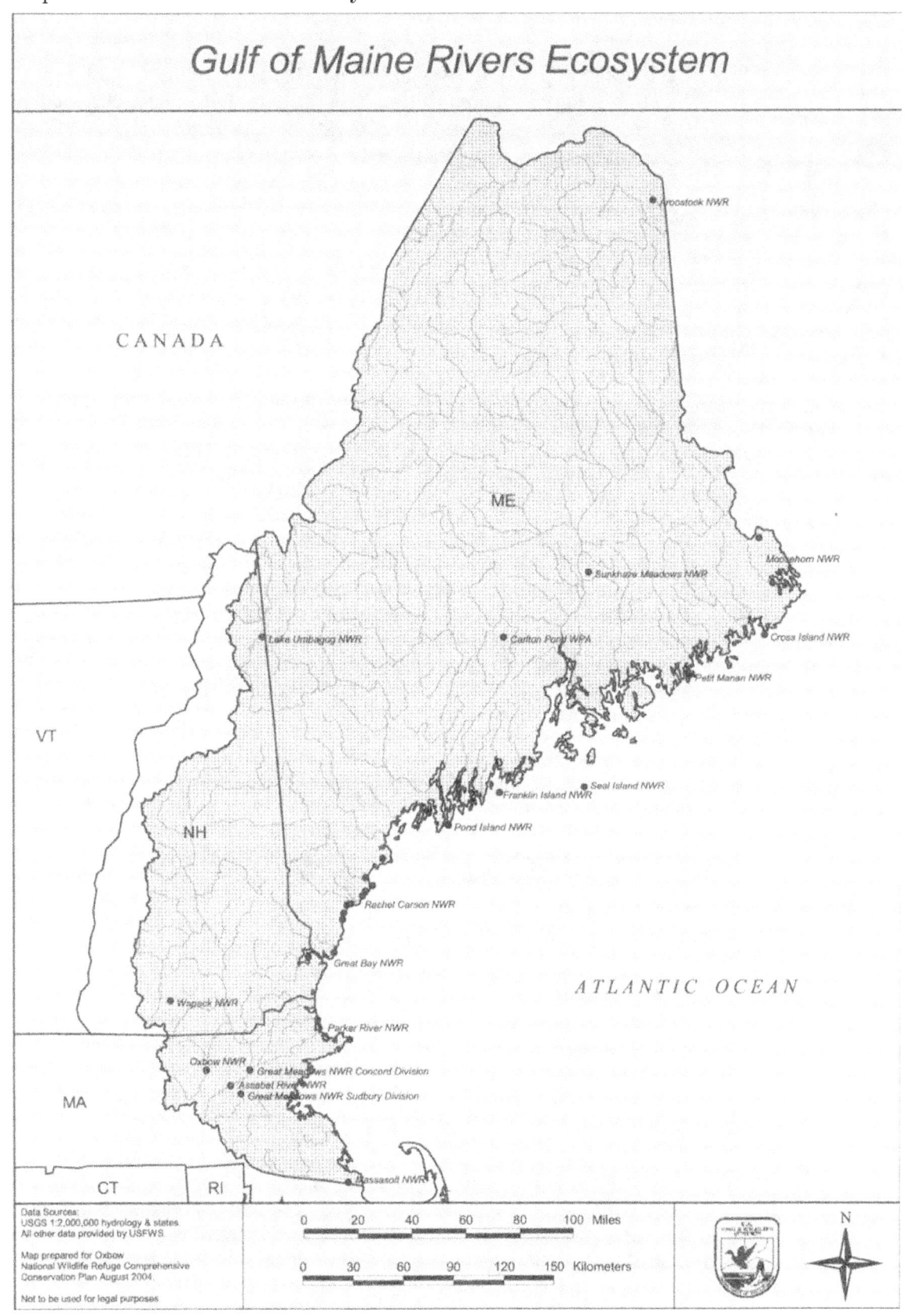

Partners in Flight Bird Conservation Plans

Partners in Flight (PIF) was initiated in 1990 as a voluntary, international coalition of agencies, organizations, institutions, industries, and other citizens dedicated to landbird conservation. The foundation for PIF's

long-term strategy for bird conservation is a series of scientifically based bird conservation plans. The goal of each PIF bird conservation plan is to ensure long-term maintenance of healthy populations of native landbirds. These plans use information on bird population trends, species' distributions, and the vulnerability of the species and their habitats to threats, to rank the conservation priority of birds occurring within a particular physiographic area.

American Goldfinch: Photo by Sandy Selesky

The PIF approach differs from many existing federal and state-level listing processes in that it (1) is voluntary and non-regulatory, and (2) focuses proactively on relatively common species in areas where conservation actions can be most effective, rather than local emphasis on rare and peripheral populations. A Landbird Conservation Plan for the southern New England physiographic area was completed in 2000, which includes all of eastern Massachusetts. This plan identifies 72 priority breeding bird species, 9 priority winter species, and 7 major habitat types as priorities for conservation in this area. Of the priority species for this physiographic area, at least 21 of the priority breeding species have been recorded as occurring on the refuge and 1 of the 9 wintering species have been recorded as wintering on the refuge. In the plan, focal species are selected for each habitat type and used in developing population and habitat objectives.

Implementation strategies and management guidelines for achieving these objectives are also included for each habitat type. Priority habitats for southern New England include maritime marshes, beaches/dunes, mature forest, early successional scrub/pine barrens, freshwater wetlands, and grasslands. The list of priority species, objectives, and conservation actions recommended in the southern New England Bird Conservation Plan will help direct landbird management on the refuge.

The North Atlantic Regional Shorebird Plan (NARSP), developed in 2001, identifies 38 priority shorebird species based upon a national scoring system that assesses population trends, relative abundance, threats and distribution patterns. The Service has recorded 4 of these species as occurring on the refuge. The NARSP builds upon the information in the U.S. Shorebird Conservation Plan (USSCP). The USSCP is a partnership involving organizations throughout the United States committed to the conservation of shorebirds. At a regional scale, the goal of the USSCP is to ensure that adequate quantity and quality of habitat is identified and maintained to support the different shorebirds that breed in, winter in, and migrate through each region. In August 2004, the USSCP was revised based upon the latest population and habitat information available. The revised list included 7 highly imperiled shorebird taxa and 23 taxa of high concern. The refuge supports 2 species of shorebirds of high concern.

Additionally, the Service has attempted to assess and integrate all the information above and compile a list of Birds of Conservation Concern for Bird Conservation Region 30, which contains the refuge. There are a total of 32 species listed, 6 of these have been recorded as occurring on the refuge.

Table 1-2: Bird Species of Concern Occurring on Oxbow NWR

Species	PIF		BCR 30	NARSP	USSCP
	Priority Breeding	Wintering	Conservation Concerns	Priority Shorebird	High Concern
Blue-winged warbler	●		●		
Wood Thrush	●		●		
Baltimore Oriole	●		●		
Scarlet Tanager					
American Woodcock	●			●	●
Rose-breasted Grosbeak	●				
Chimney Swift	●				
Eastern Wood-pewee	●				
Black-and-white Warbler	●				
Hairy Woodpecker	●				
Eastern Towhee	●				
Purple Finch	●				
American Black Duck	●	●			
Canada Warbler	●		●		
Whip-poor-will	●		●		
Sharp-shinned Hawk	●				
Pied-billed Grebe	●				
Short-eared Owl	●		●		
Osprey	●				
Great Blue Heron	●				
Killdeer				●	
Solitary Sandpiper				●	●
Spotted Sandpiper				●	
Least Sandpiper				●	

Regional Wetlands Concept Plan- Emergency Wetlands Resources Act

In 1986, Congress enacted the Emergency Wetlands Resources Act to promote the conservation of our nation's wetlands. This Act requires identification of the location and types of wetlands, and which lands should be targeted for state and federal land acquisition efforts. In 1990, the Northeast Regional Office of the Service completed a Regional Wetlands

Concept Plan to identify wetlands in the region. The Regional Plan identifies a total of 850 wetland sites and complexes in the region, two of them are within the Complex acquisition boundary. 2,000 acres of wetlands associated with the Nashua River were identified as being regionally valuable for wildlife, fisheries, recreation and water quality, quantity and flood control.

Our Irreplaceable Heritage - Protecting Biodiversity in Massachusetts, 1998

This report recommends that the State develop a biodiversity protection strategy that outlines how all native biodiversity will be conserved. It also identifies and describes eight types of natural communities that may require immediate conservation attention because of their potential vulnerability and large number of rare species they contain. Seven of the eight communities listed in the report occur within the Complex boundary.

Existing Partnerships

Throughout this CCP, we use the term "partners". In addition to our volunteers, we receive significant help from the following partners:

The Nashua River: Staff Photo

Freedom's Way Heritage Association
Friends of the Oxbow NWR
Harvard Conservation Trust
Massachusetts Department of Fish and Game (DFG), Division of Fisheries and Wildlife (MassWildlife)
Nashua River Watershed Association
Oxbow Associates
The Trust for Public Land

The Friends of the Oxbow NWR provide considerable time and effort toward accomplishment of refuge and Service goals. They participate in projects that lead to: land protection/acquisition, environmental education and outreach, provision of public use opportunities, such as guided interpretive walks, trail maintenance and kiosk maintenance/supplies, and meeting biological goals, such as assisting with surveys and habitat restoration. During fiscal year 2003, Friends of the Oxbow NWR contributed 1,301 hours of volunteer time on the refuge.

Chapter 2: The Comprehensive Conservation Planning Process

Given the mandate in the Refuge Improvement Act to develop a CCP for each NWR, we began the planning process in 1999. We started by forming a core planning team of refuge staff and Service planners from the regional office. We placed a Notice of Intent to prepare an EIS in the January 1999 Federal Register to officially kick-off our planning effort for all eight of the Complex refuges.

First, we collected information on our biological and habitat resources. While in the process of collecting information, we initiated the public scoping and involvement part of the process. We held meetings with each town's Board of Selectmen and state and federal agencies. Many of these groups provided information on natural resources and public uses on refuges in the Complex. In February of 1999, we held open houses in central locations to provide an opportunity for public comment on different issues including current and future management strategies, land protection and public uses. We were pleased with the participation at many of our meetings, which ranged from 30 people to over 100.

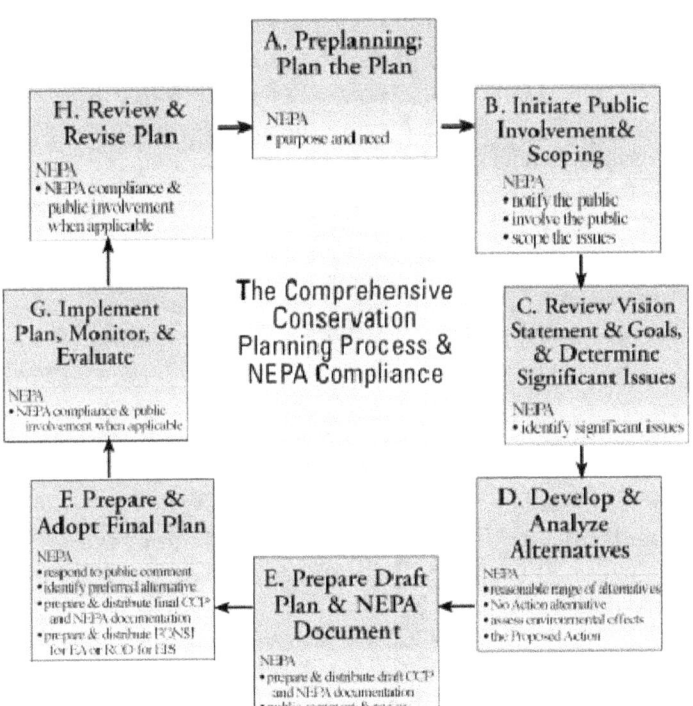

We recognized that attending our open houses would be difficult for many and designed an Issues Workbook to encourage additional comment. Over 8,000 people representing a variety of interests received workbooks. Workbooks were also available at open houses and at the refuge headquarters. We received over 660 responses.

Using the information collected from our partners and through public comment we identified significant issues to be addressed in the plan. In August of 1999, we distributed a Planning Update to everyone on our mailing list describing the key issues identified for each refuge.

Once key issues were determined and refined, we developed alternative strategies to address each one. We derived the strategies from public comment, follow-up contacts with partners and refuge staff. After a reasonable range of alternatives was identified, we evaluated the environmental consequences of each alternative.

In February of 2001 we recognized that producing a CCP/EIS for the entire Complex would be far too cumbersome to be efficient. At that time, we published a Notice of Intent to prepare a CCP/EA for five of the refuges in the Complex; Assabet River, Great Meadows, Oxbow, Mashpee and Massasoit NWRs. Additional issues and a need for more information prompted us to later split Mashpee and Massasoit NWRs from this draft as well.

The Service solicited comments on the draft CCP/EA for Great Meadows, Assabet River, and Oxbow NWRs from July 20 to September 3, 2003. We contracted with the U.S. Forest Service's Content Analysis Team (CAT) to compile the nearly 2,000 comments that we received. The CAT developed a summary report of comments (Appendix B) as well as a database of individual comments. We utilized the CAT report and comment database

Wild Indigo: Photo by Marijke Holtrop

to develop a list of substantive comments that required responses. Editorial suggestions, along with general notes of concurrence with or opposition to certain proposals that did not contain factual arguments were noted and included in the decision making process, but do not receive formal responses. We have included our responses to requests for additional information or clarification, provisions of additional information, and specific concerns as Appendix C. We have made changes to the CCP where appropriate.

The final product of the process is three stand-alone CCPs, one for each refuge. Implementation of the CCP can occur once the Finding of (No) Significant Impact (FONSI) is signed.

We will evaluate our accomplishments under the CCP, each year. Monitoring or new information may indicate the need to change our strategies. The collection of additional data at Great Meadows NWR will likely require modification and specification of the wildlife and habitat management strategies. We will modify the CCP documents and associated management activities as needed; following the procedures outlined in Service policy and NEPA requirements. The CCPs will be fully revised every 15 years or sooner if necessary.

Wilderness Assessment

The planning team conducted a Wilderness Assessment, as required under the Refuge Planning Policy, to determine if any lands and waters in fee title ownership were suitable to be proposed for designation as a Wilderness Area. During the inventory stage, we determined that the refuge does not fulfill the eligibility requirements for a Wilderness Study Area as defined by the Wilderness Act. The refuge and surrounding area has been altered in some way by man, with the imprint of man's work generally noticeable. The area is less than 5,000 contiguous acres, and is not of sufficient size as to make practicable its preservation and use in an unimpaired condition. Furthermore, permanent roads are contained within most of the areas studied. Therefore, suitability of the lands for Wilderness Designation is not analyzed further in this document.

Issues, Concerns, and Opportunities

Issues, concerns, and opportunities were brought to the attention of the refuge planning team through early planning discussions with local governments, state, and federal representatives, and through the public scoping process. We received comments from the public both verbally at open houses and in writing, through Issues Workbooks and individual letters. Some issues were identified by the Service and others were raised during the public review of the Draft CCP/EA. Many issues that are very important to the public often fall outside the scope of the decision to be made within this planning process. In some instances, the Service cannot resolve issues some people have communicated to us. We have considered all issues throughout our planning process, and have developed plans that attempt to balance the competing opinions regarding important issues.

Habitat and wildlife management

Many people were interested in our management programs. We have begun additional surveys and inventories to collect baseline information on the refuge. Our efforts at these refuges will help us develop a habitat management plan which will provide a detailed description of our goals and objectives for habitat management on the refuge.

Individuals and groups expressed a great deal of interest in how we manage Blanding's turtles and migratory birds and upland habitats. Additionally, interest was expressed in creating an additional wildlife passage under Route 2 at the refuge.

Control of invasive, injurious, and overabundant plant and animal species

Invasive species, including common reed and purple loosestrife, are a concern. These species limit the productivity of wildlife habitat. Management to control invasive species was mentioned as a watershed-wide priority to some conservation associations. We will continue efforts to control known invasives on the refuge.

Purple Loosestrife: Photo by Paul Buckley

Hunting

Requests were made at public meetings and through written comments both to allow and not to allow deer hunting on the refuge. Currently, the refuge allows hunting for migratory birds (American woodcock), big game (turkey), and upland game (ruffed grouse, rabbit and squirrel). There have been suggestions to provide additional lawful hunting opportunities on the refuge to control deer populations and deter poaching. Cooperation with local towns and hunting groups was a suggestion. Others oppose hunting of any kind on the refuge.

Bullfrog: Photo by Ken Andrews

Management of public use and access

The Complex Headquarters and Visitor Contact Station is located in Sudbury, MA. Residents near Oxbow NWR are anxious to have a visitor contact station/education center closer to their refuge. Many people requested a visitor center at Fort Devens in an effort not to build on the refuge itself. The need for environmental educational programs in local schools as well as additional interpretive opportunities where the public can learn about the refuge was raised.

The refuge has high visitation numbers. We estimated use at the refuge to be 70,000 visits in 2003. We do not have a consistent process for collecting and documenting visitation at all sites. Several non-wildlife dependent recreational activities and some unauthorized activities occur on the refuge. Some visitors use trails at the refuge for dog walking, jogging and illegally for bike riding.

Resource Protection and Visitor Safety

Many people voiced concern regarding additional protection for cultural and historical resources. Other concerns included the need to control poaching, trespassing and other refuge regulations violations.

Infrastructure and operations and maintenance

We heard from some people that the Complex doesn't have the resources and staff needed to support programs and maintenance of the refuge.

Issues and Concerns Considered Outside the Scope of This Plan

Some towns wish to develop water supply wells on refuge property.

Some towns requested access for the purpose of drilling water supply wells. Wells have been shown to draw down the surrounding water table. A 1994 study by the Massachusetts Office of Water Resources identified that "wells can have a significant impact on nearby (surface) water bodies and may affect specific biological resources." Concerns were raised by the public during CCP scoping that disturbance to wildlife, and other impacts due to the wells, or access to the wells, could occur.

Chemical control of mosquitoes on NWRs nationwide is being evaluated by the Service.

The Service has developed a draft national mosquito policy for refuge managers to apply when determining how and when mosquito populations may be managed on lands administered within the Refuge System. The science-based draft policy indicates that mosquito populations will essentially be allowed to function unimpeded as part of the wetland ecosystem. Mosquito populations may be reduced in certain circumstances and we work with state and local public health departments and mosquito abatement agencies to monitor and if necessary contain mosquito-borne diseases. Mosquito spraying to control larval mosquitoes on the refuge does not occur. Any future Service policy will be applied to Oxbow NWR.

(This page intentionally left blank)

Chapter 3: Refuge and Resource Descriptions

Socioeconomic Setting

The Refuge Revenue Sharing Act of June 15, 1935, as amended, provides annual payments to taxing authorities, based on acreage and value of refuge lands located within their jurisdiction. Money for these payments comes from the sale of oil and gas leases, timber sales, grazing fees, the sale of other Refuge System resources, and from Congressional appropriations. The Congressional appropriations are intended to make up the difference between the net receipts from the Refuge Revenue Sharing Fund and the total amount due to local taxing authorities. The actual Refuge Revenue Sharing Payment does vary from year to year, because Congress may or may not appropriate sufficient funds to make full payment.

Refuge Sign: Staff photo

The Refuge Revenue Sharing Payments are based on one of three different formulas, whichever results in the highest payment to the local taxing authority. In Massachusetts, the payments are based on three-quarters of one percent of the appraised market value. The purchase price of a property is considered its market value until the property is reappraised. The Service reappraises the value of refuge lands every five years, and the appraisals are based on the land's "highest and best use". On wetlands and formerly farmland-assessed properties, the full entitlement Refuge Revenue Sharing Payments sometimes exceeds the real estate tax. In other cases, Refuge Revenue Sharing payments may be less than the local real estate tax.

The fact that refuges put little demand on the infrastructure of a municipality, must be considered in assessing the financial impact on the municipality. For example, there is no extra demand placed on the school system and little extra demand on roads, utilities, police and fire protection, etc. Additionally, local communities may receive benefits, such as increased tourism revenues from visitors. The owner of land adjacent to refuge land, or with acquisition boundary, retains any and all the rights, privileges, and responsibilities of private land ownership. The refuge controls uses only on the properties it owns.

Table 3-1: Revenue Sharing Payments for Towns Associated with Oxbow NWR

	Ayer	Harvard	Lancaster	Shirley
2003	$918	$16,677	$6	$748
2002	$956	$17,351	$7	$778
2001	$1,023	$17,328	$7	$833
2000	$1,002	$5,193	$7	$816

	Ayer	Harvard	Lancaster	Shirley
1999	$1,136	$5,939	N/A	$927

Refuge Resources

Climate

Climatic conditions at the refuge are strongly influenced by maritime, Atlantic Ocean processes and weather patterns. The annual range in temperature is broad, with moderately hot summers and cold winters. Precipitation is distributed throughout the year. Seasonally, precipitation is greatest fall through the spring, and least during the summer. The average number of days with snow on the ground is 50 to 60 days.

The average annual temperature is 48.0 degrees Fahrenheit. January, the coldest month, has an average daily temperature of 24.3 degrees F. In July, the warmest month, the daily temperature averages 71.2 degrees F. The average, annual precipitation is 44.66 inches, with the greatest monthly average occurring in November (4.27 inches), and the lowest monthly average occurring in February (3.21 inches).

Forest habitat: Photo by Karla Thompson

Wind speed averages approximately 10 mile per hour on an annual basis. Velocities in excess of 40 miles per hour are not uncommon during summer thunderstorms or winter blizzards. Both tornados and hurricanes impact the area on infrequent intervals (U.S. Department of Justice 1995).

Geology and Topography

Oxbow NWR and the surrounding area has a glaciated topography which has produced landform characteristics of ice sheet impacts such as drumlins, kames, kame terraces, outwash plains, kettle-holes, glacial lake beds and eskers. Underlying the glacial deposits is metamorphic, sedimentary and granitic bedrock. Unconsolidated glacial deposits cover most of the bedrock, leaving little bedrock outcropping on the refuge. Topography ranges from the Nashua River, along with its associated wetlands and floodplains at approximately 200 feet above mean sea level to hilly uplands at approximately 330 feet elevation. Along the transition zone between the Nashua River floodplain and the adjacent upland, there is generally a fairly steep incline which divides these two areas. The majority of the refuge consists of the river riparian zone, its adjoining wetlands and low floodplain lands (Roberts 1995).

The surface geology of the refuge consists of glacial, alluvium, and swamp deposits overlaying bedrock. Glacial and post-glacial erosion and deposition during the Wisconsin period ice age shaped surficial geology approximately 17,500 years ago. In upland areas, glacial activity resulted in a moderately thick layer of glacial till consisting of a heterogeneous mix of clay, silt, sand, gravel and boulders, with occasional bedrock outcrops. Other glacial deposits include layers of well-sorted fine to coarse sand, fine gravel and boulders along with layers of fine sand and silt (Roberts 1995).

Alluvium and swamp deposits overlie glacial deposits on much of the area. Alluvium is light gray to white fine sand and silt with minor gravel. It is 15 feet thick in some areas and primarily found underlying the Nashua River Valley floodplain. Swamp deposits are composed of muck, peat, silt and sand overlying or mixed in with the alluvium (Roberts 1995).

Bedrock is a complex of metamorphic and granitic rocks of the Paleozoic age. Composition ranges from meta-siltstone through phyllite, slate and schist. An intrusive igneous body, the Ayer granodiorite and meta-quartzite also exist. Most contacts between formations are faults, striking northwest. The area was historically depressed under glacial loading and is rebounding (Roberts 1995).

Soils

The soils of the refuge are comprised of three generalized types. Nashua River floodplain soils are predominately the poorly drained Winooski-Limerick-Saco map unit. To the east of the Nashua River floodplain, where the majority of the refuge lies, the soils are the excessively drained outwash plain Hinckley-Merrimac-Windsor map unit. The well to moderately drained upland soils of the Paxton-Woodbridge-Canton map unit are west of the Nashua River floodplain, adjacent to the refuge.

The soils of the Winooski-Limerick-Saco map unit are very deep, nearly level soils that are moderately well drained, poorly drained, and very poorly drained on the floodplain of the river. This map unit consists of broad areas and small depressions. The soils formed in alluvium deposited by the flood waters of the Nashua River. The high water table is at the surface for the Saco soils, 6" for the Limerick soils, and between 1 ½ to 3 feet for the Winooski soils.

The soils of the Hinckley-Merrimac-Windsor map unit, which are primarily the upland soils of the refuge, are very deep, nearly level to steep soils that are excessively drained and somewhat excessively drained on the outwash plain. This map unit consists of broad plains and rolling to steep areas scattered throughout the survey area. The soils formed in water-sorted deposits of glacial outwash. Hinckley soils have a loamy surface underlain by stratified sand and gravel. Merrimac soils typically consist of 2 feet of loamy material over sand and gravel and Windsor soils are typically sandy throughout.

The soils of the Paxton-Woodbridge-Canton map unit include deep, nearly level to steep soils that are moderately well to well drained. These soils are predominately upland soils of hills and ridges. Paxton soils are gently sloping to steep with slow to very slow permeability. Woodbridge soils are nearly level to steep, and are predominately found on hill or drumlin tops. Canton soils are also gently to steeply sloping and well drained. However, they are most often associated with the toe of slopes, and have moderately rapid to rapid permeability (USDA 1985).

Hydrology

The hydrology of the refuge is essentially that of the Nashua River. All refuge lands are located along 7.5 miles of the Nashua River drainage. The Nashua River flows south to north, drains approximately 538 square miles, and is a major tributary of the Merrimack River system. The main stem of the Nashua River flowing through the refuge is formed by two branches: the north Nashua River, which originates west of Fitchburg, MA, and the south branch, which flows out of the Wachusett Reservoir. These two branches join at Lancaster, MA to the south of the refuge. Much of this section of the Nashua River is characterized by low gradient, slow moving water with numerous backwaters and wetlands. Primary tributaries of the Nashua River within its course through the refuge include: New Cranberry Pond Brook, Slate Rock Pond outlet, Phoenix Pond outlet (Catacoonamug Brook), Trout Brook, Willow Brook (a tributary of Nonacoicus Brook), Nonacoicus Brook, Morse Brook, Walker Brook, and Mulpus Brook.

Sunset: Photo by Deborah Dineen

The nearest, long-term U.S. Geological Survey gauging station on the Nashua River is located downstream of the refuge at Pepperell, MA. Flow records have been made at this station for 33 years (23,376 daily flow records). The average daily flow over this period of record is 583.5 cubic feet per second.

Numerous small freshwater ponds, vernal pools and wetlands are associated with this stretch of the Nashua River. Many small ponds along the river's course were formed by glaciers; others, e.g. oxbow wetlands, were formed as portions of the river have become silted, and the river's course changed, leaving these cut-off oxbows. Between the northern-most section of the refuge and the middle section, there is a dam, the privately owned Ice House Dam just below Shirley Road on the Nashua River. This dam has some impounding influence on the river, at least as far upstream as Route 2, and perhaps further upstream toward the southern part of the refuge.

Groundwater Resources

The groundwater hydrology of the refuge and the surrounding area is largely defined by topography and the distribution and saturated thickness of high conductivity glacial outwash deposits within the Nashua River valley and low conductivity glacial till deposits in the upland areas. This distribution of unconsolidated sediments results in steep hydraulic gradients in the upland areas with a general flattening of the water table within the regions of glacial outwash. Maintaining the base flow of the rivers and streams, groundwater flows from hills toward valleys, and discharges into streams, rivers, wetlands, and ponds. An extensive sand and gravel glacial outwash aquifer underlies most of refuge on the former North Post, the eastern portion of Main Post, and the northeastern corner of South Post, in addition to contiguous areas in adjacent towns (U.S. Army 1995).

The most productive parts of the aquifer (the high yield aquifer) are associated with the Nashua River and its tributaries. The glacial outwash deposits present in these high transmissivity areas are major sources of potable water for Devens and the towns of Shirley and Ayer. In most areas where the glacial outwash aquifer is not present, fractured bedrock resources supply water to single-family domestic wells (U.S. Army 1995).

The Devens water supply is provided by the McPherson Well on North Post, the Grove Pond Wellfield in the northeastern corner of Main Post, and the Patton and Sheboken Wells located, respectively, northeast and southwest of the mirror lakes in the southern portion of Main Post.

Groundwater in the vicinity of Devens is designated Class I groundwater by the Massachusetts Department of Environmental Protection (MADEP) and is considered to be a potable source of water. In general, the water within the main aquifer of Devens is moderately hard, requires minimal treatment and, based on tests at individual supply wells, and has met all MADEP water quality standards, with the exception of those for sodium (U.S. Army 1995).

The town of Ayer operates two wells on the southern shore of Grove Pond, to the east of the Devens Grove Pond Wellfield. In the past, these wells have functioned as a backup to Ayer's main water supply wells, which are located adjacent to Spectacle Pond in Ayer, east of Devens. The total rated capacity of the two wells is approximately 2 million gallons per day (MGD) (U.S. Army 1995).

The Shirley Water Supply District maintains two wells in the vicinity of the refuge. The Patterson Road Well, located in Shirley along Morse Brook due west of the McPherson Well, supplies approximately 225,000 gallons per day (GPD). Further west, the Catacoonamug Well supplies approximately 62,000 GPD. A supply well, operated by MCI-Shirley, is located in Shirley on the west side of the Nashua River, due west of Jackson Gate. This well is capable of supplying 720,000 GPD to the correctional facility. The extent of this zone is limited to the west side of the Nashua River (U.S. Army 1995).

Public water supply for the town of Harvard is provided by a pair of bedrock wells of limited capacity (one active well with an estimated maximum pumping rate of 43,000 GPD and a backup well with an estimated maximum pumping rate of 28,000 GPD). A third bedrock well, which pumps at less than 1,200 GPD, serves Harvard's Department of Public Works building and one private residence (U.S. Army 1995).

Floodplains

The estimated 100-year floodplain in the vicinity of the Oxbow NWR has been delineated by the Federal Emergency Management Agency (FEMA). The 100-year floodplain is most extensive along the Nashua River, reaching its greatest width in the refuge south of Route 2. The floodplain is also fairly wide along the stretch of the Nashua River near portions of the refuge within the former North Post (U.S. Army 1995).

Air Quality

The state air quality report from 2002 contains the most recent data available from the MADEP, Air Assessment Branch. The report contains data for several different pollutants: ozone (O_3); sulfur dioxide (SO_2); nitrogen dioxide (NO_2), carbon monoxide (CO), and particulate matter (10 microns (PM10) and 2.5 microns (PM2.5)). Data for O_3 and PM2.5 is available from the monitoring site in Stow; SO_2, NO_2, CO and PM10 data are from Worcester. Massachusetts levels for CO, SO_2, PM2.5, and PM10 are below the U.S. Environmental Protection Agency (USEPA) standards for these pollutants.

Eastern Bluebird: Photo by Bruce Flaig

There are two ozone standards based on two different averaging times, 1-hour and 8-hour. For almost two decades prior to 1997, the standard for ozone had been 0.12 parts per million (ppm) averaged over one hour. In 1997, USEPA set a new stricter ozone standard of 0.08 ppm averaged over an eight-hour period. Industry groups filed suit against USEPA following promulgation of the standard. In February 2001, the U.S. Supreme Court upheld the USEPA's authority for setting the new health-based ozone and particulate matter standards. In March 2002, the U.S. Court of Appeals for the District of Columbia upheld the standards themselves. However, the USEPA has not yet designated ozone nonattainment areas for the new 8-hour standard due to the delay in implementation of the new standard caused by the industry litigation. MADEP monitors for both 1-hour and 8-hour ozone levels throughout the State. Massachusetts has violated the 1-

hour ozone standard for many years. However, with the adoption of numerous control programs, progress has been made. The number and severity of the 1-hour ozone exceedances has declined significantly in recent years. As of 2002, the entire state was in violation of the 1-hour and 8-hour standards based on ozone readings for the 1999-2002 period. USEPA is expected to designate the attainment status of the State for the new 8-hour ozone standard in 2004. Massachusetts is expected to be nonattainment for the 8-hour standard.

In 2002, there were 122 exceedances of the 8-hour standard occurring on 30 days, and 22 exceedances of the 1-hour standard occurring on 5 days on a state-wide basis. A total of six 8-hour exceedances were recorded in 2002 in Stow. The trends for ozone readings in the State have been generally decreasing toward better quality since 1988.

Massachusetts has made significant progress in attaining the CO standard by implementing air pollution control programs. The last violation of the CO National Ambient Air Quality Standards (NAAQS) occurred in Boston in 1986. The Boston Metropolitan area was redesignated to attainment of the CO federal air quality standard by the USEPA in 1996. Lowell, Springfield, Waltham, and Worcester were redesignated to attainment of the CO standard by the USEPA in 2002.

In recent years there has been concern regarding the aerial deposition of mercury from atmospheric sources outside the northeast region (see for example Sweet and Prestbo 1999). Researchers have speculated that this may be the source of mercury levels found in some species and age-classes of fish in New England above the 1 ppm standard established by the U.S. Food and Drug Administration (USFDA).

The annual average concentration of lead in the air decreased substantially since 1985 from more than 300 ug/m^3 to less than 0.05 ug/m^3 (the annual average NAAQS for lead is 1.5 ug/m^3). Massachusetts is well below the standard. This result is attributed to the use of unleaded gasoline in motor vehicles, which are the primary source of airborne lead emissions (MADEP 2000). While air quality concentrations of lead have dramatically decreased, there may still be concern regarding residual lead levels in soils along heavily traveled roadways deposited prior to the change to unleaded gasoline usage.

Water Quality and Quantity

The waters of the Nashua River have been designated as Class B, warm water fisheries by the Commonwealth of Massachusetts. Class B waters are defined as being suitable for "protection and propagation of fish, other aquatic life, for wildlife, and for primary and secondary contact recreation" (MADEP 1998a). Although vastly improved in water quality character, the Nashua River has

River: USFWS photo

had a long history of water quality degradation. Through the 1960s and early 1970s, paper manufacturing facilities in Fitchburg and Pepperell, inadequately treated municipal wastewater in Fitchburg, Leominster, Clinton, and Ayer, and combined sewer overflows in Fitchburg and Leominster contributed to severe pollution of the river. While the water quality of the river has improved dramatically with closing of some of these facilities and the institution of advanced waste water treatment at others, impacts on aquatic biota and elevated bacteria levels remain problematic (MADEP 1998b).

The mainstem of the Nashua in its reach through the refuge is included in the State's list of impaired waters due to organic enrichment and low dissolved oxygen levels. Grove and Plow Shop Ponds, which are the origin of Nonacoicus Brook just above the refuge boundary, are listed as impaired due to heavy metal contamination. Mirror Lake, a kettle-hole pond located within the former Ft. Devens Main Post is also listed as impaired due to heavy metals (MADEP 1999). Mirror Lake is recharged by ground water, and does not have an apparent surface water inlet or outlet. We do not currently believe water quality within Mirror Lake would have an impact on the refuge.

The Massachusetts Department of Public Health (MADPH) has issued a fish consumption advisory for Mirror Lake due to elevated levels of mercury in fish tissue (MADPH 1999). There is also an earlier, state-wide interim fish consumption advisory for mercury that encompasses all fresh waters of the State. It is directed to pregnant women only. The general public was not considered to be at risk in this state-wide advisory (MADPH 1994).

A recent study by the Service examined heavy metal exposure in benthic invertebrates from Grove Pond, Plow Shop Pond and Nonacoicus Brook. The study found that freshwater mussels (the eastern elliptio, *Elliptio complanta*) collected from Nonacoicus Brook near its confluence with the Nashua River contained elevated levels of chromium (5.07 ug/g). Mussel tissue concentrations of arsenic, cadmium, mercury, methyl mercury and lead were found to not be elevated in comparisons with studies conducted elsewhere. However mussels tested from Nonacoicus Brook near the Nashua River exhibited higher levels of arsenic, cadmium, chromium, mercury and lead compared to samples at the inlet and outlet of Plow Shop Pond (USFWS 2000a).

In 1994, a 2.5 mile section of the Nashua River in the Fort Devens area was surveyed by the Service to check levels of contaminants in fish tissues. Polychlorinated Biphenyls (PCBs), Dichloro-diphenyl-trichloroethane (DDT) and mercury were found in fish tissues; as well as chlordane compounds and dieldrin. Chromium, arsenic, cadmium, lead and selenium were also detected at elevated levels in fish tissue. This report recommends separate evaluation of the contaminant concentrations in fish from the Fort

Devens section of the Nashua River by human health risk assessors. "Based on fish carcass and whole body analytical results, receptor groups that consume fish organ tissue or use the entire fish in meals may be at greater risk from some contaminants" (USFWS 1997).

Portions of the MADEP's Nashua River basin 1998 Water Quality Assessment Report (MADEP 2001) focusing on the mainstem of the Nashua from the confluence of the north and south branches to Squannacock River (including Still River, Nonacoicus Brook and Mulpus Brook) are attached as Appendix H to provide a synoptic view of water quality in these streams.

Biological Resources

Vegetation and Habitat Types

Oxbow NWR is located within the southern edge of the northern hardwoods forest region. The refuge is primarily a riparian community consisting of forested wetlands, shrub swamps and oxbow ponds. The Nashua River flows through a broad, low gradient floodplain with extensive wetlands. The floodplain extends up to 1,650 feet in width. Hardwood forests occur along the slopes of the floodplain valley.

Bare branches: Photo by John Grabill

A complete habitat cover type map is currently being produced in accordance with the National Vegetation Classification System (NVCS), and vegetation surveys have not been conducted on all refuge property. However, the vegetation of portions of the refuge has been examined by a number of surveys. The University of Massachusetts has conducted a plant community and vegetation analysis on portions of the Nashua River floodplain and surveys for rare plant species have been conducted (Searcy et al. 1993; Searcy 1994; and U.S. Army undated).

While the majority of work done to date has focused on wetland plant communities, the Fort Devens Natural Resource Management Office (NRMO) prepared a forest cover and condition inventory that included what is now the portions of the refuge north of Route 2 (see Maps 3-1 through 3-3). A broad description of these uplands is that they are primarily comprised of mixed oak-hardwoods, white pine-hardwoods, cherry-aspen hardwoods, red maple, shrub-land, and old field habitat (U.S. Army undated). The forest-stand condition indices reported in the Army inventory maps are likely to be outdated at this time.

The University of Massachusetts surveyed both wetland and upland plant communities along the Nashua River on the refuge north of Route 2 (Searcy et al. 1993). The study describes and evaluates upland forest and wetland plant communities within these areas of the refuge. The upland communities included two rich mesic forests, an oak-hardwood forest and a

Map 3-1: Forest and Land Cover Types (Area 1A Fort Devens)

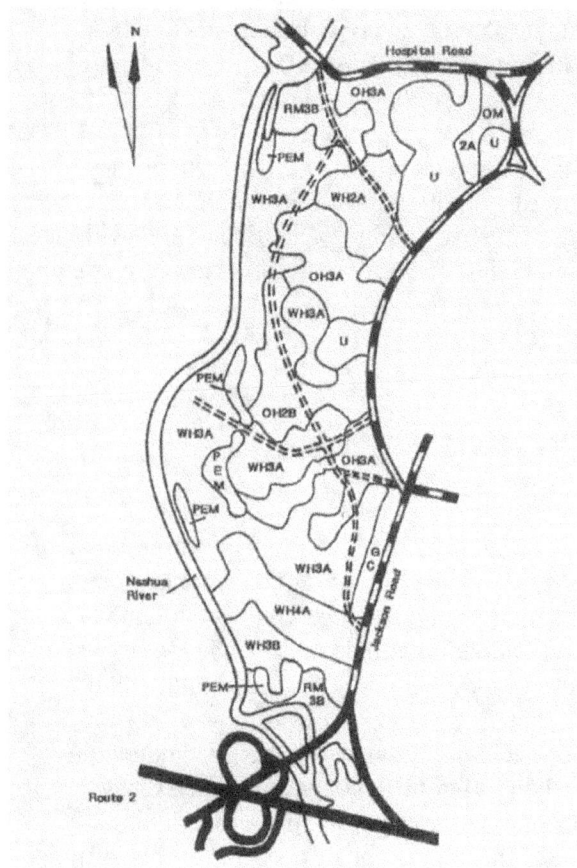

Code	Type	Acres
OH	Oak-Hardwood	64.5
OM	Mixed Oak	7.0
WH	White Pine-Hardwood	138.7
RM	Red Maple	17.4
GC	Golf Course	5.7
U	Developed Lands	35.4
PEM	Wetlands	11.0
	Total	279.7

Map 3-2: Forest and Land Cover Types (Area 1 Fort Devens)

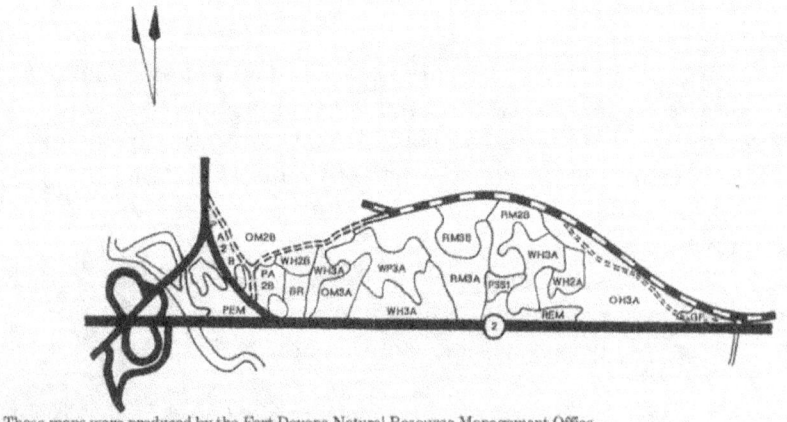

Code	Type	Acres
OH	Oak-Hardwood	23.6
OM	Mixed Oak	6.5
WH	White Pine-Hardwood	30.6
RM	Red Maple	33.6
PA	Aspen-Hardwood	6.2
WP	White Pine	10.2
GF	Grasses-Forbs	2.5
PEM	Wetlands	7.2
PSS1	Wetlands	2.5
	Total	125.9

These maps were produced by the Fort Devens Natural Resource Management Office
Mapping based upon October 1980 aerial photography

Map 3-3: Forest and Land Cover Types (Areas 2, 3, and Airfield Fort Devens)

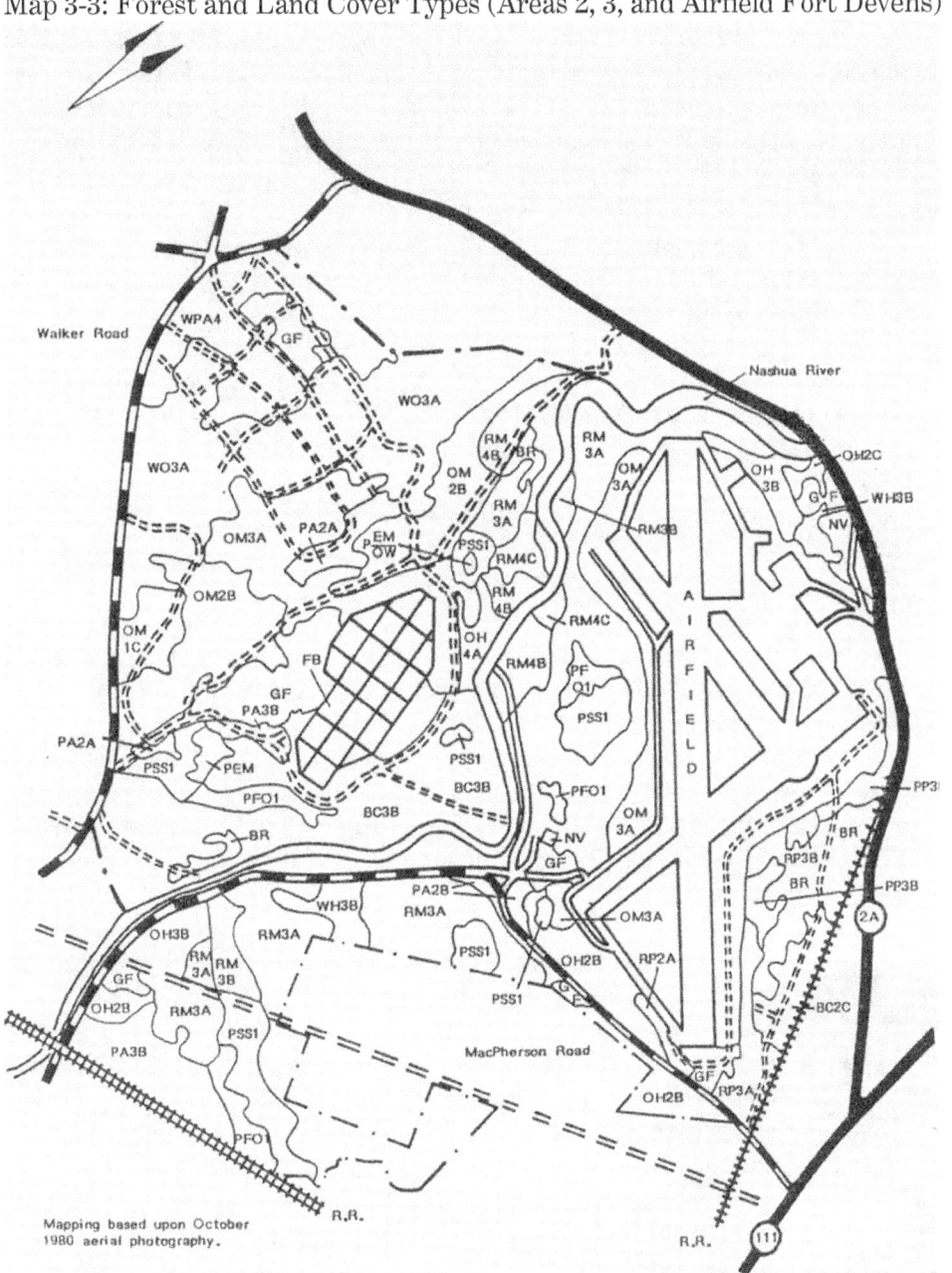

Code	Type	Acres
OH	Oak-Hardwood	42.6
OM	Mixed Oak	106.8
WO	White Pine-Oak	77.2
WH	White Pine-Hardwood	7.2
RM	Red Maple	146.4
WP	White Pine	32.6
RP	Red Pine	10.2
PP	Pitch Pine	7.2
PA	Aspen	24.4
BC	Cherry-Aspen-Hardwood	73.0

Code	Type	Acres
BR	Shrubs	20.4
	Airfield	176.0
FB	Filter Beds	31.6
NV	No Vegetation	5.5
PSS1	Wetland	25.1
PFO1	Wetland	13.6
PEM	Wetland	2.5
River	Wetland	23.4
	Total	862.3

white pine-hardwood forest. The wetland plant communities examined were classified as a red maple swamp, a southern New England floodplain, acidic seepage, and two types of oxbow pond communities. A detailed summary table providing a listing of the 174 plant taxa found in these communities, and their densities and percent cover are provided in Searcy et al., 1993.

In 1994, the portion of South Post which is adjacent to the Nashua River was more intensely surveyed. This area is directly west of the refuge. Although it is not on the refuge, many of the characteristics and features of the west side of the river also apply to the east side of the river, which is in the refuge. This includes the identification of this area as a southern New England floodplain forest, which is a high priority habitat for protection in Massachusetts. The floodplain area of this stretch of the Nashua River is flatter, wetter, and generally supports a larger more continuous area of forested wetlands (Searcy et al. 1994).

Oxbow Ponds

In 1995, the vegetation of the oxbow ponds and sloughs along the western floodplain of the Nashua River south of Route 2 were inventoried and classified as a result of a contract between the Fort Devens Military Reservation and the University of Massachusetts (Hickler 1995). The majority of the oxbows lie west of the Nashua River and are not on the refuge, however there are oxbows on the eastern floodplain which are on the southern half of the refuge. The characteristics and floristic inventories of the western oxbows can be extrapolated to the oxbows that lie east of the river, with caution.

Oxbow ponds are formed when a river cuts through the neck of a meander, leaving behind a section of river channel which forms a pond with a characteristic oxbow shape. One of the unique characteristics of these oxbow communities is the almost complete turnover of species composition between vegetation zones within one or two meters of each other. The oxbow communities have a higher variety of plant species than the adjacent upland, but more than half of those species are limited to only one or two oxbow ponds. Therefore, each pond individually contributes unique plant species to the overall biological diversity of the oxbow pond system. The oxbow communities were classified as four major vegetation types: common buttonbush (*Cephalanthus occidentalis*) swamp, wet meadow, deep marsh, and open-water aquatic.

Buttonbush and purple loosestrife:
Photo by Sandy Selesky

Common Buttonbush Swamp

Ten of the 15 ponds studied were buttonbush swamps with a well developed border of common buttonbush and a few associated forb species and tree seedlings.

Wet Meadow

Seven of the 15 ponds supported wet meadow communities. The wet meadow communities have many grass and forb plant species that vary widely between ponds and within meadows on a single pond. The most frequently occurring species in the wet meadow are cutgrass (*Leerzia oryzoides*), swampcandle (*Lysimachea terrestris*), common arrowhead (*Sagittaria latifolia*), false nettle (*Boehmeria cylindrica*), and needle rush (*Eleocharis acicularis*).

Deep Marsh

Deep marsh communities occur either as a band between meadow communities and open water, or covering large areas on shallow ponds. Deep marsh is characterized by emergent species along with floating leaved and submersed species. Pickerelweed (*Pontederia cordata*) is the most characteristic species, forming dense floating mats over large expanses on many of the ponds.

Open Water Aquatic

There are three aquatic cover types which are delineated by water depth. Shallow water areas are characterized by a dense cover of coontail (*Ceratophyllum demersum*), followed by a zone lacking emergent species with a small amount of watermeal (*Wolffia spp.*), and a second variety of coontail (*Ceratophyllum echinatum*). The deepest aquatic cover type is distinguished by a high frequency of pondweed (*Potemogeton pusillus*) and yellow water lily (*Nuphar variegatum*) (Hickler 1995).

A general description of the types of oxbow pond communities (with a cross-reference to the most similar NVCS designation) is provided in Table 3-2.

Table 3-2: Oxbow Pond Vegetation Communities

Type of Oxbow Community	NVCS Cross-reference
Buttonbush Swamp	Palustrine *Cephalanthus occidentalis* shrub thickets
Wet Meadow	Palustrine medium tall graminoid vegetation
Deep Marsh	Mixed marsh emergents community type: RI Lacustrine emergent community:ME

Vernal Pools

Vernal pools are a priority habitat type within the State of Massachusetts. Many vernal pools have been identified on Oxbow NWR, associated with the river floodplain and the adjacent forested wetlands. Vernal pools are temporary freshwater depressions which hold spring rains and snow-melt waters, and then typically dry out

Vernal Pool: Photo by Rob Vincent

during late summer. Vernal pools are critical breeding habitat for amphibian and invertebrate species due to the lack of predatory fish. The vernal pools of Oxbow NWR are confirmed breeding habitat for the state watch-listed spotted salamander (*Ambystoma maculatum*) and blue-spotted salamander (*Ambystoma laterale*), which is a state species of special concern.

Biodiversity

The Friends of the Oxbow NWR conducted a series of twenty six field trips on the refuge from March through October, 2000 (Friends of Oxbow 2000). All field trips were within the portion of the refuge located south of Route 2. These events were led by naturalists with expertise in the identification and ecology of a variety of biota. Eleven of these events examined a variety of plant groups including: lichens (27 species recorded), grasses and sedges (9 species reported), trees (39 species reported), shrubs/vines (47 species recorded), ferns/fern allies (32 species found), fungi/mushrooms (32 species reported), herbaceous plants/wildflowers (100 species), mosses (67 species reported), and liverworts (8 species recorded). A complete listing of species recorded during these biodiversity program events and by other observations on the refuge is provided in Appendix D. To date, 352 species of plants have been identified on the refuge, including 8 species that are on the Massachusetts state list of endangered (SE), special concern (SC) or watch-list (WL) of rare plants.

Invasive or Overabundant Species

Common reed (*Phragmites australis*) has invaded a portion of wetlands of Oxbow NWR. Planning to determine its rate of spread and the most effective means of control has been initiated.

Purple loosestrife: Photo by Karla Thompson

Purple loosestrife (*Lythrum salicaria*) is another extremely invasive plant species which threatens portions of the wetland habitats of the refuge. No formal surveys to determine the rate of spread have been conducted. The refuge has released *Galerucella sp.* beetles and *Hylobius transversovittatus* weevils as biological control agents. The *Galerucella* beetles are leaf-eating beetles which feed on the leaves and the new shoot growth of purple loosestrife, weakening the plant until it eventually is removed or reduced. *Hylobius tansversovittatus* is a root-boring weevil that deposits its eggs in the lower stem of purple loosestrife plants. The hatched larvae feed on the root tissue, destroying the plant's nutrient source for leaf development, which in turn leads to the destruction of the mature plant.

Additional plant species that are considered to be invasive, and that require monitoring on the refuge include: spotted knapweed (*Centaurea maculosa*), glossy buckthorn (*Rhamnus cathartica*), Oriental bittersweet (*Celastrus orbiculatus*), and autumn olive (*Elaeagnus angustifolia*).

Wildlife Resources

Migratory Birds

American woodcock at Oxbow NWR:
Staff photo

Comprehensive inventories for wintering, breeding and migratory birds have not been conducted for all avian species groups at the refuge. However, an impressive record of bird species using the refuge has been developed by staff and expert volunteer birders. A complete listing of bird species identified on Oxbow NWR to date is provided at Appendix D. In addition, the refuge staff initiated breeding American woodcock, land-bird and marsh-bird surveys on the Oxbow NWR in 2000. The latter two surveys follow regional Service sampling protocol and contribute to regional and national databases. The annual breeding season American woodcock (*Scolopax minor*) surveys also utilize standardized protocols, but are not currently a part of a regional or national series of observations.

The wetlands and open water bodies of the refuge provide important migration, feeding and nesting habitat for waterfowl species including American black duck (*Anas rubripes*), wood duck (*Aix sponsa*), mallard (*Anas platyrhynchos*), and green-winged teal (*Anas crecca*).

The wetlands along the Nashua River and its tributaries have been identified as a priority for protection under the NAWMP and the area is within one of the seven focus areas for the State of Massachusetts under this plan. Priority waterfowl species identified include American black duck, wood duck, and mallard, which nest on the refuge in upland habitat surrounding wetlands that provide brood raising habitat (USFWS 1992).

The Service Northeast Region Marshbird Callback Survey was conducted at the refuge for the first time in 2000. This survey follows a national protocol which will assist with the monitoring of marshbirds throughout the nation. The Marshbird Callback Survey specifically targets the secretive birds of wetlands that are generally missed during landbird surveys. The initial survey focused on the southern third of the refuge but will be expanded to include the newly acquired northern properties. Great blue heron (*Ardea herodias*), green heron (*Butorides virescens*) and black-crowned Night heron (*Nycticorax nycticorax*) have been observed on the refuge (Appendix D).

Great blue heron:
Photo by David
Margaretos

The Service Northeast Region Landbird Breeding Survey conducted on the refuge is similar to the National Breeding Bird Survey in which singing males are recorded at designated points along a route that traverses the refuge during the breeding season (May-July). This survey was initiated in the spring of 2000 and resulted in an initial species list of breeding land birds. The land bird survey is designed to continue for at least five years, at which time the data will be analyzed to determine the

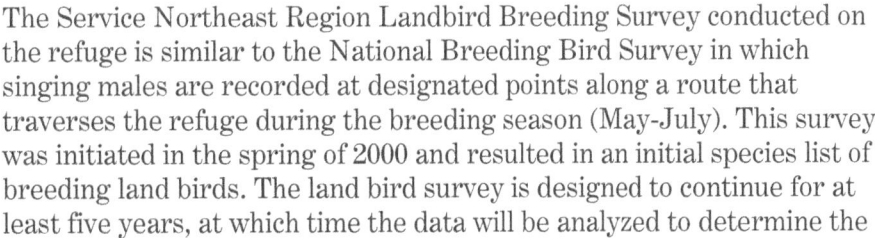

frequency at which the subsequent surveys need to be conducted to accurately monitor refuge populations.

Mammals

No formal surveys or inventories have been conducted on the refuge for mammals. However, 30 species of mammals have been identified by sight, sign or tracks on the refuge, including the presence of four bat species that need further confirmation (Friends of Oxbow 2000). A listing of these species is provided at Appendix D. In 1992, a small mammal survey was conducted on portions of the adjacent Fort Devens Military Reservation. Most of the areas that were sampled were in or adjacent to wetlands habitat in an effort to obtain specimens of the southern bog lemming (*Synaptomys cooperi*) and water shrew (*Sorex palustris*). Previously, a water shrew was captured in 1986, but in 1992 neither of these two mammals were captured (Thomas 1992). Mammals known to occur on the adjacent Fort Devens property may also occur on the refuge given the similarity in habitats (Appendix D).

Reptiles and Amphibians

Comprehensive inventories of anurans have been conducted. Additional surveys of amphibians and reptiles have not been conducted. However, observations by refuge staff, a long-term series of investigations regarding Blanding's turtles (*Emys blandingii*) and the Friends of the Oxbow NWR Biodiversity-2000 program have resulted in the compilation of a list of 17 reptile and 15 amphibian species occurring on the refuge. The species known to occur on the refuge include 4 reptiles and 1 amphibian species that are listed as threatened or of special concern by the Massachusetts Division of Fisheries and Wildlife (Mass Wildlife), Natural Heritage and Endangered Species Program (NHESP). State listed species of special concern are: spotted turtle (*Clemmys guttata*), wood turtle (*Glyptemys insculpta*), eastern box turtle (*Terrapene carolina*), and blue-spotted salamander. The Blanding's turtle is listed as state threatened.

Leopard frog: Photo by Sandy Selesky

The Service Northeast Region Anuran Call Count Survey is designed to identify breeding frog and toad species of the refuge and monitor their populations. The survey began in the spring of 2000 and focused on the southern third of the refuge, then was expanded to include the northern portions of the refuge. Surveys were originally completed by staff and are now done by volunteers. A complete list of reptiles and amphibians at Oxbow NWR is located in Appendix D.

Fish

Fish species documented in the main stem of the Nashua River include: largemouth bass (*Micropterus salmonoides*), smallmouth bass (*Micropterus dolomieui*), brown and yellow bullhead (*Ictalurus nebulosus* and *Ictalurus natalis*), yellow perch (*Perca flavescens*), chain pickerel (*Esox niger*), redfin pickerel (*Esox americanus americanus*), bluegill (*Lepomis macrochirus*), pumpkinseed (*Lepomis gibbosus*), black crappie (*Pomoxis nigromacultus*), white perch (*Morone americana*), white sucker (*Catostomus commersoni*), blacknose dace (*Rhinichtys atratulus*), spottail shiner (*Notropis hudsonius*), golden shiner (*Notemigonus crysoleucas*), tesselated darter (*Etheostoma olmstedi*), fallfish (*Semotilus corporalis*), common shiner (*Notropis cornutus*), slimy sculpin (*Cottus cognatus*) and goldfish (*Carassius auratus*) (MassWildlife 1974 and MADEP 1993). Native brook trout are found in Walker Brook (Town of Shirley 1996). The Squannacook River, which flows into the main stem of the Nashua River just north of the refuge, supports wild brook and brown trout (*Salvelinus fontinalis* and *Salmo trutta*) populations, and also gets stocked with brook, brown, rainbow (*Oncorhynchus mykiss*) and tiger trout (*Salmo trutta x salvelinus fontinalis*) (MassWildlife 1974). It is likely that some of these trout find their way into the main stem of the Nashua River. The fish species found in the Nashua River in its course through the refuge are listed in Appendix D.

In 1994, a 2.5 mile section of the Nashua River in the Fort Devens area was surveyed by the Service to check levels of contaminants in fish tissues (USFWS 1997). PCBs, DDT and mercury were found in fish tissues; as well as chlordane compounds and dieldrin. Chromium, arsenic, cadmium, lead and selenium were also detected at elevated levels in fish tissue. This report recommends separate evaluation of the contaminant concentrations in fish from the Fort Devens section of the Nashua River by human health risk assessors. "Based on fish carcass and whole body analytical results, receptor groups that consume fish organ tissue or use the entire fish in meals may be at greater risk from some contaminants."

As part of the large scale plan for fish restoration in the Merrimack River, the Nashua River Watershed is a current and future release location for river herring. Anadromous fish restoration is a cooperative effort among state agencies including the Massachusetts Division of Marine Resources, MassWildlife, and federal agencies including the Service, National Marine Fisheries Service and U.S. Forest Service. The Nashua River is considered a self-sustaining river in that it has existing fish passage facilities at dams which need to be modified or improved as part of the plan. This watershed will also be monitored and evaluated to ensure effective and efficient upstream and downstream passage of fish. Fish that would benefit from this effort include the river herring (*Alosa pseudoharengus*), American shad (*Alosa sapidissima*) and American eel (*Anquilla rostrata*).

Invertebrates

12-Spotted skimmer:
Photo by Sandy Selesky

With the exception of a 1994 inventory of moths, no formal surveys have been conducted on the refuge for invertebrate groups. However, the Friends of the Oxbow NWR Biodiversity-2000 Program, and other observations, have resulted in the compilation of a list of species that utilize the habitat resources of the refuge. This inventory list includes 9 freshwater mollusks species, one of which, the Triangle floater (*Alasmidonta undulata*), is a listed as a species of concern by the State due its low population numbers, 32 species of butterflies, 22 species of dragonflies and damselflies, and 57 other species of insects.

In 1992 and 1994, entomologists from the Lloyd Center for Environmental Studies inventoried moth species on the refuge (Mello and Peters 1993; Mello and Peters 1994). A total of 246 species of moths were recorded on the refuge. Observations of moths on the refuge were also made during the Friends of the Oxbow NWR Biodiversity-2000 Program. A total of 134 species were recorded, including 84 species not observed during the earlier inventories (Appendix D).

Threatened and Endangered Species

Rare Vertebrate Species

The Service has not conducted comprehensive surveys for threatened and endangered species on the refuge. The NHESP has identified the state endangered pied-billed grebe (*Podilymbus podiceps*) as occurring on the refuge, as well as the state threatened Blanding's turtle. The blue-spotted salamander, which is dependent on the vernal pools of the refuge, is a state species of special concern.

The pied-billed grebes in the Northeast breed in ponds, sloughs and marshes, along marshy edges of rivers, lakes and reservoirs. They prefer wetlands that are less than 5 hectares with abundant aquatic bed vegetation and open water interspersed with robust emergent vegetation. Breeding locations are scattered through much of the Northeast and are more localized and less abundant than in other regions of the U.S. In Massachusetts the pied-billed grebe is a local breeder throughout the State, but because of its rarity, the State has listed it as endangered in Massachusetts. The pied-billed grebe is identified by the Service as a migratory non-game bird of management concern in the Northeast which is representative of a biological community that is threatened in the Northeast. The greatest threat to the northeast pied-billed grebe population is the alteration and loss of wetland habitat through draining, dredging, filling, pollution, acid rain, agricultural practices, and siltation. (USFWS 2000b).

The spotty, low-density distribution of the Blanding's turtle is centered in the Great Lakes region with disjunct populations in southeastern New York, eastern New England and Nova Scotia. In New England, this turtle is found in eastern Massachusetts, southern New Hampshire and southern Maine. There are only seven known nesting sites in Massachusetts.

Blanding's turtle surfacing: Photo by David Flint

Blanding's turtles were found at the refuge in 1986, when a female and tracks were located by Brian Butler. Since that time, the population has been continually monitored. Individual turtles are uniquely identified with marginal shell notches, which allow for the calculation of local population size. Butler has estimated that approximately 25% of nesting females are new each year. This indicates a thriving population and is impressive for most species but is especially significant for the Blanding's turtle, given that females do not breed until they are about 12 years old. Habitat loss and predation on eggs are two factors limiting Blanding's turtles. Historical photos and records indicate that approximately 50% of the amount of habitat that historically was available for nesting turtles has been lost, due to the encroachment of shrubs and trees through natural succession. A high level of egg loss, as a result of fox and raccoon eating the eggs, has been a problem in many areas. During this vulnerable time, nesting areas are activity monitored and protected to reduce predation and human disturbance until the eggs hatch (Brian Butler, personal communication, Oxbow Associates, Lunenberg, MA)

In Massachusetts, the blue-spotted salamander is a species of special concern and occurs predominantly within Middlesex and Essex counties and in the adjacent eastern towns of Worcester County. This 'mole' salamander requires moist, moderately shaded environments, favoring northern hardwood/hemlock forests. The blue-spotted salamander requires vernal pools for breeding and egg laying, as well as the survival of their larvae until they metamorphose into air-breathing adult salamanders. The major threat to this species and other salamanders is the loss of wetland habitat to draining and development. Some population declines may also be attributed to sample over collection, foot and road traffic and pesticides or other toxic chemicals (MassWildlife undated).

Rare Plant Species

Although a complete plant inventory has not been conducted for the refuge, four rare plant species are known to occur on the refuge. Another three rare plants occur immediately adjacent to the refuge in habitat similar to that of the refuge. Because of the similarity of habitat on both sides of the river, there is potential that these state-listed rare plants also occur on refuge property. The Commonwealth of Massachusetts has listed ovate spike-sedge (*Eleocharis obtusa var. ovata*) as endangered. Three populations of ovate spike-sedge occur along this stretch of the Nashua

River floodplain. The largest population of ovate spike-sedge is on the refuge. There are four other areas that have been identified as potential habitat for this species along the floodplain, with one of these areas occurring on the refuge (Hunt 1991).

Climbing fern (*Lygodium palmatum*) may be abundant where it is found, however populations are rare and localized, making this a species of special concern in Massachusetts. Climbing fern does not have the characteristic shape of most ferns. It is an evergreen, ivy-like plant which sprawls over the ground or climbs clockwise short distances up shrubs and coarse herbs. This fern grows in moist pine-oak-maple woods with an open understory, moist thickets and stream margins (MDFW undated).

Wild black currant (*Ribes americanum*) typically occurs in floodplain thickets and swampy woods of the Northeast. This species has been delisted but remains on Massachusetts' watch list. A single plant was located on the northern half of the refuge within additional suitable habitat for this species to expand (Hunt 1991).

A single location of northern wild senna (*Senna hebecarpa*) is known to occur on the northern portion of the refuge. Field inspection in 2000 indicated the plants were doing well, but that shrubby overgrowth should be periodically cleared to enhance habitat conditions for the northern wild senna (Dr. William Brumback, New England Wildflower Society, October 2000, personnel communication).

Small bur-reed (*Sparganium natans L.*) occurs in shallow water throughout northern New England, but is listed as endangered in the Commonwealth of Massachusetts. Small bur-reed is known to occur in only one area of the refuge. This area was initially located in 1993, with a more intensive follow up survey in 1994 for more areas of small bur-reed. No additional areas of small bur-reed were located in 1994, and there was a decline in the patch size of the small bur-reed found in 1993. This may have been caused by an actual decline in individual plants, an increase in water level in 1994, or an algal bloom in 1994 which made it difficult to estimate the percent coverage of the small bur-reed (Searcy et al. 1994)

The range of small beggar-ticks (*Bidens discoidea*) is from Massachusetts to Virginia, Ohio, Michigan, Louisiana, and Texas. This species typically occurs in buttonbush swamps, ponds, oxbows, forested swamps and other wetlands. In Massachusetts, small beggar-ticks are currently known to occur at four sites. One site of small beggar-ticks occurs adjacent to the refuge, with suitable habitat identified adjacent Nashua River floodplain (Hunt 1991).

Bicknell's cranesbill (*Geranium bicknelli*) typically occurs in the dry rocky woods of eastern Massachusetts; however the two areas that were identified adjacent to the refuge occur in wetlands. The species is scattered in western Massachusetts and it is unclear whether or not the population found adjacent to the refuge is native (Hunt 1991). Bicknell's cranesbill is on the state species watch list.

Northern blazing star (*Liatris borealis*) is found in dry clayey or sandy soils in open woods and clearings throughout New England. Although formerly common in Massachusetts, this species is now only abundant in southeastern portions of the State. Two small populations were identified in disturbed sandy soil adjacent to the refuge and it is possible that this species may also occur in similar habitat on the refuge (Hunt 1991).

Special Designations

The Oxbow NWR and the Nashua River corridor are listed as a priority for protection under both the NAWMP and the Emergency Wetlands Resources Act of 1986.

Morning fog on the river: Photo by Sherry Fendel

The refuge and the Nashua River corridor are also included with the USEPA's priority wetlands of New England. The eight mile length of the refuge is a key component of the Nashua River Watershed Association Nashua River Greenway Designation.

The portion of the Oxbow NWR south of Route 2 lies within the 12,900 acre Central Nashua River Valley ACEC designated by the Massachusetts Secretary of Environmental Affairs due to its unique environmental characteristics and values (MADEP 1998).

Oxbow NWR, Devens Reserve, Bolton Flats Wildlife Management Area, the Nashua Greenway, Lancaster State Forest and other lands along the Nashua River have been designated as a Massachusetts Important Bird Area (IBA) for their significance to grassland species, several of which are identified under the PIF plan as priority species. Species present include grasshopper sparrow (*Ammodramus savannarum*), vesper sparrow (*Pooecetes gramineus*), upland sandpiper (*Bartramia longicauda*), bobolinks (*Dolichonyx oryzivorus*), and whip-poor-wills (*Caprimulgus voviferus*), and others. IBAs provide essential habitat for at least one or more species of breeding, wintering or migrating birds. The program highlights these important areas, but is not regulatory in nature. The primary goals of the program are listed below.

- "To identify, nominate and designate key sites that contribute to the preservation of significant bird populations or communities.
- To provide information that will help land managers evaluate areas for habitat management or land acquisition.

- To activate public and private participation in bird conservation efforts.
- To provide education and community outreach opportunities."
(http://www.massaudubon.org/birds-&-beyond/iba/iba-intro.html)

Cultural Resources

Prehistoric Period

The earliest evidence of human occupation of the Nashua River drainage dates from the paleoindian period (12,500-9,000 Before Present (BP)). The landscape during this time is characterized as postglacial with oak and spruce beginning to repopulate the area. This time period is when people first moved into the Northeast. Archaeological data for this period near the refuge consists of a single fluted point found on the surface adjacent to a small pond in Lancaster (Anthony 1978). No diagnostic artifacts have been directly associated with the river itself.

During the warmer and drier climate of the Early Archaic (9,000- 7,500 BP), the pine-hardwood forest would have seasonally made available resources that would be predictable and abundant. Some archaeological evidence suggests that a complex multi-site settlement system had been established by this period, with different site locations indicating exploitation of varied resources and environmental settings (Johnson 1984; Ritchie 1984). Populations probably increased during this period, although known sites are poorly represented in the archaeological record. Only ten sites from the Early Archaic period have been identified in this area, however, with further testing, more should be identified.

The population was slightly higher during the Middle Archaic (7,500-5,000 BP) in this region. The distribution of Middle Archaic sites indicates that seasonal settlement systems were firmly established (Glover 1993). Sites have been located along Muddy Brook and the Wachusett Reservoir at the headwaters of the Nashua River in West Boylston. Middle Archaic artifacts have also been found in Leominster, however, the site density is less than what is found along the Concord and Assabet drainage areas. By this time, the present seasonal migratory patterns of many bird and fish species had become established (Dincauze 1974) and important coastal estuaries were developing (Barber 1979).

Painted turtle: Photo by David Flint

Late Archaic period (5,000-3,500 BP) settlement in the Merrimack River basin has been documented at a number of site locations along most of the drainage's principal water courses in Massachusetts and New Hampshire. The large number of sites and artifacts attributed to the Late Archaic period, coupled with the high density of sites and their occurrence in a wide range of habitats, has been interpreted as reflecting a dense population intensively exploiting an extremely broad spectrum of resources

(Dincauze 1974; Ritchie 1985). Increase in occupation could be a possible correlation with a period of climatic warming beginning approximately 5,000 years ago (Funk 1972). Single and multi-component campsites were used for seasonal resource procurement activities. Sites from the Late Archaic are well represented in the refuge area. The majority of the sites in the refuge area appear to represent single or multicomponent campsites utilized for seasonal resource procurement activities. There are also a few quarry sites in the area that were used for raw material procurement (Glover, 1993).

Wild mushroom: Photo by Marijke Holtrop

The Transitional Archaic period (3,600-2,500 BP) was characterized in this area by the introduction of steatite (soapstone) vessels, and eventually ceramics, toward the end of this period (O'Steen 1987). Steatite vessels ceased to be manufactured with the introduction of ceramic technology; however, steatite was still used for making stone pipes (Ritchie 1985). Transitional Archaic sites in the refuge area are rare. Slightly more common, but still under represented, are Early Woodland sites.

The Early Woodland period (3,000-1,600 BP) is generally under represented in the regional archaeological record suggesting a population decline and/or poorly documented tool assemblages. Evidence for Woodland occupation of the Nashua River drainage comes from a small number of Early Woodland period sites. Along with a suspected Early Woodland deposition at several Late Archaic sites, diagnostic Meadowood and Rossville projectile points have been identified in two private collections (Glover 1993).

Middle Woodland period (1,650-1,000 BP) sites are more common indicating an increase in population, which is observed throughout New England. During this period, in this region, there were extensive long-distance social and economic interaction spheres. Horticulture appeared during this time and ceramics were commonplace. There was also a lot of movement from people traveling throughout the Northeast at this time. The Middle Woodland period activity in the Nashua drainage is represented solely at the Reedy Meadow Brook site in Pepperell. The deposition included diagnostic Fox Creek and Jack's Reef projectile points which were found in association with local and exotic stone debris including materials from Labrador and Pennsylvania (Mahlstedt 1985).

The Late Woodland period (1,000-450 BP) in this region is marked by an increase in ceramic production through improvements in technology. Some populations may not be engaged in horticulture however. The Late Woodland populations appear to be moderate around the refuge. Coastal areas and semi-permanent settlements seemed to have been preferred and larger groups lived in fortified villages. Late Woodland period artifacts represented in the archaeological record include triangular levanna points, cordwrapped stick impressed and incised collared ceramic vessels, and increasing amount of local stone materials used (MHC 1985).

By the Contact Period (450-300 BP), the Nipmuck Nation was established in the refuge region. Their settlement consisted of semipermanent villages focused on river drainages and tributary systems. Political, social and economic organizations were relatively complex and underwent rapid change during European colonization. Groups during this time, and most likely earlier times, were attracted to the anadromous fish runs in the river. The area around Harvard contained permanent camps along the river, as well as smaller, temporary camps adjacent to the natural ponds. This region, particularly the northern and western sections toward New Hampshire and Vermont, also falls within the cultural boundaries of the Western Abenaki. The Squakeag subgroup inhabited the upper Nashua River valley and became heavily involved in fur trade. The Abenaki group tended to cluster in large fortified villages (MHC 1985).

In central Massachusetts, the Contact Period is even less well documented than the rest of the Prehistoric Period. The inland location of the central uplands region precludes the availability of ethnohistorical counts by early colonial settlers visiting coastal sections of New England during the sixteenth century. By the time of direct contact with settlers in the seventeenth century, the effects of disease, isolated trade, and intertribal warfare had significantly changed the local population (Glover 1993).

Prior to European settlement in the first half of the seventeenth century, the Fort Devens section of the Nashua River Valley was primarily inhabited by the local subgroup of the Nipmuck known as the Nashaway, believed to have directly descended from pre-contact groups. Settlement patterns in the area continued to focus on the river drainages and their tributary streams during this period. Subsistence systems most likely remained oriented towards hunting and gathering of seasonally available food resources. An increased dependence on horticulture is considered likely given the appearance of semi-permanent, sometimes fortified, village settlements (MHC 1985).

Mallard with ducklings: Photo by Joseph Rhatigan

Although the gently rolling uphill terrain of the Nashua River drainage would have allowed a favorable range of movement, as well as an abundance and diversity of food resources, no prehistoric occupations from this period are documented in the area (MHC 1985). No primary or secondary Contact Period trails pass directly within the area encompassed by Fort Devens, however a major north-south trail passed to the immediate west through Lancaster and secondary north-south and east-west trails traversed present day Harvard, Ayer and Shirley. The area of present-day Lancaster, at the confluence of the Nashua and North Nashua rivers, was the site of the repeated or long-term camp of the Nashaway group, who utilized the surrounding areas from this base camp. Larger populations would also have been attracted to the area due to the presence of anadromous fish runs in the river, or to its floodplains for horticulture (MHC 1985).

Although not many sites have been reported from this region, the area has the potential to yield archaeological sites that will contribute to our understanding of prehistoric settlement in this region. Further study would supply more information about population densities and if they are found to be low for a time period, research questions can address the cause. Four prehistoric sites have been identified within the refuge boundary. The refuge area should be considered moderately to highly sensitive for archaeological resources in areas not impacted by military ordinance.

Historic Period

During the Early Historic Period, the refuge area was inhabited by a few European families engaged in farming activities. The region was heavily affected by King Philip's War in 1675. Garrisons were constructed to provide protection to the English settlers from the aggressions of the Native Americans. Attacks in Groton and Lancaster left the settlers depleted of supplies. The settlement was abandoned shortly after, and the people retreated to Concord. By 1676, the outer frontier area had crumbled (Glover 1993).

The refuge area was void of English settlement for several years after the end of the war. The death of King Philip and the English defeat of the various native groups throughout the region in the fall of 1676 meant that repopulation of the frontier was possible. The surviving Nipmucks of the Nashua River either fled westward and northwest or went to live with other groups or were reduced to subservient status. Toward the end of the 17th century, English repopulation had begun in the refuge area (Glover 1993).

This period of frontier resettlement was characterized by the demise of the nucleated English village and open field system. The trend was toward consolidating land holdings and the importance of the meetinghouse center. During the early 1700s, populations in the original territories increased steadily. Larger grants were subdivided in the process of establishing a meetinghouse, forming a government and assigning town lands (Glover 1993).

Population increases and economic growth took place at different rates in the original grants and new towns. Lancaster and Groton, the two oldest towns, were the most commercially developed population centers or core areas of settlement in the Nashua River Valley. The range of non-farm employments in these towns led to clusters of dwelling radiating out from the town center. Settlement in the late 18th century in the frontier towns reflected the regional economy of animal husbandry and extensive mixed grain cultivation. By the onset of the Revolutionary War, a number of the frontier towns in central Massachusetts were on their way to becoming important commercial and industrial regional centers (Glover 1993).

The town of Harvard was established in 1732 from parts of Lancaster, Groton, and Stow. Therefore, its historical development begins with the establishment of these colonial plantations. The Lancaster Plantation was founded in 1653, followed by the Groton Plantation in 1655. During the 1650's, Harvard served as outlying meadowland for the 35 families settled in Lancaster. The first documented evidence of colonial building on Harvard soil was the construction during the 1660's of John Prescott's Grist Mill on Nonacoicus Brook. The mill was abandoned during King Philip's War and rebuilt eastward on Stoney Brook once the territory was established (Anderson 1976).

Settlement of Harvard, which began in the late 1600's, was located in the southern section of town which remained part of Lancaster until 1732. As the population grew from 4 families in 1692 to 39 in 1723, small concentrations developed east and west of Bare Hill Pond, at Still River; at Oak Hill, and at the Old Mill. There were four garrison houses for Harvard's protection because Native American hostilities continued for several decades after the end of King Philip's War. One garrison house, which was located at Still River, was built by Major Simon Willard's son, Henry, in 1694 (MHC 1983).

By the time of Harvard's incorporation in 1732 from the eastern half of Stow Leg (the unclaimed tract of land between Groton and Lancaster plantation), the southern portion of Groton, and the northeast corner of Lancaster, there were over sixty families settled within the territory. The meetinghouse was built at the geographic center (now Harvard Center) shortly after Harvard became a town (Anderson 1976). During this planning stage, a 30-acre lot was set aside to accommodate the town's pound, stocks, cemetery and any other public facilities to come, such as the poor house (1753). Schools, taverns, and inns were also built to meet the needs of the townspeople (MHC 1983).

Harvard's predominantly agricultural economy was supplemented by a small number of artisans and support industries. Saw and gristmills were located on Bowers Brook and at Mill Road. Other town industries included a tannery, blacksmith, trip hammer, iron works and fulling mill. A blue slate quarry began operation on Pine Hill during the mid-eighteenth century, supplying slate for grave stones. Silver mining operations began on the south slope of oak hill during the 1780's (Snderson 1976).

The Shaker Community in Harvard was officially established in 1793. It was divided into four families, and had a maximum approximate membership of 200 (Andrews 1963). Some of its members were native to

Harvard, but the majority had been attracted to the community from other towns. The Shakers went on to acquire hundreds of acres, until they controlled most of the northeast corner of the town. The money for these real estate transactions came from the estates of new converts to the Shaker religion who settled in Harvard (Anderson 1976).

The Harvard Shakers dwindled in numbers due to lack of converts and orphan children. The community closed in 1918, after 127 years of existence in the town. The site of the Church Family is known today as the Shaker Village and consists of private homes. Like central Massachusetts during the federal period (1775-1830), Harvard experienced a period of population and economic growth. Between 1776 and 1830, the population increased from 1,315 to 1,600. Distinct nucleated villages developed within Harvard; at Still River, and the Shaker Village in the northeast part of town, and at Harvard Center where residences concentrated around the Commons. Beyond these villages, growth patterns remained dispersed and residents engaged in agricultural pursuits, which consisted of raising sheep, cattle and grain (MHC 1983).

Despite construction of the Worcester and Nashua Railroad in 1848, and associated depots at Still River and northwest of Harvard Center, Harvard remained essentially rural throughout the Early Industrial Period (1830-1870). The primary agricultural products were hops, hay, grains, vegetables, and fruit from apple and pear orchards. Dairying, cattle and swine raising were also major industries. By 1875, agricultural goods yielded $223,892 (MHC 1983).

Harvard was the home to two stops on the Underground Railroad, hiding slaves as they made their flight north to Canada. The list of those who supported the railroad and helped in the slaves escape is a long one and includes some of the prominent citizens of the town, including the town's reverend and deacon (Anderson 1976).

During the Late Industrial Period (1870-1917), Harvard saw a rise in industry within the town. The manufacturing peak of the period was the opening of the Union Brick Co., Union Paving Co., New England Brick Co., and Haskell's Vinegar Works, each located around Still River and the railroad. A wool knitting mill and other small-scale textile plants, and machinery shop helped support the town's industrial economy until the end of the century (Anderson 1976). Agriculture remained the town's primary income source, producing 200 products in 1905. The dairy industry continued to be an important economic asset, supported by poultry and egg production and the introduction of viticulture (grapes) (MHC 1983).

Wetland habitat: Photo by John Grabill

By 1917, the town of Harvard recorded a population of

approximately 1,000 people, supporting themselves by commercial dairying and selling vegetable and fruit products. Manufacturing played a very minor role in the economics of the town and was further reduced when the Shaker community closed in 1918 (MHC 1983). The adoption of the automobile and improvements to local roads and highways, such as Route 111 to Concord and Boston, Route 110 to Clinton and Ayer, Route 2 and interstate 495 have supported continued expansion of the residential, commercial and professional population as well as the increase in suburban development within Harvard (MHC 1983).

The refuge also extends into the towns of Ayer and Shirley (Middlesex County). Ayer was incorporated into a town in 1871 from sections of Groton and Shirley, and was part of the original colonial Groton plantation. During the mid-seventeenth century, colonial settlement of Groton consisted of a reputed fur trading house run by John Tinker located at the mouth of Nod Brook and four or five families living in a linear village established along the James Brook (Wing 1981; MHC 1980). Ayer and Shirley were unused common lands of the Groton plantation, being too far removed from the center of town. In 1659, unknown to the proprietors of the plantation, a 1,000-acre tract of Groton was granted to Major Simon Willard of Lancaster, the sergeant-major of the Middlesex County Militia, as a reward for military service and in settlement of a debt owed to him by John Sagamore, an Indian chief who lived near the site of Lowell (Glover 1993).

By the outbreak of King Philip's War in 1675, Groton was estimated to contain 300 inhabitants, 40 structures, including a meeting house, five garrison houses, including Willard's mansion, and a grist mill built by John Prescott in 1673 on Nonacoicus Brook (now in Harvard). Ayer and Shirley were still relatively uninhabited. After the war when the towns were resettled Ayer continued to be an outlying agricultural district of Groton with limited growth and settlement until after the mid-eighteenth century. The settlement of Ayer was sparse and oriented along Nonacoicus Brook. During the late eighteenth and early nineteenth century, Ayer was designated as Groton School District #5 which covered most of Ayer after 1793 (Glover 1993).

Settlement increased with an influx of Irish immigrants after 1845, and concentrated along Main and Park streets and their side streets. The first store opened in 1851, followed by the 1858 construction of Harmony Hall which consisted of stores on the first floor and a public hall on the second. The prosperous 1850's and 60's saw the construction of five churches, new school houses and a fire house (Glover 1993). During the Late Industrial Period (1870-1917), Ayer's economy and growth continued to be tied closely to the regional railroads, the town's principal employer. The Ayer railroad yards were said to be the largest classification yard in New England. Ayer was incorporated as a town in 1871 from a southern section of Groton and the portion of Shirley east of the Nashua River. The town's population grew steadily, increasing by 50%, with 20% foreign born (still mostly Irish) between 1870 and 1917. An Irish colony developed along the Nashua River in the late 1800's. New construction in Ayer Center included a town hall, new fire station and public library. Electric trolleys also connected the town center to Fitchburg, Shirley, and Lowell (MHC 1980).

By the 1900's, Ayer's fields were overworked and losing their fertility. There were "sprout land", reclaimed by forest. Only the land near the Nashua River remained fertile and contained large farms owned by Irish families. Ayer's population expanded in the early 1900's, then stabilized after 1920. The Army began leasing land in the town in 1917, and acquired large plots in the western section in 1920 to form Camp Devens. Economic disaster occurred in 1927 when the railroad yard moved out of Ayer and the tanner closed. Construction of the Moore Army Airfield on the North Post of Fort Devens brought air transport to the area. Settlement remained focused at the town center, and only recently have the undeveloped peripheral areas been subdivided (MHC 1980).

The first documented settlement of Shirley occurred in the 1720's when improved river crossings, such as Page's Bridge (1726) on the Fitchburg Road permitted settlement of the central areas of town along east-west oriented Fitchburg Road paralleling Mulpus Brook. Until this time, the Nashua River had served as a barrier to colonial settlement. A few farms were also scattered along the Squannoacook River and the west side of the Nashua River. As the frontier stabilized after 1730 there was a steady increase in the number of settlers moving into the territory. In 1747, thirty-three individuals singed a petition requesting early separation from Groton. In 1753, the district of Shirley was established. Two years later Shirley was incorporated as a town from the southwest corner of Groton and later the western half of Stow Leg (Glover 1993).

Economic activities consisted primarily of farming, supplemented by lumbering and milling. In the late 18th century, the Shakers began to influence the town's structure. Throughout the nineteenth century, the Shaker community in Shirley was considered a valuable part of the town. Their approximate maximum membership was 150, divided among the families. The Shirley Shakers were most noted for their thriving business in selling "Shaker Apple Sauce". They also had a broom shop, a mop shop, a blacksmith shop, and a house where they prepared herbs (Bolton 1914). As the numbers of the Shirley Shakers dwindled in the latter part of the nineteenth century, the few sisters and brothers subsisted mainly on money gained from selling their milk in the village (Bolton 1914). They augmented their monetary needs by maintaining a small store in the back of the office building. By the turn-of-the century, the Shaker members of the Shirley Society had nearly all passed away. The few remaining Shirley Shakers abandoned the family settlements in 1908 and went to live with the Harvard Shakers (Glover 1993).

Like Ayer, Shirley's economic base and population growth pattern was enhanced by the construction of the Fitchburg Railroad along West Main Road in 1845. During the early nineteenth century, a large scale carriage, wagon and harness factory operated on Mulpus Brook in Woodsville until it burned in 1871. The factory produced military wagons, horse drawn ambulances, and baggage wagons used in the Mexican and Civil Wars. Prairie schooners, wagons used by the pioneers crossing the prairies and Rocky Mountains as they traveled west, were also a product of the carriage factory (Glover 1993).

During the Late Industrial Period (1870-1917), Shirley experienced limited growth. The tract of land east of the Nashua River annexed to Shirley in 1789 was set off from Shirley in 1871 and annexed to the town of Ayer. After 1870, there was little new industrial development, leading to a period of economic decline. Out of the nine major factories which prospered during the mid-nineteenth century, only one cotton mill and one paper mill were still in operation by 1890. The only new industry in the 1890's was the opening of the C.A. Edgarton Suspender Factory and a cordage works. However, transportation improved when electric trolleys connected the town center to Fitchburg and Ayer (MHC 1980).

During the Modern Period (1917-present), Shirley experienced few changes in its settlement patterns or economic base. Steady, moderate population growth along with commercial strip development has occurred in peripheral areas, due in part to suburbanization and the military presence at Fort Devens after 1917. One of the most important additions to the town in the late twentieth century was the creation of MCI Shirley, south of the town center at the site of the former Shaker Village (Glover 1993).

The United States Declaration of War against Germany in April 1917 launched a massive nationwide construction campaign for the training of Army troops. Camp Devens in central Massachusetts was established as one of the 16 earliest of a total of 32 new Army cantonments nationwide. The approximately 11,000 acres of land chosen for Army training in central Massachusetts shared several common features with other selected sites across the country. It consisted of two adjoining parcels of land, known today as the Main and North Posts. These lands extended across the towns of Ayer, Shirley, Harvard, and Lancaster (Glover 1993).

The U.S. Army leased the approximate 11,000 acre tract in 1917. In 1917 the leased lands comprising the Camp Devens Reservation extended from Route 2A at the Ayer/Shirley town line south to Route 117 in Lancaster. The reservation was bounded on the east by the Boston and Maine Railroad, the Still River in Harvard and Lancaster, with the exception of a parcel of land to the east of the railroad bounded by Cold Spring Brook. It was also bounded on the west by hilly uplands west of Lunenburg Road (Glover 1993).

The Army purchase of land for a permanent training reservation began in June 1919 and was complete by 1921 (Anon 1923). The lands purchased at that time were considerably less than what Camp Devens had originally leased from 1917 to 1919. This was probably due to the deactivation status of the installation following World War I. The reduced lands purchased by the Army were situated in western Ayer, eastern Shirley, western Harvard and northeast Lancaster. The South Post lands were comprised of about 50 parcels, ranging in size from 1.5 to 93 acres with over 25 different landowners (War Department 1920).

Japanese knotweed: Photo by Marijke Holtrop

Following World War I, Camp Devens had a caretaker status until 1927, maintaining a skeleton force of personnel. In the summer months, the reservation served as a training area for the National Guard, Reservists, RPTC cadets, Civilian Military Training Camp personnel, and Regular Army. In 1927 Camp Devens received federal funding to construct permanent housing and a hospital for the purpose of troop mobilization in the northeast. The demolition of the wood-frame World War I structures and the construction of new permanent buildings began in 1928. In 1931, Camp Devens was renamed Fort Devens. The new cantonment area, built over the U-shaped system of roads formed the World War I temporary camp, included a double ring of roads, new buildings, and a parade ground. Most of these buildings are now part of the Fort Devens Historic District (Glover 1993).

A complete permanent post was built at Fort Devens between 1934 and 1939. In 1941 a large tract of land was acquired by the Army south of the permanent cantonment, in the area known as the South Post. These lands comprised the northeastern portion of the town of Lancaster, and were contiguous to those previously acquired west of the Nashua River and the former South Post Annex. In June 1946, Fort Devens was deactivated and returned to a caretaker status. Following the Korean War, Fort Devens remained an active training center for Regular Army, ROTC, and National Guard troops.

Expansion after 1965 occurred primarily on the Main Post including the barracks area, a shopping center complex, and Cutler Army Hospital. Range buildings on the South Post and Service buildings associated with the airfield and the sewage treatment plant on the North Post were constructed in the 1970's (Glover 1993). A slight reduction in the size of the South Post occurred in May, 1974, with the transfer of 662 acres of Training Area 4 to the Service to establish the Oxbow NWR. The remaining 49.03 acres of Training Area 4 (also known as the 94th ARCOM or Sylvania building area) was transferred to the Service as an addition to the Oxbow NWR in February, 1988.

The Base Closure and Realignment Act of 1990 (Public Law 101-510), and the subsequent decisions by the BRAC-1991 Commission and Congress required the closure and realignment of Fort Devens. The Army realignment action created the Devens Reserve Forces Training Area for use by Army Reserve and National Guard forces. Approximately 5,160 acres of the former 9,300 acre Fort Devens were retained for this purpose (the 4,880 acre South Post Training Area and approximately 280 acres within the former Main Post). Approximately 1,140 acres were transferred to other federal agencies, including approximately 836 acres to the Service as an addition to the Oxbow NWR, 250 acres to the Federal Bureau of Prisons for a medical center, 35 acres to the U.S. Department of Labor for a Jobs Corps Center, and 20 acres under the McKinney Act for facilities for the homeless. The remaining 3,000+/- acres were transferred to the Commonwealth of Massachusetts, and are being redeveloped as the Devens Enterprise Zone by the Massachusetts Development Finance Agency (U.S. Army 1995). In February, 1996, Congress specified (Public Law 104-106) that, if it is determined to be excess to the needs of the Department of Defense at any time in the future, the Secretary of the Army shall transfer all but 100 acres of the 4,880 acre portion of Fort Devens Military Reservation situated south of Route 2, to the Secretary of the Interior for inclusion in the Oxbow NWR.

Oxbow NWR has the potential to yield information significant in our understanding of early American culture such as the period during King Philip's War, the Shaker communities and the Early Industrial Period. The refuge has resources that can provide data for research questions for several time periods during the last 11,000 years. The historic land use patterns represent a good example of rural agricultural communities in New England. The refuge should be considered moderately to highly sensitive for archaeological materials.

Socio-economic Resources

Adjacent Communities and Land Uses

Predominant land uses within one mile east and northeast of the portions of the refuge in Ayer include high- and medium-density residential, downtown business and commerce, and light industrial areas. The land use profile of the remaining area is typical of an ex-urban, semi-rural area with a large supply of forest and agricultural land, low-density housing, and relatively undeveloped for industrial and commercial uses (U.S. Army 1995).

By far, forests are the most dominant land use, covering nearly 60 percent of the land. A distant second use, by area coverage, is single-family housing, which occupies approximately 12 percent of the area. Agriculture is still a key land use in the area, with about 10 percent devoted to cropland and pastureland (U.S. Army 1995).

Nearly 13 percent of the area is open space; this category includes parkland and water. Industrial and commercial land uses comprise less than one percent of the area each, as does multi-family housing. These land uses are more prevalent in the most urbanized communities (e.g., Nashua, Fitchburg, Leominster, and Ayer) (U.S. Army 1995).

Land use planning for communities adjacent to Fort Devens is regulated by the individual towns. The towns of Ayer, Harvard, and Shirley have developed master plans. Shirley and Lancaster have prepared open space and recreation plans (U.S. Army 1995):

- The Town of Ayer Strategic Planning Study Report addresses the affordable housing concerns and growth management provisions through updated zoning bylaws and improved subdivision regulations.

- The goals and objectives of the Harvard Town Plan (1988) are to protect environmental resources, preserve rural character, address housing needs, encourage agriculture, define the commercial area, and improve the town's management of land use.

- The goals of the Town of Shirley (1985) are to manage residential and industrial growth and balance the growth rate so there will be sufficient revenues to serve the needs of all residents. Areas of the town were targeted for protection as well as development. Since 1985, Shirley has instituted an open space and recreation plan.

- The goal of the Town of Lancaster Open Space and Recreation Plan (1993) is to preserve natural resources, maintain a balanced recreation program, and emphasize the role of agricultural land as open space. Addressed within the plan is the expansion of the Nashua River Greenway and Trail System, as well as other recreational activities.

Population and Demographic Conditions

Population trends vary considerably among the neighboring cities and towns of Ayer, Harvard, Shirley and Lancaster (U.S. Census Bureau, 2001). Overall population levels in the four towns decreased from 31,979 to 27,021 (a 14.4 percent decrease) between 1990 and 2000. The majority of this decrease occurred in Harvard due to the closure of Fort Devens (the great majority of the Fort Devens military housing and barracks areas were physically located within the town of Harvard). The population of Harvard decreased from 12,329 to 5,938 (a 51.5% decrease). The largest percent population growth occurred in Lancaster (6,661 to 7,380 or 10.8%). Ayer increased from 6,871 to 7,287 (or 6.1%), and Shirley grew by 4.2% from 6,118 to 6,373 people (U.S. Census 2001).

The greater Worcester metropolitan area grew by 33,005 people (nearly a 7% increase) to a population of 511,389 in the year 2000. The Boston-Worcester-Lawrence metropolitan area increased by 363,697 people or 6.7% to a total of 5,819,100 in 2000 (U.S. Census 2001).

Chapter 4: Management Direction

The Service manages fish and wildlife habitats considering the needs of all resources in decision-making. A requirement of the Refuge Improvement Act is to maintain the ecological health, diversity, and integrity of refuges. The refuge is a vital link in the overall function of the ecosystem. To offset the historic and continuing loss of riparian and forested floodplain habitats within the ecosystem, the refuge helps to provide a biological "safety net" for migratory non-game birds and waterfowl, threatened and endangered species, and other species of concern.

The vision and goals of Oxbow NWR translate the Refuge System Mission and Refuge Purposes into management direction. To the extent practicable, each goal is supported by objectives with strategies needed to accomplish them. Objectives are intended to be accomplished within 15 years, although actual implementation may vary as a result of available funding and staff. As one of the eight refuges in the Complex, Oxbow NWR is a vital part of the following vision and goals.

Complex Vision

The Complex will contribute to the mission of the Refuge System and support ecosystem–wide priority wildlife and natural communities. Management will maximize the diversity and abundance of fish and wildlife with emphasis on threatened and endangered species, migratory birds, and aquatic resources. The Complex will have a well-funded and community-supported acquisition program which contributes to wildlife conservation. The refuges will be well known nationally and appreciated in their communities. They will be seen as active partners in their communities, school systems, and environmental organizations which will result in high levels of support for the refuges. The refuges will be a showcase for sound wildlife management techniques and will offer top-quality, compatible, wildlife dependent recreational activities. Refuges open to the public will provide staffed visitor contact facilities that are clean, attractive, and accessible, with effective environmental education and interpretation.

Complex Goals

The following goals were developed for the Complex to support the mission of the Refuge System and the Gulf of Maine Ecosystem Priorities. These goals provide a general management direction for the refuges. Each of the goals is followed by management objectives and strategies that will help Refuge staff to meet the appropriate goals. The objectives and strategies that were developed as a part of this CCP do not adhere to the Service's guidelines for refuge goals and objectives. They are intended to provide a framework for management of the refuge. We look forward to refining many of the goals, objectives, and strategies in our various step-down management plans.

Goal 1:   Recover threatened and endangered species of the Complex.

Oxbow NWR is not home to any federally listed threatened or endangered species but does support the state listed Blanding's Turtle. Some of the strategies that are outlined for Goal 2 will specifically benefit the Blanding's Turtle and are identified as such.

Goal 2:   Protect and enhance habitats that support self-sustaining populations of federal trust species and wildlife diversity.

Objective 1:   Collect and evaluate relevant baseline habitat and wildlife data to ensure future decisions are based on sound science.

Strategy 1: Continue to participate in several region-wide and Service-wide surveys and studies including information on woodcock, marsh birds, breeding birds and anuran species. We will continue these activities as long as funding is available. We will also continue to seek any information compiled by others related to habitat and wildlife populations within the refuge and surrounding ecosystem.

Upland habitat: Photo by George Brawerman

Strategy 2: Update and expand current wildlife inventories to close data gaps including: the refuge north of Route 2, seasonality of use, habitat-type preferences, and, where practicable, estimates of population numbers. We will survey and inventory both the Service's trust resources (migratory birds and federal listed threatened and endangered species) and resident wildlife, including state listed threatened and endangered species. We expect to accomplish these concurrently; however, if necessary, surveys and inventories related to the Service's trust resources may receive priority.

Strategy 3: Continue cooperating in current, partners-based, monitoring programs for contaminants (Service Ecological Services, USEPA, MADEP) and water quality/flow levels (U.S. Geologic Survey (USGS), MADEP, and the Nashua River Watershed Association).

Strategy 4: Within 3 years, conduct a thorough survey on plants of the refuge. We will obtain aerial photography to develop a cover type map and ground truth the information in the field. The cover type map will show locations and acres for each habitat type. In addition, we will record locations of federally endangered and threatened species, other priority species, and invasive species using a global positioning system, and identified on the cover type map. We will update the map every ten years.

<u>Strategy 5: Within 5 years, census nesting bird species, migrating raptors and neotropical migrants.</u> We will conduct the raptor surveys throughout the fall, using methods and forms established by the Hawk Migration Association of North America.

<u>Strategy 6: Within 5 years, conduct a comprehensive survey of invertebrates during the spring and summer.</u> We will note any federal and state listed endangered and threatened species. We will use "sticky" sticks (paint stirrers dipped in Tanglefoot Insect Trap Coating and placed horizontally on and vertically in the substrate) to sample ground-based invertebrates throughout the refuge. We will use collecting nets to sample winged invertebrates.

Osprey: Photo by Cynthia Cronig

<u>Strategy 7: Within 7 years, we will survey small mammals using small live box traps, snap traps, and pitfall traps.</u> We will arrange the traps in a grid and will trap during the spring, summer, or fall season. If any threatened or endangered species are found, mark recapture studies may be initiated to determine a population estimate.

<u>Strategy 8: Within 7 years, we will sample freshwater fish in all the "substantial" ponds using passive and active capture gear and electro fishing.</u> Passive gear includes, but is not limited to, gill nets, trammel nets, and fyke nets. Active gear includes, but is not limited to, seines, nets, and hooks. Depending on the diversity and abundance of fish that are found in the ponds, mark and recapture studies may be initiated.

Objective 2:   *Manage aquatic and upland habitat to maintain habitat and species diversity.*

We will determine resources of concern, including focus species or species-groups and their habitat needs. Focus species and habitats are most likely to be selected based on a combination of factors such as: endangerment (federal and state-listed species); priority, national and regional Service plans (such as the NAWMP, the PIF, etc); developing Service policies/regulations such as those related to HMPs and maintenance of ecological integrity; the purpose for which the refuge was established (its value for the conservation of migratory bird species); current/historical species and habitat presence; and recommendations from MassWildlife or other partners.

<u>Strategy 1: Continue to protect nesting, wintering and migration habitat for the Service's trust resources, in particular, migratory bird species until the refuge HMP is developed.</u> We will continue to maintain approximately 25-30 acres of presently existing old-field grass/shrub habitat by mowing. We will consider maintenance of this grassland/old-field habitat with the use of fire.

Strategy 2: Selectively remove and restore to natural habitat existing roads and dirt trails that are not needed for refuge management, visitor use or fire-control purposes. We will focus these efforts within the portion of the refuge north of Route 2, which was transferred to the Service from the U.S. Army in May 1999.

Strategy 3: Within 2 years, develop a long-range HMP. The HMP will contain information for all habitats and species on the refuge, with a focus on resources of regional and national concern (based on regional and Service plans). It will provide quantitative and measurable objectives and strategies for habitat management to enhance resources of concern.

Habitat: Photo by Tim Bruce

Strategy 4: Within 5 years, complete a Habitat and Wildlife Inventory Management Plan (HWIMP). We will include an on-going monitoring component designed to measure progress toward those objectives outlined in the HMP, and to allow mid-course corrections or alterations as they may be needed. We will develop any additional step-down plans that may be required, depending on specific habitat management techniques or practices that may be recommended in the plans including chemical, mechanical or fire. We will develop protocol in this plan to be statistically sound and peer reviewed.

Strategy 5: Approximately 15-20 acres of existing, predominately mineral, sandy soil turtle nesting habitat will be maintained by mowing, discing or blading. The refuge currently supports the largest known population of the state-listed Blanding's turtle in the Northeast. Eight to ten acres of the refuge were formerly suitable turtle nesting habitat, but have succeeded to old-field vegetative type cover. In an effort to contribute to the success of this species, and complement other efforts in the area, we will restore this acreage for turtle nesting habitat. With the planning assistance of cooperating researchers, we will restore approximately eight to ten acres of turtle nesting habitat that has reverted to shrub and tree cover. These areas would be restored by removing vegetation and surface organic duff layers.

Strategy 6: Continue to seek opportunities to develop cooperative management agreements with neighboring conservation organizations and individuals. We will work with our conservation partners and, where our mission, goals, and objectives are compatible, will work together to implement habitat management and biodiversity strategies.

Objective 3: *Limit the spread of invasive and overabundant species and minimize habitat degradation.*

Strategy 1: Document presence, acreage, and location of invasive and overabundant species in conjunction with vegetation surveys and development of a cover type map. Existing stands of spotted knapweed, glossy buckthorn, cattail and common reed will be monitored to determine changes in area of extent.

Strategy 2: Develop an Integrated Pest Management Plan (IPMP), which will provide a full range of potential and alternative mechanical, biological and chemical control strategies. We will include a monitoring program as a part of the plan, which will consist of plot sampling, estimates of cover, and responses of wildlife and other plants. We will use the IPMP in concert with habitat monitoring to assess progress and the effectiveness of different techniques, and identify additional problem species. We will research alternative methods of controlling certain species as appropriate, based on monitoring results. Control strategies will be species specific and may employ biological vectors, mechanical methods (hand pulling), fire, or herbicides.

We will develop control strategies that will be species and condition specific. We may employ biological vectors such as the use of *Galerucella* beetles for purple loosestrife control, mechanical methods (e.g., hand-pulling, mowing, or discing), use of fire, or use of herbicides. We will choose the least intrusive, but effective, control practice whenever possible. The use of some herbicides may require action-specific step-down plans, and in some situations, proposed control methodologies may also require wetland permitting review and approval.

We will continue to use host-specific beetles (*Galerucella calmariensis or G. pusilla*) in a program to control purple loosestrife within a portion of a larger (240+/-ac) wetland on the refuge. Unless project-specific funding becomes available, we will continue to evaluate the effects of treatment with the beetles only by simple year-to-year photographic recording of the release site(s) on the refuge.

Strategy 3: Participate in appropriate, experimental invasive species control research programs. Such programs must be reviewed and approved by Service Regional or national biological staff and the Department of Interior's wildlife research division, the Biological Resources Division, now located within the USGS.

Strategy 4: Control populations of overabundant or non-native wildlife species. At some time prior to its transfer to the Service, a beaver colony and its dam were removed from a 25-30 acre wetland along the north side of Route 2. The wetland hydrology has been compromised with the removal of the beavers and its wildlife values have been degraded. We will work toward establishing a partnership with the Massachusetts Highway Department to re-establish a water-control structure on the Route 2 underpass culvert in order to restore this wetland. The remaining, current mix of wetland and

Beaver activity: Photo by David Margaretos

upland habitats will be protected, but allowed to mature to shrub and forest under natural successional processes.

In recent years, beaver have caused minor flooding of refuge trails and maintenance roads. To date, we have controlled such situations by manually clearing culverts, installing grates on culverts and water-control structures, and by installing beaver exclosures and "deceivers" in dams or on culverts. We will continue these practices. If more serious threats to habitat, refuge facilities, adjacent property or endangerment of health arise, we would work, in coordination with MassWildlife to either trap and relocate individual animals from problem sites, permit licensed sports trappers or hunters to reduce population numbers, remove individual beavers through trapping or shooting by refuge staff, or to permit a licensed animal damage control firm to reduce population numbers by trapping. We may need to complete a compatibility determination outlining specific requirements and conditions for beaver removal and issue a special use permit.

We will monitor mute swans on the refuge. In an effort to keep this aggressive, non-native species from becoming a resident on the refuge, territorial or nesting swans on the refuge would be lethally removed after obtaining appropriate permits from our migratory bird office.

Goal 3: **Build a public that understands, appreciates, and supports refuge goals for wildlife.**

Objective 1: *Improve the visibility of the refuge in the community and increase awareness of the Refuge System in general and the management activities and purpose of the refuge.*

As the refuge continues to contribute to the quality of life in east-central Massachusetts, strong support in the community and the region will also continue to contribute to its success. Helping hands are needed for program development, data gathering, and other opportunities discussed in these alternatives. Only with this type of assistance can the refuge fully achieve its goals and objectives, support the missions of the Refuge System and the Service, and help meet the needs of the community.

Volunteers assisting with water sampling: Staff photo

Volunteers participate in a wide variety of activities. These include wildlife and wildlands photography, assisting with or conducting educational and interpretative programs, providing information to visitors, conducting observations and surveys of wildlife species, botanical surveys, litter pick-up, trail clearing and maintenance, sign rehabilitation, and other maintenance projects.

The volunteer program at the Complex has been growing steadily. In 1990, volunteers provided more than 3,435 hours of assistance to the Complex. In 2000, volunteers provided 20,675 hours of service. Much of this volunteer work was done by core volunteers and active Friends Group members. In 2003, we again received incredible support from volunteers, which continues into 2004. Volunteers contributed 1,301 hours of service specifically to the Oxbow NWR during 2003. We are deeply indebted to all of our volunteers for their dedication and services rendered for the betterment of our nation's natural resources.

Strategy 1: Within 3 years, we will develop a Visitor Services Plan which describes all the planned public uses using standard regional guidelines. The plan will involve setting public use goals, determining measurable objectives, identifying strategies, and establishing criteria for all visitor services. The plan will also outline future funding and staffing needs. Several step-down plans will be required prior to opening or expanding public uses, including a fishing plan and hunting plan.

Strategy 2: Increase current Outreach Programs by adding sponsorship of one or more additional annual events (such as National Fishing Day, National Wildlife Refuge Week or Earth Day) designed to promote wildlife-dependent recreation and natural resource education.

Strategy 3: In cooperation with area teachers, assess the needs for, and work toward development of a refuge-specific environmental education curriculum for grades between kindergarten and the senior year of high school. We will provide an annual teacher workshop to cooperatively share experience and ideas related to these curricula.

Strategy 4: Initiate programs to provide educational and informational material and strategies related to natural resource protection and restoration to local communities and landowners. We will incorporate on-going refuge resource management practices and habitat restoration areas into all of these programs to serve as illustrations or demonstrations of resource management concepts and techniques.

Strategy 5: Work with partners and local communities to place informational kiosks related to the refuge and resource management at three off-refuge locations.

Objective 2: *Provide opportunities for wildlife observation and photography where such opportunities can be safely provided while achieving refuge purposes.*

Birder on nature trail: Photo by Sue Abrahamsen

Strategy 1: Provide opportunities for walking, snowshoeing and cross-country skiing to facilitate these wildlife-dependent opportunities on the refuge. Visitors are able to observe and photograph wildlife along approximately 2.5 miles of existing trails within the portion of the refuge located south of Route 2 (see Map 4-1). We will open an additional 5 to 6 miles of foot trails and a second canoe launch on the portion of the refuge north of Route 2. Parking

Map 4-1: Public Use at Oxbow NWR

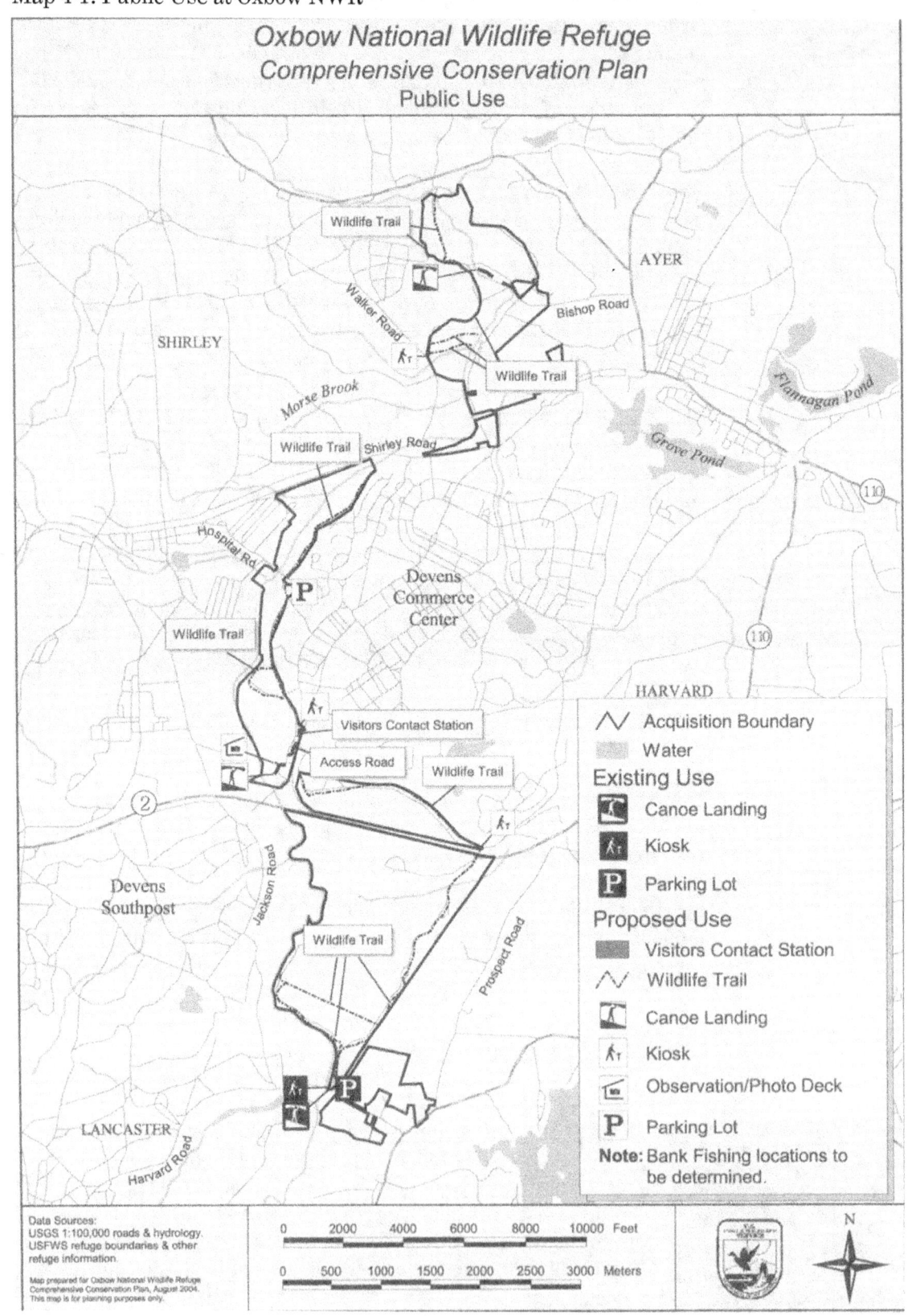

areas for these facilities will be constructed. Some areas of consideration are adjacent to Jackson, Hospital and Walker Roads.

We will evaluate the potential for a foot trail on the Watt farm. Before allowing this use, we will conduct surveys to determine what species are using the farm. We will consider a trail if our surveys show that this use would not disturb birds using the area.

Refuge staff will develop a system for evaluating proposals for new trails. This review system will provide refuge staff with the necessary tools to evaluate the need for and effects of recommended trails.

Strategy 2: Maintain and enhance canoe launching and parking areas. We will maintain the existing canoe launch and two parking areas located at the Still River Depot Road entrance. In 2003, the parking areas and canoe launch site were refurbished and a restroom was constructed. Two additional canoe launches and parking areas would be constructed within the former Fort Devens North Post (Map 4-1).

Strategy 3: Maintain the limited interpretive signing along portions of the current trails south of Route 2 (Map 4-1).

Strategy 4: Improve our current, very limited, monitoring (infrequent visitor and vehicle counts and Tank Road trail counter) to gain a rough gauge of refuge-use levels.

Objective 3:   *Provide and enhance opportunities for environmental education, interpretation, and outreach where appropriate and compatible with refuge purposes.*

Strategy 1: Continue providing environmental education oriented teacher workshops on an "as-requested" basis.

Strategy 2: Continue development and implementation of our Urban Education Program at the refuge in cooperation with the Worcester Public School System and the Friends of the Oxbow NWR. We will increase our participation in local and regional environmental education and interpretive programs. Our Urban Education Program has been conducted in cooperation with the Worcester Public School System and the Friends of Oxbow NWR. We will expand the program to include at least one additional elementary-middle or high school either from Worcester or another school system within the region. We will also endeavor to work with other school systems to provide instructional materials and presentations related to refuge resources and management programs that are occurring at Oxbow NWR. In addition, we will work with our Friends of Oxbow NWR and other partners to expand our current staff and volunteer-led interpretive

Environmental Education on the refuge: Staff photo

programs on Oxbow NWR.

Strategy 3: Continue to provide support as available for educational and interpretative programs organized and led by the Friends of Oxbow NWR and other groups.

Strategy 4: Continue to provide presentations related to the refuge and its resources to local schools, clubs, and community organizations as time and staff resources allow. We will also continue to work closely with the Friends of Oxbow NWR, to assist them in membership and program development, and to assist in the organization and leadership of volunteer programs and work activities on the refuge.

Strategy 5: Construct three informational kiosks at entrances to refuge foot trails, and a self-guided interpretive trail with signage and explanatory pamphlets. Refuge-specific informational and species list brochures will be developed and made available at refuge kiosks, visitor contact stations, and on-line at the refuge web site. The current, proposed locations of these facilities are depicted on Map 4-1.

Objective 4:   Provide opportunities for hunting and fishing where appropriate and compatible with refuge purposes.

Portions of Oxbow NWR south of Rt. 2 are currently open to hunting of big game (turkey), upland game (ruffed grouse, gray squirrel, and rabbit), and migratory birds (American woodcock). Additional portions of the Oxbow NWR will be open for hunting. Specific areas are identified below and are depicted on Map 4-2.

Before hunting is allowed on the refuge north of Rt. 2, the Code of Federal Regulations must be amended to authorize the hunting of white-tailed deer and waterfowl on Oxbow NWR. There will be a public comment period announced in the Federal Register. We anticipate an early 2005 Federal Register notice. Refuge staff will prepare a Hunt Plan before changing the location and types of hunting allowed on the refuge. No additional NEPA review is necessary to implement such changes.

Providing hunting and fishing opportunities addresses the mandates of Executive Order 12996 and the Refuge Improvement Act by providing the public with an opportunity to engage in wildlife-dependent recreation. Hunting and fishing are recognized by the Service as traditional forms of wildlife related outdoor recreation. We anticipate a low to moderate degree of hunting pressure to occur as a result of opening the refuge for these activities. The plan to permit hunting and fishing on the refuge will not affect wildlife populations in Massachusetts, as the refuges represent only a very small portion of the overall habitat available in the State.
Fishing is already allowed at the refuge.

Map 4-2: Current and Future Hunting Areas on Oxbow NWR

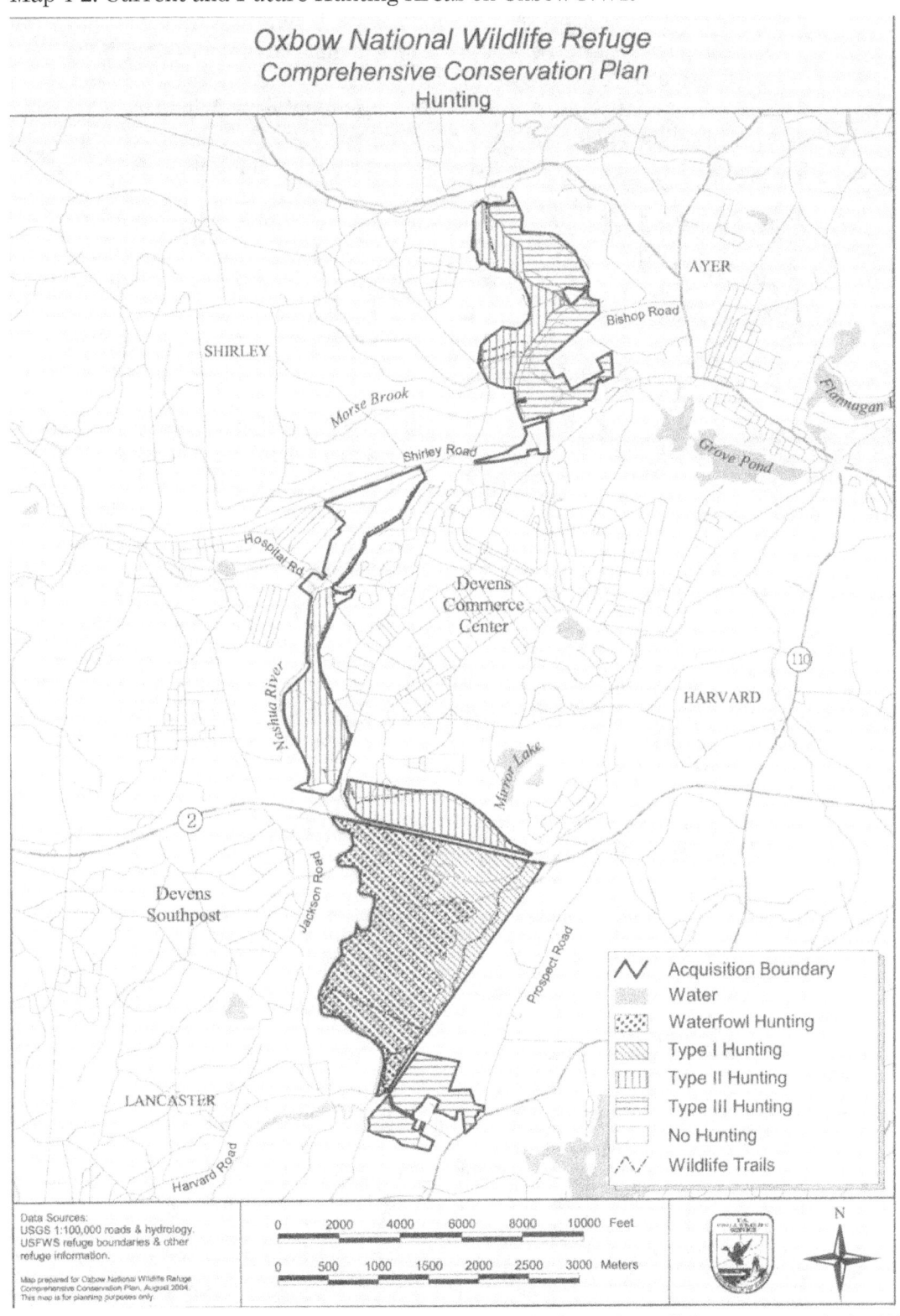

Type I Hunting = Shotgun, archery and primitive firearms hunting for deer, turkey, ruffed grouse, gray squirrel, rabbit, and woodcock
Type II Hunting = Archery deer hunting, shotgun hunting for turkey, ruffed grouse, gray squirrel, rabbit, and woodcock
Type III Hunting = Archery hunting only for deer and turkey

The refuge weighs a number of factors in opening an area to hunting or fishing, including safety considerations. The Refuge Manager may, upon annual review of the hunting program, impose further restrictions on hunting and fishing activity, recommend that the refuge be closed to hunting or fishing, or further liberalize hunting or fishing regulations within the limits of state and federal regulations. Restrictions would occur if hunting or fishing becomes inconsistent with other higher priority refuge programs or endangers refuge resources or public safety.

Trail: Photo by Stanley Klein

Annual permits will be required for hunting on the refuge. The permits will facilitate managing numbers of hunters and harvest. Fees charged for these permits will offset, but not completely cover costs associated with managing hunting programs. For additional information on the fee program, see the section on fees beginning on page 65.

Enforcement of federal and state hunting and fishing regulations will be accomplished through patrols by refuge law enforcement officers. Enforcement patrols may also be conducted by Massachusetts Environmental Police Officers. The frequency of patrols will be determined by hunter use, the level of compliance observed during patrols, and information obtained from participants, visitors and other sources. Refuge brochures and hunter orientation prior to the hunting seasons will emphasize refuge specific regulations, safety considerations and the protection of wildlife species found on the refuge.

In addition to state hunting regulations, the refuge may impose additional regulations. Examples of refuge regulations that would apply to hunting on the refuge include:

- hunters will be required to obtain permits from the refuge to hunt on the refuge;
- hunters may enter the refuge two hours before legal sunrise and must leave within 1.5 hours after legal sunset, and hunting can occur no earlier than one-half hour before sunrise and one-half hour after sunset;
- no night hunting will be allowed on the refuge;
- pre-hunt scouting of the refuge is allowed by permit, during specific time periods;
- carrying guns is not permissible during pre-hunt scouts;
- permanent blinds are not permitted on the refuge;
- all hunting materials, tree stands, and flagging must be removed at the end of each hunting day;
- no one shall insert a nail, screw, spike, wire, or other ceramic, metal, or other tree-damaging object into a tree, or may hunt from a tree into which such an object has been inserted;

- the distribution of bait and the hunting over bait is prohibited on wildlife refuge areas;
- all firearms must be unloaded outside of legal state hunting hours;
- the use of all terrain vehicles (ATV's) and snowmobiles on refuge land is prohibited;
- training of dogs on the refuge is not permitted;
- open fires are not permitted;
- use or possession of alcoholic beverages while hunting is prohibited.

Check stations will not be established on the refuge at this time, but reporting requirements may be instituted. Refuge staff will provide information about reporting forms when permits are issued.

The refuge will work with partners to provide increased hunter education through training, brochures, and news releases.

As a part of the hunt plan we will determine exactly when hunting will be allowed. The maximum amount of time that the refuge will be open for hunting is the full state seasons for each type of hunting. It is possible that we will open for a shorter duration, limited hours, or limited days of the week. In Massachusetts there is no hunting on Sundays. To illustrate the maximum potential hunting period, Table 4-1 displays the 2004 Massachusetts hunting seasons for each of the types of hunting proposed for Oxbow NWR.

Table 4-1: 2004 Massachusetts Hunting Seasons

Season	Start Date 1	End Date 1	Start Date 2	End Date 2
Deer (Archery)	10/11/2004	11/20/2004		
Deer (Primitive Firearms)	12/13/2004	12/31/2004		
Deer (Shotgun)	11/29/2004	12/11/2004		
Ducks and Regular Canada Goose	10/13/2004	11/27/2004	12/17/2004	1/8/2005
Early Canada Goose	9/7/2004	9/25/2004		
Late Canada Goose	1/15/2004	2/15/2005		
Wild Turkey	4/26/2004	5/22/2004	10/25/2004	10/30/2004
Woodcock	10/14/2004	10/30/2004	11/1/2004	11/13/2004
Ruffed Grouse	10/16/2004	11/27/2004		
Cottontail Rabbit	10/16/2004	2/28/2005		
Gray Squirrel	10/16/2004	1/1/2005		

<u>Strategy 1: Provide opportunities for hunting big and upland game species on the refuge where appropriate.</u> We will open portions of the refuge to hunting opportunities in accordance with all applicable Massachusetts state regulations and requirements. Among other restrictions, these regulations prohibit the discharge of any firearm or arrow upon or across any state or hard-surfaced highway or within 150 feet of any such highway, and any hunting within 500 feet of any dwelling or building in use, except as

authorized by the owner of occupant thereof (See Map 4-2 which depicts the general areas within the refuge where these activities will occur).

Shotgun, primitive firearms, and archery hunting of deer, ruffed grouse, turkey, rabbit, and gray squirrel will be allowed on the portions of the Oxbow NWR located south of Route 2, with the exception the "Watt Farm" addition to the east of the B&M railroad tracks. The Watt Farm area will be open only for archery hunting of deer and turkey.

The portions of the refuge from the Route 2 underpass to Hospital Road will be open for archery deer hunting. We will also permit ruffed grouse, turkey, rabbit and gray squirrel hunting on the portions of the refuge north of Route 2 and south of Hospital Road.

The portion of the refuge located on the westerly side of the Nashua River north of Shirley Road will be open for archery, shotgun, and primitive firearm deer hunting, as well as ruffed grouse, rabbit, squirrel, and turkey hunting. The portion of the refuge on the easterly side of the Nashua River north of Shirley Road, will be open only for archery deer and turkey hunting.

All state regulations and restrictions will continue to apply, and be enforced, including the safety related restrictions discussed above. In addition, the use of non-toxic shot (non-lead) will continue to be required for all areas of the refuge for all upland game seasons.

Water and pond lilies: Photo by Marijke Holtrop

We will provide a limited special season for physically handicapped hunters in accordance with state requirements for such hunts. Selected roads on the refuge will be open for vehicle traffic during this season. We believe the physical configuration of trails and roads on the refuge will allow us to provide handicapped accessible deer hunting opportunities from several of these access ways.

<u>Strategy 2: Provide opportunities for migratory bird hunting where appropriate.</u> We will permit woodcock hunting in the same areas described above for hunting of ruffed grouse, rabbit, and gray squirrel. We will also open waterfowl hunting south of Route 2 on the Nashua River and on the wetlands and ponds associated with the Nashua River in that portion of the refuge.

<u>Strategy 3: Provide opportunities for sport fishing where appropriate.</u> We will continue to provide boat and canoe fishing opportunities, in compliance with state regulations and restrictions, on the Nashua River throughout its course along and within the refuge. Fishing within refuge ponds, pools and wetlands will continue to be prohibited for wildlife nesting and habitat

protection purposes. We will increase fishing opportunities on the refuge by providing river-bank fishing at up to four areas along the Nashua River. These areas may need to receive stabilization or be provided with erosion control measures prior to being opened, and they may be closed as needed to prevent or repair bank erosion or prevent disturbance to migratory birds, if either should occur. At least one, and, based on further evaluation of their compatibility with habitat and wildlife considerations, potentially all of these locations will be made handicapped accessible.

Objective 5:   *Provide opportunities for non-wildlife dependent activities when they assist visitors in participating in wildlife dependent activities and when such use does not detract from the refuge purpose.*

Strategy 1: Continue to allow, but not encourage jogging. Staff and volunteers have observed disturbance to wildlife caused by joggers. We plan to analyze the potential impacts of jogging within the next three years on Service trust resources and priority public uses and will consider modifying or eliminating the use in the future, based on this additional analysis.

Strategy 2: Within a year, eliminate dog walking from the refuge. This use has been found to disturb wildlife and other visitors and is not considered one of the six priority uses on national wildlife refuges.

Strategy 3: Remain closed to other non-wildlife dependent activities such as bikes on trails, horseback riding, dog sledding, snowmobiling and swimming. No picnicking facilities will be provided and permits will not be issued for events, such as family reunions, where meals are a major component. Visitors will be allowed to snack and drink a beverage while on refuge trails. Bicycles are allowed in parking lots and on entrance roads. Bikes are not permitted on refuge trails.

Goal 4:   Adequately protect cultural resources that occur in the Complex.

Strategy 1: Continue evaluations or surveys of cultural resources (archeological and historical) on a refuge project-specific basis. Soil disturbance requires resource evaluation and clearance. Federal cultural resource protection laws and regulations would be enforced.

Strategy 2: Within 10 years, initiate and complete cultural and historical resource surveys and inventories on a refuge-wide basis. The archeological survey portion of this work will be designed to develop predictive models that could be applied refuge-wide in evaluating the potential of future projects to impact cultural resources.

<u>Strategy 3: Comply with Section 106 of the National Historic Preservation Act before conducting any ground disturbing activities.</u> Compliance may require any or all of the following: State Historic Preservation Records survey, literature survey, or field survey. The Service has a legal responsibility to consider the effects its actions have on archeological and historic resources.

Goal 5: **Maintain a well-trained, diverse staff working productively toward a shared refuge vision.**

We will continue to utilize Service policy, training opportunities, and other appropriate means to meet the staffing goals.

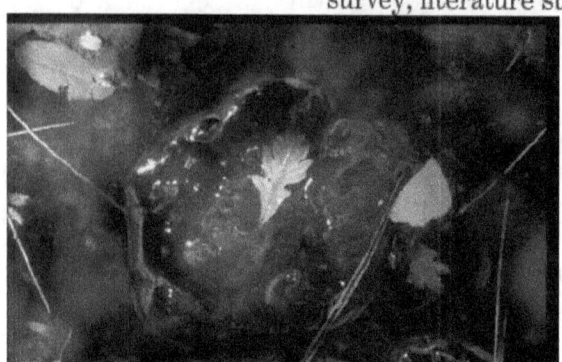

Wood frog eggs: Photo by Marijke Holtrop

General Refuge Management

The following management direction applies to various refuge goals and across program areas. Some of this direction is required by Service policy or legal mandates. Refuge management direction is organized by topic area.

Refuge Access and Fees

The Complex will charge an entrance fee at the Oxbow and Assabet River NWRs, and at the Concord impoundments of Great Meadows NWR, and a user fee for hunting on the Complex. Our fee program will be established under the Recreation Fee Demonstration Program (Fee Demo Program), a program which Congress initiated in 1997 to encourage Department of Interior agencies that provide recreational opportunities to recover costs for their public use facilities, improve visitor facilities, promote activities for visitors and address the maintenance backlog of visitor service projects (USFWS 1997a). Congress re-authorized the Fee Demo Program in 2004 for 10 years. The Fee Demo Program requires at least 70% of revenue remain at the collection site. Currently, 80% of the funds raised from user fees on a particular refuge in this region stay at the refuge. The other 20% is sent to the region to be distributed to other refuges. No more than 15% of the fees collected can be used for fee collecting or fee collection systems. The Complex has received money from these regional funds in previous years for public use facilities. If the program does become permanent, the percent of revenue remaining on site could change, however it will never be less than 70% and could be as much as 100%. Visitors with a current duck stamp, Golden Eagle Pass, Golden Age Pass or Golden Access Pass do not have to pay entrance fees.

The following entrance fee program will be initiated at the Oxbow NWR.
- A one day entrance fee will be charged per car or per group if arriving via foot or bicycle. Our proposed fee will be $4 per day.

- An annual pass for three refuges in the Complex (Assabet River, Great Meadows and Oxbow) will be available for $12.
- Daily entrance fees will be collected by refuge staff stationed on site or at self-service fee collection stations.
- Self-service fee collection stations will likely consist of a secure box with envelopes to register and pay the daily or annual fee.
- We will attempt to make purchase of the annual pass available by fax and on-line. The pass will also be available at the Refuge Headquarters.

The following Hunting Permit Fee Program will be implemented in conjunction with the hunting program described later in this chapter.

- We will charge an annual fee of $20 for a hunting permit. This permit will be valid for all unrestricted hunting seasons open on the Northern refuges (Assabet River, Great Meadows, and Oxbow NWRs). Hunters with a valid hunt permit will not have to pay an entrance fee while scouting or hunting.

- There may be a need to limit hunting during certain seasons to ensure a safe, high-quality hunt. Details of these restrictions and any application requirements will be outlined in the Hunting Management Plan. Based upon these restrictions, purchase of a permit does not guarantee the ability to hunt all seasons on all refuges. No additional fee would be required for hunting applications for restricted seasons.

- At the time of purchase of the annual hunting permit, the individual may choose to purchase an annual entrance pass for an additional $5. The combined permit/pass must be purchased jointly.

Individuals that do not purchase the combination permit/pass will be subject to entrance fees on the refuge during times when they are not hunting.

We realize that the new fee program will require an adjustment period. Our plan for instituting the fee includes an educational period, a warning period, and finally a transition to full enforcement.

Park bench: Photo by Joan Ross

We may adjust fees over the 15 year period addressed in this plan to reflect changes in administrative costs or management goals.

Accessibility

Each refuge will operate its programs or activities so that when viewed in its entirety, it is accessible and usable by disabled persons. The Rehabilitation Act of 1973, as amended, requires that programs and facilities be, to the highest degree feasible, readily accessible to, and usable by, all persons who have a disability.

Non-Wildlife Dependent Public Uses

We will eliminate dog walking opportunities from the refuge within a year of the publication of this plan. We have found dog walking to disturb wildlife and other visitors and it is not considered one of the six priority uses on national wildlife refuges. We will continue to allow jogging, but will not be encouraged. We plan to analyze the potential impacts of jogging within the next three years on Service trust resources and priority public uses and will consider modifying or eliminating the use in the future, based on this additional information. The refuge will remain closed to other non-wildlife dependent activities such as bicycling, horseback riding, dog sledding, snowmobiling and swimming. No picnicking facilities will be available. Bicycles are only allowed in parking lots and on the Still River Depot entrance road.

Fire Management

U. S. Department of the Interior and Service policy state that Refuge System lands with vegetation capable of sustaining fire will develop a Fire Management Plan (FMP) (620 DM 1.4B; 621 FW 1.1.1). The FMP, which includes Oxbow NWR, provides direction and continuity in establishing operational procedures to guide all fire management objectives as identified in the plan. This plan was finalized in March of 2003. The FMP includes descriptions of the refuges and addresses wildland and prescribed fire events. The FMP also defines levels of protection needed to ensure safety, protect facilities and resources, and restore and perpetuate natural processes, given current understanding of the complex relationships in natural ecosystems. It is written to comply with a Service-wide requirement that refuges with burnable vegetation develop a FMP (620 DM 1).

The associated EA was prepared in compliance with NEPA and the Council on Environmental Quality (CEQ) Regulations (40 CFR Parts1500 -1508). It provides a description of the purpose and need for the project, a brief background, the features of each alternative, the affected environment, and resulting effects and consequences of each alternative. The selected alternative, "prescribed fire and wildland fire suppression" is discussed in detail in the EA. Alternatives which were considered, but not selected, include differing combinations of: allowing naturally ignited fires to burn in some instances; use of prescribed burning to achieve wildlife resource and habitat objectives; and, wildland fire suppression. A "no-action" alternative of allowing all fires to burn at all times was initially considered, but dismissed as not suitable for further consideration in the development of this proposal. The no-action alternative was rejected because it fails to meet Service policy in regards to potential liability for losses of life and property, as well as its unacceptable environmental, social, and economic costs.

The mission of the Complex is to protect and provide quality habitat for fish and wildlife resources and for the development, advancement, management, and conservation thereof. By defining an appropriate level of wildland fire protection, and integrating a prescribed fire program based on biological needs, the FMP and EA are fully supportive and sensitive to the purpose of the Complex, and of benefit to the Service, in performing its activities and services.

Fall Color: Photo by Joan Ross

If you would like a copy of the FMP, or the EA, please contact the Refuge Headquarters in Sudbury.

Land Protection

The Service is currently working on a new national land conservation policy and strategic growth initiative. This policy will develop a vision and process for growth of the Refuge System, helping individual refuges better evaluate lands suitable for inclusion in the Refuge System. The process will help insure that lands the Service protects are of national and regional importance and meet certain nationwide standards and goals. Also, some of the focus of reevaluating Refuge System growth has come from the need to address nationwide operations and maintenance (O&M) backlogs on existing properties. Many refuges, including Oxbow NWR, are not fully staffed under current budgets and have significant O&M backlogs. Expanding boundaries creates a need for additional staff, O&M funds, as well as additional dollars for the land protection itself. Our Director has asked that we focus, in the interim, on acquiring inholdings within already approved boundaries, which is our proposal under all alternatives for these three refuges.

In the future, we may look at wetland, upland and river systems near Oxbow NWR which are of interest for possible private-lands habitat improvement projects, easements, and/or acquisition. All lands within the Oxbow NWR acquisition boundaries are already acquired.

Berries frozen in winter: Photo by Marijke Holtrop

The Service's land acquisition policy is to obtain the minimum interest necessary to satisfy refuge objectives. Conservation easements can sometimes be used in this context, when they can be shown to be a cost-effective method of protection. In general, conservation easements must preclude destruction or degradation of habitat, and allow refuge staff to adequately manage uses of the area for the benefit of wildlife. Because development rights must be included, the cost of purchasing conservation easements often approaches that of fee title purchase, thus rendering this method less practical. Nevertheless, donations of easements or voluntary deed restrictions prohibiting habitat destruction will be encouraged. In addition, the Service could negotiate management agreements with local and state agencies, and accept conservation easements on upland tracts.

Funding for land acquisition comes from the Land and Water Conservation Fund and the Migratory Bird Conservation Fund under the Migratory Bird Conservation Act.

Resource Protection and Visitor Safety

Protection of visitors and both natural and cultural resources will be improved. We propose to increase refuge staff by one additional, full-time Park Ranger, and provide the necessary, intensive federal law enforcement training required for dual function law enforcement responsibilities to two additional staff (e.g., an assistant manager, refuge operations specialist, or an outdoor recreation planner).

Refuge staff will complete a fire suppression contract or agreement with state or local fire suppression agencies for wildfires occurring on the refuge (see section Fire Management at the beginning of this chapter).

Special Use Permits and Memorandum of Understanding and Agreement

Guided tours, by outside groups, are permitted on the refuges if the activity is determined to be appropriate and compatible with the refuge(s) purpose. Permitting will be divided into four categories by the type of use and the regularity of the activity requested. Where appropriate, one Permit or Agreement will be developed for all three northern refuges in the Complex including Oxbow, Assabet River and Great Meadows NWRs.

Special Use Permits may be issued to user groups or individuals for annual or single events. These organizations or individuals are those who want to use the refuges for a special purpose (e.g. commercial photographer, special event or research study), or to gain access to an area otherwise closed to the public (e.g. one time entrance to closed areas to film/photograph special event or hold special wildlife celebration day on refuge). Groups will be given specific requirements and educational guidelines on materials to present to the public. The specific charge and specific requirements will be determined on a case by case basis.

A Memorandum of Understanding (MOU) or Memorandum of Agreement (MOA) may be issued to user groups/individuals who want to use the refuges for a special purpose or gain access to an area otherwise closed to the public, on a regular basis or annually. Groups will be given specific requirements and educational guidelines on materials to present to the public. The specific charge and specific requirements will be determined on a case-by-case basis.

A concession may be developed if a business operated by private enterprise is providing a public service (recreational, educational and interpretive enjoyment of our lands and waters for the visiting public), and generally requires some sort of capital investment.

Concessionaires will generally gross a minimum of $1,000 and the concession will be charged either a fixed franchise fee or a percent of gross income. Groups will also be given specific requirements and educational guidelines on materials to present to the public.

Research

The Service encourages and supports research and management studies on refuge lands that improve and strengthen natural resource management decisions. The refuge manager encourages and seeks research relative to approved refuge objectives that clearly improves land management, promotes adaptive management, addresses important management issues or demonstrates techniques for management of species and/or habitats. Priority research addresses information that will better manage the Nation's biological resources and is generally considered important to: Agencies of the Department of Interior; the Service; the Refuge System; and state Fish and Game Agencies, or important management issues for the refuge.

We will consider research for other purposes, which may not directly relate to refuge specific objectives, but may contribute to the broader enhancement, protection, use, preservation and management of native populations of fish, wildlife and plants, and their natural diversity within the region or flyway. These proposals must still pass the Service's compatibility policy.

We will maintain a list of research needs that will be provided to prospective researchers or organizations upon request. Our support of research directly relates to refuge objectives and may take the form of: funding, in-kind services such as housing or use of other facilities, direct staff assistance with the project in the form of data collection, provision of historical records, conducting of management treatments, or other assistance as appropriate.

All researchers on refuges, current and future, will be required to submit research proposals which include a detailed research proposal following Service Policy FWS Refuge Manual Chapter 4 Section 6. All proposals must be submitted at least three months prior to the requested initiation date of the project. Special Use Permits must also identify a schedule for annual

Deer abound at Oxbow NWR: Photo by Carole D'Angelo

progress reports. The Regional refuge biologists, other Service Divisions and state agencies may be asked to review and comment on proposals.

We will provide minimal on-site support for research projects. We will continue to identify other research needs to the Service's Regional Research Coordinator, and to other potential research partners (e.g., USGS, Biological Resources Division and universities).

Chapter 5: Refuge Administration

Refuge Staffing

Currently the refuge shares one refuge manager position with Assabet River NWR. The refuge also currently shares the support of two refuge biologists, an outdoor recreation planner, a natural resource planner, a law enforcement officer, two maintenance workers, two administrative technicians and seasonal employees with the Complex. We have determined that the refuge minimum staffing needs include:

- one refuge manager,
- one assistant refuge manager or refuge operations specialist,
- one outdoor recreation planner,
- one maintenance worker,
- one administrative technician,
- and one park ranger (law enforcement).

In addition, several new staff positions are required to enable us to implement the full range of programs, facilities and activities identified in our management direction. The additional needed staff includes:

- one park ranger with refuge and visitor protection responsibilities,
- one biological technician, and
- one heavy equipment operator.

The eight Eastern Massachusetts NWRs are managed as a Complex, with centrally stationed staff taking on duties at multiple refuges. The CCP examines the need for staff specific to the three refuges that were

Trail clean-up: Staff photo

organized under the Draft CCP/EA dated April 2003. A total of 39 full time personnel and a seasonal Biotech are needed to fully implement all three refuge CCPs. Permanent staff serving all three refuges may be stationed at the Refuge Headquarters in Sudbury, MA with the eventual on-site relocation of Oxbow NWR staff to the new office/visitor contact station. Appendix F identifies currently filled positions, recommended new positions, and the overall supervisory structure. The new positions identified will increase visitor services, biological expertise, and visibility of the Service on refuge lands.

Refuge Funding

Successful implementation of the CCPs for each refuge relies on our ability to secure funding, personnel, infrastructure, and other resources to accomplish the actions identified. Full implementation of the actions and strategies in all three Complex CCPs will incur one-time costs of $3 million. This includes staffing, major construction projects, and individual resource program expansions. Most of these projects have been identified as Tier 1 or Tier 2 Projects in the Refuge System's Refuge Operations Needs

System database (RONS). Appendix E lists RONS projects and their recurring costs, such as salaries, following the first year. Also presented in Appendix E is a list of projects in the Service's current Maintenance Management System (MMS) database for the Complex. Currently, the MMS database lists $3.85 million in maintenance needs for the Complex.

Refuge Buildings and Facilities

The only building on the refuge at the present time is a comfort station at the Still River Depot Road parking lot. We will work with state, private and other federal partners to obtain authorization and funding that will enable the construction of an office/visitor contact station at the refuge. This facility will likely be constructed on Jackson Road, just north of Route 2 at exit 37B. The visitor contact station could be approximately 4000 square feet in size. It will provide space for interpretative exhibits, a meeting room and administrative offices for refuge staff. The current, proposed locations of these facilities are depicted on Map 4-1.

As part of the Centennial Celebration for the Refuge System, the Service identified ten refuges in the country for new visitor centers. The Complex ranked number three on the Service's list. Refuges were ranked on a number of factors including their need for a facility and potential to provide opportunities for a large audience. The site for the new facility is not identified in this document. However, below are the criteria we will use to identify potential sites. Sites chosen will be evaluated in a later Environmental Assessment. The new center might be located at Great Meadows, Oxbow, or Assabet River NWRs or off-site in the vicinity of one of these refuges. The new facility will house exhibits focusing on a variety of environmental themes as well as refuge management activities. We will implement recommendations for interior facility design from the Complex Project Identification Document, after it is finalized. We will evaluate each potential site with the following criteria:

- Access from a major travel route (Route 2, 128, etc.)
- Access from public transportation
- Accessibility of utilities
- Presence of trust species, habitats or other important resources
- Opportunity for outdoor features associated with center, including interpretive trails
- Topography
- Potential disturbance to habitats
- Presence of hazardous wastes
- Potential impacts to neighbors
- Buffer from current or predicted commercial activity

After the new Visitor Center is built, the current headquarters on Weir Hill Road will be used for administrative purposes only by refuge staff.

Step-Down Management Plans

The Refuge Manual (Part 4, Chapter 3) lists a number of step-down management plans generally required on most refuges. These plans describe specific management actions refuges will follow to achieve objectives or implement management strategies. Some require annual revisions, such as hunt plans, while others are revised on a 5-to-10 year schedule. Some of these plans require NEPA analysis before they can be implemented. In the case of the Complex, some of the plans are developed for each refuge, while some plans are developed for the Complex with specific sections that pertain to individual refuges. In the following lists, we have identified those plans that are specific to the refuge and those that will be included in an overall Complex plan.

The following plans are either up-to-date or in progress and will be completed within 1-year of issuance of the CCP.

- Habitat Management Plan (Refuge)
- Fire Management Plan (Complex)
- Spill Prevention and Counter Measure Plan (Complex)
- Law Enforcement Management Plan (Complex)

The plans indicated in the following list either need to be initiated or are out-of-date and require complete revision. Additional management plans may be required as future Service policy dictates.

- Habitat and Wildlife Inventory Plan (Refuge)
- Integrated Pest Management Plan (Complex)
- Visitor Services Plan (Complex)
- Energy Contingency Plan (Complex)
- Hunt Plan (Refuge)
- Fishing Plan (Refuge)
- Cultural Resources Management Plan (Complex)
- Migratory Bird Disease Contingency Plan (Complex)
- Safety Management Plan (Complex)
- Continuity of Operations Plan (Complex)
- Sign Plan (Complex)

Maintaining Existing Facilities

There are no existing facilities specific to the refuge other than those at Still River Road parking area and trails. Existing facilities for the Complex that relate to the refuge include the Great Meadows NWR visitor contact station and office, Complex maintenance compound, and numerous parking areas, observation platforms, and trails. Periodic maintenance of existing facilities is critical to ensure safety and accessibility for Complex staff and visitors. Many of these facilities are not currently Americans with Disabilities Act (ADA) compliant; upgrading is needed.

Compatibility Determinations

Federal law and policy provide the direction and planning framework to protect the Refuge System from incompatible or harmful human activities and to insure that Americans can enjoy Refuge System lands and waters. The Administration Act, as amended by the Refuge Improvement Act, is the key legislation on managing public uses and compatibility. Before activities or uses are allowed on a national wildlife refuge, we must determine that each is a "compatible use." A compatible use is a use that, based on the sound professional judgment of the Refuge Manager, "...will not materially interfere with or detract from the fulfillment of the mission of the Refuge System or the purposes of the refuge." "Wildlife-dependent recreational uses may be authorized on a refuge when they are compatible and not inconsistent with public safety. Except for consideration of consistency with state laws and regulations as provided for in section (m), no other determinations or findings are required to be made by the refuge official under this Act or the Refuge Recreation Act for wildlife-dependent recreation to occur." (Refuge Improvement Act)

The Refuge Improvement Act and Regulations require that an affirmative finding be made of an activity's "compatibility" before such activity or use is allowed on a national wildlife refuge. Six priority, wildlife-dependent uses that are to be considered at each refuge are defined in the Refuge Improvement Act and Regulations. These are: hunting, fishing, wildlife observation and photography, environmental education and interpretation. These priority, wildlife-dependent uses may be authorized on a refuge when they are compatible (as defined above), and not inconsistent with public safety. Not all uses that are determined compatible must be allowed. The refuge has the discretion to allow or disallow any use based on other considerations such as public safety, policy and available funding. However, all uses that are allowed must be determined compatible.

We completed compatibility determinations (CDs) for these six priority public uses for the refuge under existing Service regulations and policy, the Act and the recent revisions of our Compatibility Regulations (Appendix G). Each (with some restrictions) was found to be compatible with both the mission of the Refuge System and the purposes for which the refuges were established. The conduct of natural history tours via special use permit has also been found to be compatible. We are issuing the final CDs, for these activities, as part of this CCP.

We have also determined non-motorized boating, snowshoeing and cross-country skiing to be compatible. These activities facilitate wildlife observation and wildlife photography. All of these means of locomotion are subject to CDs for these activities as part of this CCP.

Draft CDs were distributed (in the draft CCP/EA) for a 45 day public review in mid 2003. These CDs have since been approved, and will allow wildlife dependent recreation on the refuge. Subsequent to releasing the draft CCP/EA, we also distributed CDs for scientific research and jogging for a public review period. All comments were considered and utilized in the revision. These new CDs are now final and included in Appendix G.

Additional CDs will be developed when appropriate new uses are proposed. CDs will be re-evaluated by the Refuge Manager when conditions under which the use is permitted change significantly; when there is significant new information on effects of the use; or at least every 10 years for non-priority public uses. Priority public use CDs will be re-evaluated under the conditions noted above, or at least every 15 years with revision of the CCP.

Additional detail on the CD process is in Parts 25, 26, and 29 of Title 50 of the Code of Federal Regulations, effective November 17, 2000.

Monitoring and Evaluation

This Final CCP covers a 15-year period. Periodic review of the CCP is required to ensure that established goals and objectives are being met, and that the plan is being implemented as scheduled. To assist this review process, a monitoring and evaluation program will be implemented, focusing on issues involving public use activities, and wildlife habitat and population management.

Monitoring of public use programs will involve the continued collection and compilation of visitation figures and activity levels. In addition, we will establish research and monitoring programs to assess the impacts of public use activities on wildlife and wildlife habitat, assess conflicts between types of refuge uses, and to identify compatible levels of public use activities. We will reduce these public use activities if we determine that incompatible levels are occurring.

We will collect baseline data on wildlife populations and habitats as outlined in Chapter 4. This data will update often limited existing records of wildlife species using the refuge, their habitat requirements, and seasonal use patterns. We will use this data in the evaluation of the effects of public use and habitat management programs on wildlife populations.

We will monitor refuge habitat management programs for positive and negative impacts on wildlife habitat and populations and the ecological integrity of the ecosystem. The monitoring will assist in determining if these management activities are helping to meet refuge goals. Information resulting from monitoring will allow staff to set more specific and better management objectives, more rigorously evaluate management objectives, and ultimately, make better management decisions. This process of evaluation, implementation and reevaluation is known simply as "adaptive resource management".

Monitoring and Evaluation for this CCP occurs at two levels. The first level, which we refer to as implementation monitoring, responds to the question, "Did we do what we said we would do, when we said we would do it?" The second level of monitoring, which we refer to as effectiveness monitoring, responds to the question, "Are the actions we proposed effective in achieving the results we had hoped for?" Or, in other words, "Are the actions leading us toward our vision, goals, and objectives?" Effectiveness monitoring evaluates an individual action, a suite of actions, or an entire resource program. This approach is more analytical in evaluating management effects on species, populations, habitats, refuge visitors, ecosystem integrity, or the socio-economic environment. More often, the criteria to monitor and evaluate these management effects will be established in step-down, individual project, or cooperator plans, or through the research program. The Species and Habitat Inventory and Monitoring Plan, to be completed, will be based on the needs and priorities identified in the Habitat Management Plan.

Adaptive Management

This CCP is a dynamic document. A strategy of adaptive management will keep it relevant and current. Through scientific research, inventories and monitoring, and our management experiences, we will gain new information which may alter our course of action. We acknowledge that our information on species, habitats, and ecosystems is incomplete, provisional, and subject to change as our knowledge base improves.

Objectives and strategies must be adaptable in responding to new information and spatial and temporal changes. We will continually evaluate management actions, through monitoring or research, to reconsider whether their original assumptions and predictions are still valid. In this way, management becomes an active process of learning "what really works". It is important that the public understand and appreciate the adaptive nature of natural resource management.

The Refuge Manager is responsible for changing management actions or objectives if they do not produce the desired conditions. Significant changes may warrant additional NEPA analysis; minor changes will not, but will be documented in annual monitoring, project evaluation reports, or the annual refuge narratives.

Additional NEPA Analysis

NEPA requires a site specific analysis of impacts for all federal actions. These impacts are to be disclosed in either an EA or EIS.

Most of the actions and associated impacts in this plan were described in enough detail in the draft CCP/EA to comply

Kayaking facilitates wildlife-dependent recreation: Photo by Deborah Dineen

with NEPA, and will not require additional environmental analysis. Although this is not an all-inclusive list, the following programs are examples that fall into this category: protecting wildlife habitat, implementing priority wildlife-dependent public use programs, acquiring land, and controlling invasive plants.

Other actions are not described in enough detail to comply with the site-specific analysis requirements of NEPA. Examples of actions that will require a separate EA include: construction of a new office/visitor contact station and future habitat restoration projects not fully developed or delineated in this document. Monitoring, evaluation, and research can generally be increased without additional NEPA analysis.

Plan Amendment and Revision

Periodic review of the CCP will be required to ensure that objectives are being met and management actions are being implemented. Ongoing monitoring and evaluation will be an important part of this process. Monitoring results or new information may indicate the need to change our strategies.

The Service's planning policy (FWS Manual, Part 602, Chapters 1, 3, and 4) states that CCPs should be reviewed at least annually to decide if they require any revisions (Chapter 3, part 3.4 (8)). Revisions will be necessary if significant new information becomes available, ecological conditions change, major refuge expansions occur, or when we identify the need to do so during a program review. At a minimum, CCPs will be fully revised every 15 years. We will modify the CCP documents and associated management activities as needed, following the procedures outlined in Service policy and NEPA requirements. Minor revisions that meet the criteria for categorical exclusions (550 FW 3.3C) will only require an Environmental Action Statement.

Literature Cited

Anderson, Robert C. 1976. Directions of a Town: A History of Harvard, Massachusetts. The Harvard Common Press, The Common, Harvard, Ma.

Andrews, Edward. 1963. The People Called Shakers: A Search for the Perfect Society. Dover Publications, Inc., New York, NY.

Anon. 1923. Completion Report, December 7, 1923. On File, BRAC Office, Fort Devens, MA.

Anthony, David. 1978. The Archaeology of Worcester County: An Information Survey. Institute for Conservation Archaeology, Harvard University. Submitted to Massachusetts Historical Commission, Boston, MA.

Barber, Russell. 1979. Human Ecology and the Estuarine Ecosystem: Prehistoric Exploitation in the Merrimack Valley. Unpublished Ph.D. Dissertation, Department of Anthropology, Harvard University, Cambridge, Ma.

Bolton, Ethel Stanwood. 1914. Shirley Uplands and Intervals, Annals of a Border Town of Old Middle Sex, with Some Genealogical Sketches. George Emery Littlefield, Boston, MA.

Clarke, F. 2000. SUASCO (Sudbury, Assabet and Concord) River Watershed Biodiversity Protection and Stewardship Plan. Francis H. Clark. Under the Massachusetts Watershed Initiative of the Executive Office of Environmental Affairs. Commonwealth of Massachusetts. 2000. http://www.state.ma.us/index.html

Department of Revenue. 2000. Commonwealth of Massachusetts, Division of Local Services, Municipal Data Bank.

Dincauze, D.F. 1974. An Introduction to the Archaeology of the Greater Boston Area, Archaeology of Eastern North America, Vol. 2, No.1.

Dincauze, D.F. 1976. The Neville Site: 8,000 Years at Amoskeag...Peabody Museum Monographs 4. Cambridge.

Dincauze, D.F. 1981. Paleoenvironmental Reconstruction in the Northeast: the Art of Multidisciplinary Science. in Foundations in Northeast Archaeology, Edited By Dean R. Snow, pp 51-96.

Dincauze, D.F. 1993. Paleoindians in the Eastern Forest. in From Kostenki to Clovis: Upper Paleolithic-Paleo-Indian Adaptations, Edited by O. Soffer And N. D. Praslov. New York: Plenum. pp. 199-218.

Dincauze, D.F. And M.T. Mullholland. 1977. Early and Middle Archaic Site Distributions and Habitats in Southern New England. Annals of the New York Academy of Sciences 288: 439-456.

The Friends of the Oxbow National Wildlife Refuge. 2000. Biodiversity Days Report (A Series of Twenty Six Field Trips Led by Naturalists with Expertise in the Identification and Ecology of a Variety of Biota.) Three Volumes.

Funk, Robert. 1972. Early Man in the Northeast the Late Glacial Environment. Man in the Northeast. 4:7-39.

Glover, Suzanne. 1993. Final Report Archaeological Inventory Survey Fort Devens, Massachusetts, Volume I. Contract No.; DACA33-92-D-0005, Prepared for U.S. Army Corps of Engineers, Prepared by the Public Archaeology Laboratory, Inc.

Hickler, M. 1995. Floristic and Vegetation Analysis of the Oxbow Ponds in the Nashua River Flood-Plain Fort Devens, Massachusetts – Final Report. Department of Biology, University of Massachusetts, Amherst. Unpublished.

Johnson, Eric. 1984. Bifurcate Base Projectile Points in Massachusetts: Distribution and Raw Materials. Paper Presented at the 24th Annual Meeting of the Northeastern Anthropological Association, Hartford, CT.

Massachusetts Audubon Society. 2003. http://www.massaudubon.org Birds-&-Beyond iba-intro.html

Massachusetts Department of Environmental Quality Engineering. 1981. SUASCO River Basin Water Quality Management Plan. 94pp.

Massachusetts Department of Environmental Protection. 1993 Nashua River Watershed Biological Monitoring Survey Massachusetts Department of Environmental Protection, Bureau of Resource Protection, Division of Watershed Management, Worcester, Massachusetts, May, 1997.

Massachusetts Department of Environmental Protection. 1998. Surface Water Quality Standards: 314 CMR 4.03. Division of Water Pollution Control.

Massachusetts Department of Environmental Protection. 2001. Nashua River Basin, Water Quality Assessment Report. Report Number 81-AC-3. 125 pp.

Massachusetts Department of Environmental Protection. 1999. Final Massachusetts Section 303(D) List of Waters 1998. Division of Watershed Management. Worcester, MA

Massachusetts Department of Environmental Protection. 2000. Massachusetts 1999 Annual Air Quality Report. Air Assessment Branch, Wall Experiment Station, 37 Shattuck Street, Lawrence, Massachusetts 01843.

Massachusetts Department of Public Health. 1994. Public Health Interim Freshwater Fish Consumption Advisory. Bureau of Environmental Health Assessment. Boston, MA.

Massachusetts Department of Public Health. 1999. Freshwater Fish Consumption Advisory List. Bureau of Environmental Health Assessment. Boston, MA.

Literature Cited

Massachusetts Department of Revenue. 2001: http://www.dls.state.ma.us/allfiles.htm

Massachusetts Division of Fisheries & Wildlife. 1974 and 1999. Nashua River Fisheries Surveys.

Massachusetts Division of Fisheries and Wildlife, Natural Heritage And Endangered Species Program and the Massachusetts Chapter of the Nature Conservancy. 1998. Our Irreplaceable Heritage: Protecting Biodiversity in Massachusetts. 83 pp.

Massachusetts Division of Fish & Game. 2004. MassWildlife Abstract of the 2004 Massachusetts Fish & Wildlife Laws. Undated.

Massachusetts Division of Fisheries & Wildlife, Natural Heritage & Endangered Species Program, Westborough, Ma.

Massachusetts Executive Office of Environmental Affairs. 1998. Massachusetts Section 303(D) List of Waters (Final). 131pp.

Massachusetts Executive Office of Environmental Affairs. 2003 Air Quality Report. 88 pp.

Massachusetts Historical Commission. 1980. Ayer Reconnaissance Survey Report. Massachusetts Historical Commission, Boston, MA.

Massachusetts Historical Commission. 1983. Harvard Reconnaissance Survey Report. Massachusetts Historical Commission, Boston, MA

Massachusetts Historical Commission. 1985. Historic and Archaeological Resources of Central Massachusetts: A Framework for Preservation Decisions. Massachusetts Historical Commission, Office of the Secretary of State, Boston, MA

Mello, Mark J. and E. Peters. 1992. Survey of Lepidoptera at Fort Devens, with Notes on Sudbury Annex. Lloyd Center for Environmental Studies, South Dartmouth, MA. A Report to MA Natural Heritage And Endangered Species Program. Lloyd Center Report # 92-3.

Mello, Mark J. and E. Peters. 1993. Survey of Lepidoptera at Fort Devens, with Notes on Sudbury Annex. A Report to the Massachusetts Natural Heritage and Endangered Species Program. The Lloyd Center for Environmental Studies, South Dartmouth, MA.

Mello, Mark J. and E. Peters. 1994. The Lloyd Center for Environmental Studies, South Dartmouth, Ma. Unpublished Data.

National Weather Service. 2001.

National Wildlife Refuge Improvement Act of 1997. (16 U.S.C. § 668dd Et Seq.)

O'Steen, Lisa. 1987. Cultural Resource Literature and Research Review for the Proposed Pelham Mainline Branch of the Champlain Gas Pipeline Corridor: New Hampshire And Massachusetts. Garrow & Associates, Inc. submitted to ERT. Inc., Concord, Ma.

Population Estimates Program, Population Division, U.S. Census Bureau, Washington, DC 20233. Contact: Statistical Information Staff, Population Division, U.S. Census Bureau (301) 457-2422

Public Law 104-106. National Defense Authorization Act for Fiscal Year 1996, February 10, 1996.

Ritchie, Duncan. 1984. Musketaquied, 8,000 B.P.: Early Archaic Settlement and Resource Use in the Sudbury/Concord River Drainage. Paper presented at 24th Annual Meeting of the Northeastern Anthropological Association, Hartford, CT.

Ritchie, Duncan. 1985. Archaeological Investigations at the Hartford Avenue Rockshelter, Uxbridge, Massachusetts: The Data Recovery Program. The Public Archaeology Laboratory, Inc. Report No. 40-2. Submitted to the Massachusetts, Department of Public Works, Boston, MA.

Ritchie, Duncan. 1985 Archaeological Investigations of a Maintenance Building Site, Weir Hill Tract, Great Meadows National Wildlife Refuge, Sudbury, Massachusetts. Prepared By Public Archaeology Laboratory, Providence, Rhode Island for U. S. Fish and Wildlife Service, One Gateway Center, Suite 700, Newton Corner, MA.

Ritchie, Duncan and Ann Davin 1984 An Intensive Level Archaeological Survey of the Town of Bedford Water Treatment Facilities, Bedford, Massachusetts. Prepared by Public Archaeology Laboratory, Inc. Providence, Rhode Island, for Camp, Dresser and Mckee, Boston, Ma.

Roberts, David. 1995. Geology, Eastern North America. Peterson Field Guides. Roger T. Peterson (Editor). Houghton Mifflin CO. New York, N.Y. 368 pp.

Searcy, Karen B., B. Lindwall and T. Enz. 1993. Plant Community and Vegetation Analysis of Flood-Plain Areas Along the Nashua River, Fort Devens with Particular Emphasis on the Floodplain and Adjacent Slopes of the Nashua River between Jackson and Hospital Roads. Univ. of Massachusetts, Biology Dept., Amherst, MA. Unpublished Report. 62pp.

Searcy, Karen B., B. Lindwall and T. Enz. 1994. The Forested Wetlands on the South Post in the Flood-Plain of the Nashua River. Univ. of Massachusetts, Biology Dept., Amherst, MA. Unpublished Report. 20pp.

Sweet C.W. and E. Prestbo. 1999. Wet Deposition of Mercury in the U.S. and Canada. Presented at "Mercury In The Environment Specialty Conference", September 15-17, 1999, Minneapolis, Mn. Proceedings Published by Air and Waste Management Association, Pittsburgh, PA

Literature Cited

Thomas, H.H. 1992. Small Mammal Survey of the Sudbury Training Annex, Sudbury, Middlesex County, Massachusetts and Fort Deven Military Reservation, Lancaster, Worcester County, and Shirley, Middlesex County, Massachusetts. Unpublished Report. Dept. of Bio. Fitchburg State College, Fitchburg, Ma. 1992. (Survey 4/14-12/10/92 Report Undated In Original).

Town of Lancaster. 1993. Open Space and Recreation Plan 1993 Update.

Town of Shirley. 1996. The Shirley Conservation Commission's Open Space & Recreation Plan: 1996 - 2001.

University of Connecticut. 2000. A Provisional List of Non-Native Invasive and Potentially Invasive Plants in New England. Leslie J. Merhoff, University of Connecticut. January 1, 2000: http://www.eeb.uconn.edu/bioconctr/publications/publication-3.html

U.S. Army. 1995. Final Environmental Impact Statement, Fort Devens Disposal and Reuse. Department of the Army, Headquarters, Forces Command, Atlanta, Ga. (Prepared by the New England Division, U.S. Army Corps of Engineers, Concord, MA).

U.S. Army. 1998. Integrated Natural Resources Management Plan 1998 - 2002. Devens Reserve Forces Training Area, Massachusetts.

U.S. Census Bureau. 2001. Census 2000 Data: http://factfinder.census.gov

U.S. Department of Agriculture. 1985. Soil Survey of Worcester County Massachusetts, Northeastern Part. Soil Conservation Service (Now the Natural Resource Conservation Service).

U.S. Department of Interior. 2003. Recreation Fee Demonstration Program. http://www.ios.doi.gov/nrl/recfees/recfee.htm

U.S. Department of Justice. 1995. Final EIS, Federal Medical Center Complex, Fort Devens, Massachusetts.

U.S. Environmental Protection Agency. 2001. Office of Air Quality Planning and Standards "Airs Graphics" Web Site At http://www.epa.gov

U.S. Fish and Wildlife Service. 1985. Refuge Manual. Wash., D.C. U.S. Gov't Printing Office.

U.S. Fish and Wildlife Service. 1992. Fisheries USA. The Recreational Fisheries Policy of the U.S. Fish and Wildlife Service. Wash, D.C.,U.S. Gov't Printing Office.

U.S. Fish and Wildlife Service. 1992. Survey and Evaluation of Wetlands and Wildlife Habitat, Fort Devens, Massachusetts. February 6, 1992.

U.S. Fish and Wildlife Service. 1997. Environmental Contaminants in Fish from the Nashua River Fort Devens Ayer, Massachusetts. U.S. Fish and Wildlife Service, New England Field Office Special Project Report: FY97-NEFO-5-EC, December 1997.)

U.S. Fish and Wildlife Service. 1997a. Recreation Fee Programs Frequently Asked Questions.

U.S. Fish and Wildlife Service. 2000a. Trace Element Exposure in Benthic Invertebrates from Grove Pond, Plow Shop Pond, and Nonacoicus Brook, Ayer, Massachusetts. U.S. Fish and Wildlife Service. Maine Field Office. Special Project Report: FY00-MEFO-1-EC.

U.S. Fish and Wildlife Service. 2000b. Nongame Birds of Management Concern, 1995 List: http://migratorybirds.fws.gov/reports/speccon

U.S. Fish and Wildlife Service. 2000c. Final Compatibility Regulations and Final Compatibility Policy Pursuant to the National Wildlife Refuge System Improvement Act of 1997. 50 CFR Parts 25, 26 and 29

U.S. Fish and Wildlife Service. 2001. Policy on Maintaining Biological Integrity, Diversity, and Environmental Health of the National Wildlife Refuge System. http://policy.fws.gov/library/01FR3809.

War Department, 1920. Camp Devens, Mass. Property Map. Construction Division, War Department, Washington DC. on File, Building 1623, Fort Devens, MA.

Wing, Forrest Bond. 1981. The Shirley Story. Manuscript on File, Town of Shirley Library, Shirley, MA.

Glossary

accessibility- the state or quality of being easily approached or entered, particularly as it relates to the Americans with Disabilities Act.

accessible facilities- structures accessible for most people with disabilities without assistance; ada-accessible (e.g., parking lots, trails, pathways, ramps, picnic and camping areas, restrooms, boating facilities (docks, piers, gangways), fishing facilities, playgrounds, amphitheaters, exhibits, audiovisual programs, and wayside sites.)

adaptive management- responding to changing ecological condiditions so as to not exceed productivity limits of specific place. For example, when crop growth slows, a good farmer learns to recognize ecological signs that tell either to add more manure or to allow a field to lie fallow. Adaptive management becomes impossible when managers are forced to meet the demands of outsiders who are not under local ecological constraints (from Dodson et al., 1998)

agricultural land- nonforested land (now or recently orchards, pastures, or crops)

alternative- a reasonable way to fix an identified problem or satisfy a stated need (40 cfr 1500.2 (cf. "management alternative"))

amphidromous fish- fish that can migrate from fresh water to the sea or the reverse, not only for breeding, but also regularly at other times during their life cycle

anadromous fish- fish that spend a large portion of their life cycle in the ocean and return to freshwater to breed

aquatic- growing in, living in, or dependent upon water

aquatic barrier- any obstruction to fish passage

appropriate use- a proposed or existing use of a national wildlife refuge that (1) supports the Refuge System mission, the major purposes, goals or objectives of the refuge; (2) is necessary for the safe and effective conduct of a priority general public use on the refuge; (3) is otherwise determined under Service manual

chapter 605 FW 1 (draft), by the refuge manager and refuge supervisor to be appropriate

area of biological significance- cf. "special focus area"

best management practices- land management practices that produce desired results (n.b. usually describing forestry or agricultural practices effective in reducing non-point source pollution, like reseeding skidder trails or not storing manure in a flood plain. In its broader sense, practices that benefit target species.)

biological or natural diversity- the variety of life in all its forms

breeding habitat- habitat used by migratory birds or other animals during the breeding season

buffer zones- land bordering and protecting critical habitats or water bodies by reducing runoff and nonpoint source pollution loading; areas created or sustained to lessen the negative effects of land development on animals, plants, and their habitats

breeding habitat- habitat used by migratory birds or other animals during the breeding season

candidate species- species for which we have sufficient information on file about their biological vulnerability and threats to propose listing them

carrying capacity- the size of the population that can be sustained by a given environment

catadromous fish- fish that spend most of their lives in fresh water, but migrate to sea to reproduce

categorical exclusion- (CE, CX, CATEX, CATX) pursuant to the National Environmental Policy Act (NEPA), a category of federal agency actions that do not individually or cumulatively have a significant effect on the human environment (40 CFR 1508.4)

CFR- the Code of Federal Regulations

Challenge Cost Share Program- a Service administered grant program that provides matching funds for projects supporting natural resource education, management, restoration, or protection on Service lands, other public lands, and private lands

community- the locality in which a group of people resides and shares the same government

community type- a particular assemblage of plants and animals, named for its dominant characteristic

compatible use- "a wildlife-dependent recreational use or any other use of a refuge that, in the sound professional judgment of the Director, will not materially interfere with or detract from the fulfillment of the mission of the system or the purposes of the refuge."—National Wildlife Refuge System Improvement Act of 1997 (public law 105-57; 111 stat. 1253)

compatibility determination- a required determination for wildlife-dependent recreational uses or any other public uses of a refuge before a use is allowed

Comprehensive Conservation Plan- a document mandated by the National Wildlife Refuge System Improvement Act of 1997 that describes desired future conditions for a refuge unit, and provides long-range guidance for the unit leader to accomplish the mission of the system and the purpose(s) of the unit (p.l. 105-57; FWS manual 602 FW 1.4)

concern- cf. "issue"

conservation- managing natural resources to prevent loss or waste (n.b. management actions may include preservation, restoration, and enhancement.)

conservation agreements - voluntary written agreements among two or more parties for the purpose of ensuring the survival and welfare of unlisted species of fish and wildlife or their habitats or to achieve other specified conservation goals.

conservation easement- a legal agreement between a landowner and a land trust (e.g., a private, nonprofit conservation organization) or government agency that permanently limits uses of a property to protect its conservation values

cool-season grass- introduced grass for crop and pastureland that grows in spring and fall and is dormant during hot summer months

cooperative agreement- the legal instrument used when the principal purpose of a transaction is the transfer of money, property, services, or anything of value to a recipient in order to accomplish a public purpose authorized by federal statute, and substantial involvement between the Service and the recipient is anticipated (cf. "grant agreement")

cultural resource inventory- a professional study to locate and evaluate evidence of cultural resources present within a defined geographic area (n.b. various levels of inventories may include background literature searches, comprehensive field examinations to identify all exposed physical manifestations of cultural resources, or sample inventories for projecting site distribution and density over a larger area. Evaluating identified cultural resources to determine their eligibility for the National Register of Historic Places follows the criteria in 36 CFR 60.4 (cf. FWS manual 614 FW 1.7).)

cultural resource overview- a comprehensive document prepared for a field office that discusses, among other things, project prehistory and cultural history, the nature and extent of known cultural resources, previous research, management objectives, resource management conflicts or issues, and a general statement of how program objectives should be met and conflicts resolved (an overview should reference or incorporate information from a field offices background or literature search described in section viii of the Cultural Resource Management Handbook (FWS manual 614 FW 1.7).)

dedicated open space- land to be held as open space forever

designated wilderness area- an area designated by Congress as part of the National Wilderness Preservation System (FWS Manual 610 FW 1.5 (draft))

diadromous- fish that migrate from freshwater to saltwater or the reverse; a generic term that includes anadromous, catadromous, and amphidromous fish

easement- an agreement by which landowners give up or sell one of the rights on their property (e.g., landowners may donate rights-of-way across their properties to allow community members access to a river (cf. "conservation easement").)

ecosystem- a natural community of organisms interacting with its physical environment, regarded as a unit

ecotourism- visits to an area that maintains and preserves natural resources as a basis for promoting its economic growth and development

ecosystem approach- a way of looking at socioeconomic and environmental information based on the boundaries of ecosystems like watersheds, rather than on geopolitical boundaries

ecosystem-based management- an approach to making decisions based on the characteristics of the ecosystem in which a person or thing belongs (n.b. this concept considers interactions among the plants, animals, and physical characteristics of the environment in making decisions about land use or living resource issues.)

emergent wetland- wetlands dominated by erect, rooted, herbaceous plants

endangered species- a federal- or state-listed protected species that is in danger of extinction throughout all or a significant portion of its range

environmental education- "...education aimed at producing a citizenry that is knowledgeable about the biophysical environment and its associated problems, aware of how to help solve these problems, and motivated to work toward their solution."—Stapp et al. 1969

Environmental Assessment- (EA) a concise public document that briefly discusses the purpose and need for an action, its alternatives, and provides sufficient evidence and analysis of its impacts to determine whether to prepare an Environmental Impact Statement or Finding of No Significant Impact (q.v.) (cf. 40 CFR 1508.9)

Environmental Impact Statement- (EIS) a detailed, written analysis of the environmental impacts of a proposed action, adverse effects of the project that cannot be avoided, alternative courses of action, short-term uses of the

environment versus the maintenance and enhancement of long-term productivity, and any irreversible and irretrievable commitment of resources (cf. 40 CFR 1508.11)

estuaries- deepwater tidal habitats and adjacent tidal wetlands that are usually semi-enclosed by land but have open, partly obstructed or sporadic access to the ocean, and in which ocean water is at least occasionally diluted by freshwater runoff from land

estuarine wetlands- "the estuarine system consists of deepwater tidal habitats and adjacent tidal wetlands that are usually semi-enclosed by land but have open, partly obstructed, or sporadic access to the open ocean, and in which ocean water is at least occasionally diluted by freshwater runoff from the land."—Cowardin et al. 1979

exemplary community type- an outstanding example of a particular community type

extirpated- no longer occurring in a given geographic area

Federal land- public land owned by the Federal Government, including national forests, national parks, and national wildlife refuges

Federal-listed species- a species listed either as endangered, threatened, or a species at risk (formerly, a "candidate species") under the Endangered Species Act of 1973, as amended

Finding of No Significant Impact- (FONSI) supported by an Environmental Assessment, a document that briefly presents why a Federal action will have no significant effect on the human environment, and for which an Environmental Impact Statement, therefore, will not be prepared (40 CFR 1508.13)

fish passage project- providing a safe passage for fish around a barrier in the upstream or downstream direction

focus areas- cf. "special focus areas"

forbs- flowering plants (excluding grasses, sedges, and rushes) that do not have a woody stem and die back to the ground at the end of the growing season

forested land- land dominated by trees

forested wetlands- wetlands dominated by trees

Geographic Information System- (GIS) a computerized system to compile, store, analyze and display geographically referenced information (e.g., GIS can overlay multiple sets of information on the distribution of a variety of biological and physical features.)

grant agreement- the legal instrument used when the principal purpose of the transaction is the transfer of money, property, services, or anything of value to a recipient in order to accomplish a public purpose of support or stimulation authorized by federal statute and substantial involvement between the Service and the recipient is *not* anticipated (cf. "cooperative agreement")

grassroots conservation organization- any group of concerned citizens who come together to actively address a conservation need

habitat fragmentation- the breaking up of a specific habitat into smaller, unconnected areas (n.b. a habitat area that is too small may not provide enough space to maintain a breeding population of the species in question.)

habitat conservation- protecting an animal or plant habitat to ensure that the use of that habitat by the animal or plant is not altered or reduced

habitat- the place where a particular type of plant or animal lives

hydrologic or flow regime- characteristic fluctuations in river flows

important fish areas- the aquatic areas identified by private organizations, local, state, and federal agencies that meet the purposes of the Conte act

informed consent- "…the grudging willingness of opponents to go along with a course of action that they actually oppose."—Bleiker

Intergrated Pest Management (IPM)- sustainable approach to managing pests by combining biological, cultural, physical, and chemical tools in a way that minimizes economic, health, and environmental risks

interjurisdictional fish- populations of fish that are managed by two or more states or national or tribal governments because of the scope of their geographic distributions or migrations

interpretive facilities- structures that provide information about an event, place, or thing by a variety of means, including printed, audiovisual, or multimedia materials (e.g., kiosks that offer printed materials and audiovisuals, signs, and trail heads.)

interpretive materials- any tool used to provide or clarify information, explain events or things, or increase awareness and understanding of the events or things (e.g., printed materials like brochures, maps or curriculum materials; audio/visual materials like video and audio tapes, films, or slides; and, interactive multimedia materials, CD-Rom or other computer technology.)

interpretive materials projects- any cooperative venture that combines financial and staff resources to design, develop, and use tools for increasing the awareness and understanding of events or things related to a refuge

introduced invasive species- non-native species that have been introduced into an area and, because of their aggressive growth and lack of natural predators, displace native species

issue- any unsettled matter that requires a management decision (e.g., a Service initiative, an opportunity, a management problem, a threat to the resources of the unit, a conflict in uses, a public concern, or the presence of an undesirable resource condition.)

Issues Workbook- a packet of questions distributed in order to solicit public comments on the Refuge Complex and the planning process. Basic information on the Refuge Complex was bundled with the Issues Workbooks. Workbooks were not randomly distributed, nor were questions intended to have statistical significance.

lacustrine wetlands- "the lacustrine system includes wetlands and deepwater habitats with all of the following characteristics: (1) situated in a topographic depression or a dammed river channel; (2) lacking trees, shrubs, persistent emergents, emergent mosses or lichens with greater than 30% areal coverage; and (3) total area exceeds eight ha (20 acres)."—Cowardin et al. 1979

land trusts- organizations dedicated to conserving land by purchase, donation, or conservation easement from landowners

limiting factor- an environmental limitation that prevents further population growth

local land- public land owned by local governments, including community or county parks or municipal watersheds

local agencies- generally, municipal governments, regional planning commissions, or conservation groups

long-term protection- mechanisms like fee title acquisition, conservation easements, or binding agreements with landowners that ensure land use and land management practices will remain compatible with maintaining species populations over the long term

management alternative- a set of objectives and the strategies needed to accomplish each objective (FWS Manual 602 FW 1.4)

management concern- cf. "issue"; "migratory nongame birds of management concern"

management opportunity- cf. "issue"

management plan- a plan that guides future land management practices on a tract

management strategy- a general approach to meeting unit objectives (n.b. a strategy may be broad, it may be detailed enough to guide implementation through specific actions, tasks, and projects (FWS Manual 602 FW 1.4).)

mesic soil- sandy-to-clay loams containing moisture retentive organic matter, well drained (no standing matter)

migratory nongame birds of management concern- species of nongame birds that (*a*) are believed to have undergone significant population declines; (*b*) have small or restricted populations; or (*c*) are dependent upon restricted or vulnerable habitats

mission statement- a succinct statement of the purpose for which the unit was established; its reason for being

mitigation- actions taken to compensate for the negative effects of a particular project (e.g., wetland mitigation usually restores or enhances a previously damaged wetland or creates a new wetland.)

National Environmental Policy Act of 1969- (NEPA) requires all Federal agencies to examine the environmental impacts of their actions, incorporate environmental information, and use public participation in planning and implementing environmental actions (Federal agencies must integrate NEPA with other planning requirements, and prepare appropriate NEPA documents to facilitate better environmental decisionmaking (cf. 40 CFR 1500).)

National Wildlife Refuge Complex- (Complex) an internal Service administrative linking of refuge units closely related by their purposes, goals, ecosystem, or geopolitical boundaries.

National Wildlife Refuge System- (System) all lands and waters and interests therein administered by the Service as wildlife refuges, wildlife ranges, wildlife management areas, waterfowl production areas, and other areas for the protection and conservation of fish and wildlife, including those that are threatened with extinction

native plant- a plant that has grown in the region since the last glaciation and occurred before European settlement

non-consumptive, wildlife-oriented recreation- wildlife observation and photography and environmental education and interpretation (cf. "wildlife-oriented recreation")

non-point source pollution- nutrients or toxic substances that enter water from dispersed and uncontrolled sites

nonforested wetlands wetlands dominated by shrubs or emergent vegetation

Notice of Intent- (NOI) an announcement we publish in the Federal Register that we will prepare and review an Environmental Impact Statement (40 CFR 1508.22)

objective- a concise statement of what we want to achieve, how much we want to achieve, when and where we want to achieve it, and who is responsible for the work. Objectives derive from goals and provide the basis for determining strategies, monitoring refuge accomplishments, and evaluation the success of strategies. Make objectives attainable, time-specific, and measurable.

occurrence site- a discrete area where a population of a rare species lives or a rare plant community type grows

old fields - areas formerly cultivated or grazed, where woody vegetation has begun to invade (n.b. if left undisturbed, old fields will eventually succeed into forest. Many occur at sites originally suitable for crops or pasture. They vary markedly in the Northeast, depending on soil and land use and management history.)

outdoor education project- any cooperative venture that combines financial and staff resources to develop outdoor education activities like labs, field trips, surveys, monitoring, or sampling

outdoor education- educational activities that take place in an outdoor setting

palustrine wetlands- "the palustrine system includes all nontidal wetlands dominated by trees, shrubs, persistent emergents, emergent mosses or lichens, and all such wetlands that occur in tidal areas where salinity due to ocean-derived salts is below 0$."—Cowardin et al. 1979

Partners for Wiildlife Program- a voluntary, cooperative habitat restoration program among the Service, other government agencies, public and private organizations, and private landowners to improve and protect fish and wildlife habitat on private land while leaving it in private ownership

partnership- a contract or agreement among two or more individuals, groups of individuals, organizations, or agencies, in which each agrees to furnish a part of the capital or some service in kind (e.g., labor) for a mutually beneficial enterprise

planning updates- newsletters distributed, primarily through mailing lists,m in order to update the interested public on the status of the CCP project.

population monitoring- assessing the characteristics of populations to ascertain their status and establish trends on their abundance, condition, distribution, or other characteristics

prescribed fire- the application of fire to wildland fuels, either by natural or intentional ignition, to achieve identified land use objectives (FWS Manual 621 FW 1.7)

private land- land owned by a private individual or group or non-government organization

private landowner- cf. "private land"

private organization- any non-government organization

proposed action (or alternative)- activies for which an Environmental Assessment is being written; the alternative containing the actions and strategies recommended by the planning team. The proposed action is, for all proactival purposes, the draft CCP for the refuge.

protection- mechanisms like fee title acquisition, conservation easements, or binding agreements with landowners that ensure land use and land management practices will remain compatible with maintaining species populations at a site (cf. "long-term ~")

public- individuals, organizations, and non-government groups; officials of federal, state, and local government agencies; native american tribes, and foreign nations— includes anyone outside the core planning team, those who may or may not have indicated an interest in the issues and those who do or do not realize that our decisions may affect them

public involvement- offering to interested individuals and organizations that our actions or policies may affect an opportunity to become informed; soliciting their opinions.

public involvement plan- long-term guidance for involving the public in the comprehensive planning process

public land- land owned by the local, state, or Federal government

rare species- species identified for special management emphasis because of their uncommon occurrence

rare community types- plant community types classified as rare by any state program (as used in CCP's, includes exemplary community types.)

recommended wilderness- areas studied and found suitable for wilderness designation by both the Director (FWS) and Secretary (DOI), and recommended by the President to Congress for inclusion in the National Wilderness System (FWS Manual 610 FW 1.5 (draft))

Record of Decision- (ROD) a concise public record of a decision by a Federal agency pursuant to NEPA (N.b. a ROD includes:•the decision; •all the alternatives considered; •the environmentally preferable alternative; •a summary of monitoring and enforcement, where applicable, for any mitigation ; and, •whether all practical means have been adopted to avoid or minimize environmental harm from the alternative selected (or if not, why not).)

refuge goals- "...descriptive, open-ended, and often broad statements of desired future conditions that convey a purpose but do not define measurable units."— Writing Refuge Management Goals and Objectives: A Handbook

refuge mailing list- the "original" Great Meadows Refuge Complex mailling list which preceded the CCP process. This list contained names and addresses of people with an interest in the refuge. As part of the planning process, the list was continually updated to include conservation agencies, sporting clubs, Congressionals, workbook respondents, open house/focus group attendees, etc.

refuge purposes- "the terms 'purposes of the refuge' and 'purposes of each refuge' mean the purposes specified in or derived from the law, proclamation, Executive Order, agreement, public land order, donation document, or administrative memorandum establishing, authorizing, or expanding a refuge, refuge unit, or refuge subunit."—National Wildlife Refuge System Improvement Act of 1997

refuge lands- lands in which the Service holds full interest in fee title or partial interest like an easement

restoration- the artificial manipulation of habitat to restore it to its former condition (e.g., restoration may involve planting native grasses and forbs, removing shrubs, prescribed burning, or reestablishing habitat for native plants and animals on degraded grassland.)

riparian- of or relating to the banks of a stream or river

riparian agricultural land- agricultural land along a stream or river

riparian forested land- forested land along a stream or river (cf. note above)

riparian habitat- habitat along the banks of a stream or river (cf. note above)

riverine- within the active channel of a river or stream

riverine wetlands- generally, all the wetlands and deepwater habitats occurring within a freshwater river channel not dominated by trees, shrubs, or persistent emergents

runoff- water from rain, melted snow, or agricultural or landscape irrigation that flows over a land surface into a water body (cf. "urban runoff")

sandplain grassland- dry grassland that has resisted succession due to fire, wind, grazing, mowing, or salt spray (N.b. Characterized by thin, acidic, nutrient-poor soils over deep sand deposits, sandplains primarily occur on the coast and off-coast islands, or inland, where glaciers or rivers have deposited sands.)

Service presence- Service programs and facilities that it directs or shares with other organizations; public awareness of the Service as a sole or cooperative provider of programs and facilities

site improvement- any activity that changes the condition of an existing site to better interpret events, places, or things related to a refuge. (e.g., improving safety and access, replacing non-native with native plants, refurbishing footbridges and trail ways, and renovating or expanding exhibits.)

special focus area- an area of high biological value (N.b. fie normally direct most of our resources to SFA's that were delineated because of: 1.the presence of federal-listed endangered and threatened species, species at risk (formerly, "candidate species"), rare species, concentrations of migrating or wintering waterfowl, or shorebird stopover habitat; 2.their importance as migrant landbird stopover or breeding habitat; 3.the presence of unique or rare communities; or 4.the presence of important fish habitat.)

special habitats- as used in CCP's; wetlands, vernal pools, riparian habitat, and unfragmented rivers, forests and grasslands (N.b. many rare species are dependent on specialized habitats that, in many cases, are being lost within a watershed.)

special riparian project- restoring, protecting, or enhancing an aquatic environment in a discrete riparian corridor within a special focus area

species at risk- a species being considered for Federal listing as threatened or endangered (formerly, "candidate species")

species of concern- species not federal-listed as threatened or endangered, but about which we or our partners are concerned

State agencies- generally, natural resource agencies of State governments

State land- State-owned public land

State-listed species- cf. "Federal-listed species" (N.b. this is how to write the phrase "Federal- and State-listed species".)

step-down management plan- a plan for dealing with specific refuge management subjects, strategies, and schedules, e.g., cropland, wilderness, and fire (FWS Manual 602 FW 1.4)

stopover habitat- habitat where birds rest and feed during migration

telecommunications- communicating via electronic technology

telecommunications project- any cooperative venture that combines financial and staff resources to develop and use computer-based applications for exchanging information about a watershed with others

threatened species- a federal-listed, protected species that is likely to become an endangered species in all or a significant portion of its range

tiering- incorporating by reference the general discussions of broad topics in Environmental Impact Statements into narrower statements of environmental analysis by focusing on specific issues (40 CFR 1508.28)

tributary- a stream or river that flows into a larger stream, river, or lake

trust resource- a resource that the government holds in trust for the people through law or administrative act (N.b. a Federal trust resource is one for which responsibility is given wholly or in part to the Federal government by law or administrative act. Generally, Federal trust resources are nationally or internationally important no matter where they occur, like endangered species or migratory birds and fish that regularly move across state lines. They also include cultural resources protected by Federal historic preservation laws, and nationally important or threatened habitats, notably wetlands, navigable waters, and public lands like state parks and national wildlife refuges.)

unfragmented habitat- large, unbroken blocks of a particular type of habitat

unit objective- desired conditions that must be accomplished to achieve a desired outcome

upland- dry ground (i.e., other than wetlands)

upland meadow or pasture- areas maintained in grass for livestock grazing; hay production areas (N.b. meadows may occur naturally in tidal marshes and inland flooded river valleys or, more frequently, at upland sites where vegetation has been cleared and grasses planted. Eventually, meadows will revert to old fields and forest if they are not mowed, grazed, or burned. Grasses in both managed meadows and pastures usually are similar, but pasture herbs often differ because of selective grazing.)

Glossary

urban runoff water from rain, melted snow, or landscape irrigation flowing from city streets and domestic or commercial properties that may carry pollutants into a sewer system or water body

vernal pool- depressions holding water for at least two months in the spring or early summer, is absent of fish, and is important for amphibians during the breeding season.

vision statement- a concise statement of what the unit could achieve in the next 10 to 15 years

visitor center- a permanently staffed building offering exhibits and interpretive information to the visiting publc. Some visitor center are co-located with refuge offices, others include additional facilities such as classrooms or wildlife viewing areas

visitor contact station- compared to a visitor center, a contact station is a smaller facility which may not be permanently staffed

warm-season grass- native prairie grass that grows the most during summer, when cool-season grasses are dormant

watchable wildlife- all wildlife is watchable (N.b. a watchable wildlife program is one that helps maintain viable populations of all native fish and wildlife species by building an active, well informed constituency for conservation. Watchable wildlife programs are tools for meeting wildlife conservation goals while at the same time fulfilling public demand for wildlife-dependent recreational activities (other than sport hunting, sport fishing, or trapping).)

watershed- the geographic area within which water drains into a particular river, stream, or body of water; land and the body of water into which the land drains

well protected- a rare species or community type 75 percent or more of its occurrence sites are on dedicated open space

wet meadows- meadows located in moist, low-lying areas, often dominated by large colonies of reeds or grasses (N.b. often they are created by collapsed beaver dams and exposed pond bottoms. Saltmarsh meadows are subject to daily coastal tides.)

wetlands- "Wetlands are lands transitional between terrestrial and aquatic systems where the water table is usually at or near the surface or the land is covered by shallow water."— Cowardin et al 1979

wilderness- cf. "designated wilderness"

wildfire- a free-burning fire requiring a suppression response; all fire other than prescribed fire that occurs on wildlands (FWS Manual 621 FW 1.7)

wildland fire- every wildland fire is either a wildfire or a prescribed fire (FWS Manual 621 FW 1.3)

wildlife management- manipulating wildlife populations, either directly by regulating the numbers, ages, and sex ratios harvested, or indirectly by providing favorable habitat conditions and alleviating limiting factors

wildlife-oriented recreation- recreational experiences in which wildlife is the focus ("the terms 'wildlife dependent recreation' and 'wildlife-dependent recreational use' mean a use of a refuge involving hunting, fishing, wildlife observation and photography, or environmental education and interpretation."— National Wildlife Refuge System Improvement Act of 1997)

working landscape- the rural landscape created and used by traditional laborers (N.b. agriculture, forestry, and fishing all contribute to the working landscape of a watershed (e.g., keeping fields open by mowing or by grazing livestock).)

(This page intentionally left blank)

List of Preparers

Members of the Planning Team and Contributors

Elizabeth A. Herland
Project Leader
Eastern Massachusetts Complex

Tim Prior
Deputy Project Leader
Eastern Massachusetts Complex

Stephanie Koch
Wildlife Biologist
Eastern Massachusetts Complex

Bill Perry
Refuge Planner
Eastern Massachusetts Complex

Debra Kimbrell-Anderson
Refuge Manager
Assabet and Oxbow NWRs
Eastern Massachusetts Complex

Michael Dixon
Outdoor Recreation Planner
Eastern Massachusetts Complex

Sharon Fish Marino
Former Refuge Manager
Monomoy NWR

Carl Melberg
Land Acquisition Planner
U.S. Fish and Wildlife Service
Northeast Regional Office

Bud Oliveira
Deputy Chief of the National Wildlife Refuge
System, Region 4
Former Project Leader
Eastern Massachusetts Complex

Pamela Hess
Appalachian Mountain Club
Former Deputy Project Leader
Eastern Massachusetts Complex

Chuck Bell
Former District Manager Northeast District
Division of Fish and Game
Commonwealth of Massachusetts

Debbie Dineen, Natural Resources, Town of
Sudbury

Curt Laffin, Planning Consultant

Jack Lash
Planning and Ecology Director Department
of Environmental Management,
Commonwealth of Massachusetts

Tom Poole
Natural Resource Manager
Army at Devens Reserve Forces Training
Area

Bill Woytek
Division of Fish and Game, Commonwealth of
Massachusetts

Bruce Flaig and Marijke Holtrop
Generously allowed the refuge to use their
photographs, many of which were used in this
plan

Lindsay Krey
Assistant Planner
Former Team Leader
U.S. Fish and Wildlife Service
Northeast Regional Office

Nicole Allison
Former Wildlife Biologist
U.S. Fish and Wildlife Service
Northeast Regional Office

William Archambault
Fisheries Supervisor South
Former Regional NEPA Coordinator
U.S. Fish and Wildlife Service
Northeast Regional Office

Melissa Brewer
Former Fisheries Biologist
U.S. Fish and Wildlife Service
Northeast Regional Office

John Eaton, Cartographer
U.S. Fish and Wildlife Service
Northeast Regional Office

Andrew French
Former Realty Officer
U.S. Fish and Wildlife Service
Northeast Regional Office

Thomas Bonetti
Refuge Planner
Former Team Leader for this project.
U.S. Fish and Wildlife Service
Northeast Regional Office

Victoria Barr
Archeologist
U.S. Fish and Wildlife Service
Northeast Regional Office

Rick Jorgensen
Realty Specialist
U.S. Fish and Wildlife Service
Northeast Regional Office

Wendy Lilly-Hanson
Former Wildlife Biologist
Eastern Massachusetts Complex

Janet Kennedy
Refuge Manager Parker River NWR
Former Deputy Project Leader for Eastern
Massachusetts Complex

Deborah Long
Deputy Refuge Manager Forsythe NWR
Former Monomoy NWR Refuge Manager

Lisa Plagge
Former Bio-technician
Great Meadows, Oxbow, and Assabet NWRs
Eastern Massachusetts Complex

Pamela Rooney
Engineering Supervisor
Former Planning Team Leader
U.S. Fish and Wildlife Service
Northeast Regional Office

Rick Schauffler
Wildlife Biologist and Cartographer
U.S. Fish and Wildlife Service
New England Field Office

Janith Taylor
Regional Biologist
U.S. Fish and Wildlife Service
New England Field Office

Sharon Ware
Refuge Manager Sachuest Point NWR
Former Refuge Manager at Monomoy NWR

Mike Amaral
Senior Endangered Species Specialist
U.S. Fish and Wildlife Service
New England Field Office

Addresses

Northeast Regional Office
U.S. Fish and Wildlife Service
National Wildlife Refuge System
300 Westgate Center Dr.
Hadley, MA 01035

Eastern Massachusetts National Wildlife
Refuge Complex Headquarters
73 Weir Hill Road
Sudbury, MA 01776

New England Field Office
70 Commercial St., Ste 300
Concord, NH 03301-5087

Monomoy NWR
Wikis Way, Morris Island
Chatham, MA 02633

Appendices

(This page intentionally left blank)

Appendix A: Relevant Laws

Emergency Wetland Resources Act of 1986

This Act authorized the purchase of wetlands with Land and Water Conservation Fund moneys, removing a prior prohibition on such acquisitions. The Act also requires the Secretary to establish a National Wetlands Priority Conservation Plan, requires the States to include wetlands in their Comprehensive Outdoor Recreation Plans, and transfers to the Migratory Bird Conservation Fund amount equal to import duties on arms and ammunition.

Endangered Species Act of 1973 (16 U.S.C. 1531-1544, 87 Stat. 884), as amended

Public Law 93-205, approved December 28, 1973, repealed the Endangered Species Conservation Act of December 5, 1969 (P.L. 91-135, 83 Stat. 275). The 1969 Act had amended the Endangered Species Preservation Act of October 15, 1966 (P.L. 89-669, 80 Stat. 926). The 1973 Endangered Species Act provided for the conservation of ecosystems upon which threatened and endangered species of fish, wildlife, and plants depend, both through federal action and by encouraging the establishment of state programs. The act:
- authorizes the determination and listing of species as endangered and threatened;
- prohibits unauthorized taking, possession, sale, and transport of endangered species;
- provides authority to acquire land for the conservation of listed species, using land and water conservation funds;
- authorizes establishment of cooperative agreements and grants-in-aid to states that establish and maintain active and adequate programs for endangered and threatened wildlife and plants;
- authorizes the assessment of civil and criminal penalties for violating the act or regulations; and
- authorizes the payment of rewards to anyone furnishing information leading to arrest and conviction for any violation of the act of any regulation issued thereunder.

Executive Order 11988, Floodplain Management

The purpose of this Executive Order, signed May 24, 1977, is to prevent Federal agencies from contributing to the "adverse impacts associated with occupancy and modification of floodplains" and the "direct or indirect support of floodplain development." in the course of fulfilling their respective authorities, Federal agencies "shall take action to reduce the risk of flood loss, to minimize the impact of floods on human safety, health and welfare, and to restore and preserve the natural and beneficial values served by floodplains.

Fish and Wildlife Improvement Act of 1978

This Act was passed to improve the administration of fish and wildlife programs and amends several earlier laws, including the Refuge Recreation Act, the National Wildlife Refuge Administration Act, and the Fish and Wildlife Act of 1956. It authorizes the secretary to accept gifts and bequests of real and personal property on behalf of the United States. It also authorizes the use of volunteers on service projects and appropriations to carry out volunteer programs.

Historic Preservation Acts

There are various laws for the preservation of historic sites and objects.

Antiquities Act (16 U.S.C. 431 - 433) – The Act of June 8, 1906, (34 Stat. 225) authorizes the President to designate as National Monuments objects or areas of historic or scientific interest on lands owned or controlled by the United States. The Act required that a permit be obtained for examination of ruins, excavation of archaeological sites and the gathering of objects of antiquity on lands under the jurisdiction of the Secretaries of Interior, Agriculture, and Army, and provided penalties for violations.

Archaeological Resources Protection Act (16 U.S.C. 470aa - 470ll) -- Public Law 96-95, approved October 31, 1979, (93 Stat. 721) largely supplanted the resource protection provisions of the Antiquities Act for archaeological items.

This Act established detailed requirements for issuance of permits for any excavation for or removal of archaeological resources from Federal or Indian lands. It also established civil and criminal penalties for the unauthorized excavation, removal, or damage of any such resources; for any trafficking in such resources removed from Federal or Indian land in violation of any provision of Federal law; and for interstate and foreign commerce in such resources acquired, transported or received in violation of any state or local law.

Public Law 100-588, approved November 3, 1988, (102 Stat. 2983) lowered the threshold value of artifacts triggering the felony provisions of the act from $5,000 to $500, made attempting to commit an action prohibited by the Act a violation, and required the land managing agencies to establish public awareness programs regarding the value of archaeological resources to the Nation.

Archeological and Historic Preservation Act (16 U.S.C. 469-469c) -- Public Law 86-523, approved June 27, 1960, (74 Stat. 220) as amended by Public Law 93-291, approved May 24, 1974, (88 Stat. 174) to carry out the policy established by the historic sites act (see below), directed Federal agencies to notify the Secretary of the Interior whenever they find a Federal or Federally assisted, licensed or permitted project may cause loss or destruction of significant scientific, prehistoric or archaeological data. The Act authorized use of appropriated, donated and/or transferred funds for the recovery, protection and preservation of such data.

Historic Sites, Buildings and Antiquities Act (16 U.S.C 461-462, 464-467) -- The Act of August 21, 1935, (49 Stat. 666) popularly known as the Historic Sites Act, as amended by Public Law 89-249, approved October 9, 1965, (79 Stat. 971) declared it a National policy to preserve historic sites and objects of national significance, including those located on refuges. It provided procedures for designation, acquisition, administration and protection of such sites. Among other things, National Historic and Natural Landmarks are designated under authority of this Act. As of January, 1989, 31 national wildlife refuges contained such sites.

National Historic Preservation Act of 1966 (16 U.S.C. 470-470b, 470c-470n) -- Public Law 89-665, approved October 15, 1966, (80 Stat. 915) and repeatedly amended, provided for preservation of significant historical features (buildings, objects and sites) through a grant-in-aid program to the states. It established a National Register of Historic Places and a program of matching grants under the existing National Trust for Historic Preservation (16 U.S.C. 468-468d).

The Act established an Advisory Council on Historic Preservation, which was made a permanent independent agency in Public Law 94-422, Approved September 28, 1976 (90 Stat. 1319). That Act also created the Historic Preservation Fund. Federal agencies are directed to take into account the effects of their actions on items or sites listed or eligible for listing in the National Register.

As of January, 1989, 91 historic sites on national wildlife refuges have been placed on the National Register.

Land and Water Conservation Fund Act of 1948

This Act provides funding through receipts from the sale of surplus federal land, appropriations from oil and gas receipts from the outer continental shelf, and other sources for land acquisition under several authorities. Appropriations from the fund may be used for matching grants to states for outdoor recreation projects and for land acquisition by various federal agencies, including the Fish and Wildlife Service.

Migratory Bird Conservation Act of 1929 (16 U.S.C. 715- 715d, 715e, 715f-715r)

This Act established the Migratory Bird Conservation Commission which consists of the Secretaries of the Interior (chairman), Agriculture, and Transportation, two members from the House of Representatives, and an ex-officio member from the state in which a project is located. The Commission approves acquisition of land and water, or interests therein, and sets the priorities for acquisition of lands by the Secretary for sanctuaries or for other management purposes. Under this Act, to acquire lands, or interests therein, the state concerned must consent to such acquisition by legislation. Such legislation has been enacted by most states.

Migratory Bird Hunting and Conservation Stamp Act (16 U.S.C. 718-718j, 48 Stat. 452), as amended

The "Duck Stamp Act," as this March 16, 1934, authority is commonly called, requires each waterfowl hunter 16 years of age or older to possess a valid Federal hunting stamp. Receipts from the sale of the stamp are deposited in a special Treasury account known as the Migratory Bird Conservation Fund and are not subject to appropriations.

National and Community Service Act of 1990 (42 U.S.C. 12401; 104 Stat. 3127)

Public Law 101-610, signed November 16, 1990, authorizes several programs to engage citizens of the U.S. in full- and/or part-time projects designed to combat illiteracy and poverty, provide job skills, enhance educational skills, and fulfill environmental needs. Several provisions are of particular interest to the U.S. Fish and Wildlife Service.

American Conservation and Youth Service Corps -- as a Federal grant program established under Subtitle C of the law, the Corps offers an opportunity for young adults between the ages of 16-25, or in the case of summer programs, 15-21, to engage in approved human and natural resources projects which benefit the public or are carried out on Federal or Indian lands.

To be eligible for assistance, natural resources programs will focus on improvement of wildlife habitat and recreational areas, fish culture, fishery assistance, erosion, wetlands protection, pollution control and similar projects. A stipend of not more than 100 percent of the poverty level will be paid to participants. A Commission established to administer the Youth Service Corps will make grants to States, the Secretaries of Agriculture and Interior and the Director of ACTION to carry out these responsibilities.

National and Community Service Act -- Will make grants to states for the creation of full-time and/or part-time programs for citizens over 17 years of age. Programs must be designed to fill unmet educational, human, environmental, and public safety needs. Initially, participants will receive post-employment benefits of up to $1000 per year for part-time and $2500 for full-time participants.

Thousand Points of Light -- Creates a nonprofit Points of Light Foundation to administer programs to encourage citizens and institutions to volunteer in order to solve critical social issues, and to discover new leaders and develop institutions committed to serving others.

National Environmental Policy Act of 1969 (P.L. 91-190, 42 U.S.C. 4321-4347, January 1, 1970, 83 Stat. 852) as amended by P.L. 94-52, July 3, 1975, 89 Stat. 258, and P.L. 94-83, August 9, 1975, 89 Stat. 424).

Title I of the 1969 National Environmental Policy Act (NEPA) requires that all Federal agencies prepare detailed environmental impact statements for "every recommendation or report on proposals for legislation and other major Federal actions significantly affecting the quality of the human environment."

The 1969 statute stipulated the factors to be considered in environmental impact statements, and required that Federal agencies employ an interdisciplinary approach in related decision-making and develop means to ensure that unquantified environmental values are given appropriate consideration, along with economic and technical considerations.

Title II of this statute requires annual reports on environmental quality from the President to the Congress, and established a Council on environmental quality in the Executive Office of the President with specific duties and functions.

National Wildlife Refuge System Administration Act of 1966 (16U.S.C. 668dd-668ee) as amended

This act defines the Refuge System as including wildlife refuges, areas for protection and conservation of fish and wildlife which are threatened with extinction, wildlife ranges, game ranges, wildlife management areas, and waterfowl production areas. The Secretary is authorized to permit any use of an area provided such use is compatible with the major purposes for which such area was established. The purchase considerations for rights-of-way go into the Migratory Bird Conservation Fund for the acquisition of lands. By regulation, up to 40% of an area acquired for a migratory bird sanctuary may be opened to migratory bird hunting unless the Secretary finds that the taking of any species of migratory game birds in more than 40% of such area would be beneficial to the species. The Act requires an Act of Congress for the divestiture of lands in the system, except (1) lands acquired with Migratory Bird Conservation Commission funds, and (2) lands can be removed from the system by land exchange, or if brought into the System by a cooperative agreement, then pursuant to the terms of the agreement.

National Wildlife Refuge System Improvement Act of 1997

Public Law 105-57, amends the National Wildlife System Act of 1966 (16 U.S.C. 668dd-ee), providing guidance for management and public use of the Refuge System. The Act mandates that the Refuge System be consistently directed and managed as a national system of lands and waters devoted to wildlife conservation and management.

The Act establishes priorities for recreational uses of the Refuge System. Six wildlife-dependent uses are specifically named in the act: hunting, fishing, wildlife observation and photography, and environmental education and interpretation. These activities are to be promoted on the Refuge System, while all non-wildlife dependant uses are subject to compatibility determinations.

A compatible use is one which, in the sound professional judgment of the Refuge Manger, will not materially interfere with or detract from fulfillment of the Refuge System Mission or refuge purpose(s).

As stated in the Act, "the mission of the System is to administer a national network of lands and waters for the conservation, management, and where appropriate, restoration of the fish, wildlife, and plant resources and their habitats within the United States for the benefit of present and future generations of Americans."

The act also requires development of a comprehensive conservation plan for each refuge and management of each refuge consistent with the plan. When writing CCP, planning for expanded or new refuges, and when making management decisions, The Act requires effective coordination with other Federal agencies, state fish and wildlife or conservation agencies, and refuge neighbors. A refuge must also provide opportunities for public involvement when making a compatibility determination or developing a CCP.

North American Wetlands Conservation Act (103 Stat. 1968; 16 U.S.C. 4401-4412)

Public Law 101-233, enacted December 13, 1989, provides funding and administrative direction for implementation of the North American Waterfowl Management Plan and the Tripartite Agreement on wetlands between Canada, U.S. and Mexico.

The Act converts the Pittman-Robertson account into a trust fund, with the interest available without appropriation through the year 2006 to carry out the programs authorized by the Act, along with an authorization for annual appropriation of over $20 million plus an amount equal to the fines and forfeitures collected under the Migratory Bird Treaty Act.

Available funds may be expended, upon approval of the Migratory Bird Conservation Commission, for payment of not to exceed 50 percent of the United States share of the cost of wetlands conservation projects in Canada, Mexico, or the United States (or 100 percent of the cost of projects on Federal lands). At least 50 percent and no more than 70 percent of the funds received are to go to Canada and Mexico each year.

A North American Wetlands Conservation Council is created to recommend projects to be funded under the Act to the Migratory Bird Conservation Commission. The Council is to be composed of the Director of the Service, the Secretary of the National Fish and Wildlife Foundation, a State fish and game agency director from each flyway, and three representatives of different nonprofit organizations participating in projects under the Plan or the Act. The Chairman of the Council and one other member serve ex officio on the Commission for consideration of the Council's recommendations.

The Commission must justify in writing to the Council and, annually, to Congress, any decisions not to accept Council recommendations.

Oil Pollution Act of 1990

Public Law 101-380 (33 U.S.C. 2701 et seq.; 104 Stat. 484) established new requirements and extensively amended the Federal Water Pollution Control Act (33 U.S.C. 1301 et. seq.) to provide enhanced capabilities for oil spill response and natural resource damage assessment by the Service. It required Service consultation on developing a fish and wildlife response plan for the National Contingency Plan, input to Area Contingency Plans, review of Facility and Tank Vessel Contingency Plans, and to conduct damage assessments associated with oil spills.

One aspect of particular interest to the Service involves the identification of ecologically sensitive areas and the preparation of scientific monitoring and evaluation plans. Research conducted by the Service is to be directed and coordinated by the National Wetland Research Center.

National Wildlife Refuge System Centennial Cct of 2000

This Act paves the way for a special, nationwide outreach campaign. The law calls for a Centennial Commission of distinguished individuals to work with partners in carrying out the outreach campaign. The law also calls for a long-term plan to address the major operations, maintenance, and construction needs of the Refuge System

These centennial activities will help broaden visibility, strengthen partnerships, and fortify facilities and programs for wildlife and habitat conservation and recreation. They will build a stronghold of support for the National Wildlife Refuge System to sustain it in a new era of both challenge and opportunity.

Refuge Recreation Act of 1962

This Act authorizes the Secretary of the Interior to administer refuges, hatcheries, and other conservation areas for recreational use, when such uses do not interfere with the area's primary purposes. It authorizes construction and maintenance of recreational facilities and the acquisition of land for incidental fish and wildlife oriented recreational development or protection of natural resources. It also authorizes the charging of fees for public uses.

Refuge Revenue Sharing Act (16 U.S.C. 715s)

Section 401 of the Act of June 15, 1935, (49 stat. 383) provided for payments to counties in lieu of taxes, using revenues derived from the sale of products from refuges.

Public Law 93-509, approved December 3, 1974, (88 Stat. 1603) required that moneys remaining in the fund after payments be transferred to the Migratory Bird Conservation Fund for land acquisition under provisions of the Migratory Bird Conservation Act.

Public Law 95-469, approved October 17, 1978, (92 Stat. 1319) expanded the revenue sharing system to include National Fish Hatcheries and Service research stations. It also included in the Refuge Revenue Sharing Fund receipts from the sale of salmonid carcasses. Payments to counties were established as:

1) on acquired land, the greatest amount calculated on the basis of 75 cents per acre, three-fourths of one percent of the appraised value, or 25 percent of the net receipts produced from the land; and

2) on land withdrawn from the public domain, 25 percent of net receipts and basic payments under Public Law 94-565 (31 U.S.C. 1601-1607, 90 Stat. 2662), payment in lieu of taxes on public lands.

This amendment also authorized appropriations to make up any difference between the amount in the Fund and the amount scheduled for payment in any year. The stipulation that payments be used for schools and roads was removed, but counties were required to pass payments along to other units of local government within the county which suffer losses in revenues due to the establishment of refuges.

Transfer of Certain Real Property for Wildlife Conservation Purposes Act of 1948

This Act provides that upon determination by the Administrator of the General Services Administration, real property no longer needed by a Federal agency can be transferred, without reimbursement, to the Secretary of the Interior if the land has particular value for migratory birds, or to a state agency for other wildlife conservation purposes.

Rehabilitation Act of 1973 (29 U.S.C. 794)as amended

Title 5 of Public Law 93-112 (87 Stat. 355), signed October 1, 1973, prohibits discrimination on the basis of handicap under any program or activity receiving Federal financial assistance.

The Volunteer and Community Partnership Act

The Volunteer and Community Partnership Act of 1998 brings recognition and additional authorities to the volunteer program and community partnerships, as well as supports education programs. Under this Act, refuges can now more easily conduct business with community partners under the auspices of the newly authorized and streamlined administrative processes. Leveraging Federal dollars and staff, Refuge Managers can operate and construct services through cooperative agreements, deposit donations in individual accounts at the refuge, and match donations.

Youth Conservation Corps Act (16 U.S.C. 1701-1706, 84 Stat. 794)

Public Law 91-378, approved August 13, 1970, declares the YCC pilot program a success and establishes permanent programs within the Departments of Interior and Agriculture for young adults who have attained the age of 15, but not the age of 19, to perform specific tasks on lands and waters administered under jurisdiction of these Secretaries. Within the Fish and Wildlife Service, YCC participants perform various tasks on national wildlife refuges, national fish hatcheries, research stations, and other facilities.

The legislation also authorizes the Secretary of Interior and the Secretary of Agriculture to establish a joint grant program to assist states employing young adults on non-Federal public lands and waters throughout the U.S.

Requires the Secretaries of Interior and Agriculture to prepare a joint report to the President and Congress prior to April 1 of each year.

Wilderness Act of 1964

Public Law 88-577, approved September 3, 1964, directed the Secretary of the Interior, within 10 years, to review every roadless area of 5,000 or more acres and every roadless island (regardless of size) within national wildlife refuges and national parks for inclusion in the National Wilderness Preservation System.

Appendix B: U.S. Forest Service Content Analysis Team Summary Report

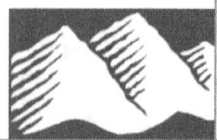

Analysis of Public Comment

CAT
Content
Analysis
Team

**November 26
2003**

200 E
Broadway
Room 301
P.O. Box 7669
Missoula, MT
59807
406-329-3038

U.S. Department of the Interior, Fish & Wildlife Service

The Eastern Massachusetts National Wildlife Refuge Complex

Assabet River, Great Meadows, Oxbow Wildlife Refuges

Draft Comprehensive Conservation Plan and Environmental Assessment

Table of Contents

Introduction

The contracted U.S. Forest Service Content Analysis Team report summarizes public comment submitted on the Draft Comprehensive Conservation Plan and Environmental Assessment (hereafter Draft CCP/EA) prepared to describe the alternatives for the Assabet River, Great Meadows, and Oxbow refuges in the Eastern Massachusetts National Wildlife Refuge Complex. This report provides a narrative review of concerns raised as well as appendices detailing the coding process for reviewing public comments, analyzing demographic information derived from responses, and listing individuals responsible for the analysis. The narrative summary provides an overview of pervasive themes in public sentiment rather than a comprehensive description of each public concern.

Public input on the Draft CCP/EA is documented, analyzed, and summarized using a process called content analysis. This is a systematic method of compiling and categorizing the full range of public viewpoints and concerns regarding a plan or project. This process makes no attempt to treat comments as votes. In no way does content analysis attempt to sway decision makers toward the will of any majority. Content analysis ensures that every comment is considered at some point in the decision process. Content analysis is intended to facilitate good decision-making by helping the planning team to clarify, adjust, or incorporate technical information into the final guidelines. The process facilitates agency response to comment.

All responses (i.e., letters, emails, faxes, oral testimony, and other types of input) are included in this analysis. In the content analysis process, each response is given a unique identifying number, which allows analysts to link specific comments to original letters. Respondents' names and addresses are then entered into a project-specific database program, enabling creation of a complete mailing list of all respondents. The database is also used to track pertinent demographic information such as responses from special interest groups or federal, state, tribal, county, and local governments.

All input is considered and reviewed by an analyst. Comments are then entered into the database. In preparing the final summary analysis, public statements are reviewed again using database printouts. These reports track all coded input and allow analysts to identify a wide range of public concerns and analyze the relationships between them in a narrative summary.

The U.S. Fish and Wildlife Service solicited comments on the Draft CCP/EA from July 20, 2003 to September 3, 2003.

During the comment period, 1,907 responses, oral and written, were received. Twenty-five responses were duplicates; therefore 1882 responses were entered into the comment database. Organized response campaigns (forms) represented 70 percent (1,334 of 1,907) of the total responses.

Summary of Comments

Synopsis

The general tenor of comments is appreciative and laudatory. Typically, respondents endorse Alternative B. While there are many specific exceptions to these trends, the two most common are opposition to new or increased hunting on the refuge, and opposition to proposed limits on non-motorized recreation on the refuge, such as dog-walking and picnicking. Endorsement of Alterative B is often couched with provisos, such as that it eliminate hunting on the refuge.

Where analysts were able to identify unit-specific comments (such as those about the Great Meadows), the database includes that identification; FWS may wish to review unit-specific comments. In general, however, analysts do not discern any appreciable difference in comments addressed to the various units. The overall themes of comments are the same, and most specific suggestions could apply equally to all three refuges. Where site-specific suggestions or concerns are relevant to this summary, they are identified.

Planning Processes

General Planning

Although respondents are generally complimentary of U.S. Fish and Wildlife Service (FWS) staff and the CCP/EA, commentors provide some suggestions and various criticisms of the document. Respondents also request an opportunity to revisit the plan after its implementation and make any necessary changes.

Time frame for planning/length of comment period

Some respondents are disappointed in the comment period, arguing that holding the comment period during the summer months limits the informed input that communities and individuals can give. Specifically, the Suasco Watershed Community Council states, "The summer timing of this public review may have inadvertently and unfortunately limited public comment." Also, some respondents want more time to review the "technical and voluminous" conservation plan so that they may submit more informed comments. Respondents are also disappointed that the agency failed to adequately inform the public of the comment period. One respondent from Concord, for example, wanted notice of the comment period posted on the bulletin board at the Great Meadows Refuge. The FWS, some argue, should extend the comment period and improve outreach efforts so that communities and individuals may provide well-informed and useful comments.

Public Involvement

Many respondents feel satisfied with the FWS's level of public involvement and education; they praise the agencies past efforts and eagerly anticipate additional opportunities for interest groups and communities to stay involved in the refuge's management. One Maynard respondent affirms, "Your efforts to involve the local communities are appreciated and should benefit us all." There are, however, a significant number of respondents who believe the FWS could improve their public involvement and education efforts. One individual states, "Community members in the towns abutting the land appear to have very little knowledge about your proposal, and therefore have had very little input." Respondents urge the FWS to hold more public meetings in schools, libraries, senior centers, and town offices, as well as take advantage of the media to improve public involvement and educate communities. "[Great Meadows Refuge] is a wonderful opportunity for public outreach—a place to engage dedicated environmentalists in a dialogue with U.S. Fish and Wildlife and to recruit new support for the service and its mission."

Civic and conservation organizations express interest in collaborating with the FWS on management issues. The City of Marlborough Conservation Commission, for example, would like to work cooperatively with the FWS in managing the Refuge Complex and the Memorial Forest and Desert Natural Area "to enhance biodiversity and wildlife while allowing public access where suitable." Conservation commissions from other towns express interest in collaborative management as well. Similarly, respondents nominate the Massachusetts Audubon Society, the Trustee of Reservations, the Friends of Assabet River Wildlife Refuge, The Friends of the Oxbow National Wildlife Refuge, The Great Meadows Neighborhood Association, Bay State Trail Riders Association, and the Sudbury Valley Trustees as good candidates for public involvement.

Relationship to Regional Planning Efforts

Respondents ask for clarification of the CCP's compatibility with other regional management efforts, such as: the Maynard Open Space by-law for the Maynard portion of the Sudbury Annex in 1987 and its hunting restrictions; the Freedom's Way Association bill currently before congress to formally designate 43 communities as a national heritage area near the Great Meadows complex; wildlife management and conservation restrictions near Bolton Flats and Devens South Post; the goals of Wild and Scenic River designations; and the original intent of the O'Rourke farm "river reservation."

Statutory Authority

Respondents sometimes address real or perceived conflicts between the CCP and federal or state law. Some respondents remind the FWS that projects proposed "within the Oxbow boundary are subject to the Massachusetts Endangered Species Act," and that the National Wildlife Refuge Improvement Act of 1997 permits hunting as "one of six priority wildlife-dependent uses."

Trust and Integrity

Some respondents question the intent of the agency, and are disappointed that the land management decisions proffered in the CCP do not reflect the historical uses of the land. "I know that I would not have voted for FWS to take the land if I had believed that I would never have access to that property for recreational use. You duped the residents of these towns so that you could get this property," exclaims one respondent.

Other respondents, however, praise the FWS staff and their efforts. These respondents trust the agency to make appropriate land management decisions based on expertise and dedication.

Clarity/Organization of Planning Documents

Many respondents approve of the CCP and commend the agency. "I would like to say that it is an impressive document [and] remarkably well-written," comments one typical respondent. Commentors also support the document's consideration of and compatibility with neighboring areas.

Some respondents express disappointment, however, in the agency's website performance and the size of the electronic document.

Technical & Editorial

Respondents suggest the agency provide clearer, more accurate maps. Respondents also provided editorial suggestions. For example, "Correction: The Commission would like to point out an error on the map on page 2-71. A parking lot is shown on Maple St. north of the service road. This site is in fact a private home. There is a parking lot across the street on Greenough Conservation Land existing there." Another respondent wrote, "Please correct the capitalization on Sudbury section maps 2-6, 2-7, 2-16 to Sherman Bridge Road. It is two words. It's a street in Wayland."

Purpose and Need

Range of Issues

Some respondents feel that FWS is making a mistake in classifying certain issues as beyond the scope of the EA. These respondents want the FWS to evaluate and mitigate noise and air pollution impacts on visitors and wildlife caused by Hanscom Field air traffic. One commentor states, "The CCP should include a plan to evaluate impacts to waterfowl, especially during nesting seasons, from air traffic at Hanscom Field. The CCP should identify noise from Hanscom Field as an issue with which the U.S. Fish and Wildlife staff should be more involved." Respondents protest the expansion of Hanscom Field and its related impacts to the visitor experience; and ask that FWS partner with local communities and federal agencies—the Department of Transportation and the Federal Aviation Administration—to analyze the impacts of the expansion. One conservation organization asks the FWS to participate in the evaluation of jet ski impacts to recreation and wildlife on the Concord River.

Guiding Policy for Public Lands

Respondents repeatedly describe the agency's mission as one of wildlife protection, and assert that human activities and development should be limited. "In establishing the permitted uses for the refuge, you must not bow to public pressure. You must follow the charter of a NWR. To do that, you need to establish what the sensitive species are in the refuge, and how they are best managed. You must define what additional resources should be involved to preserve habitat for the animals. This might include re-establishing topographical features, acquiring adjacent land, procuring easements on neighboring lands, or managing tourists." Respondents emphasize the history of the land and its importance to local communities, and suggest that informed management decisions that benefit biodiversity would best preserve the refuge. To accomplish this, respondents suggest the agency "recognize areas in proximity to the refuge and consider such in managing refuge resources," as wildlife and ecosystems do not recognize political boundaries.

The land that makes up the Assabet River, Great Meadows, and Oxbow Wildlife Refuges is important to the people in the neighboring communities. Many respondents feel connected to the land, historically, spiritually, and personally.

Alternatives

Many respondents either support Alternative A or B, while little is said regarding Alternative C. Proponents of Alternative A are concerned about expanding or limiting specific activities such as hunting and dog-walking. Some of these respondents request not expanding or allowing hunting. Other respondents ask to retain, rather than prohibit, existing "non-wildlife" dependent activities. In general, these respondents desire Refuge Complex management to continue as is.

Respondents support Alternative B more for its management approach than allowed activities. Many of these respondents favor active management for invasive species and wildlife habitat. Additionally, supporters of Alternative B approve of the levels of funding and staffing proposed. Respondents are divided about the benefits of the phased opening of the refuge. Other concerns stemming from Alternative B include additional fees, allowed uses, and land acquisitions. Repeatedly, respondents endorse Alternative B while asking that it permit non-motorized uses such as dog-walking, and prohibit hunting.

Some respondents feel that no alternative considered is adequate. New alternatives suggested include: emphasizing non-consumptive, non-lethal approaches to population control; promoting the refuge as "open space," not a hunting preserve; and providing more local level decision-making.

Affected Environment

General resources

One respondent requests that the FWS include in its bibliography the respondent's publication, "A Bibliography of the Biodiversity and the Natural History of the Sudbury River- Concord River Valley, including the Great Meadows, the Estabrook Woods, and Walden Woods."

One respondent avows support for "projects that deal with restoring the native ecology to the area."

Water quality

One respondent requests protection of water quality and quantity in the Assabet River corridor and drainage. Related to the issue of quantity, one respondent raises the issue of connected aquifers: "Areas outside the scope of the CCP and town water supply wells (Pg. 1-24): Protecting the remaining base flow—the groundwater that supplies flow to the streams during dry times—in the tributaries and main stem of the Assabet River is critical to protecting water quality and aquatic habitat in the watershed . . . therefore, we suggest that any requests for access to the refuges for the purpose of drilling new water supply wells be reviewed for impacts to the wetlands and tributary streams on and off the refuges and suggest using the groundwater model of the Assabet River watershed currently being developed by the US Geological Survey (Northborough) to evaluate potential habitat impacts of proposed increased withdrawals."

One respondent argues that water quality degradation should be a critical part of the CCP/EA, rather than being considered out of scope: "I thought the water quality section was weak. Having raised the red flag that the rivers are heavily contaminated, I did not feel that the text clearly explained what that meant for the public and for wildlife in the refuge, and what the prospects for correction are. For example, I had thought that a major current issue was discharge of excessive nutrients from waste water treatment plants leading eutrophication and low-oxygen conditions."

Vegetation

Respondents request that the FWS complete proposed cover-type maps to assess species occurrence and distribution. One respondent provides extensive advice: "Biological Inventories and Mapping Alternative B calls for a thorough inventory of all species on the refuges: It would be ideal to be that comprehensive. If priorities are needed, we suggest the following order of importance: Reptiles, especially turtles; Complete documentation of vernal pools; Invertebrates: Select representative habitats to inventory macro invertebrates in order to provide a representational picture of invertebrates in the different habitats on the refuge and to identify any rare species. Invertebrates can also serve as indicators of overall ecosystem health; Benthic macro invertebrates: select representative habitats for river, stream, pond and wetland surveys within the refuge; Field invertebrates: select a methodology that targets representative field types, such as wet meadow and upland field."

Several respondents suggest that the refuge should sustain and enhance grassland and shrubland habitat on all three units to promote early-successional species, many of which are in decline in the Northeast. One respondent suggests creation of a butterfly refuge on the south side of the patrol road running from the Hudson Road gate to the radar station.

Invasives

The need to inventory refuge resources is connected by one respondent to the need to control invasives: "The Service's proposal to complete a comprehensive invasive plant inventory by 2007 will help guide species-specific management. Many exotic and invasive plant species in the watershed have become discouragingly pervasive. SVT recommends that the Service prioritize its efforts on species that are threatening rare habitats, out-competing rare or state-listed species, or are still in low density numbers. The need for exotic species control research is great and the Service's proposal to participate in experimental invasive species control could result in new innovative methods."

Many respondents support efforts to eliminate invasive non-native species. Indeed, a number urge the FWS to help catalyze a regional control effort in cooperation with abutters, state, federal, and town authorities, and non-profits, arguing that, "Without a systematic treatment of this issue, invasive plants will continue to be dispersed throughout the area by wildlife, people, and mechanical means."

Several respondents raise concerns about invasives at Puffer Pond, given new fishing access to Puffer. One respondent writes: "At present Puffer Pond is pristine and free from invasive species such as milfoil and water chestnut that have infected other waterways within Massachusetts, especially in local ponds including nearby Lake Boon. Allowing canoes previously used in these infected waterways increases the probability of infecting Puffer Pond with these invasives. Canoe portage presents still another problem in that Puffer Pond is a fair distance from the existing entrances. If auto canoe portage were allowed to the pond, temporary parking (allowing driving on the refuge proper) for canoe launch would have to be provided. This could (would) become permanent parking because of the undesirability of leaving the canoe and its contents to move the canoe carriers to an approved parking area after launch and then walking back to the canoe launch area."

Concerns about targeted species are raised in two cases: one respondent argues that cattails are native, and should not be removed; a number of respondents argue that mute swans are harmless and should be

Wildlife Management

The most commonly offered input regarding wildlife management reflects an overwhelming sense of community and a desire to harmonize refuge planning efforts with past, present, and future local and regional land management activities. As one respondent summarizes, "The physical configuration and multiple ownership (plus the unique natural history heritage) of the valley demands a common vision and a systems and team approach. If all the landowners will work together in supporting and adding to the enormous environmental, natural resource and knowledge base that has already been put in place by past generations, the resulting synergy will produce a 'refuge' of far greater proportions and impact than could ever occur if each property owner goes off on his/her own." This sentiment is reflected over and over in comments. Often, people state, "our town" or "our organization" already has wildlife survey data, or "our town/community" wishes to expand its knowledge of natural resources in the area. These respondents encourage FWS to utilize existing data and established management practices when making decisions for the refuge, and frequently urge FWS to "coordinate," "consult," and "share information."

A related theme touched on by many respondents is the quality of wildlife species data provided in the CCP. Respondents request consistently high-quality data, and some respondents request that FWS provide the most up-to-date species information possible.

Some respondents argue that the agency is drifting away from what they perceive to be its central mission: providing "refuge" for wildlife. A number of people assert that in a wildlife refuge, wildlife needs should take precedence over human needs. Echoing this view, many people request that FWS conduct thorough wildlife assessments to determine what kinds of human activities (if any) might be appropriate on the refuge. A number of respondents believe that hunting and trapping for wildlife population control are not appropriate. Some people encourage non-lethal—or at least humane—population control methods.

All respondents who comment on wildlife monitoring support Alternative B; however, these people encourage FWS to provide more detail regarding how, when, and where monitoring will occur.

Refuge Administration

General Suggestions

A number of respondents urge FWS to address refuge management from a regional perspective, encouraging the FWS to integrate refuge management with the management of surrounding lands through community partnerships. Several people ask the FWS to justify splitting the Great Meadows refuge into two units. They argue that this area is all part of one ecosystem and, accordingly, should be managed as one unit.

The few people who address historical and archaeological sites simply ask the FWS to inventory these resources and to preserve and enhance them when possible.

Land Acquisition

Many respondents comment on the proposed land acquisition boundaries, with the majority of people in favor of expanding them. A typical respondent argues that, "In a plan that purports to run for the next 15 years, it seems shockingly shortsighted to limit land acquisition (including through donations) by the refuge." Some respondents suggest that expansion is the best way to protect whole ecosystems and waterways, while others encourage an expanded refuge area to protect threatened and endangered species and wildlife corridors. Some people ask the FWS to include specific areas, such as the former Fort Devens South Post area and parts of the Assebet and Nashua rivers, in the land acquisition boundaries.

Some respondents discourage the FWS from expanding the land acquisition boundaries. Typically these sentiments stem from disagreement with FWS management choices, such as limits on horseback use.

Buildings and Facilities

Respondents voice a myriad of opinions regarding what kinds of buildings and facilities should be provided at the refuge. Suggesting that visitor education is an important component of gaining public support for the refuge, a number of respondents encourage the FWS to build a visitor center or at the least, a contact station. Some of these respondents make more specific suggestions, such as using existing buildings for a contact station/visitor center or locating such a facility at Hudson Road or at Deven's near Jackson Gate. A number of people support the idea of an administration building on the refuge.

Citing the importance of public education, many people ask the FWS to locate kiosks at strategic locations throughout the refuge. Comments regarding refuge parking focus on lot location with many people discouraging parking at Heard Pond. These respondents contend that there has been too much garbage dumping and vandalism at the Heard Pond site to make it a desirable parking place. One respondent asks the FWS to place portable toilets at all parking facilities in the refuge. A number of people support development of an observation deck. A few other specific refuge management suggestions offered by respondents include:

remove barbed wire from the refuge, use smaller information signs, establish a picnic area with a bear-proof garbage can, and construct fire hydrants on White Pond Road and along Sudbury Road.

Staffing and Funding

Although one respondent believes that the refuge should not have rangers because they merely ". . . harass old ladies . . .," most people feel that adequate refuge staffing is essential. While many people assert that Alternative B will meet desired staffing levels, a number of other respondents contend that proposed staffing levels are too low. These people cite anticipated user conflicts, present refuge hazards, and the current downsizing trend in government as reasons to increase proposed staffing levels. Some respondents suggest utilizing community groups and/or to form partnerships with volunteer organizations to supplement staffing needs.

With regard to refuge management funding, the only direction provided by respondents is a request that the FWS ensure its adequacy.

Enforcement

Respondents who comment on enforcement say that the level of enforcement on the refuge needs to increase. Some respondents suggest that implementation of some programs be delayed until adequate enforcement is in place. Others recommend developing a contingency plan in case proposed enforcement levels are not effective. An additional suggestion offered by some people is that the FWS have a backup force in place of either volunteers and/or community officers.

The key areas identified by respondents as needing increased policing efforts are off-highway vehicle trespass, poaching, dumping, trespass, and vandalism. As a typical respondent writes, "Preventing illegal use by ATVs is a major enforcement challenge for properties with large borders surrounded by suburban landscapes and with many potential entry points."

Wild and Scenic Rivers

The one concern regarding wild and scenic river designation expressed by several respondents is that hunting is incompatible with this designation and should be prohibited within these areas.

Priority Public Uses

Analysis of Existing Conditions and Need for Further Analysis

Several respondents question CCP visitor estimates and request better calculations, one respondent suggesting that based on personal experience the estimate of 70,000 people per year visiting Oxbow is "wildly incorrect. It is probably more like 7,000."

Numerous respondents request that scientific analysis of wildlife populations take place prior to any hunting or trapping. One conservation organization suggests that the CCP be driven entirely by wildlife surveys: "We suggest three overarching management priorities when considering policies about public use activities: 1. Public uses allowed under the CCP should be based on the findings of wildlife inventory and habitat management step-down plans. Public use plans should be based on wildlife inventory and habitat management plans; 2. The Service should monitor and adjust allowed public uses based on impacts to wildlife and habitat during the drafting/revision of step-down plans; 3. Public use should be coordinated among partner organizations with land holdings in the vicinity of refuges."

Several respondents argue that ongoing monitoring will be critical to management of wildlife-dependent recreation, typically: "The proposed additional monitoring projects in Alternative B for all three refuges must include at least that level of detail about how the monitoring and evaluation will be carried out. For example: The CCP states on pages 2-29, 2-68, and 2-95 that the Visitor Services Plans, to be completed by 2007, for Assabet River, Great Meadows, and Oxbow Refuges would include a monitoring program to evaluate the intensity and potential impacts of all the wildlife-dependent public uses on the refuges. What data have you collected to date on this issue and what has your analysis of the results shown? What steps are now being taken or will be taken until 2007 when the monitoring program is in place to ensure that current management of wildlife-dependent uses is not having an adverse effect on the resources?"

General Management Direction

Respondents offer a number of suggestions for general management direction of the Refuge Complex relating to priority public uses, typically defining the extent to which they believe various recreational activities should be permitted. Many respondents, for example, argue that the refuge should be "open to the public," by which they typically mean members of the public who undertake non-motorized recreation such as picnicking and jogging. For many, this is their defining test of the value of the refuge and a natural consequence of it being public land, e.g., since we pay taxes we get to use it.

For a few respondents, general access to the refuge is part payback for the original government acquisition of the land. For many more, there is a significant level of anger at the prospect of restriction of passive uses, e.g., "[Great Meadows] has been used with great respect and affection by the local public for well over the thirty years that we've lived here. I can't imagine what reason or right the Federal Government might think it has to interfere with that use."

Some respondents acknowledge the mission of the refuge, and couch their suggestions in terms of "wildlife-dependent uses." These respondents suggest that jogging, dog-walking, picnicking, and bicycling are dependent on wildlife.

Many other respondents functionally argue that the purpose of the refuge should be redefined, making other arguments for permitting non-motorized recreation. For example, although few respondents articulate the thought as clearly and plainly, many implicitly advanced an argument in consonance with this comment: "The following suggestions are based upon the assumption that the primary purpose of the refuge is to preserve native species and habitat, but that other compatible uses are acceptable if they support and do not significantly interfere with the primary use."

Other respondents implicitly or explicitly question the priority attached to those activities defined as wildlife-dependent, e.g., "The boundary between wildlife-dependent and non-wildlife dependent activities is not always clear. The more important distinction, in our view, is between outdoor activities that have an adverse effect on the health and diversity of populations of natural organisms, and those that have little or no such impact."

Related to the assertion that only harmful public uses should be restricted, one respondent suggests that permitting only harmless uses would mean "hiking, skiing, snowshoeing, and not much else." A significant number of respondents asserted that off-highway vehicle use— legal and illegal—results in harm, and should be prohibited.

Some respondents offer support for the general direction of the FWS preferred alternative or general confidence in the agency's ability to sort things out. Some respondents ask the agency to monitor use and make appropriate judgments down the line, saying that the agency should continually evaluate relationship between recreational uses, ensure that all legal uses receive fair consideration and access, and minimize conflict.

Refuge Access

Again, many respondents argue for "access" to the Refuge Complex, by which they usually mean easy entrance for non-motorized recreation. While some respondents assert that certain specific activities (dog-walking, jogging, etc.) may negatively impact the refuge, most argue that non-motorized uses are harmless.

Regarding infrastructure, some respondents request that the FWS eliminate the maximum number of trails and roads to protect wildlife. Some respondents assert that off-trail access should be by permit only. One respondent asks that access be limited where it may impact state-listed rare species, such as Blanding's turtles, and argues that the FWS should survey for rare reptiles and amphibians before opening areas or new infrastructure for recreation access.

According to one respondent, "It would be nice if one long trail could be paved for handicapped people in wheelchairs."

Respondents provide many suggestions for specific access points and trails they would like to see developed.

Fees

A considerable number of respondents support fees for use of the Refuge Complex. As one respondent said at a public meeting, "They are great areas; I enjoy walking them a lot. I'd be happy to give somebody twenty bucks tonight to walk in them the rest of the year." Some of those who support user fees hinge continued support on clear and appropriate local application of funds, or on fee levels remaining stable.

A considerable number of respondents also oppose user fees at the refuge. Some respondents oppose fees based on their perception that the FWS is effectively double-dipping; quote one respondent, "We've already paid through taxes."

Respondents oppose user fees for a number of other reasons, arguing variously that fees will deter use (especially by low-income individuals) or alienate local residents and collaborators. Some perceive fees as a barrier, e.g.: "I am very much opposed to the plans for Great Meadows. This land has been use and enjoyed for many years, and I cannot fathom that access may be impeded by restricted hours and fees. The community benefits greatly from a refuge that is easily and freely accessible to all." "It belongs to all of us," another respondent writes, "not the few who are able to pay admission costs." A number of respondents argue that fees change the nature of a recreational experience, e.g., "It destroys the soul of the experience."

With regard to both opposition to fees and concern about the proposed fee schedule, it is worth noting that a number of respondents appear unaware of or uninterested in the possibility of purchasing an annual pass instead of paying upon each entrance to the park. For some respondents, then, fees may appear deceptively exorbitant.

With regard to fee schedules, several suggestions are advanced. Several respondents propose that local residents be exempted from fees. Some respondents suggest that volunteers receive free passes. A number of respondents suggest that hunting fees be higher than other entrance fees. Some respondents complain that a car full of hunters (for example) would be charged less for entrance than a family of bicyclists, and argue that non-motorized arrivals are less intrusive and solve parking problems, and should be admitted for lower charges than motor vehicles. One respondent suggests charging a parking fee, rather than an entrance fee.

Several respondents request clarification of fee schedules, in one case asking whether there are any fee differences between Alternatives B and C, and in another asking whether a $15 annual duck stamp wouldn't obviate the need to pay $20 for an annual permit.

Respondents also offer suggestions and concerns regarding the mechanics of fee collection and enforcement. A number of respondents argue that enforcement will be impractical and expensive, arguing that self-service doesn't work and that all refuge entrances will have to be staffed. Likewise, a number of respondents question whether entrance gates will work in a refuge with as many porous boundaries between local residences and conservation land as the refuge has. Several respondents ask whether fee income will be outweighed by financial and goodwill costs, and ask the FWS to provide a detailed analysis of costs and benefits.

Hunting

Hunting was the issue most frequently addressed in comments on the EMNWR CCP. The hunting issue most frequently raised by respondents was safety—many residents and recreationists fear that hunting will put them in danger. These responses merit close scrutiny, which follows in a section on public safety. However, many other issues were raised vis-à-vis hunting, and they will be discussed here.

Hunting advocates

Although lesser in number than those opposed to hunting, a number of both area residents and others voiced support for hunting on the Refuge. Some respondents assert that the purpose of refuges is conservation—not preservation—and that hunting should be allowed on all wildlife refuges. Others argue that hunting is plainly a wildlife-dependent activity, and one with important cultural and educational values. One respondent writes, "Hunting should also be recognized and allowed as a legitimate wildlife-dependent recreational activity. Pursuing wild game for sport and table fare is an American tradition as old as our country itself. Family bonds are forged and strengthened as parents pass on to their children valuable lessons in conservation and outdoor ethics. Hunting is a total wildlife-dependent experience that fosters an intimate knowledge of game and habitat and teaches a wide variety of wilderness skills."

Other respondents argue that sportsmen and women have "been the primary source of funding" for many conservation efforts, provide money to FWS, and therefore deserve entry to the refuge complex. Some respondents assert that hunters have been losing territory to development in northeast Massachusetts for decades, and argue that the refuge complex should, in fairness, and to relieve hunting pressure on other areas, be available.

Addressing the issue of displacement, several respondents indicate that hunting does not impact other recreationists. As a typical respondent states, "If you're worried about compatibility issues on the river as to being able to share, I hunt the Sudbury River, and people go by in their kayaks, I don't shoot when they're paddling by. I wave to them. They don't wave back, but I wave to them. I'm sitting there with my dog just, you know, letting them go on by."

Some hunting advocates also seek to allay safety concerns, arguing that hunting is an extremely safe sport. "Some local people have concerns about the opening of these areas to hunting. It is important to inform the public of the safeguards, rules and restrictions that will be associated with the harvest of resident wildlife. . . . If practiced safely hunting is no more dangerous than many other daily activities."

Some respondents (hunters and non-hunters alike) suggest that the Refuge permit bow hunting only, .e.g., "Once the abutters have an understanding of how close one must be to their quarry to execute a lethal shot, they will also understand that before a shot is made, and there is no question about what it is the archer is taking aim at. So there will be no mistaking a human or household pet for a deer. . . . It is not some beer-guzzling bubba sitting in wait for the first thing that moves but rather responsible people who have been through state-mandated training in the sport of bow hunting and who are dedicated to the sport who wish every hunt to be a safe incident free experience for themselves and anybody they share the woods with."

Respondents also offer suggestions for ensuring safe hunts, such as banning buckshot and limiting magazine capacity. Some respondents suggest using testing, expense, and the willingness of hunters to assist with Refuge goals to ensure that only a safe and ethical subset of hunters have access to the Refuge.

Advocates of hunting also claim that hunting provides effective population control for nuisance species, arguing that waterfowl befoul water and recreation areas, and that deer cause traffic accidents, browse crops and ornamentals, and carry lyme disease-infected ticks.

Hunters also assert that their activities are humane, asserting that overpopulation will be addressed either through lingering, painful deaths by starvation or disease, or through quick and painless execution.

Some respondents support hunting but are concerned that access to Oxbow may be being increased too much, and ask that use be monitored and adjusted as necessary. Some respondents ask the agency to limit expansion to what can be handled by existing enforcement capability. Some respondents ask that waterfowl hunting at Oxbow include "the marshes and potholes," as well as Hop Brook near the train tracks. One respondent urges that there be no limits on waterfowling.

One respondent suggests that pheasant stocking continue at Oxbow, but not be expanded to Assabet.

Opposition to hunting

Opposition to hunting at the EMNWR is intense and widespread, at least within the subset of individuals who provided comment on the CCP. When respondents differentiate between game species, opposition to hunting turkey and grouse is common, but support for a limited deer hunt is more common. Leaving aside public safety, and the associated question of displacement, comments which question the wisdom of permitting (or expanding existing) fall into four broad categories: requests for additional analysis; concern over impacts; moral outrage; and concerns about iniquitous treatment of recreationists.

Additional Analysis

Some respondents don't plainly oppose hunting, but ask for additional analysis to justify and focus hunting. For example, one respondent says, "I am not in favor of hunting in that area unless it is required to control species that have no natural means of control, and justified by appropriate studies." Some respondents suggest that hunting not be regarded as recreation, but as wildlife population management, and that therefore it should be utilized only where comprehensive biological surveys and analysis indicate it would be of value for biodiversity or habitat protection. These respondents argue that only species with real overpopulations should be hunted (and ask for hard evidence, rather than anecdotes of browsed ornamentals), excluding species—such as woodcocks—that appear to be in decline. Some respondents question whether scientific analysis will indicate that hunting in such a limited area will have real impacts on area populations.

Some respondents assert that the CCP inadequately analyzes the impact of hunting. Respondents request more data on the cost of ministering to hunters, on impacts on public safety, habitat, and species, and on methods of implementation. Some respondents ask the FWS to evaluate the economic impacts of hunting, positing that displacement of other recreationists' results in negative impacts. Respondents ask for boundary clarifications and improved maps of available hunting areas. Respondents ask whether the agency has assessed its liability for hunting accidents.

Connected with the sense that analysis is inadequate is the argument that the "cure" is inappropriate to the problem. Respondents suggest that beavers be controlled through non-lethal means, which they argue have been proven more effective than trapping.

Impacts

Several respondents oppose hunting based on perceived impacts to other resources. As one respondent writes, "A great number of migratory birds rely on this sanctuary for breeding, as do many amphibians, reptiles, fish and mammals. Loud noise such as gun shot is known to interfere with breeding. Such interference seems in direct conflict with the intent of this land as sanctuary." Numerous area residents complain that the sound of gun shots is aesthetically disturbing as well as frightening.

Several respondents express concern about the impact of lead shot on wildlife and water quality. Several respondents argue that hunting off-trail with or without dogs will cause damage, and suggest that off-trail use be as limited for hunters as it is for other recreationists. Several respondents argue that many migratory birds are in decline, and ask that none be hunted.

Moral objections

Comments from both area residents and apparent respondents to a campaign by animal rights organizations indicate revulsion at the idea of hunting, particularly on a national wildlife refuge. For example: "Of all the violent, destructive activities in the world, hunting is right up at the top of the list. I am really disgusted at these proposed changes, as is the rest of my family. We live very close to Great Meadows, and I'm sure that the last thing we want to hear in the middle of a peaceful Saturday afternoon is gunfire ripping though the air followed by the squeal of a helpless animal gasping its last breath." Or: "Hunting, especially trapping, is an unnecessary and cruel attack on nature's innocent creatures. To permit people to entertain themselves by cruelly destroying the lives of other beings is unconscionable. Hatred, selfishness, and violence tear the world we live in today. Encouraging people to hunt and to kill does nothing to heal our wounds and move us toward a better world."

Respondents argue that hunting should not be permitted, because, they allege: it benefits a small constituency; fees for sportsmen and women are a minor part of overall conservation funding; hunters kill two animals for each they harvest, leaving the others to die suffering, lingering deaths; hunters present a danger to non-game species; in terms of population control, predators better select prey; hunting stresses wildlife.

Respondents are particularly angered by the idea of hunting on a refuge, which they perceive to be directly in conflict with the purpose and definition of a refuge. One typical respondent describes shooting wildlife on a wildlife refuge as "oxymoronic."

Iniquity

A strong sentiment running through the comments is a sense that there is something inconsistent, unfair, and hypocritical about permitting hunting on the EMNWR while prohibiting activities such as dog-walking, jogging, and picnicking on the basis of their wildlife impacts. As one respondent writes, "It makes absolutely no sense to me that hunting will be allowed in the refuge, but dogs on leashes and bike riding will not be allowed. How in the world are dogs on leashes and people on bicycles considered dangerous to wildlife, yet people with guns are okay?" Or as a conservation group writes, "Inconsistent or arbitrary management of public use could lead to confusion and resentment. Why could someone who is hunting grouse have a dog (unleashed!) whereas non-hunters must leave their canine friends at home? Can a birdwatcher take along a sandwich, or is that considered picnicking? If the pace of a jogger spooks wildlife, then why can someone cross-country ski?"

Many respondents assert that quiet recreation opportunities are rare, but that adequate hunting is already available.

Hunting and Public Safety

Many respondents argue that expanded hunting will threaten the safety of area residents and other recreationists. It is easiest to consider these comments in two categories: threats to people, and displacement of recreationists.

Threats to people

Many respondents, including many local residents, argue that a) they will feel unsafe if hunting is permitted on the Refuge, and b) that people or animals will be injured or killed by friendly fire. A typical comment: "I was brought up learning how to handle a gun, including shotguns, and remember going deer hunting with my father in Lincoln, Lexington and other towns west of Boston—albeit over 50 years ago. . . . Without prejudice one way or the other about the justification for hunting, I think the CCP fails to address the important issue of public safety and the dangers resulting to adjacent schools, roadways and homes in the Refuge area. Clearly, MetroWest is already too overbuilt to allow for the extended hunting proposed in the CCP." Or: "I do not want to be shot hanging clothes in my back yard."

To protect visitors to other conservation lands, some respondents suggest that hunters be prohibited from using public access points to other lands (such as Foss Farm and Greenough Conservation lands). Local abutters and area residents are particularly concerned about stray or mistargeted bullets, and raise concerns regarding a number of specific sites such as the Maynard public school campus and the southern portion of the Sudbury unit.

One respondent raises concerns regarding the resources local law enforcement will expend as a result of increased hunting: "As the Chief of Police in the Town of Billerica I am concerned about proposed hunting on and around the Concord River. This has been a safety and noise concern for residents of west Billerica for many years. I feel that this proposed change will increase these problems. Please take into consideration that this end of the refuge is a populated area and hunting can pose safety risks. Additionally this will cause an influx of Police calls to the area to determine if hunters are on private property or refuge land. Does the plan have any contingency to compensate the town for this added use of resources?"

Displacement

Many respondents aver that they will be unable to use the Refuge during hunting season. One respondent asks that the FWS "Expand the Compatibility Determination analysis to include an assessment of recreational compatibility. This should include a determination that the conditions that motivated the past Refuge Manager to ban hunting have been alleviated." Respondents argue that creating an exclusive use for significant portions of the year is unfair and unwise. Some respondents express significant concern for area recreationists over unmarked and porous boundaries between the Refuge, conservation land, and residences, particularly where hunters might go off-trail. A typical respondent writes, "I am also opposed to hunting, not for moral reasons, but for safety reasons. I and my dogs were the target of a hunter at Great Meadows several years ago. I had to hit the ground and crawl behind a tree for safety. He didn't see me, though when he heard me, he took off in a hurry."

Some respondents complain that hunting season occupies optimal use times for the Refuge, one respondent stating that no one uses refuges in summer because "the deer flies will kill you." Several respondents think along similar lines, suggesting reduced hunting opportunities to permit other recreation: "Maybe hunting could be limited to a few weekends per season," writes one, while another suggests a couple days of hunting per week. Another respondent suggests things would be better "if you had one or two hunting days where experienced hunters signed up to do a 'cull' if you could actually get them to kill sick, old and slow individuals instead of the healthiest, biggest and most impressive animals—and those days be highly publicized so innocent people wouldn't be hurt."

Some respondents suggest that the only safe course of action is to close the Refuge to other uses during hunting season.

To alleviate these concerns, some respondents argue that hunting should only be done by professionals paid by the refuge for wildlife management: "If the refuge needs to use deadly force to carry out the mission, have that applied by trained professionals and not by anyone with ten bucks and a shotgun."

Several respondents mention the need to educate both hunters and area residents on the schedule and placement of legal hunting. Several respondents talk about the need to increase law enforcement to deal with increased hunting, and some assert that the Refuge's record of successful interdiction of motorized trespass and vandalism indicates a current inability to enforce laws, and little confidence that hunting can be safely policed.

Dogs and Public Safety

A number of respondents offer intensely felt comments advocating continued use of dogs on the refuge as a matter of personal safety. These respondents, all women, state that prohibiting dogs effectively prohibits their use of the refuge, e.g., "I am a woman and very aware that when I am in the woods—I am an easy prey object for defective human types. I would never walk alone in the woods without my dog—a 120 pound dog at my side is a huge deterrent to even trying something. I have been approached in the past by questionable behavior and my dog at that time did place himself between me and the man creeping up behind me. The man turned and left. By banning dogs on-leashes at Great Meadows you effectively ban all women."

Fishing

With the exception of the occasional "let us fish anywhere we want," most fishing comments are restricted to Puffer Pond on the Assabet River. There is considerable support for fishing on Puffer Pond, and for the proposal to do so, and some respondents argue that anglers infrequently transport invasives.

There are also a number of respondents who request that fishing be prohibited on Puffer Pond. Respondents argue that anglers will disturb nesting birds, erode the shore, trample vegetation, bring in invasives, and drag boats through the refuge. As one respondent writes, "Little consideration has been given to the effect [fishing] would have upon Puffer Pond's habitat. The shoreline risking areas would gradually be expanded by use, destroying additional shoreline habitat and pond plants. Trash that is left behind such as beverage containers, fishing gear wrappers, tangled fish line in trees, on the ground and in the water, are a danger to birds, waterfowl, and other wildlife. How a shoreline fishing area would be made handicapped accessible is not discussed. Catch and release is an ideal fishing concept. However, it can prove to be fatal to many fish due to hook swallowing and extraction. Enforcement of catch and release will be difficult. Due to the small size of the pond, the popularity of fishing, and the high density of the area, the pond would soon be in danger of being greatly depleted. This rapid removal of fish would affect other wildlife populations that depend upon the pond for food. These would include the colony of great blue herons currently residing in the refuge near the pond, raccoon, and other water and fish dependent animals."

Respondents concerned about impacts to Puffer Pond, but not categorically opposed to fishing, suggest very limited shoreline access to the Pond, to reduce impacts, and in one case a prohibition on the use of treble hooks. One respondent offers extensive recommendations for minimizing the threat of invasives.

Several respondents ask how the agency intends to adequately enforce restrictions and monitor impacts at Puffer Pond.

Environmental Education

A large majority of respondents who chose to address this section of the CCP support the environmental efforts and facilities proposed in Alternative B, advocating more environmental education for people of all ages. Several respondents encourage completion of the proposed Sudbury River interpretive canoe trail. Several respondents encourage the FWS to think bigger, and develop its educational plan in concert with other regional entities and efforts, such as a Sudbury-Concord River valley regional conservation study and education effort. One respondent urges that "a full-scale information/education center is included as part of the future considerations for the Oxbow. . . . The Oxbow is also significant because it offers the additional opportunity for linkages with other state, private and town owned lands. And it is also situated in the center of the proposed Freedom's Way National Heritage Area." One respondent urges the FWS to use the refuge principally for biological studies.

With regard to facilities, one respondent is "very interested in the potential development of a visitor center in the area of Great Meadows NWR. We would like to explore any opportunities to increase the public understanding of the Sudbury, Assabet River and Concord Wild and Scenic Rivers within the educational materials and displays presented at the visitor center." One respondent urges the FWS to continue historical tours: "These have been very popular and have provided a way by which some of Maynard's older residents can view the refuge. Several such tours a year would provide access to history and wildlife through use of a motorized van or bus."

One organization requests clarification on facilities development "The proposed management of public outreach is unclear. The only designated public outreach position is slotted for Great Meadows. Does this position support all three refuges, or Great Meadows, or the complex as a whole? Does this individual coordinate volunteer efforts and recruit volunteers for all three refuges, or Great Meadows, or the complex as a whole?"

Some respondents complain that recreational restrictions undermine opportunities for education at the refuge, and urge that leashed dogs and off-trail nature study and photography be permitted. Several respondents urge the FWS to close some areas to hunting to permit educational tours in spring and fall.

Recreation

Due to the refuge's proximity to heavily populated areas, and an already existing recreational trail system, accessing the refuge for recreation is a major concern of many respondents. Some respondents even see the refuge as a sort of town park. Many local residents that responded did not expect restrictions on recreation when they supported FWS's offer to buy the property. Others support the concept that wildlife sanctuary should be the priority, and use limitations should be imposed.

Some respondents see access for recreation at the refuge as a means to an end: "Through controlled access to refuges you can create and sustain a community of citizens who will not only care for the refuges but also support the Fish and Wildlife Service in its struggle to maintain them."

Some respondents want the refuge to be used for quiet sports only, and ask that motors be prohibited to reduce noise, air and water pollution, erosion of soil, and to increase safety. As one respondent states, "I urge you to support making the refuge into a place where passive recreation can take place. By that I mean prohibiting motorized vehicles and hunting. The land is a treasure for hikers, bikers, runners, birdwatchers, nature lovers and, as such, should be preserved for this and future generations."

Snowmobiling

Snowmobilers describe themselves as law-abiding recreationists that are respectful of others and wildlife. One local snowmobile club would like to establish a trail through the refuge, maintained by the club, for the club's enjoyment. This club goes on to point out that snowmobiling will not harm the terrain or wildlife because snowmobiling usually occurs from the beginning of January to the beginning of April (at the latest) and only when there is a minimum of four inches of snow. Further, snowmobiling is already governed by Massachusetts laws requiring, among other things, that snowmobiles stay on the trail. Snowmobiling, the club concludes, is a traditional use in the area and ask the FWS to let snowmobilers use traditional trails.

Jogging

Joggers view the refuge as a safe, peaceful place to pursue their activity, and are confused as to why jogging would be banned. One respondent states that the refuge ". . . is a beautiful place to jog, particularly because it is one of the few off-road places with no early morning traffic. It would be shame if joggers were not allowed to use the paths of the Wildlife refuge." Another respondent asserts that, "The joggers I've seen are respectful of walkers, seems inconsistent when hiking, snowshoeing, and cross-country skiing are allowed." Another respondent writes: "If anyone ever asks, I guess I'll just tell folks, 'Oh no, I'm not running, I'm just hiking real fast.'"

Picnicking

Picnicking is viewed by many respondents as a harmless past time that allows people to enjoy the refuge's beauty. As one respondent puts it, "Is this really such a huge problem? On my daily walks I never see any trash along the trails. . . . What is so bad about taking a family, a lunch basket, and enjoying a couple of hours surrounded by nature?" These respondents ask the FWS to allow picnicking within the refuge.

Bicycling

Similar to jogging, many respondents assert that the refuge offers a safe, traffic-free environment for bicycling. These respondents also point out that bicycling is already an important component of the surrounding towns, and that many local residents have moved into the area because of its extensive town trail system. By not allowing bicycling in the refuge, FWS will be creating a gap in the local trail systems. For example, the nearby areas of the Stow Town Forest, the Sudbury State Forest, the Memorial Forest Reservation, and Desert Natural Area allow bicyclists on the trails. The addition of the refuge to this significant resource would yield excellent opportunities for exercise and enjoyment of the natural setting, by allowing cyclists to connect with other available areas. Therefore, respondents ask that the refuge acknowledge the local trail systems' benefits by allowing responsible cyclists to use the refuge's roads. Some cyclists are willing to be flexible as to when and where they can pursue their sport. One respondent suggests FWS provide signage to indicate allowed routes and speed limits to help restrict bicycling that may conflict with wildlife activities. Another proposes that the FWS set aside periods during the day when bicycling would be permitted. Others suggest allowing cycling on paved roads only.

Other respondents aren't as sympathetic to cyclists, and would like to see bicycles kept off the refuge. One respondent asserts that riding a bike is a poor way to observe wildlife, and that if the refuge allows cycling, many cyclists would speed through or venture off designated paths.

Horseback Riding

As with the cyclists, equestrians are concerned that not allowing horseback riding in the refuge will compromise access to other conservation/state/local forest trails immediately surrounding the refuge, such as the Stow Town Forest, Sudbury State Forest, Marlboro State Forest, Sudbury Conservation Land, and the Desert Memorial Forest. The refuge is located directly in the middle these properties, and presently corridors allow horseback riders to travel from one conservation land to another. Further, this group asserts that horseback riding has not impacted other uses in the aforementioned areas. These trail riders ask that the refuge be open to horseback riding, and that consideration be given to an access trail so riders may traverse the refuge to access other conservation areas. Another respondent asks FWS to work with various trail riding and breed organizations in Massachusetts, to establish a horseback riding plan that serves the needs of wildlife and those who enjoy nature from horseback. Further, the Bay State Trail Riders offer to help with the maintenance of any connector trails with volunteer work days and funds if necessary.

Some respondents point out the economic benefits of horseback riding, stating that equine activities are engaged in by a large number of Massachusetts citizens and also make a significant contribution to the Massachusetts economy. For example, they assert that equine agriculture provides over $200 million per year in direct spending into the Massachusetts economy, over 5,000 jobs and more than $13.2 million in state and local tax revenues. Limiting horseback riding would harm the economy.

Equestrians state that they oppose expansion of the refuge's boundaries as long as it limits horseback riding.

Dog-Walking

Many respondents assert that given the popularity and demand for areas to walk dogs, and the fact that parts of the refuge have been used responsibly for decades by dog-walkers; FWS should make part of the refuge available for this pastime. These dog walking enthusiasts request that leashed dog-walking be allowed on refuge trails in appropriate areas, and that strict fines are in place for anyone releasing a dog or failing to pick up after their animal. Others are willing to allow an exclusion of dogs during the most sensitive times, when wildlife surveys identify an impact on nesting birds or other animal life. Many of these respondents view dog-walking as meditative and a way of connecting to the natural beauty of the earth, something that is consistent with refuge goals. These respondents assert that without substantial evidence that dog-walkers are threatening the integrity of the refuge it is unjust and an act of discrimination to prohibit dog-walking. On the other hand, one respondent would like to see dogs banned from the refuge, stating that many dog owners don't obey leash rules to the detriment of wildlife, and further, even on a leash dogs frighten animals.

Birdwatching

Birdwatchers and nature photographers are concerned that they will be confined strictly to trails when observing wildlife, while hunters would not. If hunters are allowed off trail, they assert, birders should be allowed off trail as well.

Trapping

Some respondents ask that the Refuge be open to beaver and muskrat trapping, asserting that modern traps are instant and humane, and arguing that small game threatens children, pets, and livestock, and that beavers "cause extensive property damage."

Some respondents ask whether and under what circumstances which furbearers could be trapped, and what constitutes an invasive species and appropriate control methods. Some respondents oppose trapping on the grounds that it is inhumane; other respondents perceive trapping as ham-fisted interference in natural systems that function best on their own.

Socioeconomic Concerns

Several respondents applaud Alternative B for helping to make Maynard a "destination." One respondent requests permission to graze in the Oxbow unit, and one requests continued cooperative farming.

Several area residents request development of an "abutter policy," without clearly articulating what the components of such a policy would be.

Several respondents urge consideration of impacts to area parking, specifically at Monsen Road at Great Meadows, and at the east gate of Assabet River off Old Marlborough Road. Some respondents are concerned about refuse at entry points.

Appendix A
Coding Structure and Demographic Codes

Eastern Massachusetts National Wildlife Refuge Complex Draft CCP/EA

Header Information

Coders will identify organization type, number of signatures, response type and delivery type on all letters by filling in the proper box. Use **CIC** (Common Interest Class) field only if this information is requested by the Administration. Fill in additional fields when necessary.

Header Order: MID, OT, S, and **RT**, and **DT** fields are required. **IA, UT, LG, F, CIC, RI,** and **CE** fields are optional fields and used only where necessary. The **TS** (Total Signatures) field will tally automatically in Oracle. A stamp containing these fields will be placed on the working copy.

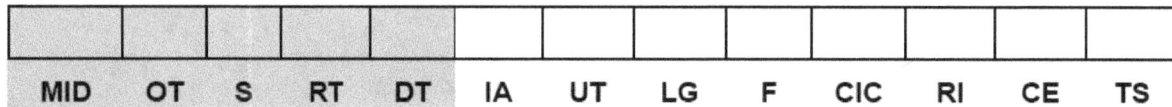

| MID | OT | S | RT | DT | IA | UT | LG | F | CIC | RI | CE | TS |

Mail Identification (MID)

The Mail Identification number is a unique respondent number assigned in the CAET Oracle Program. The Oracle form contains mailing information needed to create mailing labels and obtain project specific demographic information about a respondent.

Organization Types (OT)

The Organization Type code identifies a specific type of organization, association, government agency, elected official, or individual.

Government Agencies and Elected Officials

F	Federal Agency
N	International Government/International Government Association
S	State Government Agency/Elected Official/Association
C	County Government Agency/Elected Official /Association
T	Town/City Government Agency/Elected Official/Association
Q	Tribal Government/Elected Official/Tribal Member/Association
E	Government Employees Organizations/Unions

FW	Fish Wildlife Service Employee
XX	Regional/other governmental agency (multi-jurisdictional)

Business and Industry

A	Agriculture Industry or Associations (Farm Bureaus, Animal Feeding)
B	Business (my/our, Chamber of Commerce)
G	Range/Grazing Orgs and Permittees
HT	Hunting/trapping Industry or Org
M	Mining Industry/Assn (locatable)
O	Energy Industry (Oil, Gas, Coal, Pipeline)
U	Utility Group or Org (water, electrical, gas)
L	Timber or Wood Products Industry/Assn

Other Organizations

AD	Academic
AR	Animal Rights
CH	Church/Religious Groups
D	Placed Based Groups (Multi-issue, focused on a specific region—i.e., QLG)
H	Consultants/legal representatives
J	Civic Organizations (Kiwanis, Elks, Community Councils)
K	Special Use Permittees (Outfitters, Concessions, Ski Areas)
P	Preservation/Conservation Organization
PA	Professional Association/Society
QQ	Tribal Non-Governmental Organization/Member
RB	Mechanized Recreation (bicycling)
RC	Recreational/Conservation (Trout Unlimited, Elk Foundation, Ducks Unlimited)
RM	Recreational - Motorized
RN	Recreational - Non-Motorized (hiking, biking, horseback riding)
SC	All Schools
X	Conservation Districts
Y	Other (Organization with an indecipherable focus—i.e., Ice Cream Socialist Party)
Z	Multiple Use/Wise Use

Unaffiliated

I	Unaffiliated Individual or Unidentifiable Respondent

Number of Signatures (S)

The number of signatures is the total count of names associated with a mail identification (Mail ID) number. The procedure for determining the number of signatures for a Mail ID number is consistent across all response types. In other words, letters, forms, and other types will be treated the same for determining the number of signatures. Each individual name associated with one Mail ID is counted as one signature. When a Mail ID has an incomplete name associated with it, such as an anonymous letter or an email address, it is counted as one signature. Mr. and Mrs. X are counted as two signatures.

Response Type (RT)

The Response Type identifies the specific format of correspondence.

1   Letter
2   Form or Letter Generator
3   Resolution
4   Action Alert
5   Transcript (dictated Audio, Video, Telephone response)

Delivery Types and Descriptions (DT)

The Delivery Type identifies the method of delivery for the correspondence.

E   Email
F   Fax
H   Hand-delivered/oral testimony (personally delivered)
M   Mail or commercial carrier (includes video, audio, letter format)
T   Telephone
U   Unknown

User Type (UT)

The User Type identifies the purpose for which an individual, organization, or agency uses public lands/refuge.

A   Area Residents
B   Businesses and Services
D   Dog Walkers
E   Environmental Educational
K   Bikers
F   Anglers
H   Hikers
P   Photographers
W   Non-motorized Recreation
M   Motorized Recreation
S   Horseback Riding
T   Hunters
X   Non-identifiable

Early Attention (IA)

Early Attention codes are applied only to those documents requiring an early response from the ID team. The Early Attention codes are listed in order of priority. If more than one code applies to a single document, the code with the highest priority is attached.

1   **Threat of harm** – Any response that threatens physical harm to administration, agency, or project personnel.

2   **Notice of appeal or litigation** – Any response that describes the respondents' intent to appeal an action or bring legal suit against the agency.

3   **Freedom of Information Act (FOIA) requests** – Any response that officially requests information and documentation under the FOIA.

4   **Provides proposals for new alternatives** – Any response that suggests a new alternative to the proposed action. These do not include critiques of alternatives or partial changes of existing alternatives.

5   **Requires detailed review** – Any response that requires detailed review. These responses may include detailed scientific or technical analysis, or significant enclosures.

5A   **Provides extensive technical edits** – includes extensive use of lined out text, suggestions to delete text, and/or replace text.

5M   **Provides maps** – Any response that includes map enclosures.

6   **Government entities** – Any response from an elected official, writing in his/her official capacity, representing a Federal, State, county, or municipal government. Also includes official correspondence from any government agency.

6A   **Requests for cooperating agency status from a government entity**.

7   **Public hearing** – Any response that requests a public hearing.

Information Request (RI)

Information Request codes are applied only to those documents with specific requests for information pertaining to the proposal.

A   Mailing List Only/Nothing to Code
B   Request to be Removed from the Mailing List
C   Request for Copy of Federal Register Notice
D   General Request for Other Information
E   Request for Confirmation of Receipt of Letter

Comment Extension Request (CE)

Comment Extension codes are used when a respondent has a specific request for extending the comment period.

0   Request to Extend the Comment Period

Eastern Massachusetts National Wildlife Refuge Complex Draft CCP/EA

The coding structure is a topical outline with alpha and numeric codes attached. It is a tool to identify public comments and sort them into recognizable topic categories. Once comments are assigned codes, they are then entered into a database from which they can be reported and sorted in any combination needed for analysis.

The coding structure is organized into required fields called subject and category codes. Subject codes are five-character alpha codes that represent broad themes associated with a project. Category codes are five-digit numeric codes that define specific subtopics within each subject code, and they are generally arranged from the general to specific with subcategories nested within categories.

PLANN (Subject Code) - Introduction - Chapter 1 and Coordination with Others - Chapter 5

10000   (Category Code) Planning Process and Policy

- 10100 Timeframes for planning/Length of comment period *(adequacy of, timing)*
- 10200 Public Involvement *(General strategies, methods & techniques, collaborative efforts, pre-EIS/CCP consultation)*
- 10300 Scoping *(General comments, planning before the EIS)*
- 10400 Relationship to other planning processes *(Conflicts with other area projects, general planning)*
- 10500 Statutory Authority *(Compliance with laws and regulations; general references to/ violations of NEPA, APA, NFMA, Planning Regs. For resource-specific regulations, code to resource)*
- 10600 Science/Resource-Based Decision-Making *(Use of science in Decisionmaking; general references to use of science and scientific documents)*
- 10700 Budgetary Ramifications *(References to the cost of implementing the proposed rule, project funding)*
- 10800 Agency Organization, Structure and Staffing *(General comments not specific to project, includes trust and integrity issues)*
  - 10810 Trust and Integrity
- 10900 Coordination & Consultation *(Interagency, State, Private, Tribal)*
- 11100 Clarity/organization of planning documents
- 11200 Technical and Editorial Comments

12000 Purpose and Need *(General references to the purpose and need of the CCP/EA and needs for further analysis; if specific, code to the resource).*

- 12100 Project Area *(Scope of project)*
- 12200 Proposed Action/ Decision to be Made *(What it should/should not include)*

12300 Range of Issues Identified through Public Scoping *(General; Comments specific to resource areas go to AFFEC)*

12400 Issues and Concerns Considered Outside the Scope of This Analysis

12500 Permits and Agency Approvals Required

12600 Guiding Policy for Public Lands *(General land management philosophies)*

ALTER - Alternatives - Chapter 2

13000 Alternatives (Comments that simply vote, without rationale)

13100 Alternative A: Current Management *(General comments not specific to a resource; Assumptions made in the analysis)*

13200 Alternative B: Proposed Action

13300 Alternative C

13400 Formulating Alternatives *(Issues used, Design criteria, Development, etc.)*

13500 Features common to all Alternatives

13600 Features common to Action Alternatives only (B & C)

13700 Alternatives Considered But Not Given Detailed Study *(Same as eliminated alternatives)*

13800 Range/Comparison of Alternatives *(General comments, adequacy of range; I like A &C better than B)*

13900 New Alternatives *(Support for or recommendation for a new one)*

13910 Alternative Matrices *(Including Map comments and references)*

AFFEC - Affected Environment - Chapter 3, and Environmental Consequences - Chapter 4

14000 Physical, Biological, and Socio-Economic Resources (general Climate comments, extensive lists)

15000 Geology/Topography

15100 Analysis of Existing Conditions and Need for Further Analysis

15200 General Management Direction *(including other Management Impacts on this Resource)*

15300 Cumulative Impacts

15400 Mitigation and Monitoring

16000 Soils

16100 Analysis of Existing Conditions and Need for Further Analysis

16200 General Management Direction *(including other Management Impacts on this Resource)*

16300 Cumulative Impacts

16400 Mitigation and Monitoring

17000 Hydrology

17100 Analysis of Existing Conditions and Need for Further Analysis

17200 General Management Direction *(including other Management Impacts on this Resource)*

17300 Cumulative Impacts

17400 Mitigation and Monitoring

18000 Air Quality

18100 Analysis of Existing Conditions and Need for Further Analysis

18200 General Management Direction *(including other Management Impacts on this Resource)*

18300 Cumulative Impacts

18400 Mitigation and Monitoring

19000 Water Quality

19100 Analysis of Existing Conditions and Need for Further Analysis

19200 General Management Direction *(including other Management Impacts on this Resource)*

19300 Cumulative Impacts

19400 Mitigation and Monitoring

20000 Vegetation and Habitat Types

20100 Analysis of Existing Conditions and Need for Further Analysis

20200 General Management Direction *(including other Management Impacts on this Resource)*

20300 Forested and Shrub Dominated Wetlands

20400 Vernal Pools and Ponds

20500 Bordering Communities *(Uplands, Marshes, Swamps)*

20600 Invasive or Overabundant Species

20700 Cumulative Impacts

20800 Mitigation and Monitoring

21000 Wildlife and Fisheries

21100 Analysis of Existing Conditions and Need for Further Analysis (Fencing)

21200 General Management Direction *(including other Management Impacts on this Resource; general habitat comments.*

21300 Migratory Birds

21400 Mammals

21500 Reptiles and Amphibians

21600 Fisheries

21700 Invertebrates

21800　Cumulative Impacts

21900　Mitigation and Monitoring

22000　Cultural Resources and Special Designations (focus areas)

22100　Analysis of Existing Conditions and Need for Further Analysis

22200　General Management Direction *(including other Management Impacts on this Resource)*

22210　Land Acquisitions

22300　Refuge Buildings and Facilities

22400　Refuge Administration and Staffing

22410　Volunteers

22420　Enforcement

22500　Wild & Scenic River Plan / Designation

22600　Cumulative Impacts

22700　Mitigation and Monitoring

23000　Priority Public Uses

23100　Analysis of Existing Conditions and Need for Further Analysis

23200　General Management Direction *(including other Management Impacts on this Resource)*

23210　Access

23220　Fees

23230　Passes and Permits

23240　Visitor Safety

23241　Hunting

23242　Dog Walking

23300　Hunting *(If safety concern, code to 23241)*

23310　Big and Upland Game Hunting

23320　Migratory Bird Hunting

23400　Fishing

23500　Wildlife Observation and Photography

23600　Environmental Education and Interpretation

23610　Natural and Cultural History Tours

23620　Outreach for Public Awareness

23700　Cumulative Impacts

23800　Mitigation and Monitoring

24000　Recreation and Other Opportunities

24100　Analysis of Existing Conditions and Need for Further Analysis

24200　General Management Direction *(including other Management Impacts on this Resource)*

24300 Motorized Recreation
   24310 Snowmobiling
24400 Non-Motorized Recreation
   24410 Snowshoeing / X-Country Skiing
   24420 Walking/Jogging
   24430 Picnicking
   24440 Biking
   24450 Horseback Riding
   24460 Dog-Walking, general *(if safety concern, code to 23242)*
   24470 Bird Watching
24500 Cumulative Impacts
24600 Mitigation and Monitoring

25000 Socio-Economic Resources

25100 Analysis of Existing Conditions and Need for Further Analysis
25200 General Management Direction *(including other Management Impacts on this Resource)*
25300 Population and Demographic Conditions
25400 Schools
25500 Neighboring Communities
   25510 Infrastructure *(Roads, Plazas, Utility Corridors, etc.)*
   25520 Revenue Sharing
25600 Cumulative Impacts
25700 Mitigation and Monitoring

26000 Appendices *(General Comments and Technical/Editorial)*

ATTMT – Attachments

27000 [Attachment No., Title, Author's name]

Site Specific 1

The Site Specific 1 code is an up to four digit alpha/numeric comment specific code. For this project, the alpha-code is used to indicate which refuge the comment addresses.

A   Assabet River NWR
G   Great Meadows NWR
O   Oxbow NWR
X   Multiple NWRs/Null

Appendix B
Demographics

Demographic coding allows managers to form an overall picture of who is submitting comments, where they live, their general affiliation with various organizations or government agencies, and the manner in which they respond. The database can be used to isolate specific combinations of information about public comment. For example, a report can include public comment only from people in Massachusetts or a report can identify specific types of land users such as recreational groups, agricultural organizations, or businesses. Demographic coding allows managers to focus on specific areas of concern linked to respondent categories, geographic areas, and response types.

Although demographic information is captured and tracked, it is important to note that the consideration of public comment is not a vote-counting process. Every comment and suggestion has value, whether expressed by one or a thousand respondents. All input is considered, and the analysis team attempts to capture all relevant public concerns in the analysis process. The Content Analysis Team processed 1,907 responses. Because 28 responses are duplicates, the team entered 1,882 responses into the database representing 1,959 signatures, for the Draft CCP/EA.

In the tables displayed below, please note that demographic figures are given for number of responses, respondents, and signatures. For the purposes of this analysis, the following definitions apply: "response" refers to a discrete piece of correspondence; "respondent" refers to each individual or organization to whom a mail identification number is assigned (e.g., a single response may represent several organizations without one primary author); and "signature" simply refers to each individual who adds his or her name to a response, endorsing the view of the primary respondent(s).

Geographic Representation

Geographic representation is tracked for each response during the course of content analysis. Letters and emails were received from 49 of the United States, the District of Columbia, and one foreign country. The response format did not reveal geographic origin for 102 respondents.

Table C1 - Geographic Representation of Respondents by Country and State

Country	State	Number of Respondents	Number of Signatures
Costa Rica		1	1
United States	Alabama	9	9
	Alaska	2	2
	Arizona	22	22
	Arkansas	6	6

Country	State	Number of Respondents	Number of Signatures
	California	201	208
	Colorado	16	16
	Connecticut	19	19
	Delaware	1	1
	District of Columbia	4	6
	Florida	63	65
	Georgia	16	16
	Hawaii	4	4
	Idaho	2	2
	Illinois	45	45
	Indiana	16	16
	Iowa	3	3
	Kansas	10	10
	Kentucky	4	4
	Lousiana	7	7
	Maine	8	9
	Maryland	36	39
	Massachusetts	710	752
	Michigan	30	32
	Minnesota	21	21
	Mississippi	2	2
	Missouri	17	17
	Montana	2	2
	Nebraska	2	3
	Nevada	12	12
	New Hampshire	16	16
	New Jersey	35	38
	New Mexico	6	6
	New York	110	111
	North Carolina	28	29
	Ohio	30	31
	Oklahoma	6	6
	Oregon	14	14
	Pennsylvania	58	60
	Rhode Island	10	10
	South Carolina	13	14

Country	State	Number of Respondents	Number of Signatures
	South Dakota	1	1
	Tennessee	8	8
	Texas	68	69
	Utah	6	6
	Vermont	6	6
	Virginia	19	20
	Washington	29	29
	West Virginia	5	5
	Wisconsin	21	21
	Wyoming	2	2
	Unidentified	102	106
	Total	**1,884**	**1,959**

Organizational Affiliation

Responses were received from various organizations and unaffiliated individuals. Respondents include conservation organizations, wood products associations, as well as unaffiliated individuals and others. Organization types were tracked for each response.

Table C2 - Number of Respondents/Signatures by Organizational Affiliation

Organization Field	Organization Type	Number of Respondents	Number of Signatures
AR	Animal Rights	5	7
B	Business	1	1
D	Place-Based Group	6	6
F	Federal Agency/Elected Official	2	2
HT	Hunting/Trapping Organization	8	8
I	Unaffiliated Individual or Unidentifiable Respondent	1,820	1,885
J	Civic Organization	2	2
P	Preservation/Conservation Organization	14	14
RB	Recreational – Mechanized	1	1
RC	Recreational – Conservation Organization	2	2
RM	Recreational - Motorized	2	2
RN	Recreational – Non-motorized/Non-mechanized	2	2

Organization Field	Organization Type	Number of Respondents	Number of Signatures
S	State Government Agency	6	6
SC	Schools	1	1
T	Town/City Government Agency/Elected Official	12	20
Total		**1,884**	**1,959**

Response Type

Response types were tracked for each response received on the project. Responses were received as letters and public meeting transcripts.

Table C3 - Number of Responses/Signatures by Response Type

Response Type #	Response Type	Number of Responses	Number of Signatures
1	Letter	497	543
2	Form	1,334	1,365
5	Transcript	51	51
Total		**1,882**	**1,959**

Delivery Type

Delivery types were tracked for each response received on the project. Responses were received as email, fax, hand-delivered, standard mail, and one telephone call. Delivery type was not revealed for 11 responses.

Table C4 - Number of Responses/Signatures by Delivery Type

Delivery Type Code	Delivery Type	Number of Responses	Number of Signatures
E	Email	1,630	1,677
F	Fax	1	1
H	Hand-delivered	67	67
M	Mail or commercial carrier	172	202
T	Telephone	1	1
U	Unknown	11	11
Total		**1,882**	**1,959**

User Type

User type was tracked for each response received on the project. User types include anglers, bikers, area residents, dog walkers, photographers and others.

Table C5 - Number of Responses/Signatures by User Type

User Type Code	User Type	Number of Responses	Number of Signatures
A	Area Residents	202	220
B	Businesses and Services	1	2
D	Dog Walkers	14	15
E	Environmental Education	2	2
F	Anglers	2	2
H	Hikers	19	23
K	Bikers	7	7
M	Motorized Recreation	3	3
P	Photographers	2	2
S	Horseback Riding	25	26
T	Hunters	39	39
W	Non-motorized Recreation	8	8
X	No Identifiable Type	1,558	1,610
Total		**1,882**	**1,959**

Appendix C
Early Attention Letters

The early attention designation is attached to public responses in the content analysis database for a variety of reasons. Our intent is to identify responses that fall into certain key categories, such as threats of litigation or comments from government officials, etc. These designations alert the project team members to public concerns or inquiries that may require an agency response or may necessitate detailed project team review for policy, political, or legal reasons.

The early attention designated responses are primarily intended for an internal audience. The categories of responses selected are designed to meet project team needs. This report is not intended to, nor should it be construed to, obviate the need to review all responses.

CAT identified seven early attention categories. The relevant designations are outlined below and followed by report tables.

1   **Threat of harm** – Any response that threatens physical harm to administration, agency, or project personnel.

2   **Notice of appeal or litigation** – Any response that describes the respondents' intent to appeal an action or bring legal suit against the agency.

3   **Freedom of Information Act (FOIA) requests** – Any response that officially requests information and documentation under the FOIA.

4   **Provides proposals for new alternatives** – Any response that suggests a new alternative to the proposed action. These do not include critiques of alternatives or partial changes of existing alternatives.

5   **Requires detailed review** – Any response that requires detailed review. These responses may include detailed scientific or technical analysis, or significant enclosures.

5A   **Provides extensive technical edits** – includes extensive use of lined out text, suggestions to delete text, and/or replace text.

5M   **Provides maps** – Any response that includes map enclosures.

6   **Government entities** – Any response from an elected official, writing in his/her official capacity, representing a Federal, State, county, or municipal government. Also includes official correspondence from any government agency.

6A   **Request for cooperating agency status from a government entity**.

7   **Public hearing** – Any response that requests a public hearing.

Table D1 – (4) Proposes a New Alternative

Letter Number	Name and Address	Remarks
41	Bette Stallman, Wildlife Scientist Linda Huebner, Program Coordinator Humane Society of the United States New England Regional Office 2100 L St. NW Washington, DC 20037	Respondent requests that the USFWS prohibit hunting and trapping in wildlife refuges. Respondent requests the inclusion of an alternative that emphasizes non-consumptive land uses.

Table D2 – (6) Government Entities

Letter Number	Name and Address	Remarks
97	Brenda Kelly Conservation Commission Chair 10 Mudge Way Bedford, MA 01730-2144	Respondent expresses concern for resident safety with regard to nearby hunting and asks the USFWS to address this issue.
98	Tricia Smith Carlisle Conservation Commission Chair P.O. Box 827 66 Westford Street Carlisle, MA 01741	Respondent expresses concern for public safety from proposed hunting on USFWS land. Also, respondent expresses concern regarding access for hunters across private land.
99	Ann Thompson Maynard Board of Selectmen Chair Municipal Building 195 Main Street Maynard, MA 01754	Respondent requests additional allowed uses of the refuge and encourages consistency with local planning processes.
100	Maureen Valente Town Manager 288 Old Sudbury Road Sudbury, MA 10776-1843	Respondent encourages increased refuge use for passive recreation activities; no hunting with firearms; and additional law enforcement.
101	Brian Monahan Wayland Conservation Commission Conservation Administrator Town Building 41 Cochituate Road Wayland MA 01778	Respondent requests no, or strictly regulated hunting in the refuge. Respondent also encourages the USFWS to increase its number of staff.

Letter Number	Name and Address	Remarks
102	John Dwyer Maynard Conservation Commission 4 Durant Ave Maynard, MA 01754	Respondent expresses concern regarding hunting impacts on public safety, wildlife populations, and other recreation activities.
103	Pamela Resor Massachusetts Senate State Senator District Office P.O. Box 1110 Marlborough, MA 01752	Respondent discourages hunting and trapping in the refuge.
104	Susan Pope The Commonwealth of Massachusetts House of Representatives State Representative State House, Boston 02133-1020	Respondent requests that hunting not be allowed in the refuge for safety and environmental reasons. Also, respondent discourages the USFWS from charging user fees.
106	Kathleen Farrell Board of Selectmen Chair 380 Great Road Stow, MA 01775	Respondent requests expansion of the proposed refuge acquisition boundary. Respondent also requests limitations on hunting as well as increased law enforcement for hunting activities.
108	Priscilla Ryder Conservation Commission Conservation Officer 140 Main Street Marlborough, MA 01752	Respondent encourages expansion of the proposed refuge acquisition boundary, increased law enforcement for unauthorized land use, and public education regarding the proposed introduction of hunting to the refuge.
109	William Galvin Massachusetts Historical Commission Secretary of the Commonwealth Massachusetts Archives Building 220 Morrissey Boulevard Boston, MA 02125	Respondent commends the proposed Draft CCP's compliance with Section 6 of the National Historic Preservation Act of 1966.
110	Wayne MacCallum Division of Fisheries and Wildlife Director	Respondent expresses concern for rare, threatened, and endangered species in the refuge, and encourages the USFWS to update species information.
111	Anne Gagnon Conservation Commission Conservation Administrator	Respondent encourages expansion of the proposed refuge acquisition boundary, and increased staffing to decrease user conflicts.
105	Charlie Gorss Conservation Commission Chair	Respondent supports proposed Alternative B.

Letter Number	Name and Address	Remarks
407	Patricia Perry Conservation Commission Administrative Assistant 380 Great Road Stow, MA 01775	Respondent encourages expansion of the proposed refuge acquisition boundary, discourages hunting within the refuge, and encourages coordination of refuge management with local communities.

Appendix D
Information Requests

Requests for additional information, excluding Freedom of Information Act requests, are presented in this appendix. CAT identified five information request categories. The relevant designations are outlined below and followed by report tables. In addition, requests for extension of the comment period are displayed below.

A   Mailing List Only/Nothing to Code
B   Request to be Removed from the Mailing List
C   Request for Copy of Federal Register Notice
D   General Request for Other Information
E   Request for Confirmation of Receipt of Letter

Table E1 – (D) General Requests for Information

Letter Number	Name and Address	Remarks
4	Kate Wheeler Maynard Open Space Planning Committee Chair 31 Harrison St Maynard, MA 01754	Respondent requests specific agency response to the Committee's concerns and notification of the final documents release.
18	Bonnie and John Chandler 183 Prospect Hill Road Harvard, MA 01451	Respondents request information on leasing part of the cow field across from their house for sheep and goat grazing.
117	Daniel Cassidy danc@arguscl.com	Respondent requests a copy of the Draft CCP and EA, and would like to be notified of any public hearings on the subject.
132	Edmund Schofield P.O. Box 598 Boylston, MA 01505-0598	Respondent requests hard copy of the Draft CCP and EA.
200	John Dwyer mjohn.dwyer@verizon.net	Respondent requests Lindsay Krey's email address.
307	Jason Hetherington hetherjw@yahoo.com	Respondent requests online links to information regarding the proposed project.
342	David Stepp 69 Peabody Dr. Stow, MA 01775	Respondent requests information regarding proposed types of hunting and seasons for the refuge.
353	Sally Hewitt Sarah.Hewitt@Simonandschuster.com	Respondent requests notification regarding meetings or plans about bicycling in the Assabet River NWR.

Table E2 – (E) Request for Confirmation of Receipt

Letter Number	Name and Address	Remarks
374	Steve Parker 109 Moore Road Sudbury, MA 01776	Respondent requests confirmation of receipt of letter.

Table E3 – Requests for Comment Period Extension

Letter Number	Name and Address	Remarks
13	Michael Ojemann Great Meadows Neighborhood Association 153 Monsen Road Concord, MA 01742	Respondent requests extension of comment period, no specific length of time specified.
69	Hope Luder 5 Edgehill Road Billercia, MA 01862	Respondent requests extension of comment period, no specific length of time specified.
138	Kathleen Farrell 267 Sudbury Road Stow, MA 01775	Respondent requests extension of comment period, no specific length of time specified.
121	Louise Berliner Strongwhitepine@aol.com	Respondent requests extension of comment period, no specific length of time specified.
232	Rob Aldape Joropab1@mac.com	Respondent requests extension of comment period, no specific length of time specified.

Appendix E
Organized Response Report

Organized response campaigns (forms) represent 70 percent (1,334 of 1,907) of the total responses received during the public comment period for the proposal.

Forms are defined as five or more responses, received separately, but containing nearly identical text. Once a form is identified, a "form master" is entered into the database with all of the content information. All responses with matching text are then linked to this master form within the database with a designated "form number." If a response does not contain all of the text presented in a given form, it is entered as an individual letter. Duplicate responses from four or fewer respondents are also entered as individual letters.

Table F1 – Description and Number of Signatures for Each Form

Number of Form	Number of Signatures	Description of Form
1	11	FWS should reconsider the determination that horseback riding is not compatible with the purpose of the refuge. Opposes acquisition boundaries expansion.
2	1,104	FWS should not increase hunting/trapping in Oxbow National Wildlife Refuge, and prohibit hunting/trapping in the Assabet River and Great Meadows National Wildlife Refuges.
3	250	FWS should not increase hunting/trapping in Oxbow National Wildlife Refuge, and prohibit hunting/trapping in the Assabet River and Great Meadows National Wildlife Refuges. FWS should focus on habitat improvement and non-lethal methods of wildlife management.
Total:	**1,365**	

Appendix F
List of Preparers

Content Analysis Team

Project Coordination

Shari Kappel, Team Leader

John Adams, Assistant Team Leader

Program Coordination

Jody Sutton, Coordinator

James MacMillen, Contracting

Content Analysts

John Adams, Editor/Analyst

Angela Concepcion, Writer/Analyst

Theodore Hughes, Writer/Analyst

Anne Jensen, Writer/Analyst

Holly Schneider, Writer/Analyst

Karl Vester, Coder/Analyst

Database Administration

Buell Whitehead, Technical Support

Information Systems

Lori Warnell, Project Lead/Response Processing/Data Technician

Julie Easton, Data Technician

Kay Flink, Data Technician

Jon Hardes, Data Technician

Geraldine Hill, Data Technician

Linda Kenaston, Data Technician

Shanna Robison, Data Technician

Barbie Gibson, CD Production

Appendix B: U.S. Forest Service Report

(This page intentionally left blank)

Oxbow National Wildlife Refuge

Appendix C: Responses to Substantive Comments

Planning Process

Length of comment period

Some commentors were unhappy with the timing and length of the comment period.

The comment period was 45 days long, which is a standard period for a document such as a CCP. Unfortunately, the timing of the draft CCP release came during the summer months. We knew that there were many people eagerly anticipating its release and focused on releasing the plan to the public as quickly as we could. While, there were requests to extend the comment period, they came at the very end of the comment period. The notification process to ensure that all individuals and groups were aware of an extension could not have been completed before the scheduled end of the comment period. Despite the concerns of some commentors, we did receive nearly 2,000 comments and we feel confident that we heard from all viewpoints.

Public Involvement

Many respondents feel satisfied with the FWS's level of public involvement and education; they praise the agencies past efforts and eagerly anticipate additional opportunities for interest groups and communities to stay involved in the refuge's management. Civic and conservation organizations express interest in collaborating with the FWS on management issues.

We look forward to continued involvement and collaboration as we implement the provisions of the CCP, continue day-to-day operations, and develop necessary step-down plans.

Planning Vision

Relationship to Regional Planning Efforts and Legislation

Some respondents ask for clarification of the CCP's compatibility with other regional management efforts and role in an ecosystem context.

We realize that we are one of several conservation partners in a regional ecosystem. Where appropriate, we have worked with surrounding landowners and communities to ensure management that complements adjacent lands. Unfortunately, the missions of adjacent landowners do not always match the mission and purposes of the refuge. Because of these differences, there will be times when activities that are allowed in one area are prohibited in another, or vice versa.

We look forward to continuing to work with our various conservation partners. Our management actions are focused on the NWRs by design. Our jurisdiction and planning efforts include only these lands. We will continue to consider the effects our management actions have on the surrounding landscape. The patchwork of lands that create these refuges creates unique challenges and partnerships. The Service mission and refuge purposes must be our first priority. We understand that this priority does not always mesh with adjacent landowners' wishes and concerns. We are a part of the larger Refuge System and must consider not only our role in the surrounding ecosystem, but our role in the Refuge System, as well.

Priority Public Uses

Hunting – General

Hunting was the issue most frequently addressed in comments on the draft CCP. General hunting comments include advocates for hunting on public lands and individuals that are opposed to hunting in any form.

The National Wildlife Refuge System Improvement Act of 1997 (Refuge Improvement Act) lists hunting as one of six priority, wildlife-dependent public uses to receive enhanced and preferential consideration in refuge planning and management. In addition to hunting, other priority uses include fishing, wildlife observation and photography, environmental education and interpretation. Our mandate is to provide high-quality opportunities for these priority uses where they are compatible with respective refuge purposes, goals, and other management priorities.

Regardless of individual opinions about the appropriateness of hunting on the refuges, the Refuge Improvement Act requires that we give preferential consideration to the six priority, wildlife-dependent uses. We are also concerned about the potential for hunting to impact other priority uses. There appears to have been some confusion about where we are proposing to allow hunting. We have outlined the areas where hunting is to be allowed on the maps that are included as a part of the CCP.

We have included some of the additional details in regard to hunting in the Final CCPs. In order to open the refuges to additional hunting opportunities, Federal regulations will need to be changed. There will be an additional public comment period when proposed hunting regulations are released in the Federal Register. This will likely occur during the winter/spring of 2005.

Additionally, we will be developing a Hunt Management Plan for each Refuge that will outline all of the details for each specific hunting program.

Each plan will be completed in cooperation with the Massachusetts Department of Fish and Game (MA DFG), Division of Fisheries and Wildlife. Refuge areas that meet certain criteria have been evaluated to determine tracts of land that have the ability to support a high quality public hunt. We have determined that certain areas are appropriate for certain types of hunting and not others. The criteria used included: 1) an area of sufficient size to insure public safety; 2) an area more than 500 feet from occupied dwellings (Massachusetts state law); and 3) an area that provides reasonable opportunities for a successful hunt. An additional consideration that was considered in some instances is whether hunting of an area of the refuge is consistent with or complements other hunted areas in surrounding towns.

Hunting – Safety and Conflicts with Other Users

There were a large number of individuals that expressed concerns about safety and hunting. Some individuals expressed concerns about safety while using the refuge during hunting season and the assertion that the non-hunting public will not participate in other wildlife dependent activities during the hunting seasons. Other people indicated their concerns about the proximity to the refuge boundary of homes, schools, and conservation areas. Additionally, individuals raised the possibility of hunters accessing non-refuge lands or misguided arrows, shotgun slugs, or pellets injuring someone not on the refuge.

There will be areas on the refuges where no hunting will be allowed. In some cases, these are highly used areas, such as the Concord Impoundments at Great Meadows NWR. In others, we have restricted hunting because of the mandated safety zones. We realize that there may be people that will not visit the refuges during specific seasons. As mentioned previously, we have a responsibility to facilitate all forms of wildlife-dependent public use on the refuges, when possible, and there may be days when people engaged in hunting will have preferential access to parts of the refuges. National policy encourages refuges to follow state hunting regulations, but we do have the authority to set our own dates and times if needed and we can limit the number of hunting permits issued. We will evaluate these options in the development of the Hunt Management Plan for each refuge, but do not anticipate a need to include such restrictions at this time.

We strive to achieve a balance between consumptive and non-consumptive uses on the refuges. Because Massachusetts does not allow hunting on Sunday, at a minimum non-hunters will be free to enjoy our nature trails with no concern about possible hunting conflicts on those days during the hunting seasons. In addition, experience managing hunts both at Oxbow Refuge and at other refuges within the system shows that many areas can safely support both hunting and non-consumptive uses, such as wildlife observation, at the same time. We are confident that we can develop a hunting program that will safely provide opportunities for wildlife-dependent public use to a majority of our refuge visitors.

We contacted the Massachusetts Division of Fisheries and Wildlife to obtain hunting accident statistics. We considered investigating such statistics in other states, but decided that Massachusetts has a higher population density than the majority of other states with readily available accident statistics such as Pennsylvania, North Carolina, and Texas. According to Massachusetts Law, any person involved in a hunting accident or any person with knowledge of a hunting accident must file a report with the state or local police, who, in turn, must file a report with the Division of Law Enforcement. The Massachusetts Environmental Police, Hunter Education Program reports hunting accidents in the *Hunting Accident Report: 1995 – 2002.* During the reporting period, there were 38 hunting accidents. None of the accidents were fatal and none involved any individuals who were not hunting at the time of the accident. According to the *2001 National Survey of Fishing, Hunting, and Wildlife-Associated Recreation,* there were 1.58 million days of hunting that occurred in Massachusetts in 2001. During that year there were 3 hunting accidents, the corresponding accident rate is extremely low.

Specific areas were mentioned by local residents as being of concern. Some commentors indicated distances that bullets travel when fired from a rifle (effective range). The areas that were mentioned by commentors as being potential safety areas were:

Great Meadows NWR
Concord Impoundments
O'Rourke, Greenough, and Foss Properties in Carlisle
Dudley Road area in Bedford
Area along the Concord River in Billerica
Areas adjacent to Wayland Conservation Property
Heard Pond

Assabet River NWR
Stearns Lane and Hudson Road in Sudbury
The Maynard School Complex
Firecut Lane area in Sudbury

Based upon the concerns expressed in response to the draft, we reviewed the most up-to-date aerial photographs available. We analyzed the locations of the 500-foot safety zones around existing homes to determine whether or not a reasonable hunting area could be provided given the constraints associated with the safety zones. In addition to the aerial photo analysis, we went to the refuges to determine how visible the homes near the refuge are from inside the refuge. We would like to remind individuals that by state regulation there is a 500 foot zone around any inhabited structure. *Hunting, whether by gun or bow, is not allowed in this area unless the hunter received permission from the owner of the building. It is the hunter's responsibility to ensure that he/she is more than 500 feet from any such buildings.* There are times in which the safety zone extends into the refuge. Hunting will not be allowed within these areas.

However, the Service will assist hunters in delineating any areas where there may be confusion as to the actual location of the safety zone. The information that we gathered enabled us to make informed decisions about the appropriateness of areas for different hunting activities. We will require hunters to obtain an annual hunting permit. We may prepare maps showing the hunt areas in detail. Areas with adjacent homes can be depicted on the maps as a further guide to inform hunters of safety zones adjacent or within the refuge.

Also, there is some confusion as to whether or not hunting is being proposed in certain locations. We would like to clarify our original proposal and highlight the following changes:

- o Hunting is <u>not</u> proposed for the Concord Impoundments.

- o The waterfowl hunting area on the Concord River and associated wetlands starts at the Route 225 Bridge and extends upstream to the area where refuge ownership ends on the west side of the Concord River in the town of Carlisle. This is the area at the northern end of the O'Rourke property. The area along the Concord River in Billerica has been removed from consideration for waterfowl hunting. The entire river in that area is within the 500 foot safety zone required by state hunting regulations. Hunting on the river in that area is illegal.

o   We understand the concern regarding hunting on the Greenough property. We will ensure that the boundary is clearly marked. The deer hunting opportunities on the property will be limited to archery only.

o   The area adjacent to private and conservation property in the vicinity of Dudley Road in Bedford is proposed as archery only for deer hunting.

o   In the Sudbury Division of the refuge, the proposed waterfowl hunting area south to Route 20 has been reduced. The waterfowl hunting opportunities adjacent to refuge lands ou to the center line of the Sudbury River south of Route 20 have bee reduced from 193 acres to 77. Additionally, no waterfowl hunting will be allowed between Route 20 and the Wayland School Complex. Waterfowl hunting will be allowed in a limited area upstream of the school along the Sudbury River south of Heard Pond. The revised hunting area will be a minimum of 1,000 feet from the school playing fields. Please see the maps in the Great Meadows NWR CCP for a depiction of this area.

o   In the South section of the Assabet River NWR, we have changed the designation to Archery Only.

o   Based upon the comments that we received regarding Hudson Road and Stearns Lane, we made a revision to the hunting areas on the North section of the Assabet River NWR. The area outside of the entire Patrol Road has been designated Archery Only.

Hunting – Various Species

Commentors indicated that it was necessary for the Service to conduct detailed surveys of wildlife populations before implementing a hunt program.

The hunting of migratory bird species is managed from a national point of view. The Service monitors the population status of all migratory bird game species and works with the States to set season lengths and harvest limits. Hunting is managed in a way that does not contribute to a decline in waterfowl and other migratory game bird populations.

The hunting of resident species, such as deer, rabbits, and squirrels, falls within the responsibility of state fish and wildlife agencies, which also monitor and manage populations to ensure healthy ecosystems, sustainable populations, and a certain level of hunter success. We work in partnership with the Massachusetts Division of Fisheries and Wildlife and rely on their knowledge and expertise to determine the appropriateness of hunting seasons. Any decisions we make to limit or prevent the harvest of resident species on any refuge is based on other management concerns and not on a concern about the population of a given species. State fish and wildlife agencies have an excellent record of sound, professional wildlife management, and this is true in Massachusetts as well.

Fishing

Most fishing comments are directed toward the proposal to allow fishing at Puffer Pond on the Assabet River NWR. There is considerable support for fishing on Puffer Pond. There are also a number of respondents who request that fishing be prohibited on Puffer Pond. These individuals argue that anglers will disturb nesting birds, erode the shoreline, trample vegetation, contribute to the spread of invasives, and drag boats through the refuge.

Fishing is one of the priority wildlife dependent uses for national wildlife refuges, where compatible. As such, the staff has determined that fishing is compatible with refuge purposes. Staff from Assabet River NWR will finalize the details of fishing on Puffer Pond as a part of the Fishing Management Plan. Staff will ensure that impacts to the resources in and surrounding the pond are minimized. This is evidenced by the stipulations already included in the draft plan. No motorized boats will be allowed, greatly reducing the likelihood of invasive species being brought to the pond. Public use in general causes some disturbance of vegetation and wildlife. We will manage all public uses, including fishing, to minimize the disturbance and ensure that the level of disturbance does not materially interfere with the purposes of the refuges. We share the concern about the potential introduction of invasive species, as well as other types of disturbance. We will continue to monitor disturbance caused by public uses of the refuges and take any action that we deem necessary or appropriate.

Environmental Education

A majority of commentors who chose to address environmental education support the efforts and facilities proposed in Alternative B, advocating more environmental education for people of all ages. Several respondents encourage completion of the proposed Sudbury River interpretive canoe trail. Some of the commentors encourage the FWS to think bigger, and develop its educational plan in concert with other regional entities and efforts.

Environmental education is one of the priority wildlife dependent uses for national wildlife refuges. As such, the staff has determined that it is compatible with refuge purposes and will continue to work to provide these opportunities. The staff is encouraged by the support that individuals and groups have shown for environmental education. We look forward to continuing and expanding educational opportunities associated with the refuges.

Wildlife Observation Trails

Some of the organizations and towns that commented on the CCP included requests for trails to be developed in specific areas that would connect to adjacent trail systems. In some cases, the requests are for formalizing trails that have been created by individuals for unauthorized access. In other cases, the requests are for new trails that would provide access to new areas.

Refuge staff will develop a system for evaluating such requests. This review system will provide refuge staff with the necessary tools to evaluate the need for and effects of recommended trails.

Non-wildlife Dependent Public Uses

Dog Walking

A large number of commentors assert that given the popularity and demand for areas to walk dogs, and the fact that parts of the refuge have been used responsibly for decades by dog-walkers, FWS should continue to allow dog walking and should authorize it at Assabet River NWR. Some commentors express support for a ban of dogs from the refuge; they cited safety concerns, conflicts between dog walkers and bird watchers, and owners that do not clean up after their dogs.

All of the refuges in the Eastern Massachusetts National Wildlife Refuge Complex were created with purposes related to protecting, managing, and conserving native wildlife. The 1997 Refuge Improvement Act establishes the mission of the Refuge System as "to preserve a national network of lands and waters for the conservation and management of fish, wildlife, and plant resources of the United States for the benefit of present and future generations." The Refuge Improvement Act further stipulates that all activities occurring on refuges must be compatible with wildlife conservation and the specific purposes for which a refuge was established. This is an important distinction from other public lands and recreation areas; refuges have a narrow management focus and are not multi-purpose lands. Six public uses were identified by the Refuge Improvement Act as the priorities for receiving enhanced consideration on refuges. Dog walking is not one of the six priority public uses, nor are dogs (except hunting, seeing or hearing dogs) necessary to support the safe, practical, and effective conduct of the priority public use programs we would be implementing on the refuge.

Dogs running off leash and piles of dog waste left on trails or tossed in the bushes are consistent problems, not isolated incidences. Several circumstances prompted the elimination of this activity on the refuges, including
- Dogs can intimidate other refuge visitors, and deprive them of the peace that refuges provide. Visitation to the National Wildlife Refuges is expanding, potentially aggravating user conflicts;
- Dog feces left on trails are an unhealthy and unsightly nuisance to refuge visitors and impact refuge vegetation. The presence of dog feces on public trails is one of the most common complaints we receive;
- Dogs, whether leashed or unleashed, conflict with refuge efforts to provide recreational opportunities for a diversity of visitors, including those limited to handicapped accessible trails, and the many school groups which visit the refuges for environmental education;
- Dog walking has resulted in user conflicts with persons engaged in priority public uses (bird watching, photography, see below);

- Instinctively, dogs want to chase wildlife. Unleashed dogs commonly chase nesting wildlife, which can result in destruction of ground nests and young. Dogs may step on nests or young chicks, as they "freeze" in response to danger;
- Many dog owners consistently remove their dogs from leashes when they are away from the parking lots and believe they are unlikely to be observed by a refuge ranger;
- Wildlife can't distinguish between dogs on leashes and unleashed dogs. In the presence of a dog, many species will abandon their nests or young, leaving them vulnerable to be killed by predators, or die from starvation or exposure.

We realize that many dog owners are responsible owners and have a strong emotional connection to the refuge and to walking their dog on the refuge. We realize that many people will not be happy with this decision. Nevertheless, we firmly believe that the overall adverse impacts from dog walking on wildlife and other visitors engaged in wildlife-dependent public use justify this prohibition. Our decision is also consistent with land managers throughout the State who manage lands specifically for wildlife. Massachusetts Audubon Society and State of Massachusetts wildlife sanctuary lands also do not allow pets.

Horseback Riding

A large number of commentors are opposed to a prohibition on horseback riding on any of the refuges. They are concerned that not allowing horseback riding in the refuge will compromise access to other conservation/state/local forest trails immediately surrounding the refuge. In addition, they point to the economic benefits of horseback riding.

We have decided to maintain our prohibition of horseback riding on refuge trails. This activity does not promote wildlife conservation, is not one of our six priority public uses, nor is it necessary to support the safe, practical, and effective conduct of a priority public use on the refuges.

While we appreciate the desire for horseback riding opportunities on Assabet River, Great Meadows, and Oxbow National Wildlife Refuges, we do not believe that these relatively small refuges are appropriate places for horseback riding. Existing refuge trails are not designed to accommodate horses. Most of our trails are not wide enough for riders and walkers to avoid each other, nor are trails designed to withstand the impact of horses. This is especially true in wetter areas. Another issue with horse use is the waste left on trails. It is well-documented that horse waste introduces seeds from non-native and invasive vegetation. Further, the horse waste is unsightly and detracts from other visitors' experiences when they have to watch for and avoid stepping in it. We are supporting an appropriate level and type of public use on our refuges by maintaining our focus on wildlife-dependent public uses.

Jogging

Joggers view the refuge as a safe, peaceful place to pursue their activity, and would like more information as to why jogging would be banned.

As indicated in the draft CCP/EA, we will be investigating the impacts of jogging to determine whether or not this is an appropriate use and a compatible use. Jogging is not a priority public use nor is it necessary to support one of the six priority public uses. Currently, there are a relatively high number of individuals that participate in jogging on the refuges. Other refuges have documented impacts to wildlife caused by jogging. We have issued a compatibility determination that indicates that, based on our current knowledge, jogging is compatible with refuge purposes. If we gather information to the contrary, we will issue a new compatibility determination with appropriate public comment opportunities.

Picnicking

Some respondents view picnicking as a harmless past time that allows people to enjoy the refuge's beauty.

We would like to take this opportunity to clarify our position on picnicking. We believe that the draft CCP/EA conveyed a change that we did not intent. We do not intend to prohibit a refuge visitor from sitting on a bench or under a tree and eating a snack or drinking a beverage. However, we will not issue permits for large events, such as family reunions, where a meal is a normal part of the event to occur on the refuges, nor will we provide picnic tables or specific locations for picnicking.

Bicycling

Similar to jogging, a number of commentors assert that the refuge offers a safe, traffic-free environment for bicycling. By not allowing bicycling on the refuges, it is asserted that the FWS will be creating a gap in the local trail systems. Some cyclists are willing to be flexible as to when and where they can pursue their sport. Some of the commentors suggest allowing cycling on paved roads only. Of greatest interest to many of the commentors are the Patrol Road on Assabet River NWR and the Tank Road on Oxbow NWR.

Bicycling is not compatible with the refuge purposes for each of the 3 refuges. Bicycles frighten wildlife and cause changes in behavior that have potential adverse impacts to species. While there are places where bicycling can enhance wildlife dependent opportunities, in general the intention of a visitor on a bicycle is to engage in the act of cycling or transportation, not to observe wildlife. The refuges are small enough that bicycling is not needed to facilitate a wildlife-dependent public use. Additionally, while there may be some existing roads on the refuges (particularly Assabet River NWR) which seem to lend themselves to cycling, our long term plans for the refuges will include some road removal and return to a natural state.

Snowmobiling

Snowmobilers describe themselves as law-abiding recreationists that are respectful of others and wildlife. One local snowmobile club would like to establish a trail through the refuge, maintained by the club, for the club's enjoyment.

Snowmobiling is not a wildlife-dependent use of the refuges. Snowmobiles tend to frighten wildlife and can adversely impact wintering species. The refuges are small enough that non-motorized use (such as cross-country skiing or snowshoeing) would be the preferred method of travel for facilitation of wildlife dependent uses of the refuges during winter months.

Gathering

One respondent requested permission to collect mushrooms and suggested a daily limit for individuals that would like to collect them.

The picking of fruit, plants, and mushrooms is not allowed on the refuges. These plants and fungi are components of the natural ecosystem and can provide food for refuge wildlife. With the large volumes of refuge visitors, there could be significant depletion of certain plants and mushrooms as well as unauthorized access off-trail to collect these specimens if this were allowed. Our intention in managing these refuges is to allow natural processes to occur as much as possible, with specific land management techniques to maintain or restore specific habitat types for wildlife. Gathering of plants, mushrooms and other refuge resources (such as rocks found on stone walls) is not appropriate.

Fees

Commentors provided a number of arguments for and against fees. Additionally, some commentors questioned the viability of a fee system for the refuges. Some of the concerns raised include the appropriateness of fees on Federal land, a potential deterrence of visitors from low-income families or neighborhoods, and the costs of enforcement. Others point out the need to support local lands that are under-funded by Federal budgets.

In response to concerns expressed about the cost of a pass, we have lowered the annual pass fee from $20 in our original proposal to $12. Additional detail about the fees has been added to the final CCPs for each of the refuges.

Fees will be used to support local projects on the refuges. The only way the Service will be able to achieve, maintain and provide a high quality of visitor service in the future is with additional funds. Unfortunately, our budget is insufficient to meet our visitor services needs. Failure to receive additional revenues will have a significant impact on our ability to provide quality opportunities for visitors to engage in wildlife-dependent public uses. Fees are fair because they are paid by refuge users.

Land Acquisition

A large number of commentors expressed concern over the lack of additional lands within the proposed acquisition boundary. Some individuals specifically mentioned the Devens South Post land that has been identified as part of the Base Closure and Realignment Act as land to be transferred to Oxbow NWR. Other individuals expressed concern that some town conservation lands adjacent to the existing refuges were within the acquisition boundary. These individuals expressed a preference that the land remains in town control.

Assabet River, Great Meadows, and Oxbow NWRs are a part of the much larger Refuge System. The Service is developing a plan for strategic growth of the Refuge System. This plan will allow the Service to prioritize land acquisition and boundary expansions for the System as a whole. The process for changing land acquisition boundaries is long and complex and takes a great deal of staff time. The plan for strategic growth will also allow Refuge System staff to focus boundary expansion efforts to those areas that are of greatest value to the System as a whole. Certainly, the refuges encompassed in the draft CCP/EA contribute a great deal to fulfilling the Refuge System mission. Any boundary expansion must also be shown to have a necessary contribution. Staff will continue to work toward boundary expansions within Service policy and guidelines.

Expansion of the boundaries at locations that provide important habitats is still possible. Staff will need to pursue these acquisition boundary issues as a separate process. Congress has specifically identified the Devens South Post land as appropriate for transfer to the Service. The transfer would not be hindered by the lack of an acquisition boundary around that land.

We would like to point out that the acquisition boundary identifies natural areas that are important to the purposes of the refuges. However, the Service does not plan to condemn land that is being protected by other entities. In the event that a group or individual, such as a town conservation commission, is attempting to sell some of this land, the Service would be interested in acquiring the land rather than allowing it to be developed.

Buildings and Facilities

Respondents voiced a myriad of opinions regarding what kinds of buildings and facilities should be provided at the refuge. Citing the importance of public education, many people ask the FWS to locate kiosks at strategic locations throughout the refuge. Comments regarding refuge parking focus on lot location with a number of people discouraging parking at Heard Pond. These respondents contend that there has been too much garbage dumping and vandalism at the Heard Pond site to make it a desirable parking place.

We are sensitive to the fact that there are a wide variety of opinions regarding development of buildings, restroom facilities, and parking areas at the refuges. We will work to ensure that buildings are sited to provide the greatest benefit to the groups that will use them, while at the same time reducing any associated impacts. Where appropriate, we will site and build kiosks to provide educational and informational opportunities. We understand the concern over past activities at Heard Pond. The proposed parking lot will be located along the road and not set back like the previous lot. We have proposed a limited expansion of no more than 6 cars depending on available area that will allow more visitors to enjoy the area.

NHESP suggested working cooperatively with the Service for review of impacts to state-listed species when construction or demolition projects are proposed.

The Service will continue to include NHESP in review of appropriate projects.

Staffing

Most commentors feel that adequate refuge staffing is essential. While many people assert that Alternative B will meet desired staffing levels, a number of other respondents contend that proposed staffing levels are too low. These people cite anticipated user conflicts, present refuge hazards, and the current downsizing trend in government as reasons to increase proposed staffing levels. Some respondents suggest utilizing community groups and/or to form partnerships with volunteer organizations to supplement staffing needs.

We appreciate the support for increased staffing levels. We have proposed the level of staffing that we feel is appropriate to implement the programs outlined in the CCP.

Wild and Scenic Rivers

The one concern regarding wild and scenic river designation expressed by several respondents is that hunting is incompatible with this designation and should be prohibited within these areas.

The Wild & Scenic Rivers Act (WSR) does not prohibit hunting, nor does it indicate that hunting is incompatible with the intent of the WSR designation.

Enforcement

Respondents who comment on enforcement indicate that the level of enforcement on the refuge needs to increase. The key areas identified by respondents as needing increased policing efforts are off-highway vehicle trespass, poaching, dumping, trespass, and vandalism.

We are aware of a number of violations that occur on refuge lands. Our law enforcement staff is working to correct these violations and are bringing in outside help when necessary. The number of violation notices issued during the past year is a testament to our focused law enforcement efforts. We look forward to implementation of the CCP and the opportunity to expand our law enforcement presence through the potential addition of staff, agreements with local law enforcement agencies, and continued cooperation with State environmental police officers.

Invasives

Many respondents support efforts to eliminate invasive non-native species. Several respondents raise concerns about invasives at Puffer Pond, given new fishing access. Concerns about targeted species are raised in two cases: one respondent argues that cattails are native, and should not be removed; a number of respondents argue that mute swans are harmless.

We will develop specific strategies to deal with control and elimination of invasive species as a part of the Habitat Management Plan. We are aware of the problem with invasives at nearby lakes and ponds. We have proposed to allow only non-motorized boats on Puffer Pond to help ensure that new invasive species are not introduced to the pond.

State Listed Species

The Massachusetts Natural Heritage and Endangered Species Program (NEHSP) provided changes and edits to the Species Lists for each of the refuges, especially concerning the state listed species.

We have reviewed the suggestions and incorporated them into the species lists.

Wildlife Surveys

NEHSP suggested that we complete surveys to determine areas that should be closed to public use and prior to opening roads or trails for use.

Staff will continue to use survey information, along with local knowledge and known locations of sensitive species to determine whether there is a need to close areas of the refuge that are open or before opening areas to new public access opportunities.

Literature Cited

An individual suggested inclusion of a comprehensive bibliography of biodiversity for the Great Meadows NWR area that has been published.

We have included a reference to this bibliography in the Great Meadows NWR CCP.

Editorial/Corrections

A number of commentors made suggestions that were editorial or that offered corrections to place names, geography, or history.

We have made the corrections where appropriate.

Alternatives

The Humane Society of the Unites States expressed concern that the CCP/EA did not consider a reasonable range of alternatives. HSUS urged the Service to "give full consideration to an alternative that would emphasize non-consumptive uses, non-lethal approaches to conflicts with wildlife, aggressive acquisition of land that could provide important habitat for refuge wildlife, and removal of invasive plant species.

We worked hard to ensure consideration of the reasonable range of alternatives that were presented in the draft CCP/EA. Each of the items mentioned was considered and the majority are included in the final CCP. We analyzed the effects of continuing no-hunting on Assabet River and Great Meadows NWR, along with maintaining the existing level of hunting on Oxbow NWR as a part of Alternative A. Our current management plan is a balance of consumptive and non-consumptive uses with a focus on non-consumptive uses only for the majority of the year. All of our alternatives emphasize non-lethal approaches to wildlife conflicts with lethal control only utilized when our managers and biologists have determined that non-lethal controls have not been effective. Similarly, we will continue to acquire land as dictated by Service policy and as outlined under the "land acquisition" heading earlier in this section. Finally, removal of non-native invasive plant species is included in our final CCP and will be outlined further in our Habitat Management Plan.

Support for each alternative [No response required]

A number of commentors expressed support for all or portions of specific alternatives without citing specific reasons for doing so. The greatest number of such respondents indicated support for Alternative B or variations of Alternative B.

Appendix D: Species Lists

Table D-1: Birds at Oxbow NWR

Scientific Name	Common Name	Status	References
Phalacrocorax auritus	Double-creasted cormorant		Friends of Oxbow 2000
Branta canadensis	Canada goose		Lockwood 2000; Friends of Oxbow 2000
Anas platyrhynchos	Mallard	NAWCA	Friends of Oxbow 2000; Lockwood - BBS 2000
Aix sponsa	Wood duck	NAWCA	Lockwood - BBS 2000; Friends of Oxbow 2000
Anas rubripes	American black duck	NAWCA	Friends of Oxbow 2000
Anas crecca	Green-winged Teal	NAWCA	
Ardea herodias	Great Blue Heron	SRC	Friends of Oxbow 2000; Lockwood - BBS 2000
Butorides striatus	Green heron	SRC	Friends of Oxbow 2000
Nycticorax nycticorax	Black-crowned night heron		Friends of Oxbow 2000
Actitis macularia	Spotted sandpiper		Friends of Oxbow 2000
Tringa solitaria	Solitary sandpiper		Friends of Oxbow 2000
Charadrius vociferus	Killdeer		Lockwood - BBS 2000
Accipiter striatus	Sharp-shinned hawk		Friends of Oxbow 2000
Buteo jamaicensis	Red-tailed hawk		Friends of Oxbow 2000; Lockwood - BBS 2000
Buteo platypterus	Broad-winged hawk		Friends of Oxbow 2000
Falco sparverius	American kestrel	SRC	Friends of Oxbow 2000
Pandion haliaetus	Osprey		Friends of Oxbow 2000
Cathartes aura	Turkey vulture		Friends of Oxbow 2000
Bonasa umbellus	Ruffed grouse		Friends of Oxbow 2000
Phasianus colchicus	Ring-necked pheasant		Friends of Oxbow 2000
Scolopax minor	American woodcock	SRC	Plagge 2000; Friends of Oxbow 2000
Asio flammeus	Short-eared owl	NGSMC	Friends of Oxbow 2000
Zenaida macroura	Mourning dove		Friends of Oxbow 2000; Lockwood - BBS 2000
Columba livia	Rock dove		Friends of Oxbow 2000
Caprimulgus vociferus	Whip-poor-will	SRC	Plagge 2000; Lockwood - BBS 2000
Archilochus colubris	Ruby-throated hummingbird		Friends of Oxbow 2000
Megaceryle alcyon	Belted kingfisher		Friends of Oxbow 2000; Lockwood - BBS 2000
Colaptes auratus	Northern flicker	NGSMC	Friends of Oxbow 2000; Lockwood - BBS 2000
Picoides pubescens	Downy woodpecker		Friends of Oxbow 2000; Lockwood - BBS 2000
Picoides villosus	Hairy woodpecker		Friends of Oxbow 2000; Lockwood - BBS 2000
Contopus virens	Eastern Wood-pewee		Lockwood - BBS 2000
Myiarchus crinitus	Great-crested flycatcher		Lockwood - BBS 2000
Empidonax minimus	Least flycatcher		Friends of Oxbow 2000
Empidonax traillii	Willow flycatcher		Lockwood - BBS 2000
Tyrannus tyrannus	Eastern kingbird		Friends of Oxbow 2000; Lockwood - BBS 2000
Tachycineta bicolor	Tree swallow		Friends of Oxbow 2000; Lockwood - BBS 2000
Hirundo rustica	Barn swallow		Friends of Oxbow 2000; Lockwood - BBS 2000
Chaetura pelagica	Chimney swift		Friends of Oxbow 2000
Sayornis phoebe	Eastern phoebe		Friends of Oxbow 2000; Lockwood - BBS 2000
Cyanocitta cristata	Blue jay		Friends of Oxbow 2000; Lockwood - BBS 2000
Corvus brachyrhynchos	American crow		Friends of Oxbow 2000; Lockwood - BBS 2000
Parus bicolor	Tufted titmouse		Friends of Oxbow 2000; Lockwood - BBS 2000
Parus atricapillus	Black-capped chickadee		Friends of Oxbow 2000; Lockwood - BBS 2000
Sitta carolinensis	White breasted nuthatch		Friends of Oxbow 2000; Lockwood - BBS 2000
Certhia americana	Brown creeper		Lockwood 2000
Thryothorus ludovicianus	Carolina Wren		Friends of Oxbow 2000

Comprehensive Conservation Plan

Troglodytes aedon	House wren	Lockwood - BBS 2000
Regulus calendula	Ruby-crowned kinglet	Friends of Oxbow 2000
Polioptila caerulea	Blue-gray gnatcatcher	Friends of Oxbow 2000; Lockwood - BBS 2000
Mimus polyglottos	Northern mockingbird	Friends of Oxbow 2000
Sialia sialis	Eastern bluebird	Friends of Oxbow 2000
Dumetella carolinensis	Gray catbird	Friends of Oxbow 2000; Lockwood - BBS 2000
Turdus migratorius	American robin	Friends of Oxbow 2000; Lockwood - BBS 2000
Hylocichla mustelina	Wood thrush NGSMC	Friends of Oxbow 2000; Lockwood - BBS 2000
Catharus fuscescens	Veery	Friends of Oxbow 2000; Lockwood - BBS 2000
Seiurus aurocapillus	Ovenbird	Friends of Oxbow 2000; Lockwood - BBS 2000
Catharus guttatus	Hermit Thrush	Lockwood - BBS 2000
Seiurus noveboracensis	Northern Waterthrush	Friends of Oxbow 2000
Bombycilla cedrorum	Cedar Waxwing	Friends of Oxbow 2000; Lockwood - BBS 2000
Dendroica pinus	Pine warbler	Friends of Oxbow 2000; Lockwood - BBS 2000
Mniotilta varia	Black-and-white warbler	Friends of Oxbow 2000; Lockwood - BBS 2000
Dendroica palmarum	Palm warbler	Friends of Oxbow 2000
Dendroica magnolia	Magnolia warbler	Friends of Oxbow 2000
Dendroica coronata	Myrtle warbler (Yellow-rumped)	Friends of Oxbow 2000; Lockwood 2000
Setophaga ruticilla	American redstart	Friends of Oxbow 2000; Lockwood - BBS 2000
Vireo solitarius	Blue-headed (solitary) vireo	Lockwood 2000
Vireo gilvus	Warbling vireo	Friends of Oxbow 2000; Lockwood - BBS 2000
Vireo olivaceus	Red eyed vireo	Lockwood - BBS 2000
Vireo flavifrons	Yellow throated vireo	Lockwood - BBS 2000
Dendroica virens	Black-throated green warbler	Friends of Oxbow 2000; Lockwood - BBS 2000
Dendroica pensylvanica	Cheastnut-sided warbler	Friends of Oxbow 2000; Lockwood - BBS 2000
Vermivora pinus	Blue-winged warbler NGSMC	Friends of Oxbow 2000; Lockwood 2000
Geothlypis trichas	Common Yellowthroat	Friends of Oxbow 2000; Lockwood - BBS 2000
Dendroica petechia	Yellow warbler	Friends of Oxbow 2000; Lockwood - BBS 2000
Wilsonia canadensis	Canada warbler	Friends of Oxbow 2000
Cardinalis cardinalis	Northern cardinal	Friends of Oxbow 2000; Lockwood - BBS 2000
Melospiza georgiana	Swamp sparrow SRC	Friends of Oxbow 2000; Lockwood - BBS 2000
Melospiza melodia	Song sparrow	Friends of Oxbow 2000; Lockwood - BBS 2000
Zonotrichia leucophrys	White-crowned sparrow	Lockwood 2000
Zonotrichia albicollis	White-throated sparrow	Lockwood 2000; Friends of Oxbow
Spizella passerina	Chipping Sparrow	Lockwood - BBS 2000
Pipilo erythrophthalmus	Eastern towhee	Friends of Oxbow 2000; Lockwood - BBS 2000
Carduelis tristis	American goldfinch	Friends of Oxbow 2000; Lockwood - BBS 2000
Agelaius phoeniceus	Red-winged blackbird	Friends of Oxbow 2000; Lockwood - BBS 2000
Euphagus carolinus	Rusty blackbird	Friends of Oxbow 2000
Molothrus ater	Brown-headed cowbird	Friends of Oxbow 2000; Lockwood - BBS 2000
Quiscalus quiscula	Common grackle	Friends of Oxbow 2000; Lockwood - BBS 2000
Carpodacus purpureus	Purple finch	Lockwood 2000
Sturnella magna	Eastern Meadowlark NGSMC	Friends of Oxbow 2000
Icterus galbula	Baltimore Oriole	Friends of Oxbow 2000; Lockwood - BBS 2000
Piranga olivacea	Scarlet tanager	Friends of Oxbow 2000; Lockwood - BBS 2000
Pheucticus ludovicianus	Rose-breasted grosbeak	Friends of Oxbow 2000; Lockwood - BBS 2000
Podilymbus podiceps	Pied-billed grebe	Refuge Staff

Table D-2: Mammals at Oxbow NWR

Scientific name	Common name	Reference
Blarina brevicauda	Northern short-tailed shrew	Friends of Oxbow 2000

Scalopus aquiaticus	Eastern mole	Friends of Oxbow 2000
Tamias striatus	Eastern chipmunk	Friends of Oxbow 2000
Tamiasciurus hudsonicus	Red squirrel	Friends of Oxbow 2000
Sciurus carolinensis	Eastern gray squirrel	Friends of Oxbow 2000
Sylvilagus floridanus	Eastern Cottontail Rabbit	Friends of Oxbow 2000
Castor canadensis	American beaver	Plagge & Lockwood 2000; Friends of Oxbow 2000
Microtus pennsylvanicus	Meadow vole	Friends of Oxbow 2000
Microtus spp.	Vole spp.	Friends of Oxbow 2000
Ondatra zibethicus	Common muskrat	Baseline Study 1993; Friends of Oxbow 2000
Mus musculus	House mouse	Baseline Study 1993
Rattus noregicus	Norway rat	Baseline Study 1993
Napaeozapus insignis	Woodland jumping mouse	Baseline Study 1993
Erethizon dorsatum	Common porcupine	Baseline Study 1993
Canis latrans	Eastern Coyote	Friends of Oxbow 2000
Vulpes fulva	Red fox	Plagge & Lockwood 2000
Urocyon cinereoargenteus	Gray fox	McCarter, 2000
Procyon lotor	Common raccoon	Friends of Oxbow 2000
Mustela vison	American mink	Friends of Oxbow 2000
Lutra canadensis	Northern river otter	Friends of Oxbow 2000
Martes pennanti	Fisher	Friends of Oxbow 2000; Lockwood 2000
Lynx rufus	Bobcat	Baseline Study 1993; Friends of Oxbow 2000
Odocoileus virginiana	White-tailed deer	Friends of Oxbow 2000
Alces alces	Moose	Lockwood 2000
Eptesicus fuscus	Big brown bat	Baseline Study 1993; Friends of Oxbow 2000
Lasiurus borealis	Eastern red bat (*)	Baseline Study 1993
Lasiurus cinereus	Hoary bat (*)	Baseline Study 1993
Myotis lucifugus	Little brown bat	Baseline Study 1993; Friends of Oxbow 2000
Myotis keenii	Keen's myotis (*)	Baseline Study 1993
Pipistrellus subflavus	Eastern pipistrelle (*)	Baseline Study 1993

* not positive ID

Dr. Howard Thomas Research at Fort Devens

Scientific Name	Common Name	Status	References
Didelphis virginiana	Virginia opossum		Thomas 1992
Sorex cinereus	Masked shrew		Thomas 1992
Sorex palustris	Common water shrew	SC	Thomas 1992
Parascalops breweri	Hairy-tailed mole		Thomas 1992
Condylura cristata	Star-nosed mole		Thomas 1992
Sylvilagus floridanus	Eastern cottontail		Thomas 1992
Lepus americanus	Snowshoe hare		Thomas 1992
Glaucomys volans	Southern flying squirrel		Thomas 1992
Marmota monax	Woodchuck		Thomas 1992
Peromyscus leucopus	White-footed mouse		Thomas 1992
Microtus pinetorum	Woodland vole (Pine vole)		Thomas 1992
Clethrionomys gapperi	Southern red-backed vole		Thomas 1992
Zapus hudsonius	Meadow jumping mouse		Thomas 1992
Ursus americanus	Black bear		Thomas 1992
Mustela erminea	Ermine		Thomas 1992
Mephitis mephitis	Striped skunk		Thomas 1992
Blarina brevicauda	Northern short-tailed shrew		Thomas 1992
Tamias striatus	Eastern chipmunk		Thomas 1992

Microtus pennsylvanicus	Meadow vole		Thomas 1992
Canis latrans	Eastern coyote		Thomas 1992
Procyon lotor	Common raccoon		Thomas 1992
Mustela vison	American mink		Thomas 1992
Lutra canadensis	Northern river otter		Thomas 1992
Odocoileus virginiana	White-tailed deer		Thomas 1992
Tamiasciurus hudsonicus	Red squirrel		Thomas 1992
Sciurus carolinensis	Eastern gray squirrel		Thomas 1992
Martes pennanti	Fisher		Thomas 1992

Table D-3: Reptiles at Great Meadows NWR

Scientific Name	Common Name	Status	References
Coluber c. constrictor	Northern black racer		Baseline Study 1993
Diadophis punctatus	Northern ringneck snake		Baseline Study 1993
Elaphe guttata	Corn snake		Baseline Study 1993
Lampropeltis triangulum	Eastern milk snake		Baseline Study 1993
Nerodia s. sipedon	Northern water snake		Baseline Study 1993; Friends of Oxbow 2000
Opheodrys vernalis	Smooth green snake		Baseline Study 1993
Storeria dekayi	Northern brown snake		Baseline Study 1993
Storeria occipitomaculata	Northern redbelly snake		Baseline Study 1993
Thamnophis sauritus	Northern ribbon snake		Baseline Study 1993; Friends of Oxbow 2000
Thamnophis s. sirtalis	Common garter snake		Baseline Study 1993; Friends of Oxbow 2000
Chelydra serpentina	Snapping turtle		Baseline Study 1993; Friends of Oxbow 2000
Chrysemys picta	Painted turtle		Baseline Study 1993; Friends of Oxbow 2000
Clemmys guttata	Spotted turtle	SC	Baseline Study 1993
Clemmys insculpta	Wood turtle	SC	Baseline Study 1993
Terrapene carolina	Eastern box turtle	SC	Baseline Study 1993
Emydoidea blandingii	Blanding's turtle	ST	Baseline Study 1993; Friends of Oxbow 2000
Sternotherus odoratus	Stinkpot		Baseline Study 1993

Table D-4: Amphibians at Oxbow NWR

Scientific Name	Common name	Status	Reference
Ambystoma laterale	Blue-spotted salamander	SC	Baseline Study 1993; Friends of Oxbow 2000
Ambystoma maculatum	Spotted salamander		Baseline Study 1993; Friends of Oxbow 2000
Bufo americanus	American toad		Baseline Study 1993; Friends of Oxbow 2000
Bufo woodhousei fowleri	Fowler's toad		Baseline Study 1993
Hyla crucifer	Spring peeper		Baseline Study 1993; Friends of Oxbow 2000
Hyla versicolor	Gray treefrog		Baseline Study 1993
Desmognathus fuscus	Dusky salamander		Baseline Study 1993
Eurycea bislineata	Two-lined salamander		Baseline Study 1993

Plethodon cinereus	Red Backed salamander	Baseline Study 1993
Rana catesbeiana	Bullfrog	Baseline Study 1993; Friends of Oxbow 2000
Rana clamitans	Green frog	Baseline Study 1993; Friends of Oxbow 2000
Rana palustris	Pickerel frog	Baseline Study 1993; Friends of Oxbow 2000
Rana pipiens	Northern leopard frog	Baseline Study 1993; Friends of Oxbow 2000
Rana sylvatica	Wood frog	Baseline Study 1993; Friends of Oxbow 2000
Notopthalmus viridescens	Red spotted newt	Baseline Study 1993; Friends of Oxbow 2000

Table D-5: Moths at Oxbow NWR

Scientific Name	Status	References
Drepana arcuata		Mello & Peters 1994
Drepana bilineata		Mello & Peters 1994
Oreta rosea		Mello & Peters 1994
Eumacaria latiferrugata		Mello & Peters 1994
Itame pustularia		Mello & Peters 1994
Semiothisa aemulitaria		Mello & Peters 1994
Semiothisa minorata		Mello & Peters 1994
Semiothisa bisignata		Mello & Peters 1992
Semiothisa granitata		Mello & Peters 1994
Glena cognataria		Mello & Peters 1994
Anacamptodes humaria		Mello & Peters 1994
Anavitrinelia pampinaria		Mello & Peters 1994
Ectropis crepuscularia		Mello & Peters 1994
Melanolophia signataria		Mello & Peters 1994
Eufidonia nototaria		Mello & Peters 1994
Erannis tiliaria		Mello & Peters 1994
Cabera variolaria		Mello & Peters 1994
Euchlaena serrata		Mello & Peters 1994
Campaea perlata		Mello & Peters 1994
Ennomos magnaria		Mello & Peters 1994
Petrophora subaequaria		Mello & Peters 1994
Homochlodes discoventa		Mello & Peters 1994
Metanema inatomaria		Mello & Peters 1994
Cepphis decoloraria		Mello & Peters 1994
Anagoga occiduaria		Mello & Peters 1994
Probole amicaria		Mello & Peters 1994
Plagodis serinaria		Mello & Peters 1994
Plagodis alcoolaria		Mello & Peters 1994
Besma endropiaria		Mello & Peters 1994
Eusarca confusaria		Mello & Peters 1994
Prochoerodes transversata		Mello & Peters 1994
Antepione thiosaria		Mello & Peters 1994
Nematocampa limbata		Mello & Peters 1994
Nemoria bistriaria		Mello & Peters 1994
Chlorochlamys chloroleucaria		Mello & Peters 1994

Cyclophora pendulinaria	Mello & Peters 1994
Scopula cacuminaria	Mello & Peters 1994
Scopula purata	Mello & Peters 1994
Scopula limboundata	Mello & Peters 1994
Eulithis diversilineata	Mello & Peters 1994
Thera juniperata	Mello & Peters 1994
Xanthorhoe lacustrata	Mello & Peters 1994
Orthonama obstipata	Mello & Peters 1994
Orthonama centrostrigaria	Mello & Peters 1994
Operophtera bruceata	Mello & Peters 1994
Heterophelps triguttaria	Mello & Peters 1994
Calledapteryx dryopterata	Mello & Peters 1994
Tolype velleda	Mello & Peters 1994
Tolype laricis	Mello & Peters 1994
Dryocampa rubicunda	Mello & Peters 1994
Callosamia promethea	Mello & Peters 1994
Sphinx gordius	Mello & Peters 1994
Paonias myops	Mello & Peters 1994
Pachysphinx modesta	Mello & Peters 1994
Clostera albosigma	Mello & Peters 1994
Costera inclusa	Mello & Peters 1994
Costera apicalis	Mello & Peters 1994
Nadata gibbosa	Mello & Peters 1994
Hyperaeschra georgica	Mello & Peters 1994
Peridea angulosa	Mello & Peters 1994
Peridea ferruginea	Mello & Peters 1994
Notodonta scitipennis	Mello & Peters 1994
Nerice bidentata	Mello & Peters 1994
Gluphisia septentrionis	Mello & Peters 1994
Macrurocampa marthesia	Mello & Peters 1994
Schizura badia	Mello & Peters 1994
Schizura unicornis	Mello & Peters 1994
Oligocentra semirufescens	Mello & Peters 1994
Oligocentra lignicolor	Mello & Peters 1994
Hypoprepia fucosa	Mello & Peters 1994
Holomelina aurantiaca	Mello & Peters 1994
Spilosoma congrua	Mello & Peters 1994
Spilosoma virginica	Mello & Peters 1994
Phragmatobia fuliginosa	Mello & Peters 1994
Apantesis carlotta	Mello & Peters 1994
Apantesis figurata	Mello & Peters 1994
Apantesis arge	Mello & Peters 1994
Halysidota tessellaris	Mello & Peters 1994
Cycnia oregonensis	Mello & Peters 1994
Cisseps fulvicollis	Mello & Peters 1994
Orgyia leucostigma	Mello & Peters 1994
Lymantria dispar	Mello & Peters 1994
Idia americalis	Mello & Peters 1994
Idia aemula	Mello & Peters 1994
Idia rotundalis	Mello & Peters 1994
Idia julia	Mello & Peters 1994
Idia diminuendis	Mello & Peters 1994

Oxbow National Wildlife Refuge

Idia lubricalis	Mello & Peters 1994
Zanclognatha protumnusalis	Mello & Peters 1992
Zanclognatha jacchusalis	Mello & Peters 1992
Zanclognatha ochreipennis	Mello & Peters 1992
Chytolita petrealis	Mello & Peters 1992
Hormisa absorptalis	Mello & Peters 1994
Hormisa litophora	Mello & Peters 1994
Hormisa bivittata	Mello & Peters 1994
Hormisa orciferalis	Mello & Peters 1994
Hormisa loiusiana	Mello & Peters 1994
Phalaenostola metonalis	Mello & Peters 1994
Phalaenostola larentioides	Mello & Peters 1994
Bleptina caradrinalis	Mello & Peters 1994
Renia factiosalis	Mello & Peters 1994
Renia flavipunctalis	Mello & Peters 1994
Lascoria ambigualis	Mello & Peters 1994
Palthis angulalis	Mello & Peters 1994
Palthis asopialis	Mello & Peters 1994
Rivula propinqualis	Mello & Peters 1994
Colobochyla interpuncta	Mello & Peters 1994
Melanoma aurinctaria	Mello & Peters 1994
Hypenodes caducus	Mello & Peters 1994
Hypenodes fractilinea	Mello & Peters 1994
Hypenodes palustris	Mello & Peters 1994
Hypenodes sombrus	Mello & Peters 1994
Dyspyralis puncticosta	Mello & Peters 1994
Bomolocha baltimoralis	Mello & Peters 1994
Lomanaltes eductalis	Mello & Peters 1994
Plathypena scabra	Mello & Peters 1994
Pangrapta decoralis	Mello & Peters 1994
Ledaea perditalis	Mello & Peters 1994
Metalectra discalis	Mello & Peters 1994
Gabara subnivosella	Mello & Peters 1994
Drasteria occulta	Mello & Peters 1994
Zale helata	Mello & Peters 1994
Zale horrida	Mello & Peters 1994
Parallelia bistriaris	Mello & Peters 1994
Caenurgina crassiuscula	Mello & Peters 1994
Caenurgina erechtea	Mello & Peters 1994
Catocala antinympha	Mello & Peters 1994
Catocala unijuga	Mello & Peters 1994
Catocala cara	Mello & Peters 1994
Catocala concumbens	Mello & Peters 1994
Catocala andromedae	Mello & Peters 1994
Catocala ultronia	Mello & Peters 1994
Pseudoplusia includens	Mello & Peters 1994
Autographa precationis	Mello & Peters 1994
Anagrapha falcifera	Mello & Peters 1994
Plusia putnami	Mello & Peters 1994
Plusia contexta	Mello & Peters 1994
Plusia venusta	Mello & Peters 1994
Baileya ophthalmica	Mello & Peters 1994

Lithacodia bellicula		Mello & Peters 1994
Lithacodia muscosula		Mello & Peters 1994
Lithacodia albidula		Mello & Peters 1994
Lithacodia carneola		Mello & Peters 1994
Homophoberia cristata		Mello & Peters 1994
Homophoberia apicosa		Mello & Peters 1994
Neotarache curvata		Mello & Peters 1994
Tarachidia candefacta		Mello & Peters 1994
Panthea pallescens		Mello & Peters 1994
Raphia frater		Mello & Peters 1994
Acronicta lepusculina		Mello & Peters 1994
Acronicta noctivaga		Mello & Peters 1994
Acronicta distans		Mello & Peters 1994
Acronicta oblinita		Mello & Peters 1994
Harrisimemna Trisignata		Mello & Peters 1994
Crymodes burgessi		Mello & Peters 1994
Eremobina hilli		Mello & Peters 1992
Oligia exhausta		Mello & Peters 1994
Oligia bridghami		Mello & Peters 1994
Oligia mactata		Mello & Peters 1994
Oligia illocata		Mello & Peters 1994
Meropleon diversicolor		Mello & Peters 1994
Lemmeria digitalis	WL	Mello & Peters 1992
Archanara oblonga		Mello & Peters 1992
Helotropha reniformis		Mello & Peters 1994
Papaipema impecuniosa		Mello & Peters 1994
Papaipema lysimachiae		Mello & Peters 1994
Papaipema speciosissima		Mello & Peters 1994
Papaipema inquaesita		Mello & Peters 1992
Papaipema birdi		Mello & Peters 1994
Bellura gortynoides		Mello & Peters 1994
Bellura obliqua		Mello & Peters 1994
Euplexia benesimils		Mello & Peters 1994
Phlogophora periculosa		Mello & Peters 1992
Nedra ramosula		Mello & Peters 1992
Fagitana littera		Mello & Peters 1994
Callopistria mollissima		Mello & Peters 1994
Amphipyra pyramidoides		Mello & Peters 1994
Amphipyra glabella		Mello & Peters 1994
Proxenus miranda		Mello & Peters 1994
Platyperigea multifera		Mello & Peters 1994
Platysenta videns		Mello & Peters 1994
Platysenta vecors		Mello & Peters 1994
Cosmia calami		Mello & Peters 1994
Xylena curvimacula		Mello & Peters 1994
Lithophane solidaginis		Mello & Peters 1994
Lithophane querquera		Mello & Peters 1994
Lithophane tepida		Mello & Peters 1994
Lithophane antennata		Mello & Peters 1994
Lithophane grotei		Mello & Peters 1994
Lithophane fagina		Mello & Peters 1994
Pyreferra hesperidago		Mello & Peters 1994

Eupsilia morrisoni	Mello & Peters 1994
Metaxaglaea semitaria	Mello & Peters 1994
Epiglaea decliva	Mello & Peters 1994
Epiglaea apiata	Mello & Peters 1994
Chaetaglaea tremula	Mello & Peters 1994
Chaetaglaea sericea	Mello & Peters 1994
Psectraglaea carnosa	Mello & Peters 1994
Eucirroedia pampina	Mello & Peters 1994
Sunira bicolorago	Mello & Peters 1994
Anathix ralla	Mello & Peters 1994
Xanthia togata	Mello & Peters 1994
Sutnya privata	Mello & Peters 1994
Cucullia convexipennis	Mello & Peters 1994
Lacanobia legitima	Mello & Peters 1994
Lacinipolia meditata	Mello & Peters 1994
Faronta diffusa	Mello & Peters 1994
Aletia oxygala	Mello & Peters 1994
Pseudaletia unipuncta	Mello & Peters 1992
Leucania linda	Mello & Peters 1992
Leucania multilinea	Mello & Peters 1994
Nephelodes minians	Mello & Peters 1994
Ulolonche modesta	Mello & Peters 1994
Agrotis vetusta	Mello & Peters 1994
Agrotis venerabilis	Mello & Peters 1994
Agrotis stigmosa	Mello & Peters 1994
Feltia jaculifera	Mello & Peters 1994
Feltia subgothica	Mello & Peters 1994
Feltia herilis	Mello & Peters 1994
Feltia geniculata	Mello & Peters 1994
Longivesica messoria	Mello & Peters 1992
Euxoa velleripennis	Mello & Peters 1994
Euxoa tessellata	Mello & Peters 1992
Euxoa albipennis	Mello & Peters 1994
Euxoa violaris	Mello & Peters 1994
Euxoa bostoniensis	Mello & Peters 1994
Euxoa obeliscoides	Mello & Peters 1994
Orchopleura plecta	Mello & Peters 1994
Euagrotis illapsa	Mello & Peters 1994
Peridroma saucia	Mello & Peters 1994
Spaelotis clandestina	Mello & Peters 1994
Xestia adela	Mello & Peters 1994
Xestia dolosa	Mello & Peters 1994
Xestia smithii	Mello & Peters 1992
Xestia bicarnea	Mello & Peters 1992
Anomogyna elimata	Mello & Peters 1994
Anomogyna dilucida	Mello & Peters 1994
Eugraphe subrosea opacifrons	Mello & Peters 1994
Protolampra brunneicollis	Mello & Peters 1994
Euretagrotis perattenta	Mello & Peters 1994
Abagrotis alternata	Mello & Peters 1994
Rhynchagrotis cupida	Mello & Peters 1994
Derrima stellata	Mello & Peters 1994

Schinia spinosae	Mello & Peters 1992	
Schinia lynx	Mello & Peters 1994	
Schinia arcigera	Mello & Peters 1994	

MOTHS—Biodiversity 2000 (* Previously Recorded by Mello & Peters, 1224)

Scientific Name	Common Name	Status	References
Acronicta americana	American dagger		Friends of Oxbow 2000
Cosmia calami	American dun-bar		Friends of Oxbow 2000
Idia americalis	American idia		Friends of Oxbow 2000
Bomolocha baltimoralis	Baltimore bomolocha		Friends of Oxbow 2000
Pantograpta limata	Basswood leafroller		Friends of Oxbow 2000
Bleptina cardrinalis	Bent-winged owlet		Friends of Oxbow 2000
Paonias excaecatus	Blinded sphinx		Friends of Oxbow 2000
Hemicleuca maia	Buck moth		Friends of Oxbow 2000
Melanolopha candaria	Canadian melanolophia		Friends of Oxbow 2000
Udea rubigalis	Celery leaftier		Friends of Oxbow 2000
Catocala blandula	Charming underwing		Friends of Oxbow 2000
Schizura badia	Chestnut chiizura		Friends of Oxbow 2000
Peridea ferruginea	Chocoloate prominent		Friends of Oxbow 2000
Chytonix palliatricula	Cloaked marvel		Friends of Oxbow 2000
Gluphisia septentrionis	Common gluphisia		Friends of Oxbow 2000
Idia aemula	Common Idia		Friends of Oxbow 2000
Petrophordae sp.	Common petrophora		Friends of Oxbow 2000
Zanclognatha obscuripennis	Dark zancolognatha		Friends of Oxbow 2000
Pangrapta decoralis	Decorated owlet		Friends of Oxbow 2000
Datana drexelli	Drexel's datana		Friends of Oxbow 2000
Malacosoma americanum	Eastern tent catapillar		Friends of Oxbow 2000
Ennomos subsignaria	Elm spanworm		Friends of Oxbow 2000
Hyphantria cunea	Fall webworm		Friends of Oxbow 2000
Pheosia rimosa	False sphinx		Friends of Oxbow 2000
Amolita fessa	Feeble grass moth		Friends of Oxbow 2000
Hydria prunivorata	Fergerson's scallop shell		Friends of Oxbow 2000
Bomolocha manalis	Flowing-line bomolocha		Friends of Oxbow 2000
Chrysanympha formosa	Formosa looper		Friends of Oxbow 2000
Renia flavipunctalis	Fraternal renia		Friends of Oxbow 2000
Probole amicaria	Friendly probole		Friends of Oxbow 2000
Polia goddelli	Godells' arches		Friends of Oxbow 2000
Desmia funeralis	Grape leaf folder		Friends of Oxbow 2000
Aglossa cuprina	Grease moth		Friends of Oxbow 2000
Nadata gibbosa	Green oak caterpillar		Friends of Oxbow 2000
Peridea angulosa	Green oak caterpillar		Friends of Oxbow 2000
Lymantria dispar	Gypsy		Friends of Oxbow 2000
Harrisimemna trsignata	Harris's three spot		Friends of Oxbow 2000
Acronicta haesitata	Hesitant dagger		Friends of Oxbow 2000
Acronicta ovata	Hesitant dagger moth complex		Friends of Oxbow 2000
Nematocampa resistaria	Horned spanworm		Friends of Oxbow 2000
Zale horrida	Horrid zale		Friends of Oxbow 2000
Hemaris thysbe	Hummingbird moth		Friends of Oxbow 2000
Catocala ilia	Ilia underwing		Friends of Oxbow 2000
Phrrharetia isabella	Isabella tiger moth catapiller		Friends of Oxbow 2000
Phyllodesma americana	Lappet		Friends of Oxbow 2000
Scopula limboundata	Large lacked border		Friends of Oxbow 2000

Scientific Name	Common Name	References
Prochoerodes transversata	Large maple spanworm	Friends of Oxbow 2000
Lithacodia muscosula	Large mossy lithacodia	Friends of Oxbow 2000
Zeuzera pyrina	Leapord moth	Friends of Oxbow 2000
Itame pustularia	Lesser maple sapnworm	Friends of Oxbow 2000
Acronicta longa	Long-winged dagger	Friends of Oxbow 2000
Ledaea perditalis	Lost owlet	Friends of Oxbow 2000
Parallelia bistriaris	Maple looper	Friends of Oxbow 2000
Locmaeus bilineata	Marble prominent	Friends of Oxbow 2000
Drepana bilineata	Masked birch caterpillar	Friends of Oxbow 2000
Euchactias	Milkweed tiger moth caterpillar	Friends of Oxbow 2000
Schizura ipomoeae	Morning glory prominent	Friends of Oxbow 2000
Pero morrisonaria	Morrison's pero	Friends of Oxbow 2000
Macrurocampa marthesia	Mottled prominent	Friends of Oxbow 2000
Lapara bombycoides	Northern pine sphinx	Friends of Oxbow 2000
Lapara coniferarum	Northern sphnix	Friends of Oxbow 2000
Hetrocampa obliqua	Oblique heterocampa	Friends of Oxbow 2000
Zale orbliqua	Oblique zale	Friends of Oxbow 2000
Hypagytis unipunctata	One-spotted variant	Friends of Oxbow 2000
Idia diminuendis	Orange spotted idia	Friends of Oxbow 2000
Halysidota tessellaris	Pale tussock	Friends of Oxbow 2000
Eudryas unio	Pearly wood nymph	Friends of Oxbow 2000
Lithacodia carneola	Pink barred lithacodia	Friends of Oxbow 2000
Callopistria mollissima	Pink shaded fern moth	Friends of Oxbow 2000
Antheraea polyphemus	Polyphemus moth	Friends of Oxbow 2000
Protoboarmia porcelaria	Porcelain gray	Friends of Oxbow 2000
Panopoda rufimargo	Red-lined panopoda	Friends of Oxbow 2000
Dryocampa rubicunda	Rosy maple moth	Friends of Oxbow 2000
Phragmatabia fuliginosa	Ruby tiger	Friends of Oxbow 2000
Ectropis crepuscularia	Saddleback looper	Friends of Oxbow 2000
Euchaena serrata	Sawwing	Friends of Oxbow 2000
Hypoprepia fucosa	Scarlet winged lilchen moth	Friends of Oxbow 2000
Eueretagrotis sigmoides	Sigmoid dart	Friends of Oxbow 2000
Callopistria cordata	Silver spotted fern moth	Friends of Oxbow 2000
Paonias astylus	Small eyed spinx	Friends of Oxbow 2000
Eugonobapta nivosaria	Snowy geometer	Friends of Oxbow 2000
Catocala sordida	Sordid underwing	Friends of Oxbow 2000
Euclea delphinii	Spiny oak slug	Friends of Oxbow 2000
Dasychira obligata	Streaked tussock	Friends of Oxbow 2000
Cyclophora pendulinaraia	Sweetfern geometer	Friends of Oxbow 2000
Panthea pallescens	Tufted white pine caterpllar	Friends of Oxbow 2000
	Tussock moth	Friends of Oxbow 2000
Ctenucha virginica	Virginia ctenuchid	Friends of Oxbow 2000
Laothoe juglandis	White sphinx	Friends of Oxbow 2000
	Woodland moth	Friends of Oxbow 2000
Pyrrharctia isabella	Woolybear (Isabella tiger moth)	Friends of Oxbow 2000
Spilosoma viginica	Yellow bear tiger	Friends of Oxbow 2000
Colobochyla interpuncta	Yellow lined owlet	Friends of Oxbow 2000
Agrotis ipsilon	Ypsilon dart (cutworm)	Friends of Oxbow 2000

Scientific Name	Status	References
Abagrotis alternata		Friends of Oxbow 2000
Acrobasis stigmella		Friends of Oxbow 2000

Comprehensive Conservation Plan

Appendix D: Species Lists

Amolita roseola	Friends of Oxbow 2000
Anaplectoides prasina	Friends of Oxbow 2000
Anomogyna praevia	Friends of Oxbow 2000
Callima argenticinctella	Friends of Oxbow 2000
Choristoneura pinus	Friends of Oxbow 2000
Chrystoteucha topiaria	Friends of Oxbow 2000
Dasychira cinnamomea	Friends of Oxbow 2000
Efermaladia giradellus	Friends of Oxbow 2000
Euchlaena muzaria	Friends of Oxbow 2000
Eufernalda agitatellus	Friends of Oxbow 2000
Eulithis explanata	Friends of Oxbow 2000
*Euliths diversilineata	Friends of Oxbow 2000
*Gabara subnivosella	Friends of Oxbow 2000
Heptagrotis phyllophora	Friends of Oxbow 2000
Herculia binodularis	Friends of Oxbow 2000
Herpetogramma aegealis	Friends of Oxbow 2000
Herpetogramma pertextalis	Friends of Oxbow 2000
Holomelina opella	Friends of Oxbow 2000
*Idia rotundalis	Friends of Oxbow 2000
Leucania insueta	Friends of Wildlife 2000
Lithacodes fascola	Friends of Oxbow 2000
Macrochilo litophora	Friends of Oxbow 2000
*Nemorim bistriaria	Friends of Oxbow 2000
*Noctura pronuba	Friends of Oxbow 2000
Olethreutes lacunara	Friends of Oxbow 2000
*Orgyia leucostigma	Friends of Oxbow 2000
*Paonias myops	Friends of Oxbow 2000
Peoria approximella	Friends of Oxbow 2000
Redectis vitrea	Friends of Oxbow 2000
Renia salusalis	Friends of Oxbow 2000
*Scopula cacuminaria	Friends of Oxbow 2000
*Semiothisa granitata	Friends of Oxbow 2000
Semiothisa pinistrobata	Friends of Oxbow 2000
*Semiothisda bisgnata	Friends of Oxbow 2000
*Semiothsa minorata	Friends of Oxbow 2000
Tetralopha asperatella	Friends of Oxbow 2000
Zanclognatha laevigata	Friends of Oxbow 2000
*Zanclognatha protumnusalis	Friends of Oxbow 2000

Table D-6: Butterflies at Oxbow NWR

Scientific Name	Common Name	Status	References
Celestrina ladon	Spring azure		Friends of Oxbow 2000
Nymphalis antiopa	Mourning cloak		Friends of Oxbow 2000
Nymphalis antiopa	Mourning cloak		Friends of Oxbow 2000
Megisto cymela	Little wood satyr		Friends of Oxbow 2000
Vanessa virginiensis	American lady		Friends of Oxbow 2000
Celastrina ladon neglecta	Summer azure		Friends of Oxbow 2000
Phyciodes tharos	Pearl crescent		Friends of Oxbow 2000
Speyeria cybele	Great spangles fritterlary		Friends of Oxbow 2000
Vanessa atalanta	Red admiral		Friends of Oxbow 2000
Ebidua anthedon	Northern Pearly eye		Friends of Oxbow 2000

Danaus plexippus	Monarch	Friends of Oxbow 2000
Papilio polyxenes	Black swallowtail	Friends of Oxbow 2000
Pieris rapae	Cabbage white	Friends of Oxbow 2000
Colias philodice	Clouded sulphur	Friends of Oxbow 2000
Colias philodice	Clouded sulphur (white)	Friends of Oxbow 2000
Coenonnypha tullia	Common ringlet	Friends of Oxbow 2000
Colias philodice	Common sulphur (albino)	Friends of Oxbow 2000
Euphyes vestris	Dun skipper	Friends of Oxbow 2000
Polygonia comma	Eastern comma	Friends of Oxbow 2000
Papilio glaucus	Eastern tiger swallowtail	Friends of Oxbow 2000
Sattrides eurydice	Eyed brown satyr	Friends of Oxbow 2000
Strymon melinus	Gray hairstreak	Friends of Oxbow 2000
Feniseca tarquinius	Harvester	Friends of Oxbow 2000
Poanes hobomok	Hobomok skipper	Friends of Oxbow 2000
Ancyloxpha numitor	Least skipper	Friends of Oxbow 2000
Thorybes pylades	Northern cloudywing	Friends of Oxbow 2000
Colias eurytheme	Orange sulphur	Friends of Oxbow 2000
Polygoina interrogationis	Question mark	Friends of Oxbow 2000
Limenitis arthemis astyanax	Red-spotted purple	Friends of Oxbow 2000
Epargyreus clarus	Silver-spotted skipper	Friends of Oxbow 2000
Satyrium liparops	Striped hairstreak	Friends of Oxbow 2000
Limenitis archippus	Viceroy	Friends of Oxbow 2000

Table D-7: Dragonflies and Damselflies at Oxbow NWR

Scientific Name	Common Name	Status	References
Lestes rectangularis	Spreadwing		Friends of Oxbow 2000
Pachydiplax longipennis	Blue Dasher		Friends of Oxbow 2000
Sympetrum spp.	Meadow Hawk		Friends of Oxbow 2000
Everes comyntas	Eastern tailed blue		Friends of Oxbow 2000
Stylunus spiniceps	Arrow clubtail		Friends of Oxbow 2000
Gomphus spp.	Clubtail		Friends of Oxbow 2000
Hagenius brevistylus	Common dragon hunter		Friends of Oxbow 2000
Libellula luctosa	Common ringlet		Friends of Oxbow 2000
Ischnura verticalis	Eastern forktail		Friends of Oxbow 2000
Erythemis simplicicollis	Eastern pondhawk (green jacket)		Friends of Oxbow 2000
Calopenyx maculata	Ebony jewelwing		Friends of Oxbow 2000
Ischnura posita	Fragile foxtail		Friends of Oxbow 2000
Leucorrhinia frigida	Frosted whiteface		Friends of Oxbow 2000
Porocordulia libera	Racket tailed emerald		Friends of Oxbow 2000
Sympetrum ribiculdulum	Ruby meadowhawk		Friends of Oxbow 2000
Libellula incesta	Slaty skimmer		Friends of Oxbow 2000
Lestes rectangularis	Slender spreadwing		Friends of Oxbow 2000
Nehalennia gracilis	Sphagnum sprite		Friends of Oxbow 2000
Argia fumiphennis	Violet dancer		Friends of Oxbow 2000
Libellula lustucosa	Widow skimmer dragonfly		Friends of Oxbow 2000
Sympetrum vicinum	Yellow legged meadownhawk		Friends of Oxbow 2000
Stylunus scudderi	Zebra clubtail		Friends of Oxbow 2000

Table D-8: Insects at Oxbow NWR

Scientific Name	Common Name	Status	References
Carabidae sp.	Ground Beetle		Friends of Oxbow 2000
Chrysomealinae sp.	Flower Beetle (red spotted)		Friends of Oxbow 2000
Chrysomealinae sp.	Flower Beetle (yellow striped)		Friends of Oxbow 2000
Lycosidae sp.	Running Wolf Spider		Friends of Oxbow 2000
Salticidae sp.	Jumping Spider		Friends of Oxbow 2000
Dytiscus harrisi	Predacious Diving Beetle		Friends of Oxbow 2000
Acilius sp.	Water Tigers		Friends of Oxbow 2000
Tropisternus sp.	Water Scavenger Beetle		Friends of Oxbow 2000
Eubranchipus vernalis	Fairy Shrimp		Friends of Oxbow 2000
Limnephilidae sp.	Caddis Fly		Friends of Oxbow 2000
Stratiomyidae sp.	Soldier Fly		Friends of Oxbow 2000
Haliplidae sp.	Crawling Water Beetle		Friends of Oxbow 2000
Malacosoma disstria	Tent Caterpillers		Friends of Oxbow 2000
Ixodes scapularis	Deer Ticks		Friends of Oxbow 2000
Simuliidae spp.	Black flies		Friends of Oxbow 2000
Bombus spp.	Bumble bee		Friends of Oxbow 2000
Halictidae family	Burrowing bees		Friends of Oxbow 2000
Chironomidae family	Midges		Friends of Oxbow 2000
Locusta spp.	Locust		Friends of Oxbow 2000
Magicicada spp.	Cicada		Friends of Oxbow 2000
(?)	Metwing Beetle		Friends of Oxbow 2000
Alaus oculatus	Eastern click beetle		Friends of Oxbow 2000
Myrmeleon spp.	Ant Lions		Friends of Oxbow 2000
	Birch leaf minor		Friends of Oxbow 2000
Leioburnun spp.	Daddy long-legs Spider		Friends of Oxbow 2000
	Potato Leaf Hopper		Friends of Oxbow 2000
Calopteron recticulatum	Banded Netwing Beetle		Friends of Oxbow 2000
Chrysops spp.	Deer fly		Friends of Oxbow 2000
Camponotus pennsylvanicus	Carpenter ant		Friends of Oxbow 2000
	Hover fly		Friends of Oxbow 2000
	Scorpion fly		Friends of Oxbow 2000
Populla japonica	Japanese beetle		Friends of Oxbow 2000
Cicindela punctulata	Tiger beetle		Friends of Oxbow 2000
Photuris pennsylvanicus	Firefly		Friends of Oxbow 2000
	Rose leaf hopper		Friends of Oxbow 2000
	Snout beetle		Friends of Oxbow 2000
Placoadella sp.	Turtle Leech		Friends of Oxbow 2000
Placoadella sp.	Turtle Leech		Friends of Oxbow 2000
Macrobdella decora	American Mediainal Leech		Friends of Oxbow 2000
Pyrrharetia isabella	Wooly bear (Isabella tiger moth catapiller)		Friends of Oxbow 2000
Psylla alni	American alder pysllid		Friends of Oxbow 2000
Eliss pennanut (calithemeis elisa)	Calico pennant		Friends of Oxbow 2000
Dernacebtor spp	Eastern wood tick		Friends of Oxbow 2000
Culex pipineas	House mosquito		Friends of Oxbow 2000
	Leaf beetles		Friends of Oxbow 2000
Trichloptera	Log cabin caddishfly		Friends of Oxbow 2000
Sympetrum sp.	Meadowhawk		Friends of Oxbow 2000

Philaenus spumarius	Meadown spittlebug	Friends of Oxbow 2000
Lygaeus kalmii	Milkweed bug	Friends of Oxbow 2000
Culicidae (family)	Mosquito	Friends of Oxbow 2000
	Silk worm	Friends of Oxbow 2000
Cincindela sexguttata	Six spotteed tiger beetle	Friends of Oxbow 2000
Lygaeus kalmii	Small mildweed bug	Friends of Oxbow 2000
Collembola	Springtails	Friends of Oxbow 2000
	Tortis shell catepiller	Friends of Oxbow 2000
Eylais sp.	Water mites	Friends of Oxbow 2000
	Wild cheery leaf rolling plant hopper	Friends of Oxbow 2000

Table D-9: Freshwater Mollusks at Oxbow NWR

Scientific Name	Common Name	Status	References
Physella heterostroyha	Freshwater Snails		Friends of Oxbow 2000
Planorbidae gyrauls	Coiled Snail		Friends of Oxbow 2000
Elliptio complanate	Eastern elliptio		Friends of Oxbow 2000
Lampsilis radiata	Eastern lampmussel		Friends of Oxbow 2000
Alasmidonta undulata	Triangle floater	SC	Friends of Oxbow 2000
Andononta implicata	Alewife floater		Friends of Oxbow 2000
Margaritifera margaritifera	Eastern pearlshell		Friends of Oxbow 2000
Amnicola limnosa	Little pond snail		Friends of Oxbow 2000
Sphaerium occidentalle	Fingernail clam		Friends of Oxbow 2000
Orconectes rusticas	Crayfish		Friends of Oxbow 2000

Table D-10: Vascular Plants at Oxbow NWR

Scientific Name	Common Name	Status	References
Athyrium filix-feminia	Northern Lady fern		Friends of Oxbow 2000
Botrychium dissectum obliquum	Dissected fern		Sorrie, 1987
Cystopteris tenuis	Fragile fern		Friends of Oxbow 2000
Cystopteris tenuis	Brittle Fern		Friends of Oxbow 2000
Dennstaedtia punctilobula	Hay-scented fern		Friends of Oxbow 2000
Deparia acrostichoides	Silvery spleenwort		Sorrie, 1987
Diphasiastrum digitatum	Southern ground-cedar		Friends of Oxbow 2000
Diphasiastrum habereri	Hybrid clubmoss		Friends of Oxbow 2000
Diphasiastrum tristachyum	Slender ground-cedar		Friends of Oxbow 2000
Dryopteris carthusiana	Spinulose woodfern		Friends of Oxbow 2000
Dryopteris cristata	Crested woodfern		Friends of Oxbow 2000
Dryopteris intermedia	Grandular woodfern (intermediate)		Friends of Oxbow 2000
Dryopteris marginalis	Marginal woodfern		Friends of Oxbow 2000
Lygodium palmatum	Climbing Fern	SC	Sorrie, 1987
Drypolteris spinulosa	Wood fern		Friends of Oxbow 2000
Equisetaceae fluviatile	River horsetail		Friends of Oxbow 2000
Equisetaceae hyemale	Scouring horsetail		Friends of Oxbow 2000
Equisetum arvense	Common horsetail		Friends of Oxbow 2000
Equisetum fluviatile	Swamp horsetail		Friends of Oxbow 2000
Equisetum hyemale	Rough horsetail		Friends of Oxbow 2000
Equisteum sp.	Horsetail		Friends of Oxbow 2000
Huperzia lucidula	Shining clubmoss		Friends of Oxbow 2000
Lycopodium clavatum	Common clubmoss		Friends of Oxbow 2000

Lycopodium complanatum	Running pine		Friends of Oxbow 2000
Lycopodium hickeyi	Hickey's princess pine		Friends of Oxbow 2000
Lycopodium obscurum	Princess pine		Friends of Oxbow 2000
Lycopodium spp	Club moss		Friends of Oxbow 2000
Matteuccia struthiopteris	Ostrich fern		Friends of Oxbow 2000
Oncoclea sensibilis	Sensitive fern		Friends of Oxbow 2000
Osmunda cinnamomea	Cinnamon fern		Friends of Oxbow 2000
Osmunda claytoniana	Interrupted fern		Friends of Oxbow 2000
Osmunda regalis	Royal fern		Friends of Oxbow 2000
Platyneuron	Ebony spleenwort		Friends of Oxbow 2000
Polystichum acrostichoides	Christmas fern		Friends of Oxbow 2000
Pteridium aquilinum	Bracken fern		Friends of Oxbow 2000
Thelypteris noveboracensis	New York fern		Friends of Oxbow 2000
Thelypteris pdustris	Marsh fern		Friends of Oxbow 2000
Thelypteris simulata	Massachusetts fern		Friends of Oxbow 2000
Eleocharis ovata	Ovate Spike Sedge	SE	Hunt 1991
Abies balsamea	Balsam fir		Friends of Oxbow 2000
Juniperus spp.	Juniper		Friends of Oxbow 2000
Pinus rigida	Pitch pine		Sorrie, 1987
Pinus strobus	White pine		Friends of Oxbow 2000
Aralia nudicaulis	Wild sasparilla		Friends of Oxbow 2000
Arisaema atrorubens	Jack-in-the-pulpit		Friends of Oxbow 2000
Calamagrostis coarctata	Bluejoint Reed		Friends of Oxbow 2000
Carex crinita	Fringed sedge		Friends of Oxbow 2000
Carex stricita	Tussock sedge		Friends of Oxbow 2000
Cypripedium acaule	Pink Lady's slipper		Friends of Oxbow 2000
Dulichium arundianaceum	Three-way sedge		Friends of Oxbow 2000
Epipactis helleborine	Helleborine		Friends of Oxbow 2000
Eriocaylon septangulare	Pipe Wort		Friends of Oxbow 2000
Erythronium americanum	Trout Lily (Yellow alder's tongue)		Friends of Oxbow 2000
Goodyera pubescens	Downy rattlesnake plantain		Friends of Oxbow 2000
Iris versicolor	Blue flag iris		Friends of Oxbow 2000
Juncus effusus	Soft rush		Friends of Oxbow 2000
Leersia oryzoides	Rice cut-grass		Friends of Oxbow 2000
Lemna minor	Lesser Duckweed		Friends of Oxbow 2000
Lilium philadelphicum	Wood lily		Friends of Oxbow 2000
Nughar variegatum	Yellow cow lily		Friends of Oxbow 2000
Phalaris arundinacea	Reed canary grass		Friends of Oxbow 2000
Plantago spp.	Water Plantain		Friends of Oxbow 2000
Saggitaria latifolia	Arrowhead		Friends of Oxbow 2000
Schizachyrium scoparium	Little bluestem		Friends of Oxbow 2000
Scirpus atrovirens	Black Bulrush		Friends of Oxbow 2000
Scirpus cyperinus	Bulrush		Friends of Oxbow 2000
Sparganiaceae spp.	Bur-reed spp.		Friends of Oxbow 2000
Spirodela polyrrhiza	Greater Duckweed		Friends of Oxbow 2000
Symplocarpus foetidus	Skunk Cabbage		Friends of Oxbow 2000
Sparganium minimum	Small Bur-Reed	SE	Searcy 1994
Typha latifolia	Cat-tails		Friends of Oxbow 2000
Veratrum viride	False Hellebore		Friends of Oxbow 2000
Acer rubrum	Red maple		Friends of Oxbow 2000
Acer saccharinum	Silver maple		Friends of Oxbow 2000
Aesculus hippocastanum	Horse chestnut		Friends of Oxbow 2000

Alnus rugosa	Speckled alder		Friends of Oxbow 2000
Betula papyrifera	Paper birch		Friends of Oxbow 2000
Betula papyrifera	White birch		Friends of Oxbow 2000
Betula populifloria	Grey birch		Friends of Oxbow 2000
Carpinus carolinana	Ironwood (Blue Beech)		Friends of Oxbow 2000
Castanea dentata	American chestnut		Sorrie, 1987
Carya ovata	Shagbark hickory		Friends of Oxbow 2000
Comandra umbellata	Bastard-toadflax		Sorrie, 1987
Comptonia peregrina	Sweet fern		Friends of Oxbow 2000
Corylus americana	American hazelnut		Friends of Oxbow 2000
Crataegus spp	Hawthorne		Friends of Oxbow 2000
Fraxinus americana	White ash		Friends of Oxbow 2000
Hamamelis virginiana	Witch hazel		Friends of Oxbow 2000
Malus prunifolia	Plum-leaf apple		Friends of Oxbow 2000
Malus pumila	Apple		Friends of Oxbow 2000
Myrica gale	Sweet gale		Sorrie, 1987
Ostrva virginiaia	Hop-hornbeam (Ironwood)		Friends of Oxbow 2000
Overcus bicolor	Swamp white oak		Friends of Oxbow 2000
Pinus rigida	Pitch pine		Friends of Oxbow 2000
Platanus occidentalis	American sycamore		Friends of Oxbow 2000
Populus deltoides	Cottonwood		Friends of Oxbow 2000
Populus grandidentata	Big-toothed aspen		Friends of Oxbow 2000
Populus tremuloides	Quaking aspen		Friends of Oxbow 2000
Populus balsamifera	Balsam Poplar	WL	Hunt 1991
Prunus serotina	Black Cherry		Friends of Oxbow 2000
Quercus alba	White oak		Friends of Oxbow 2000
Quercus palustris	Pin Oak		Friends of Oxbow 2000
Quercus coccinea	Scarlet oak		Friends of Oxbow 2000
Quercus prinus	Chestnut oak		Friends of Oxbow 2000
Quercus rubra	Red oak		Friends of Oxbow 2000
Quercus velutina	Black oak		Friends of Oxbow 2000
Salix discolor	Willow		Friends of Oxbow 2000
Salix nigra	Black willow		Friends of Oxbow 2000
Sorbus americana	Mountain-ash		Friends of Oxbow 2000
Tilia americana	Basswood		Friends of Oxbow 2000
Ulmus americana	American elm		Friends of Oxbow 2000
Viburnum dentatum	Arrowood viburnum		Friends of Oxbow 2000
Elaeagnus angustifolia	Autumn olive		Friends of Oxbow 2000
Berberis vulgaris	European barberry		Friends of Oxbow 2000
Myrica pensylvanica	Bayberry		Friends of Oxbow 2000
Verbena hastata	Blue vervain		Friends of Oxbow 2000
Rubus spp	Bramble		Friends of Oxbow 2000
Arctium minus	Burdock		Friends of Oxbow 2000
Cephalanthus occidentalis	Buttonbush		Friends of Oxbow 2000
Rhamnus cathartica	Common buckthorn		Friends of Oxbow 2000
Sambucus canadensis	Common elderberry		Friends of Oxbow 2000
Rubus flagellaris	Dewberry		Friends of Oxbow 2000
Elaeagnus sp	Eleganus		Friends of Oxbow 2000
Vitis labrusca	Fox-grape		Friends of Oxbow 2000
Rhamnus frangula	Glossy buckthorn		Friends of Oxbow 2000
Crataegus sp	Hawthorne shrub		Friends of Oxbow 2000
Vaccinium corymbosum	Highbush blueberry		Friends of Oxbow 2000

Lonicera spp	Honeysuckle		Friends of Oxbow 2000
Berberis thunbergii	Japanese barberry		Friends of Oxbow 2000
Lonicera japonica	Japanese honeysuckle		Friends of Oxbow 2000
Vaccinium vacillans	Lowbush blueberry		Friends of Oxbow 2000
Lyonia ligustrina	Maleberry		Friends of Oxbow 2000
Spiraea latifolia	Meadowsweet		Friends of Oxbow 2000
Kalmia latifolia	Mountain laurel		Friends of Oxbow 2000
Rose multiflora	Multiflora rose		Friends of Oxbow 2000
Viburnum lentago	Nannyberry		Friends of Oxbow 2000
Celastrus orbiculatus	Oriental bittersweet		Friends of Oxbow 2000
Cornus racemosa	Panicked dogwood		Friends of Oxbow 2000
Juniperus communis	Pasture juniper		Friends of Oxbow 2000
Toxicodendron radicani	Poison ivy		Friends of Oxbow 2000
Salix discolor	Pussy Willow		Friends of Oxbow 2000
Actaea rubra	Red Baneberry		Friends of Oxbow 2000
Uitis riparia	Riverbank grape		Friends of Oxbow 2000
Amelanchier canadensis	Shad		Friends of Oxbow 2000
Amelanchier laevis	Shadbush		Friends of Oxbow 2000
Cornus sp.	Shrubby dogwood		Friends of Oxbow 2000
Cornus amomum	Silky dogwood		Friends of Oxbow 2000
Rhus glabra	Smooth sumac		Friends of Oxbow 2000
Rhus typhia	Staghorn sumac		Friends of Oxbow 2000
Spiraea tomentosa	Steeplebush		Friends of Oxbow 2000
Chimaphila maculata	Striped wintergreen		Friends of Oxbow 2000
Rosa palustris	Swamp rose		Friends of Oxbow 2000
Parthenocissus quinquefolia	Virginia creeper		Friends of Oxbow 2000
Clematis virginiana	Virgins bower		Friends of Oxbow 2000
Verbena urticifolia	White verbain		Friends of Oxbow 2000
Cornus racemosa	White Dogwood		Friends of Oxbow 2000
Ribes americanum	Wild currant		Friends of Oxbow 2000
Viburnum rudum var. cassinoidos	Wild raisin		Friends of Oxbow 2000
Rosa sp.	Wild rose		Friends of Oxbow 2000
Rhus copallinum	Winged Sumac		Friends of Oxbow 2000
Ilex vertecillata	Winterberry		Friends of Oxbow 2000
Acelepias syricaca	Milkweed		Friends of Oxbow 2000
Achillea millefolium	Yarrow		Friends of Oxbow 2000
Actaea pachypoda	White baneberry (Doll's eyes)		Friends of Oxbow 2000
Ambrosia artemisiifolia	Common Ragweed		Friends of Oxbow 2000
Anemone quinquefolia	Wood anemone		Friends of Oxbow 2000
Apios americana	Groundnut		Friends of Oxbow 2000
Arctium minus	Burdock (common)		Friends of Oxbow 2000
Aster cordifolius	Heart leaved aster		Friends of Oxbow 2000
Aster divaricatus	White wood aster		Friends of Oxbow 2000
Aster ericoides	Many flowered aster		Friends of Oxbow 2000
Aster linariifolius	Stiff aster		Friends of Oxbow 2000
Aster novae-angliae	New England aster		Friends of Oxbow 2000
Liatris borealis	New England Blazing Star	SC	Hunt 1991
Aster novi-belgii	New York aster		Friends of Oxbow 2000
Aster pilosus	Heath aster		Friends of Oxbow 2000
Aster umbellatus	Flat top white aster		Friends of Oxbow 2000
Baptisia tinctoria	Wild indigo		Friends of Oxbow 2000

Barbarea spp.	Winter cress		Friends of Oxbow 2000
Bidens coronata	Tickseed sunflower		Friends of Oxbow 2000
Bidens frondosa	Beggar ticks		Friends of Oxbow 2000
Geranium bicknellii			
var. *bicknelli*	Bicknell's Cranesbill	WL	Hunt 1991
Boehmeria cylindrica	Bog-hemp (fasle nettle)		Friends of Oxbow 2000
Centaurea jacea	Brown knapweed		Friends of Oxbow 2000
Centaurea maculosa	Spotted knapweed		Friends of Oxbow 2000
Chelone glabra	White turtlehead		Friends of Oxbow 2000
Chimiaphila maculata	Variegated pipsissewa		Friends of Oxbow 2000
Chimiaphila umbellata	Pipsissewa		Friends of Oxbow 2000
Chrysanthemum			
leucanthemum	Oxye daisy		Friends of Oxbow 2000
Cichorium intybus	Chicory		Friends of Oxbow 2000
Cicuta maculata	Water hemlock		Friends of Oxbow 2000
Circaea lutetiana	Enchanter's Nightshade		Friends of Oxbow 2000
Cirsium arvense	Canadian thistle		Friends of Oxbow 2000
Cirsium vulgare	Common Thistle		Friends of Oxbow 2000
Clematis virginiana	Clematis		Friends of Oxbow 2000
Cuscuta gronovii	Common Dodder		Friends of Oxbow 2000
Cusuta gronovii	Dodder		Friends of Oxbow 2000
Daucus carota	Queen Annes lace		Friends of Oxbow 2000
Desmodium canadense	Showy tick trefoil		Friends of Oxbow 2000
Dianthus armeria	Deptford pink		Friends of Oxbow 2000
Erigeron annuus	Daisy fleabane		Friends of Oxbow 2000
Erigeron sp.	Fleabane		Friends of Oxbow 2000
Eupatorium dubium	Eastern Joe-Pye weed		Friends of Oxbow 2000
Eupatorium maculatum	Joe-pye weed		Friends of Oxbow 2000
Eupatorium perfoliatum	Boneset		Friends of Oxbow 2000
Euthamia graminifolia	Grass leaved (lace-leaved) goldenrod		Friends of Oxbow 2000
Fragaria virginiana	Wild Strawberry		Friends of Oxbow 2000
Galium mollugo	Bedstraw - wild madder		Friends of Oxbow 2000
Galium spp trifidum	Tree lobed bedstraw (small)		Friends of Oxbow 2000
Galium tinctorium	Stiff Marsh-bedstraw		Friends of Oxbow 2000
Galium tomctproi	Clayton's bedstraw		Friends of Oxbow 2000
Gentiana clausa	Bottle gentian		Friends of Oxbow 2000
Glechoma hederacea	Ground ivy		Friends of Oxbow 2000
Helianthus tuberosus	Jerusalem artichoke		Friends of Oxbow 2000
Hepatica nobilis var. obtusa	Hepitica round leafed		Friends of Oxbow 2000
Hesperis matronalis	Dame's Rocket		Friends of Oxbow 2000
Houstonia caerulea	Bluets (quaker lady)		Friends of Oxbow 2000
Hypericum perforatum	St. Johnswort		Friends of Oxbow 2000
Hypericum punctatum	St. Johnswort, spotted		Friends of Oxbow 2000
Hypericum virginiacum	Marsh St. Johns wort		Friends of Oxbow 2000
Impatiens capensis	Jewelweed (touch-me-not)		Friends of Oxbow 2000
Lactuca biennis	Tall blue lettuce		Friends of Oxbow 2000
Lactuca canadensis	Wild lettuce		Friends of Oxbow 2000
Linaria canadensis	Blue toadflax		Friends of Oxbow 2000
Lycopus spp.	Water Horehound		Friends of Oxbow 2000
Lysimachia ciliata	Fringed loosestrife		Friends of Oxbow 2000
Lysimachia quadrifolia	Whorled loosestrife		Friends of Oxbow 2000
Asarum canadense	Wild ginger	WL	Friends of Oxbow 2000

Comprehensive Conservation Plan

Lysimachia terrestris	Swamp Candle		Friends of Oxbow 2000
Lythrum salicaria	Purple loosestrife		Friends of Oxbow 2000
Maianthemum candaense	Canada mayflower		Friends of Oxbow 2000
Matricaria discoidea	Pineapple-weed		Friends of Oxbow 2000
Melilotus alba	White sweet clover		Friends of Oxbow 2000
Mentha arvensis	Wild mint		Friends of Oxbow 2000
Mimulus ringens	Blue Monkey Flower		Friends of Oxbow 2000
Monotropa uniflora	Indian Pipe		Friends of Oxbow 2000
Nuphar variegata	Yellow water-lily		Friends of Oxbow 2000
Oenothera perennis	Small Sundrops		Friends of Oxbow 2000
Bidens discoidea	Small Beggar-Ticks	WL	Hunt 1991
Oenothera sp.	Evening primrose		Friends of Oxbow 2000
Phytolacca americana	Pokeweed		Friends of Oxbow 2000
Pilea pomila	Clearweed		Friends of Oxbow 2000
Plantago major	Plantain		Friends of Oxbow 2000
Plantago major var. major	Common Plantain		Friends of Oxbow 2000
Polygonum punctatum	Smartweed		Friends of Oxbow 2000
Potentilla norvegica	Rough Cinquefoil		Friends of Oxbow 2000
Potentilla simplex	Old field cinquefoil		Friends of Oxbow 2000
Prunella vulgaris	Self heal		Friends of Oxbow 2000
Pyrola elliptica	Elliptic Shinleaf		Friends of Oxbow 2000
Ranunculus abortivus	Small flowered buttercup (crowsfoot)		Friends of Oxbow 2000
Rubus idaeus	Black raspberry		Friends of Oxbow 2000
Rubus idaeus	Red raspberry		Friends of Oxbow 2000
Rudbeckia serotina	Black eyed susan		Friends of Oxbow 2000
Rumex acetosella	Sheep sorrel		Friends of Oxbow 2000
Rumex crispus	Curled dock		Friends of Oxbow 2000
Sanguinaria canadensis	Bloodroot		Friends of Oxbow 2000
Saponaria officinalis	Bouncing bet		Friends of Oxbow 2000
Solanum dulcamara	Bittersweet Nightshade		Friends of Oxbow 2000
Solidago caesia	Blue stemmed goldenrod		Friends of Oxbow 2000
Solidago canadensis	Canada goldenrod		Friends of Oxbow 2000
Solidago juncea	Early goldenrod		Friends of Oxbow 2000
Solidago patula	Rough-leaved goldenrod		Friends of Oxbow 2000
Solidago puberula	Downy goldenrod		Friends of Oxbow 2000
Solidago rugosa	Rough-stemmed goldenrod		Friends of Oxbow 2000
Solidago spp.	Field goldenrod		Friends of Oxbow 2000
Tanacetum vulgare	Tansy		Friends of Oxbow 2000
Taraxacum officinale	Dandelion		Friends of Oxbow 2000
Thalictrum polygamum	Tall meadow rue		Friends of Oxbow 2000
Tragopogon porrifolius	Goat's Beard (Oysterplant)		Friends of Oxbow 2000
Trientalis borealis	Starflower		Friends of Oxbow 2000
Trifolium arvense	Rabbitfoot clover		Friends of Oxbow 2000
Trifolium pratense	Red clover		Friends of Oxbow 2000
Trifolium procumbens	Hop clover		Friends of Oxbow 2000
Trifolium repens	White clover		Friends of Oxbow 2000
Trifolium spp.	Clover		Friends of Oxbow 2000
Urtica dioica	Stinging nettle		Friends of Oxbow 2000
Urtica procera	Tall nettle		Friends of Oxbow 2000
Urtica sp.	Nettle		Friends of Oxbow 2000
Verbascum thapsus	Common mullen		Friends of Oxbow 2000
Verbena urticifolia	White vervain		Friends of Oxbow 2000

Veronica officinalis	Common speedwell	Friends of Oxbow 2000
Vicia craecca	American vetch	Friends of Oxbow 2000
Vicia spp.	Vetch	Friends of Oxbow 2000
Viola septentrionalis	Violet, northern blue	Friends of Oxbow 2000
Viola spp	Violet (long leaved)	Friends of Oxbow 2000
Viola spp.	Blue violet	Friends of Oxbow 2000
Virginia otenucha	Native loosestrife	Friends of Oxbow 2000
Vitis spp.	Wild Grape	Friends of Oxbow 2000
Ganoderma applanatum	Artists conch	Friends of Oxbow 2000
Poloyporus betulinus	Birch polypore	Friends of Oxbow 2000
not found	Black knot of cherry	Friends of Oxbow 2000
Cantharellus cinnabarinus	Cinnabar-red	Friends of Oxbow 2000
Laccaria laccata	Common lacara	Friends of Oxbow 2000
Galerina autumnalis	Deadly galerina	Friends of Oxbow 2000
Geastrum spp	Earth star	Friends of Oxbow 2000
Russula emetica	Emetic russula	Friends of Oxbow 2000
Scutellinia scutellata	Eyelash cup	Friends of Oxbow 2000
Monotropa uniflora	Indian pipes	Friends of Oxbow 2000
Ganoderma lucidum	Ling chih	Friends of Oxbow 2000
Pleurotus ostreatus	Oyster	Friends of Oxbow 2000
Lycoperdon umbrium	Pear shaped	Friends of Oxbow 2000
Scleroderma citrinum	Pigskin poison puffballs	Friends of Oxbow 2000
Mirasmius sp	Pinwheel	Friends of Oxbow 2000
not found	Scaly pugskin puffball	Friends of Oxbow 2000
Nymphodies	Spagnum moss	Friends of Oxbow 2000
Collybia maculata	Spotted collybia	Friends of Oxbow 2000
Tricentalis borealis	Starflower	Friends of Oxbow 2000
Daedalea conjiagosa	Thin mazae flat poloypore	Friends of Oxbow 2000
Thametes versicolor	Turkey tail	Friends of Oxbow 2000
not found	Vescolor polypores	Friends of Oxbow 2000
Poloyoporus albellus	White chese polypore	Friends of Oxbow 2000
Tremella mesenterica	Witches butter	Friends of Oxbow 2000
Cladonia cristatella	British soldiers	Friends of Oxbow 2000
Candelariella sp	Egg yoke lichen	Friends of Oxbow 2000
Evernia mesomorpha	Flabby antler lichen	Friends of Oxbow 2000
Trapeliopsis granulosa	Gray earth lichen	Friends of Oxbow 2000
Amandinea punctata	Gret stupple lichen	Friends of Oxbow 2000
not found	Haircap moss	Friends of Oxbow 2000
Cladonia cervicornis	Lichen (Cladonia cervicornis)	Friends of Oxbow 2000
Cladonia grayi	Lichen (Cladonia grayi)	Friends of Oxbow 2000
Cladonia rei	Lichen (Cladonia rei)	Friends of Oxbow 2000
Lecanora dispersa	Lichen (Lecanora dispersa)	Friends of Oxbow 2000
Micaria sp.	Lichen (Micaria sp).	Friends of Oxbow 2000
Peltigra didactyla	Lichen (Peltigra didactyla)	Friends of Oxbow 2000
Placynthiella icmalea	Lichen (Placynthiella icmalea)	Friends of Oxbow 2000
Placynthiella oligotropha	Lichen (Placynthiella oligotropha)	Friends of Oxbow 2000
Trapelia involuta	Lichen (Trapelia involuta)	Friends of Oxbow 2000
Verrucaria sp	Lichen (Verrucaria)	Friends of Oxbow 2000
Caloplaca sp.	Orange lichen (fire dots)	Friends of Oxbow 2000
Dibaeis baeomhyces	Pink earth lichen	Friends of Oxbow 2000
Cladonia conicoraea	Power horn lichen	Friends of Oxbow 2000
Hypogymnia physodes	Puffed shield lichen	Friends of Oxbow 2000

Cladina rangiferina	Reindeer lichen	Friends of Oxbow 2000
Cladina subtenuis	Reindeer lichen	Friends of Oxbow 2000
Micarea erratica	Rock tar lichen	Friends of Oxbow 2000
Physcia stellaris	Rosette lichen	Friends of Oxbow 2000
Placynthiella uliginosa	Tar lichen	Friends of Oxbow 2000
Cladonia macilenta	White pine lichen	Friends of Oxbow 2000
Flavoparmelia caperata	Wrinkled shield lichen	Friends of Oxbow 2000
Anthoceros laevis	not found	Friends of Oxbow 2000
Ptilidium pulcherrimum	not found	Friends of Oxbow 2000
Bazzania trilobata	not found	Friends of Oxbow 2000
Norwellia curvifolia	not found	Friends of Oxbow 2000
Geocalyx graveolens	not found	Friends of Oxbow 2000
Lophozia capitata	not found	Friends of Oxbow 2000
Porella pinnata	not found	Friends of Oxbow 2000
Frullania	not found	Friends of Oxbow 2000

References Used for the Oxbow NWR Species List

Baseline Study 1993 *Biological and Endangered Species Baseline Study Fort Devens*, Massachusetts. ABB Environmental Services, Inc. August 1993

Mello & Peters 1994 Mello, Mark J. and Edward Peters. List of Macrolepidoptera collected at Oxbow Wildlife Refuge in 1994.

Mello & Peters 1992 Mello, Mark J. and Edward Peters. *Survey of Lepidoptera at Fort Devens with notes on Sudbury Annex.* Lloyd Center for Environmental Studies. April - November 1992.

Thomas 1992 Thomas, Howard H. , PhD. *Small Mammal Surveys of the Sudbury Training Annex, Sudbury, Middlesex County, Massachusetts and Fort Devens Military Reservation, Lancaster, Worcester County, and Shirley, Middlesex County, Massachusetts.* Fitchburg State College. April - December 1992.

USFWS 1999 USFWS Fisheries Sections for Comprehensive Conservation Plan "Affected Environment". David A Tilton and Melissa Brewer

Brewer 2000 Correspondance from Melissa Brewer dated January 11, 2000 (An update to the fish species list in the Nashua River)

Hunt 1991 David M. Hunt. *Floristic Survey with Emphasis on Rare Species of Fort Devens, Massachusetts.* December 1991

Searcy 1994 Karen Searcy, Matthew Hickler and Bruce Lindwell. *Progress Report: Critical Habitata and Floristics Survey of Fort Devens, Massachusetts, 1994 continuation.* Biology Department, University of Massachusetts. October 15, 1994

Lockwood 2000 Observations by Ron Lockwood while birding on refuge land during field season.

Lockwood - BBS 2000 Year 2000 survey results from breeding bird survey by Ron Lockwood & Lisa Plagge

Friends of Oxbow 2000 Observations by the Friends of Oxbow NWR during Biodiversity Days 2000 Programs (John McCarter 3/19; Bryan Windmiller 4/15; Wayne Peterson 4/29; Elizabeth Bagdonas 4/29; Roy Christoph 5/12, Peter Alden 5/13, Russ Cohen 6/17, Kathy Leahy 7/19, Joe Choinere 7/29, Kate O'Brien 7/29, Richard Hartley 8/12, John McCarter 8/13, Ray Abair & Dan Lubin 8/13, Paul Wanta 8/13

Plagge 2000 Observations by Lisa Plagge, Biological Technician at Great Meadows NWR while completing wildlife field surveys

McCarter 2000 Mammals documented at Oxbow NWR, Summer 1998 - Winter 2000 by Jon McCarter

KEY TO "STATUS" COLUMN NOTATIONS

FE	Federally Endangered
FT	Federally Threatened
SE	State (MA) Endangered
ST	State (MA) Threatened
SC	State (MA) Special Concern
WL	State (MA) Watch List Species
NAWCA	North American Waterfowl Management Plan Priority Species
NGSMC	US Fish & Wildlife Service Region 5 Nongame Species of Managemtent Concern
SRC	US Fish & Wildlife Service Region 5 Species of Regional Concern

Friends of the Oxbow National Wildlife Refuge
Biodiversity 2000
Naturalist Leaders Resumes

Ray Abair - Ferns and Mosses
Ray Abair began studying plants in 1989 and has since taken many courses at the New England Wildflower Society and The Arnold Arboretum. He received Certificates ' Native Plant Studies, Field Botany and Floristic Survey Techniques from the New In England Wildflower Society where he also conducts field trips and teaches fems and mosses. He studied mosses at the Farlow Herbarium. Membersh'ps include the Arnold Arboretum, Friends of the Farlow, New England Wildflower Society and the New England Botany Club.

Peter Alden - Envasive Plants, Birds, General Ecology
Peter Alden was the sparkplug for the July 1998 Biodiversity Day in Concord and Lincoln, Massachusetts. He is working with the Secretary of Environmental Affairs to implement a state-wide program. Peter is nationally recognized naturalist and has written several field guides for the National Audubon Society such as the "Field Guild to African Wildlife." Closer to home, he the recently wrote the National Audubon Society "Field Guide to New En land."

Elizabeth Bagdonas - Emeruent Spring Plants
Elizabeth Bagdonas is a wetlands biologist and Conservation Administrator for the town of Bedford, Massachusetts. She has taught botany at the Worcester Horticultural Society Tower Hill facility and lead workshops on vernal pools and wetlands for the Massachusetts Association of Conservation Commissions.

Rona Balco - Vernal Pools and Wildflowers
Rona Balco has a long history of teaching the natural world to children. She has led a project resulting in the restoration of a dam and associated freshwater marsh on local conservation land and conducted plant and animal inventories. Rona is a guide teacher for the Massachusetts Audubon Society Wachusett Meadow Wildlife Sanctuary. She has a Certificate in Native Plant Studies from the New England Wildflower Society and is a graduate of the University of Massachusetts Coverts Program. She has also served as a Director of the Bolton Land Trust and been an Associate Member of the Bolton Conservation Commission.

Joe Choiniere - Nesting Birds and General Ecology
Joe Choinere is Director of the Massachusetts Audubon Society Wachusett Meadow Wildlife Sanctuary. In addition to managing all aspects of Sanctuary operations, he develops and teaches natural history programs on New England pants and animals. At Wachusett he has lead programs focused on bringing school age children to the Sanctuary to provide on-the-ground natural history experiences. Joe trains and supervises undergraduate college intems in field biology. He has been guest lecturer on old growth forests and wildlife management at colleges and universities throughout the region and has a degree in Natural History from the University of Massachusetts.

Gene Christoph - Mushrooms
ene Christoph is a retired science teacher. He has been active in community affairs, serving on the Lancaster Planning Board and is a member of the Lancaster Land Trust.

Rov Chistorph - Birds
Inspired by at teacher when he was 8 years old, Roy Chn'stoph has been a bird lover specializin- in warblers. He has a BS degree in biology from Atlantic Union Collece.

Russ Cohen - Edible Plants
Russ has been a wild foods enthusiast since his high school years. He leads dozens of wild foods teachin- pro,-rams yearly. He holds a Bachelors Degree in land use planniny from Vasser College and a law degree from Ohio State University. Russ works in the Riverways Program of the Massachusetts Department of Fisheries, Wildlife and Law Enforcement. Among his awards are: the Environmental Achievement Award from Save the Bay, Environmental Service Award from the Massachusetts Association of Conservation Commissions and the Public Servant of the Year Award from the Environmental League of Massachusetts.

Al Ferry - Mushrooms
Al Ferry is a member of the North American Mycology Association, has co-chaired the North East Mushroom Foray for more 15 years and has been on the Identification Committee of the Boston Mycological Club, the oldest such organization in North America.

Richard Hartley - Fishes
Mr. Hartley has been the Massachusetts State Warm and Coldwater Project Leader for 9 years. He is a 1990 graduate from the University of Maine with a Masters Degree in Zoology, with a concentration in fisheries.

Pat Huckery - Mollusks
Ms. Huckery has worked as Conservation Biologist for the Massachusetts Natural Heritage and Endangered Species Program for 10 years where she conducts surveys for state-protected rare vertebrates and invertebrates and oversees vernal pool certification and education. She is a leader in freshwater mussel conservation and coordinated the publication of the first Massachusetts Freshwater Mussel Atlas. Ms. Huckery has a Bachelors Degree from Florida Southern College and a Masters Degree in Environmental Science from the University of Massachusetts. She is a Professional Wetlands Scientist and is member of the National Biological Society

Elizabeth Knieper - Lichens
Ms.KnelperhasaMastersinBioloo,ydegree,withspecialty'nlichenology. She is a teacher at the New England Wildflower Society Garden in the Woods focusing on lichens and their habitat, is a volunteer at the Harvard University Herbarium and is a member of the New England Lichen Network-. Ms. Knelper conducts lichen inventories as a consultant and participated in the 1998 pilot "Blodiversity" program in Concord and Lincoln Massachusetts.

Kathleen Leahy- Day Insects
Kathleen Leahy is an orchard ecosystem consultant who works with over twenty growers in central New England, including, the Bolton/Harvard area. She is a specialist is Integrated Pest Manacement, a technique for managing pests in ways that are least disruptive to the ecosystem. Most of her clients refer to her as "the ladv bug."

Bob Leverett - Trees and Shrubs
An expert on New England's old growth forests, Bob Leverett has lead educational programs for the Massachusetts Audubon Society, Appalachian Mountain Club and other conservation organizations. Co-founder of the Eastern Native Tree Society, he has written extensively about ancient forests in the northeast. His works include co-authoring "Eastern Old Growth Forests - Prospects for Rediscovery and Recovery", "Stalking the Forest Monarch - A Guide to Measuning Champion Trees" and "Re-Wildlng the Northeast - A New Wilderness Paradigm." The Massachusetts Natural Heritace Program recognizes Bob as the discoverer of most of the 40 odd known old growth stands in Massachusetts.

Don Lubin - Ferns and Mosses
Don Lubin has a BA degree in physics from Brandeis University with lonc, experience identifying and cataloging fems. He has found uncommon hybrid wood fems and collected specimens for the New England Botanical Club collection at the Asa Gray Herbarium. Don leads classes and field trips for the New England Wildflower Society and is conducting a census of fems and fem allies the Wachusett Mountain Reservation. He has conducted surveys for the Massachusetts Natural Heritage Program, Metropolitan District Commission, Sudbury Valley Trustees, Nature Conservancy and Trustees of Reservations.

Mark Mello - Night Insects
Mark Mello is a Director of the Lloyd Center for Environmental Studies in South Dartmouth, Massachusetts.

John McCarter - Mammals
Animal tracker John McCarter is a staff instructor for Paul Rezendes Photography and Nature programs. He has taught for Outdoor Recreation Services in Carlisle and has lead outings for the Friends of the Oxbow National Wildlife Refuce.

Kate O'Brien - Emergent Wetlands Plants
Kate O'Brien received her Masters in Wildlife Ecology from the Yale School of Forestry and Environmental Studies. Her projects have included studies of the Hawaiian monk seal, moose and deer in the boreal forests of Saskatchewan and sonc7bird research in South Carolina. She specializes in quantifying wildlife habitat by surveying vegetation. Kate works for the U.S. Fish and Wildlife Service at the Rachel Carson National Wildlife Refuge in Maine.

Jessie Panek - Wildflowers
Jessie Panek leads tours at the Garden in the Woods, the display garden of the New England Wildflower Society. She has taken numerous courses there, and designed their exhibit for the New England Flower Show in 1997. She has studied at Radcliffe's Landscape Design Program, and works as a landscape designer. Her interest in wildflowers grew out of a love of gardening and birdwatching.

Wayne Peterson - Birds
Wayne Peterson is Field Omitholoaist with the Massachusetts Audubon Society. Throughout his career, he has led trips and tours, lectured and conducted birdiny workshops throughout North America. His tour leading experience has taken him from arctic Canada to South America, Antarctica, Iceland, Africa and Madagascar. Wayne is vice President of the American Birding Association, past Chairman of the Massachusetts Avian Report Committee, and is a New Encland Regional Editor for North American Birds. His writing projects have included co-authoring Birds of Massachusetts (with Richard Veit), contributor to the Audubon Society Master Guide to Birding, and writing the National Audubon Society's Pocket Guide to Songbirds and Familiar Backyard Birds (East).

Scott Reyonlds - Bats
D. Scott Reynolds is a populations biologist and holds a PhD in biology. He manges his own consulting company, New England Ecological Sciences.

David Small - Birds, Butterflies and Dragonflies
David Small is Supervisor of Watershed Maintenance at the Quabbin Reservoir for the Metropolitan District Commission. He is a lifelong naturalist and President of the Athol Bird and Nature Club.

Jeremiah R. Trimble - Dragonflies and Damselflies
Jeremiah Trimble is symbolic of our hope for the future. A recent Connecticut College graduate majoring in zoology, he has established himself as a leading New England dragonfly expert. He served on the Zoology Advisory Board of the Connecticut College Zoology Department. Project work included profiling species of endangered dragonflies and damselflies for the Massachusetts Endangered Species Program and collecting data and conducting impact studies on odondates as part of the environmental impact statements at the former Otis Air Force Base. As a research assistant, he conducted studies on feeding habits of dragonflies, surveyed moth and butterflies at the Massachusetts Audubon Society Wellfleet Bay Wildlife Sanctuary, researched the abundance and diversity of breeding birds on St. John in the U.S. Virgin Islands and

developed dragonfly conservation plans. He is also a field trip leader for the Massachusetts Audubon Society.

Paul Wanta - Mammals
Paul Wanta teaches wilderness skills at the Tracking Project in Albuquerque, New Mexico, and for Paul Renzendes of Royalston, Massachusetts. He has fourteen years tracking experience and study. During his biodiversity program young people and their parents discovered tracks and other indications of animals who live on the Refuge. Participating trackers move quietly, camouflaging themselves in the terrain, and elevate their perceptions to detect animal signs. With Paul's help young trackers gain an important element of outdoor literacy — the abillty to read the clues left behind by our animal neighbors.

Jack Whelan - Vernal Pools
Jack Whelan is a member of the Harvard Conservation Commission and has taught vernal pool certication programs. He is a graduate of the University of Massachusetts Coverts program. As a trail guide in the town of Harvard, he works with elementary school children in introducing them to the joys of understanding the natural world.

Bryan Windmiller - Salamanders, Turtles, Snakes
Bryan Wildmiller is the principal herpetologist of Hyla Associates, an environmental consulting firm that he founded. The company serves local conservation commission and state and federal environmental agencies in matters pertaining to the conservation and protection of amphibians, reptiles and vernal pools. Mr. Windmiller is an expert in the 1998 Concord/Lincoln Biodiversity Day and served on the Concord Natural Resource Commission.

(This page intentionally left blank)

Oxbow National Wildlife Refuge

Appendix E: RONS and MMS

The Refuge Operations Needs System (RONS) lists refuge projects over $20,000. The Management Maintenance System (MMS) identifies maintenace needs on refuges. Projects on both lists are prioritized and initated as funding becomes available. Funding is allocated through the Service's Northeast Regional Office and is based on Congressional appropriation to the Service.

Project: this list includes projects currently in the RONS database and projects proposed in the CCP.

FTE: full time staffing equivalent. One fte equals one person working full time for one whole year; seasonal employees are considered 0.5 fte. (note: staff are often "shared" by multiple rons projects)

Cost, year 1: estimated costs incurred during the first year of a project - typically higher than recurring costs, due to construction, equipment purchase, or other start-up expenses.

Cost, recurring: estimated average annual project cost for subsequent years; includes recurring salary and maintenance costs.

Project duration: estimated length of time for each project. Since this CCP will be revised in 15 years, the "maximum project duration" is 15 years, even though some projects may continue into the next planning cycle

Table E-1: Projects currently in the RONS database and proposed projects to be included for Oxbow NWR

Project	FTE	Startup cost x1,000	Annual cost x 1,000	Duration (years)
Oversee refuge management, planning, programs, administration and maintenance	GS 11 Refuge Ops. Spec.	139	74	15
Provide wildlife and habitat management planning, implementation, and evaluation	GS 11 Wildlife Biologist	133	68	15
Collect essential biological data to efficiently manage the refuge	GS 9 Biol. Tech.	123	58	15
Provide planning and implementation of wildlife-dependent public use programs	GS 11 Outdoor Rec. Planner	133	68	15
Provide refuge visitor protection and law enforcement	GS 7 (LE) Park	114	49	15

Project	FTE	Startup cost x1,000	Annual cost x 1,000	Duration (years)
	Ranger			
Provide refuge maintenance and facilities repair	WG 8 Maint. Worker	118	53	15
Provide habitat restoration, maintenance, and facilities repair	WG 5 Main. Worker	110	45	15
Provide refuge Visitor Contact Station support, administrative programs, and visitor services	GS 5 Admin Tech.	107	42	13
Assessment and monitoring of hazardous waste landfills		21	0	1
Inventory and evaluate status of key wildlife species		55	55	2
Develop Habitat Inventory and Management Plan		50	12	2
Conduct cultural resources overview of refuge		40	5	3
Conduct wetland habitat restoration and maintenance		72	15	15
Conduct upland habitat restoration and maintenance		143	25	15
Increase security through new gates		28	14	2
Construct, improve and maintain visitor trails, wildlife viewing platforms, and photography blinds		180	20	15
Construct and maintain three on-site interpretive kiosks		45	4	15
With partners, construct and maintain three off-site interpretive kiosks		25	2	15
Construct exhibits and operate Visitor Contact Station		95	25	2
Restore and maintain grassland habitat		25	6	15
Provide for seasonal employee/volunteer housing		225	15	13
Survey of mussels on the Nashua River		30	5	5
Conduct essential migratory bird surveys for sound management		43	8	15
Reptile, amphibian, and invertebrate surveys		45	10	5
Control exotic and invasive species		85	25	8
Develop and maintain parking areas and canoe launches		120	12	15
Total		2,304	715	

Table E-2: Projects currently backlogged in the MMS for Oxbow NWR

Project # (SAMMS)	Project Name	Cost Estimate ($1,000)
00104419	Replace gates	50
00104407	Rehab powerline trail	38
01110810	Remove military foundations	43
00104406	Nashua River trail	41
01111833	Replace 1991 Blazer	28
00110309	Office/VCS	1,357
00	Manufactured home	254
00123753	Accessible trail	90
00123753	Two parking areas	108
Total		**2,009**

Table E-3: Projects currently backlogged in the MMS for the Eastern Massachusetts Refuge Complex

Project # (SAMMS)	Project Name	Cost Estimate ($1,000)
01113926	Replace 1979 tractor trailer	55
99104362	Replace 1992 S-10	32
99104364	Replace 1991 Suburban	37
00104409	Replace 17' aluminum boat	27
00104417	Replace 23' Sea Ox	42
00104412	Replace Boston Whaler	26
01111811	Replace 00 Suburban	40
01111813	Replace 00 Durango	37
02120884	Replace 01 1-ton pickup	42
02120936	Replace 19' Carolina skiff	29
02120939	Replace 02 crew cab pickup	28
02120942	Replace 01 ½ ton pickup	25
00110311	Visitor center phase I	522
00110344	Visitor center phase II	908
00110539	Visitor center phase III	5,386
Total		**7,026**

(This page intentionally left blank)

Oxbow National Wildlife Refuge

Appendix F: Eastern Massachusetts National Wildlife Refuge Complex Staffing Chart

Appendix F: Staffing charts

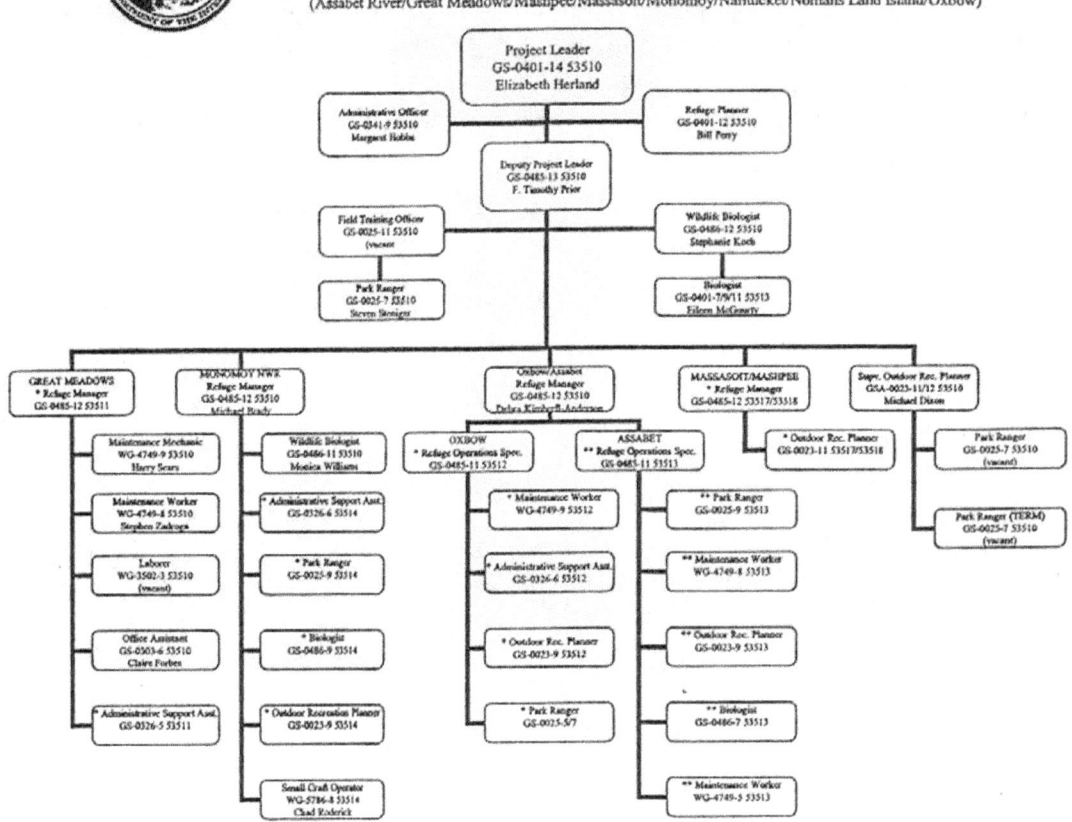

U.S. Fish and Wildlife Service
Northeast Region
Regional Chief, National Wildlife Refuge System
Eastern Massachusetts National Wildlife Refuge Complex
(Assabet River/Great Meadows/Mashpee/Massasoit/Monomoy/Nantucket/Nomans Land Island/Oxbow)

_____   _____
Refuge Manager   Date   Refuge Supervisor   Date

_____   _____
Regional Chief, NWRS   Date   Regional Director   Date

* Essential Staff

** New/Expanded Staff

Eastern Massachusetts National Wildlife Refuge Complex
Assabet River, Great Meadows, and Oxbow National Wildlife Refuges
Proposed Staffing Chart

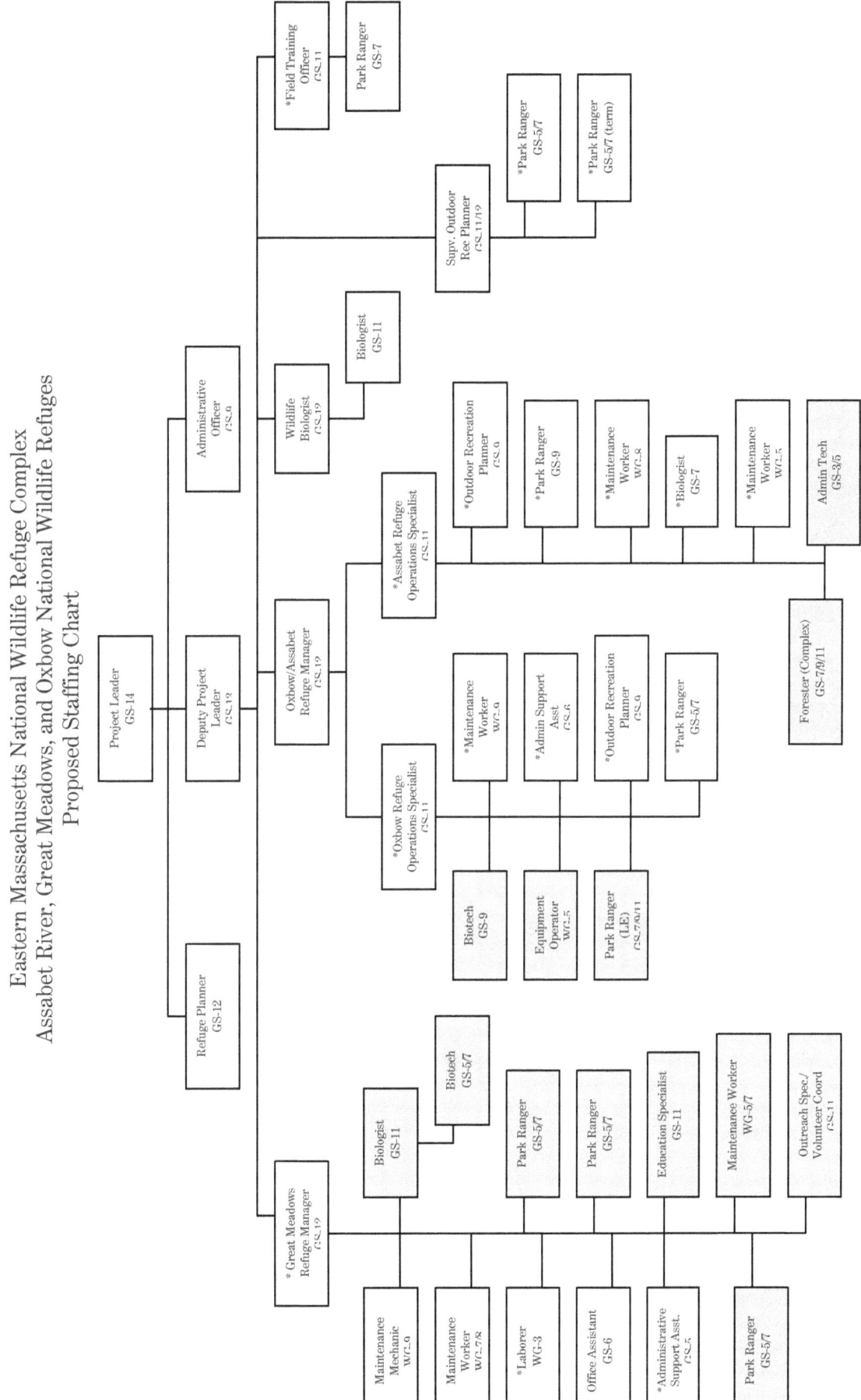

Highlighted boxes show proposed positions.
This chart does not depict additional staff for Mashpee, Massasoit, Monomoy, Nomans Land Island, and Nantucket NWRs
* Positions that are currently vacant.

Appendix G: Final Compatibility determinations

(This page intentionally left blank)

Appendix G: Final Compatibility Determinations

Compatibility Determination

Use: Environmental Education and Interpretation

Refuge Name: Oxbow National Wildlife Refuge

Establishing Authority: Oxbow National Wildlife Refuge was established in 1974 under an Act Authorizing the Transfer of Certain Real Property for Wildlife, or Other Purposes. (16 U.S.C. 667b).

Refuge Purpose: Oxbow NWR's purpose is its "...particular value in carrying out the national migratory bird management program." (16 U.S.C. 667b-d, as amended)

National Wildlife Refuge System Mission: To administer a national network of lands and waters for the conservation, management, and where appropriate, restoration of the fish, wildlife, and plant resources and their habitats within the United States for the benefit of present and future generations of Americans.

Description of Use: Environmental education includes activities which seek to increase public knowledge and understanding of wildlife and the importance of habitat protection and management. Typical activities include teacher or staff-guided on-site field trips, off-site programs in classrooms, and nature study, such as teacher and student workshops and curriculum-structured instruction, and interpretation of wildlife resources. The refuge also conducts an Urban Education program which offers these programs to students from the Boston and Worcester schools.

Interpretation includes those activities and supporting infrastructure that explain management activities, fish and wildlife resources, ecological processes, and cultural history among other topics to public users. Programs and activities may be developed, sponsored and supervised by the Friends of Oxbow NWR.

Access to the refuge for these activities is achieved through walking, snowshoeing or cross-country skiing.

The refuge will continue the activities above plus provide additional volunteer led interpretive and education programs on the refuge. Additionally, the Urban Education Program may be expanded to other regional school systems. An annual teacher workshop, refuge-specific EE curriculum, and refuge-sponsored interpretive and educational events on the refuge might also be conducted. The Service will place three additional kiosks on the refuge as well as self- guided interpretive walking and canoe trails. Additionally, a visitor contact station could be built in a prime location to offer educational and interpretive programs to the greater Boston area.

Availability of Resources: Environmental education and interpretation occur through the use of existing staff, resources, and facilities. Existing resources include staff, interpretive kiosks and displays, environmental education programs carried out through extensive help of volunteers, displays, and trails. The amount and character of environmental and interpretive programming will be a direct reflection of the refuge's staff and funding levels. The following components of an environmental education and interpretation program will need to be developed to fully implement the program outlined in the Comprehensive Conservation Plan. Additional components may be added at later dates. Specific costs will be determined as implementation of specific programs occurs.

- Planning and implementation of wildlife oriented public use and outreach programs
- Interpretive and educational programs (cost of Park Rangers)
- Construction of visitor contact station
- Provide refuge visitor contact station support, administrative programs and services
- Construction and maintenance of three new kiosks
- Exhibits and operation visitor contact station

Anticipated Impacts of the Use: On-site activities by teachers and students using trails and environmental education sites may impose low-level impacts such as trampling of vegetation, removing vegetation, littering and temporary disturbance to wildlife. In the event of persistent disturbance to habitat or wildlife the activity will be restricted or discontinued.

Placement of kiosks may impact small areas of vegetation. Kiosks will be placed where minimal disturbance will occur.

Providing additional interpretive and educational brochures and materials may result in increased knowledge of the refuge and its resources. This awareness and knowledge may improve the willingness of the public to support refuge programs, resources, and compliance with regulations.

There will be impacts from building a new visitor contact station. These impacts will be analyzed in an appropriate NEPA compliance environmental document after potential sites for the building are identified.

Public Review and Comment: The compatibility determination was included in the Draft CCP/EA. The Draft CCP/EA was available for comment from July 20 through September 3, 2003. Refuge staff held four public meetings to collect public comments, written and verbal, on the draft CCP/EA, including all compatibility determinations.

Determination:
Use is not compatible ___.
Use is Compatible with the following stipulations _X_.

The following stipulations are required to ensure compatibility: Activities will be held in areas where minimal impact will occur. Periodic evaluation of sites and programs will be conducted to assess if objectives are being met and to prevent site degradation. If evidence of unacceptable adverse impacts appears, the location(s) of activities will be rotated with secondary sites, curtailed or discontinued. The known presence of a threatened or endangered species will preclude the use of an area until the refuge manager determines otherwise.

Special use permits will be issued to organizations conducting environmental education or interpretive tours or activities. A fee may be charged for the special use permit. The areas used by such tours will be closely monitored to evaluate the impacts on the resource. If adverse impacts appear, the activity will be moved to secondary locations or curtailed or discontinued. Specific conditions may apply depending upon the requested activity and will be addressed through the special use permit.

Guidelines to ensure the safety of all participants will be issued in writing to the teacher or group leader responsible for the activities and will be reviewed before the activity begins.

Law enforcement patrol of public use areas should continue to minimize the above-mentioned types of violations. The current "Refuge open ½ hour before sunrise to ½ hour after sunset" regulation restricts entry after daylight hours, and should be maintained along with "Public Use Restricted to Trails Only".

Justification: The National Wildlife Refuge System Improvement Act of 1997 (P.L. 105-57) identifies six legitimate and appropriate uses of wildlife refuges: environmental education, interpretation, hunting, fishing, wildlife observation and wildlife photography. These priority public uses are dependent upon healthy wildlife populations. Where these uses are determined to be compatible, they are to receive enhanced consideration over other uses in planning and management.

Environmental education and interpretation activities generally support Refuge purposes and impacts can largely be minimized (Goff et al., 1988). The minor resource impacts attributed to these activities are generally outweighed by the benefits gained by educating present and future generations about refuge resources. Environmental education is a public use management tool used to develop a resource protection ethic within society. While it targets school age children, it is not limited to this group. This tool allows us to educate refuge visitors about endangered and threatened species management, wildlife management and ecological principles and communities. A secondary benefit of environmental education is that it instills an 'ownership' or 'stewardship' ethic in visitors and most likely reduces vandalism, littering and poaching; it also strengthens Service visibility in the local community. Environmental education (outdoor classroom) is listed in the Refuge Manual (U.S. Fish and Wildlife Service, 1985) as the highest priority visitor use activity throughout the National Wildlife Refuge System.

These activities will not materially interfere with or detract from the mission of the National Wildlife Refuge System or the purposes for which the refuge was established.

Literature Cited:

Goff, G.R., D.J. Decker And G. Pomerantz. 1988. A Diagnostic Tool for Analyzing Visitor Impacts on Wildlife Refuges: A Basis for a Systematic Approach to Visitor Management. Trans. Northeast Sect. Wildl. Soc. 45:82.

U.S. Fish and Wildlife Service. 1985. Refuge Manual. Wash., D.C. U.S. Gov't Printing Office.

Signature - Refuge Manager:_____ /s/ Elizabeth A. Herland 12/21/2004
                                     (Signature and Date)

Concurrence - Regional Chief: _____ /s/ Anthony D. Léger 12/27/2004
                                     (Signature and Date)

Mandatory 15-year Reevaluation Date: _____ December 27, 2019

Compatibility Determination

Use: Fishing

Refuge Names: Oxbow National Wildlife Refuge

Establishing Authority: Oxbow National Wildlife Refuge (NWR) was established in 1974 under an Act Authorizing the Transfer of Certain Real Property for Wildlife, or Other Purposes. (16 U.S.C. 667b).

Refuge Purpose: Oxbow NWR's purpose is its "...particular value in carrying out the national migratory bird management program." (16 U.S.C. 667b-d, as amended)

National Wildlife Refuge System Mission: To administer a national network of lands and waters for the conservation, management, and where appropriate, restoration of the fish, wildlife, and plant resources and their habitats within the United States for the benefit of present and future generations of Americans.

Description of Use: Fishing at Oxbow NWR is currently only allowed only on the Nashua River. Additional fishing access will be provided at designated river bank locations in the future. Fishing on the refuge is in compliance with State regulations. Fishing is a priority public use of the refuge.

Availability of Resources: This program can be run with existing staff, although the hiring of additional public use and law enforcement staff would assist in managing the program and ensuring compliance. Maintenance costs for this activity are small. Costs which may occur include maintenance to trails and river access areas, as well as costs to stabilize designated river bank fishing sites.

Anticipated Impacts on Refuge Purpose: The designated areas for fishing may need stabilization to prevent erosion before being opened and or to curb erosion after use of these areas has begun. Potential and actual refuge impacts include trampling vegetation, creation of unauthorized trails and subsequent erosion or over-harvesting. Some disturbance of roosting and feeding birds will probably occur (Burger, 1981) but is considered minimal. Discarded fishing line and other fishing litter can entangle migratory birds and cause injury and death (Gregory, 1991). Additionally, litter impacts the visual experience of refuge visitors (Marion and Lime, 1986). Law enforcement issues include illegal taking of fish, littering, illegal fires at night, fishing without a license, and disorderly conduct.

Public Review and Comment: The compatibility determination was included in the Draft CCP/EA. The Draft CCP/EA was available for comment from July 20 through September 3, 2003. Refuge staff held four public meetings to collect public comments, written and verbal, on the draft CCP/EA, including all compatibility determinations.

Determination:
Use is not compatible ___.
Use is Compatible with the following stipulations _X_.

The following stipulations are required to ensure compatibility: The designated areas for fishing may need stabilization to prevent erosion before being opened and or to curb erosion after use of these areas has begun.

Enforcement will be conducted to help curb illegal fires, disorderly conduct and littering. Enforcement will also help to ensure that fishing regulations are observed, reduce creation of unauthorized trails and serve as a direct contact to the fishing public. Public meetings with local fishing clubs and interested parties will also be required to reinforce refuge regulations. If these measures do not curb unauthorized activities, other measures will be implemented to control activities and fishermen.

Law enforcement patrol of public use areas should minimize the above-mentioned types of violations. The current "Refuge open ½ hour before sunrise to ½ hour after sunset" regulation restricts entry after daylight hours, and should be maintained along with "Public Use Restricted to Trails Only".

Justification: The National Wildlife Refuge System Improvement Act of 1997 (P.L. 105-57) identifies six legitimate and appropriate uses of wildlife refuges: fishing, environmental education, interpretation, hunting, wildlife observation and wildlife photography. These priority public uses are dependent upon healthy wildlife populations. Where these uses are determined to be compatible, they are to receive enhanced consideration over other uses in planning and management.

Fishing is a wildlife-oriented activity that provides substantial recreational opportunities to the public (U.S. Fish and Wildlife Service, 1992 and U.S. Fish and Wildlife Service, 1997). Fishing is a traditional form of outdoor recreation.

These activities will not materially interfere with or detract from the mission of the National Wildlife Refuge System or the purposes for which the refuge was established.

Literature Cited:

Burger, J. 1981. The Effect of Human Activity on Birds at a Coastal Bay. Biol. Conserv. 21:231-241.

Gregory, M.R. 1991. The Hazards of Persistent Marine Pollution: Drift Plastics and Conservation Islands. J. Royal Soc. New Zealand. 21(2):83-100.

Marion, J.L. And D.W. Lime. 1986. Recreational Resource Impacts: Visitor Perceptions and Management Responses. pp. 239-235. Kulhavy, D.L. and R.N. Conner, Eds. in Wilderness and Natural Areas in the Eastern United States: A Management Challenge. Center for Applied Studies, Austin State Univ., Nacogdochesz, TX. 416pp.

U.S. Fish and Wildlife Service. 1992. Fisheries USA. The Recreational Fisheries Policy of the U.S. Fish and Wildlife Service. Wash, D.C.,U.S. Gov't Printing Office.

U.S. Fish and Wildlife Service. 1997a. Recreation Fee Programs Frequently Asked Questions.

Signature - Refuge Manager: _____ /s/ Elizabeth A. Herland 12/21/2004___
                            (Signature and Date)

Concurrence - Regional Chief: _____ /s/ Anthony D. Léger 12/27/2004_____
                             (Signature and Date)

Mandatory 15-year Reevaluation Date: _____ December 27, 2019_____

Compatibility Determination

Use: Hunting – Big Game, Upland Game, Migratory Bird

Refuge Names: Oxbow National Wildlife Refuge

Establishing Authority: Oxbow National Wildlife Refuge (NWR) was established in 1974 under an Act Authorizing the Transfer of Certain Real Property for Wildlife, or Other Purposes. (16 U.S.C. 667b).

Refuge Purpose: The purpose of the Oxbow NWR is its "...particular value in carrying out the national migratory bird management program." (16 U.S.C. 667b-d, as amended)

National Wildlife Refuge System Mission: To administer a national network of lands and waters for the conservation, management, and where appropriate, restoration of the fish, wildlife, and plant resources and their habitats within the United States for the benefit of present and future generations of Americans.

Description of Proposed Use:

Migratory Bird: Waterfowl and Woodcock

This activity involves the taking of waterfowl along the Nashua River and associated wetlands and pools south of Route 2. Waterfowl hunting involves the use of calls and decoys to bring in waterfowl. Dogs and canoes may be used in areas to retrieve downed birds. No permanent blinds are allowed. Waterfowl hunting activities will be conducted according to State regulations and restrictions.   Non-toxic shot is required.

This activity also involves the taking of American woodcock south of Route 2, the area between Route 2 and Hospital Road, and the westerly side of the Nashua River north of Shirley Road.

Big Game Hunting: White-tailed Deer and American Turkey

Archery, shotgun and primitive firearm deer hunting opportunities would be provided on portions of Oxbow NWR in accordance with Massachusetts State regulations and requirements. Portions of the refuge located south of Route 2, except the "Watt Farm" addition, would be open for all three deer seasons and spring turkey. The Watt Farm would be open for the archery deer hunting only and for turkey (by archery only) in the spring season. The portions of the refuge from the Route 2 underpass to Hospital Road would be open for the turkey and archery deer season only. The portion of the Refuge from Hospital Road to Shirley Road would not be open for hunting. The portion of the refuge located on the westerly side of the Nashua River north of Shirley Road would be open for turkey and all three deer seasons, and the portion of the refuge on the easterly side of the Nashua River in this area would be open only for the archery deer season and archery turkey.

Upland Game: Ruffed Grouse, Rabbit, Squirrel

This activity involves the taking of ruffed grouse, rabbit, and gray squirrel. All applicable State hunting regulations are in force on the refuge. These animals are taken through traditional means with shotguns only; non-toxic shot is required. The use of unleashed dogs is permitted only while under the control of individuals actively engaged in hunting.

Areas open to hunting at Oxbow NWR are south of Route 2, the area north of Route 2 and south of Hospital Road, and the westerly side of the Nashua River north of Shirley Road.

All applicable Federal (50 CFR Part 32) and State hunting regulations will be in force on the refuge, including the discharge of firearms or arrows across or within 150 feet of any highway and the possession or discharge of any firearm or arrow within 500 feet of any dwelling or building in use. The use or possession of alcoholic beverages while hunting will be strictly prohibited. Hunting will occur within designated State seasons but could be restricted by time or day if determined necessary by the refuge manager to address resource or visitor use issues. All hunters will be required to obtain a permit from the refuge prior to scouting or hunting. The permit could contain both refuge-specific information, maps, and/or additional refuge requirements for hunter compliance. This may be modified on an annual basis if necessary. A fee will be charged for the permit.

Access to the refuge for all hunt seasons is through walking, cross-country skiing or snowshoeing. Cutting of vegetation is prohibited.

A limited special season for physically handicapped hunters, in accordance with State requirements for such hunts, will be provided. The physical configuration of trails and roads will allow us to provide accessible hunting opportunities in certain parts of the refuge.

Availability of Resources: See Appendix F of the Final CCP for recurring cost estimates and duration of the proposed projects.

The cost involved in offering this wildlife dependent activity is minimal. Hunting on the refuge will be by annual permit. The refuge will be collecting an annual fee of $20 for all hunting seasons on the refuge. One fee is valid for all the refuges in the Complex open to hunting. Fee money collected will help recover costs for funding the program. The refuge anticipates hiring a full time law enforcement officer to assist with managing priority public uses including the hunt program and will assist in refuge habitat projects.

Anticipated Impacts on Refuge Purpose: The impacts of allowing hunting may include disturbance of non-target species in the course of tracking game, the trampling of vegetation, possible creation of unauthorized trails by hunters, littering and possible vandalism.

White-tailed deer number about 90,000 in Massachusetts. In some areas, deer density is as high as 25-30 deer per square mile. Many landowners suffer landscape damage due to deer on a regular basis, transmission of Lyme disease becomes a significant issue with large numbers of deer, starvation is a possibility when deer numbers are high as food supplies dwindle in bad weather and deer-vehicle collisions become more common and problematic. Woodcock and waterfowl populations are managed at a national level, with seasons and bag limits set annually to reflect population status and trends.

The harvest of white-tailed deer, upland game, woodcock and waterfowl will not significantly decrease the populations of these game species.

During the hunting season, non-hunters may limit refuge visits to Sundays or to portions of the refuge not open for hunting. River users may adjust their non-hunting use of the Nashua River to periods when hunters are not active or to Sundays. Some people may avoid the refuge or the river altogether to avoid any potential interaction with hunters.

Public Review and Comment: The compatibility determination was included in the Draft CCP/EA. The Draft CCP/EA was available for comment from July 20 through September 3, 2003. Refuge staff held four public meetings to collect public comments, written and verbal, on the draft CCP/EA, including all compatibility determinations. Many people wrote in to express opposition to hunting in general. Others recommended hunting be restricted to archery deer hunting. Others either support hunting specifically or supported the preferred alternative, which included establishing new and expanding existing hunt programs.

Determination:
Use is not compatible ___.
Use is Compatible with the following stipulations _X_.

The following stipulations are required to ensure compatibility:
- All hunters must obtain all necessary State, Federal, and refuge permits.

- Hunters must abide by all applicable refuge, State, and Federal regulations.

- Refuge staff will develop a Hunt Plan and amend the Code of Federal Regulations before permitting hunting on the refuge.

- Staff will monitor hunting activities to determine any adverse impacts to refuge resources and adjust the hunt program as necessary.

- Waterfowl hunting is permitted from on the Nashua River and in associated wetlands. Enforcement will be necessary to ensure compliance with refuge and State regulations regarding hunting of waterfowl.

- Cutting of vegetation is prohibited. The use of unleashed dogs is permitted only while under the control of individuals actively engaged in hunting.

Justification: The National Wildlife Refuge System Improvement Act of 1997 (P.L. 105-57) identifies six legitimate and appropriate uses of wildlife refuges; hunting, environmental education, interpretation, fishing, wildlife observation and wildlife photography. These priority public uses are dependent upon healthy wildlife populations. Where these uses are determined to be compatible, they are to receive enhanced consideration over other uses in planning and management.

Hunting of big game (white-tailed deer and turkey), upland game (rabbit, squirrel and ruffed grouse), and migratory bird (waterfowl and woodcock) on Oxbow NWR is justified within refuge objectives by providing wildlife-oriented recreation and promoting appreciation of wildlife and the outdoors.

These activities will not materially interfere with or detract from the mission of the National Wildlife Refuge System or the purposes for which the refuge was established.

Signature - Refuge Manager: _____ /s/ Elizabeth A. Herland 12/21/2004 ___
        (Signature and Date)

Concurrence - Regional Chief: _____ /s/ Anthony D. Léger 12/27/2004 ____
        (Signature and Date)

Mandatory 15-year Reevaluation Date: _____ December 27, 2019 ___

Compatibility Determination

Use: Jogging/Running

Refuge Names: Oxbow National Wildlife Refuge

Establishing Authority: Oxbow National Wildlife Refuge (NWR) was established in 1974 under an Act Authorizing the Transfer of Certain Real Property for Wildlife, or Other Purposes (16 U.S.C. 667b).

Refuge Purpose: Oxbow's purpose is its "...particular value in carrying out the national migratory bird management program." (16 U.S.C. 667b-d, as amended)

National Wildlife Refuge System Mission: To administer a national network of lands and waters for the conservation, management, and where appropriate, restoration of the fish, wildlife, and plant resources and their habitats within the United States for the benefit of present and future generations of Americans.

Description of Use: Jogging or running on refuge trails. Maps showing these trail systems are included in the refuge brochure for Oxbow NWR. Jogging occurs year-round on the refuge with the majority of use from April through October. At Oxbow NWR, jogging occurs mainly on the Tank Road. Occasionally, joggers stop at the informational kiosk to obtain refuge or wildlife viewing information. Use is heaviest during the summer months and occurs more frequently early in the morning and in the evening when individuals jog before and after work and while the weather is more pleasant. Exact numbers are currently not available. The activity is primarily athletic in nature. It is likely that some joggers observe wildlife while they are jogging on the refuge. However, such observation tends to be incidental to the primary activity of jogging.

Availability of Resources: Maintenance of the trails and facilities include costs. These costs are not directly related to jogging or running. Jogging and running may cause incremental needs for additional trail maintenance activities. The major portion of the funds needed to support this activity is in the form of salaries to maintain the trails for wildlife observation. Additional funds are needed for maintenance materials and other supplies. Also, funds are needed to provide resource protection and monitoring. The prorated portion of the cost for law enforcement, resource protection and monitoring is approximately $3,000.

Anticipated Impacts on Refuge Purpose: Jogging or running as conducted on Oxbow NWR has not been studied in a rigorous fashion. Jogging has the potential of impacting shorebird, waterfowl, marshbird, and other migratory bird populations feeding and resting near the trails during certain times of the year. Use of upland trails is more likely to impact songbirds than other migratory birds. Human disturbance to migratory birds has been documented in many studies in different locations.

Conflicts arise when migratory birds and humans are present in the same areas (Boyle and Samson 1985). Response of wildlife to human activities includes: departure from site (Owen 1973, Burger 1981, Korschgen et al 1985, Henson and Grant 1991, Kahl 1991, Klein 1993), use of sub-optimal habitat (Erwin 1980, Williams and Forbes 1980), altered behavior (Burger 1981, Korschen et al. 1985, Morton et al. 1989, Ward and Stehn 1989, Havera et al. 1992, Klein 1993), and increase in energy expenditure (Morton et al. 1989, Belanger and Bedard 1990). McNeil et al. (1992) found that many waterfowl species avoid disturbance by feeding at night instead of during the day.

The location of recreational activities impacts species in different ways. Miller et al. (1998) found that nesting success was lower near recreational trails, where human activity was common, than at greater distances from the trails. A number of species have shown greater reactions when pedestrian use occurred off trail (Miller, 1998). In addition, Burger (1981) found that wading birds were extremely sensitive to disturbance in the northeastern U.S. In regard to waterfowl, Klein (1989) found migratory dabbling ducks to be the most sensitive to disturbance and migrant ducks to be more sensitive when they first arrived, in the late fall, than later in winter. She also found gulls and sandpipers to be apparently insensitive to human disturbance, with Burger (1981) finding the same to be true for various gull species.

For songbirds, Gutzwiller et. al. (1997) found that singing behavior of some species was altered by low levels of human intrusion. Jogging can impact normal behavioral activities, including feeding, reproductive, and social behavior. Studies have shown that ducks and shorebirds are sensitive to jogging activity (Burger 1981, 1986). Resident waterbirds tend to be less sensitive to human disturbance than migrants, and migrant ducks are particularly sensitive when they first arrive (Klein 1993). In areas where human activity is common, birds tolerated closer approaches than in areas receiving less activity.

Public Review and Comment: The draft compatibility determination was available for public review and comment period by 1) a notice posted on the refuge kiosk bulletin board for a period of 30 days, 2) a notice included in a planning update sent to all of the individuals on the comprehensive conservation plan mailing list, and 3) posted on the refuge website. The comment period was from June 21, 2004 to July 20, 2004. We received no comments on the compatibility determination.

Determination:
Use is not compatible ___.
Use is Compatible with the following stipulations _X_.

The following stipulations are required to ensure compatibility: Joggers and runners will utilize only established trails and other areas open to the public and not venture into closed areas. The current "refuge open ½ hour before sunrise to ½ hour after sunset" regulation restricts entry after daylight hours, and should be maintained along with "Public Use Restricted to Trails Only".

We will be undertaking research to examine whether or not there are site specific impacts on the refuge. We will examine impacts to wildlife and impacts to other recreationists participating in wildlife dependent recreational activities. We will reexamine the compatibility of jogging and running after this research is completed.

Justification: The National Wildlife Refuge System Improvement Act of 1997 (P.L. 105-57) identifies six legitimate and appropriate uses of wildlife refuges: environmental education, interpretation, hunting, fishing, wildlife observation and wildlife photography. These priority public uses are dependent upon healthy wildlife populations. Where these uses are determined to be compatible, they are to receive enhanced consideration over other uses in planning and management.

Jogging and running are to be used only as a means to facilitate the priority public uses identified above.

These activities will not materially interfere with or detract from the mission of the National Wildlife Refuge System or the purposes for which the refuge was established.

Literature Cited:

Belanger, L., and J. Bedard. 1990. *Energetic cost of man-induced disturbance to staging snow geese.* Journal of Wildlife Management. 54:36-41

Boyle, S. A., F. B. Samson. 1985. *Effects of nonconsumptive recreation on wildlife: A review.* Wildlife Society Bulletin 13:110-116

Burger, J. 1981. *The effect of human activity on birds at a coastal bay.* Biological Conservation. 21:231-241.

Burger, J. 1986. *The effect of human activity on shorebirds in two coastal bays in northeastern United States.* Environmental Conservation. 13:123-130.

Erwin, R. M. 1980. *Breeding habitat by colonially nesting water birds in 2 mid-Atlantic U.S. regions under different regimes of human disturbance.* Biological Conservation. 18:39-51.

Gutzwiller, K.J., R.T. Wiedenmann, K.L. Clements, 1997. *Does human intrusion alter the seasonal timing of avian song during breeding periods?* Auk 114:55-65.

Havera, S. P., L. R. Boens, M. M. Georgi, and R. T. Shealy. 1992. *Human disturbance of waterfowl on Keokuk Pool, Mississippi River.* Wildlife Society Bulletin. 20:290-298.

Henson, P. T., and A. Grant. 1991. *The effects of human disturbance on trumpeter swan breeding behavior.* Wildlife Society Bulletin. 19:248-257.

Kahl, R. 1991. *Boating disturbance of canvasbacks during migration at Lake Poygan, Wisconsin.* Wildlife Society Bulletin. 19:242-248.

Klein, M.L. 1993. *Waterbird behavioral responses to human disturbances.* Wildlife Society Bulletin. 21:31-39.

Korschen, C. E., L. S. George, and W. L. Green. 1985. *Disturbance of diving ducks by boaters on a migrational staging area.* Wildlife Society Bulletin. 13:290-296.

McNeil, Raymond; Pierre Drapeau; John D. Goss-Custard. 1992. *The occurrence and adaptive significance of nocturnal habitats in waterfowl.* Biological Review. 67: 381-419

Miller, S.G., R.L. Knight, and C.K. Miller. 1998. *Influence of recreational trails on breeding bird communities.* Ecological Applications. 8(1) 162-169.

Morton, J. M., A. C. Fowler, and R. L. Kirkpatrick. 1989. *Time and energy budgets of American black ducks in winter*. Journal of Wildlife Management. 53:401-410.

Owen, M. 1973. *The management of grassland areas for wintering geese.* Wildfowl. 24:123-130.

Ward, D. H., and R. A. Stehn. 1989. Response of Brant and other geese to aircraft disturbance at Izembek Lagoon, Alaska. U.S. Fish and Wildlife Service, Alaska Fish and Wildlife Research Center. Final report to the Minerals Management Service. Anchorage, Alaska. 193 pp.

Williams, G. J., and E. Forbes. 1980. *The habitat and dietary preferences of dark-bellied Brant geese and widgeon in relation to agricultural management.* Wildfowl. 31:151-157.

Signature - Refuge Manager: _____/s/ Elizabeth A. Herland 12/21/2004___
                                         (Signature and Date)

Concurrence - Regional Chief: _____/s/ Anthony D. Léger 12/27/2004_____
                                         (Signature and Date)

Mandatory 5-year Reevaluation Date: _____December 27, 2009___

Compatibility Determination

Use: Natural History Tours

Refuge Name: Oxbow National Wildlife Refuge

Establishing Authority: Oxbow National Wildlife Refuge (NWR) was established in 1974 under an Act Authorizing the Transfer of Certain Real Property for Wildlife, or Other Purposes. (16 U.S.C. 667b).

Refuge Purpose: Oxbow NWR's purpose is its "...particular value in carrying out the national migratory bird management program." (16 U.S.C. 667b-d, as amended)

National Wildlife Refuge System Mission: To administer a national network of lands and waters for the conservation, management, and where appropriate, restoration of the fish, wildlife, and plant resources and their habitats within the United States for the benefit of present and future generations of Americans.

Description of Use:
(a) What is the use? Is the use a priority public use?
This activity consists of a group of people with a leader or guide walking or driving on refuge property to learn about plant and wildlife species, natural processes and wetlands and other habitats. Natural history tours will facilitate wildlife observation and photography, and environmental interpretation and education, which are priority public uses of the refuge.

(b) Where would the use be conducted?
Natural history tours would normally occur on established refuge trails or roads. However, tours could be conducted in other areas of the refuge with approval from the refuge manager.

(c) When would the use be conducted?
Natural history tours would normally be conducted only during hours when the refuge is open, generally ½ hour before sunrise to ½ hour after sunset. Activities held at night, such as an owl prowl, would require approval from the refuge manager.

(d) How would the use be conducted?
Natural history tours would occur either by foot or motor vehicle.

(e) Why is this use being proposed?
Natural history tours offer an opportunity to expose visitors to the refuge purposes and Refuge System mission. Some of the tours may specifically be birding trips. Participants gain an extra understanding and appreciation for the Refuge and the environment.

Availability of Resources: Before groups may conduct tours on the refuge they must obtain a special use permit (SUP). The cost of preparing the SUPs for natural history tours will be minimal. Maintenance of the trails and facilities will be encompassed in costs associated with routing refuge operations and maintenance activities.

Anticipated Impacts on Refuge Purpose: The impacts associated with this activity are trampling of vegetation, littering, possible vandalism and temporary disturbance to wildlife in the area of the group. These impacts are minor in light of the appreciation and knowledge gained by participants in these activities. The known presence of a threatened or endangered species will preclude the use of an area until the refuge manager determines otherwise.

Public Review and Comment: The compatibility determination was included in the Draft CCP/EA. The Draft CCP/EA was available for comment from July 20 through September 3, 2003. Refuge staff held four public meetings to collect public comments, written and verbal, on the draft CCP/EA, including all compatibility determinations.

Determination:
Use is not compatible ___.
Use is Compatible with the following stipulations _X_.

The following stipulations are required to ensure compatibility:
An SUP will be issued to the organization conducting the tour. A fee may be charged for the SUP. The areas used by such tours will be closely monitored to evaluate the impacts on the resource. If adverse impacts appear, the activity will be moved to secondary locations or curtailed entirely. Specific conditions may apply depending upon the requested activity and will be addressed through the SUP.

Law enforcement patrol of public use areas should minimize the above-mentioned types of violations. The current "Refuge open ½ hour before sunrise to ½ hour after sunset" regulation restricts entry after daylight hours, and should be maintained along with "Public Use Restricted to Trails Only", unless specifically authorized by an SUP.

Justification: The National Wildlife Refuge System Improvement Act of 1997 (P.L. 105-57) identifies six legitimate and appropriate uses of wildlife refuges: environmental education, interpretation, hunting, fishing, wildlife observation and wildlife photography. These priority public uses are dependent upon healthy wildlife populations. Where these uses are determined to be compatible, they are to receive enhanced consideration over other uses in planning and management.

Natural history activities generally support refuge purposes and impacts can largely be minimized. The minor resource impacts attributed to these activities are generally outweighed by the benefits gained by educating present and future generations about refuge resources. Natural history activities are a public use management tool used to develop a resource protection ethic within society. This tool allows us to educate refuge visitors about endangered and threatened species management, wildlife management and ecological principles and communities. A secondary benefit of natural history activities is that it instills an 'ownership' or 'stewardship' ethic in visitors and most likely reduces vandalism, littering and poaching; it also strengthens Service visibility in the local community.

These activities will not materially interfere with or detract from the mission of the National Wildlife Refuge System or the purposes for which the refuge was established.

Appendix G: Final Compatibility determinations

Signature - Refuge Manager: _____/s/ Elizabeth A. Herland 12/21/2004___
                                         (Signature and Date)

Concurrence - Regional Chief: _____/s/ Anthony D. Léger 12/27/2004____
                                         (Signature and Date)

Mandatory 10-year Reevaluation Date: _____December 27, 2014_____

Compatibility Determination

Use: Non-motorized Boating

Refuge Names: Oxbow National Wildlife Refuge

Establishing Authority: Oxbow National Wildlife Refuge (NWR) was established in 1974 under an Act Authorizing the Transfer of Certain Real Property for Wildlife, or Other Purposes (16 U.S.C. 667b).

Refuge Purpose: "...particular value in carrying out the national migratory bird management program." (16 U.S.C. 667b-d, as amended)

National Wildlife Refuge System Mission: To administer a national network of lands and waters for the conservation, management, and where appropriate, restoration of the fish, wildlife, and plant resources and their habitats within the United States for the benefit of present and future generations of Americans.

Description of Use:
(a) What is the use? Is the use a priority public use?
Non-motorized boating consists of the use of canoes, kayaks, or row boats across open water. The use is not a priority public use, but would be allowed to facilitate participation in a variety of priority wildlife-dependent activities, including fishing, hunting, wildlife observation and wildlife photography.

(b) Where would the use be conducted?
Non-motorized boating would be conducted only on the Nashua River, not in refuge wetland pools or other ponds.

(c) When would the use be conducted?
Non-motorized boating would occur during times when the refuge is open and access is provided.

(d) How would the use be conducted?
Access would be provided via a boat launch and from upstream or downstream of the refuge boundary.

(e) Why is this use being proposed?
Non-motorized boating will facilitate participation in priority wildlife-dependent recreation.

Availability of Resources: The costs of infrastructure associated with facilitating non-motorized boating are discussed in the compatibility determinations for the respective wildlife dependent public uses. These costs are also included in Appendix E of the Comprehensive Conservation Plan (CCP) for the Oxbow NWR. Minor improvements and maintenance will be accomplished by refuge staff and volunteers from the Friends of the Oxbow NWR. At Oxbow Refuge, two additional canoe launches and parking areas may be constructed. The estimated cost of these facilities is $120,000.

Anticipated Impacts on Refuge Purpose: Non-motorized boating at Oxbow NWR will be monitored to ensure the activity will not have adverse impact on wildlife habitat, or the management of migratory birds and other wildlife species. This activity will facilitate wildlife-dependent recreation.

Public Review and Comment: The compatibility determination was included in the Draft CCP/EA. The Draft CCP/EA was available for comment from July 20 through September 3, 2003. Refuge staff held four public meetings to collect public comments, written and verbal, on the draft CCP/EA, including all compatibility determinations.

Determination:
Use is not compatible ___.
Use is Compatible with the following stipulations _X_.

The following stipulations are required to ensure compatibility: Non-motorized boaters will utilize only established trails and other areas open to the public and not venture into closed areas. The current "refuge open ½ hour before sunrise to ½ hour after sunset" regulation restricts entry after daylight hours, and should be maintained along with "Public Use Restricted to Trails Only".

Justification: The National Wildlife Refuge System Improvement Act of 1997 (P.L. 105-57) identifies six legitimate and appropriate uses of wildlife refuges: environmental education, interpretation, hunting, fishing, wildlife observation and wildlife photography. These priority public uses are dependent upon healthy wildlife populations. Where these uses are determined to be compatible, they are to receive enhanced consideration over other uses in planning and management.

Non-motorized boating is to be used only as a means to facilitate the priority public uses identified above.

These activities will not materially interfere with or detract from the mission of the National Wildlife Refuge System or the purposes for which the refuge was established.

Signature - Refuge Manager: _____/s/ Elizabeth A. Herland 12/21/2004_____
                              (Signature and Date)

Concurrence - Regional Chief: _____/s/ Anthony D. Léger 12/27/2004_____
                              (Signature and Date)

Mandatory 10-year Reevaluation Date: _____December 27, 2014_____

Compatibility Determination

<u>Use:</u>   Scientific Research

<u>Refuge Names:</u> Oxbow National Wildlife Refuge

<u>Establishing Authority:</u> Oxbow National Wildlife Refuge (NWR) was established in 1974 under an Act Authorizing the Transfer of Certain Real Property for Wildlife, or Other Purposes (16 U.S.C. 667b).

<u>Refuge Purpose:</u> Oxbow's purpose is its "...particular value in carrying out the national migratory bird management program." (16 U.S.C. 667b-d, as amended)

<u>National Wildlife Refuge System Mission:</u> To administer a national network of lands and waters for the conservation, management, and where appropriate, restoration of the fish, wildlife, and plant resources and their habitats within the United States for the benefit of present and future generations of Americans.

<u>Description of Use:</u>

(a) What is the use? Is the use a priority public use?
The use is research conducted by non-Service personnel. The purposes of research conducted on the refuge are to further the understanding of the natural resources and to improve the management of such resources on the refuge or within the National Wildlife Refuge System (Refuge System). Priority will be given to research which is applicable to wildlife, habitat, or public use management on and near the refuge. Research conducted by non-Service personnel is not a priority public use of the Refuge System.

(b) Where would the use be conducted?
The location of the research will vary depending on the individual research project that is being conducted. The entire refuge may be made available for specific scientific research projects. However, an individual research project is usually limited to a particular habitat type, plant or wildlife species. On occasion research projects may encompass an assemblage of habitat types, plants or wildlife. The research location will be limited to only those areas of the refuge that are necessary to conduct any specific, approved research project.

(c) When would the use be conducted?
The timing of the research will depend on the individual research project that is being conducted. Scientific research may be allowed to occur on the refuge throughout the year. An individual research project could be short-term in design, requiring one or two visits over the course of a few days. Other research projects could be multiple-year studies that require daily visits to the study site. The timing of each individual research project will be limited to the minimum required to complete the project. If a research project occurs during a refuge hunting season, special precautions or limitations may be required to ensure the safety of researchers or staff.

(d) How would the use be conducted?
The methods of a research project will depend on the individual project that is being conducted. The methods of each research project will be evaluated before it will be allowed to occur on the

refuge. No research project will be allowed to occur if it does not have a study plan approved by the refuge manager, or if the refuge manager determines the project may adversely affect wildlife, wildlife habitat, on-going or planned refuge management activities, previously approved research programs, approved priority public uses, or public health and safety.

(e) Why is this use being proposed?
Research by non-Service personnel is conducted by colleges, universities, Federal, State, and local agencies, non-governmental organizations, and qualified members of the general public. The purposes of research conducted on the refuge are to further the understanding of the natural resources and to improve the management of such resources on the refuge or within the National Wildlife Refuge System. Priority will be given to research which is applicable to wildlife, habitat, or public use management on and near the refuge.

Most research projects on the refuges comprising the Eastern Massachusetts NWR Complex examine management of avian resources, various public uses, and rare, threatened or endangered species. Currently, research by non-Refuge staff is concentrated on 5 of the Refuges in Eastern Massachusetts NWR Complex: Great Meadows, Assabet River, Oxbow, Monomoy, and Massasoit. Much of the research is focused on management of migratory birds, or resident herptiles and mammals, but other more specific research projects have also been implemented. In addition, much of the research conducted at the Refuges is part of larger, landscape based projects. At Great Meadows NWR, Special Use Permits (SUP) have been issued for research which has included: investigating deer populations and movements, particularly in the winter months; investigating Blanding's turtle populations, movements, and habitat occupancy during the non-nesting season; mapping the spread of West Nile Virus; and evaluating mercury contamination in the Sudbury and Concord Rivers. At Assabet River and Oxbow NWRs, research activities have included establishing presence, documenting habitat use, and monitoring impacts to productivity of Blanding's Turtles, Spotted Turtles, Box Turtles, and Wood Turtles. At Monomoy NWR, research has covered the breadth of biological resources including: neurological studies involving horseshoe crabs; movement patterns and use of the Refuge by grey and harbor seals; and tern phenology, behavior, and productivity on Monomoy (a control site for oil spill studies occurring in Buzzards Bay). At Massasoit NWR, research has focused on the natural history of the federally listed Northern red-bellied cooter. Although no SUPs have been issued to date for biological research on Nomans Land Island, Mashpee, and Nantucket NWRs, it is likely that research will occur on these sites in the future.

The Service will encourage and support research and management studies on refuge lands that improve and strengthen natural resource management decisions. The refuge manager will encourage and seek research relative to approved refuge objectives that clearly improves land management and promotes adaptive management. Information that enables better management of the Nation's biological resources and is generally considered important to agencies of the Department of Interior, including the U.S. Fish and Wildlife Service, the Refuge System, and State Fish and Game Agencies, and that addresses important management issues or demonstrate techniques for management of species and/or habitats, will be the priority.

The refuge may also consider research for other purposes which may not be directly related to refuge-specific objectives, but would contribute to the broader enhancement, protection, use, preservation and management of populations of fish, wildlife and plants, and their natural diversity within the region or flyway. These proposals must comply with the Service's compatibility policy.

The refuge may develop a list of research needs that will be provided to prospective researchers or organizations upon request. Refuge support of research directly related to refuge objectives may take the form of funding, in-kind services such as housing or use of other facilities, direct staff assistance with the project in the form of data collection, provision of historical records, conducting of management treatments, or other assistance as appropriate.

Availability of Resources: The bulk of the cost for research is incurred in staff time to review research proposals, coordinate with researchers, write SUPs, and review the research results. In some cases, a research project may only require one day of staff time to write an SUP. In other cases, a research project may require weeks of staff time. Currently, a senior refuge biologist spends an average of seven weeks a year working full time on research projects conducted by outside researchers. At an hourly wage of approximately $30 (for a GS-12), this adds up to about $8,500 annually for resources spent on outside research.

Anticipated Impacts of the Use: Disturbance to wildlife and vegetation by researchers could occur through observation, a variety of wildlife capture techniques, banding, and accessing the study area by foot or vehicle. It is possible that direct or indirect mortality could result as a by-product of research activities. Mist-netting or other wildlife capture techniques, for example, can cause mortality directly through the capture method or in-trap predation, and indirectly through capture injury or stress caused to the organism.

Overall, however, allowing well designed and properly reviewed research to be conducted by non-Service personnel is likely to have very little impact on refuge wildlife populations. If the research project is conducted with professionalism and integrity, potential adverse impacts are likely to be outweighed by the knowledge gained about an entire species, habitat or public use.

Public Review and Comment: This compatibility determination has been made available for public review by posting on the refuge bulletin board for a period of thirty days, including information about the release of the compatibility determination in a planning update that was sent to all of the individuals on the comprehensive conservation plan mailing list, and posted on the refuge website. The comment period was from June 21, 2004 to July 20, 2004.

Determination (check one below):

___ Use is Not Compatible

_X_ Use is Compatible With Following Stipulations

Stipulations Necessary to Ensure Compatibility: All researchers will be required to submit a detailed research proposal following Service Policy (FWS Refuge Manual Chapter 4 Section 6, as may be amended). The refuge must be given at least 45 days to review proposals before initiation of research. If collection of wildlife is involved, the refuge must be given 60 days to review the proposal. Proposals will be prioritized and approved based on need, benefit, compatibility, and funding required.

An SUP will be issued for all research conducted by non-Service personnel. The SUP will list the conditions that the refuge manager determines to be necessary to ensure compatibility. The SUP will also identify a schedule for progress reports and the submittal of a final report or scientific paper.

Regional refuge biologists, other Service Divisions, State agencies or non-governmental organizations and biologists may be asked to provide additional review and comment on any research proposal.

All researchers will be required to obtain appropriate State and Federal permits.

All research related Special Use Permits will contain a statement regarding the Service's policy regarding disposition of biotic specimen. The current Service policy language in this regard (USFWS, 1999) is, *"You may use specimens collected under this permit, any components of any specimens (including natural organisms, enzymes, genetic material or seeds), and research results derived from collected specimens for scientific or educational purposes only, and not for commercial purposes unless you have entered into a Cooperative Research and Development Agreement (CRADA) with us. We prohibit the sale of collected research specimens or other transfers to third parties. Breach of any of the terms of this permit will be grounds for revocation of this permit and denial of future permits. Furthermore, if you sell or otherwise transfer collected specimens, any components thereof, or any products or any research results developed from such specimens or their components without a CRADA, you will pay us a royalty rate of 20 percent of gross revenue from such sales. In addition to such royalty, we may seek other damages and injunctive relief against you."*

Any research project may be terminated at any time for non-compliance with the SUP conditions, or modified, redesigned, relocated or terminated, upon a determination by the refuge manager that the project is causing unanticipated adverse impacts to wildlife, wildlife habitat, approved priority public uses, or other refuge management activities.

Justification: The Service encourages approved research to further understanding of refuge natural resources. Research by non- Service personnel adds greatly to the information base for refuge managers to make proper decisions. Research conducted by non-Service personnel will not materially interfere with or detract from the mission of the National Wildlife Refuge System or the purposes for which the refuge was established.

Literature Cited:

U.S. Fish and Wildlife Service. 1985. Refuge Manual. Washington, D.C.: U.S. Government Printing Office.

U.S. Fish and Wildlife Service. 1999. Director's Order No. 109: Use of Specimens Collected on Fish and Wildlife Lands. March 30, 1999.

Signature - Refuge Manager: _____/s/ Elizabeth A. Herland 12/21/2004___
                                                    (Signature and Date)

Concurrence - Regional Chief: _____/s/ Anthony D. Léger 12/27/2004____
                                                    (Signature and Date)

Mandatory 10-year Re-evaluation Date: ____December 27, 2014___

Compatibility Determination

Use: Snowshoeing and cross country skiing

Refuge Names: Oxbow National Wildlife Refuge

Establishing Authority: Oxbow National Wildlife Refuge was established in 1974 under an Act Authorizing the Transfer of Certain Real Property for Wildlife, or Other Purposes (16 U.S.C. 667b).

Refuge Purpose: Oxbow's purpose is its "...particular value in carrying out the national migratory bird management program." (16 U.S.C. 667b-d, as amended)

National Wildlife Refuge System Mission: To administer a national network of lands and waters for the conservation, management, and where appropriate, restoration of the fish, wildlife, and plant resources and their habitats within the United States for the benefit of present and future generations of Americans.

Description of Use: These uses are not priority public uses, but would facilitate wildlife observation, wildlife photography, and interpretive programs, which are priority public uses, during winter months. The trail systems are not plowed, because of the cost and because of the habitat disturbance plowing would entail. The use simply involves foot-travel over the surface of the snow with the use of snowshoes and cross country skis on the refuge trail system. Maps showing these trails are included in the refuge brochure.

Availability of Resources: The cost of trail and facilities maintenance are not directly related to showshoeing or cross country skiing. Costs for activities that are facilitated by these methods of locomotion are discussed under their respective compatibility determinations.

Anticipated Impacts on Refuge Purpose: Snowshoeing and cross country skiing as conducted on Oxbow NWR have no adverse impact on the management of migratory birds or other wildlife species. These activities will only be done in conjunction with wildlife-dependent recreation. These will likely create similar disturbances as people walking on the trails.

Public Review and Comment: The compatibility determination was included in the Draft CCP/EA. The Draft CCP/EA was available for comment from July 20 through September 3, 2003. Refuge staff held four public meetings to collect public comments, written and verbal, on the draft CCP/EA, including all compatibility determinations.

Determination:
Use is not compatible ___.
Use is Compatible with the following stipulations _X_.

The following stipulations are required to ensure compatibility: Snowshoers and cross country skiers will utilize only established trails and other areas open to the public and not venture into closed areas. The current "refuge open ½ hour before sunrise to ½ hour after sunset" regulation restricts entry after daylight hours, and should be maintained along with "Public Use Restricted to Trails Only".

Justification: The National Wildlife Refuge System Improvement Act of 1997 (P.L. 105-57) identifies six legitimate and appropriate uses of wildlife refuges: environmental education, interpretation, hunting, fishing, wildlife observation and wildlife photography. These priority public uses are dependent upon healthy wildlife populations. Where these uses are determined to be compatible, they are to receive enhanced consideration over other uses in planning and management.

Snowshoeing and cross country skiing are to be used only as a means to facilitate the priority public uses identified above.

These activities will not materially interfere with or detract from the mission of the National Wildlife Refuge System or the purposes for which the refuge was established.

Signature - Refuge Manager: _____/s/ Elizabeth A. Herland 12/21/2004_____
                                    (Signature and Date)

Concurrence - Regional Chief: _____/s/ Anthony D. Léger 12/27/2004_____
                                    (Signature and Date)

Mandatory 10-year Reevaluation Date: _____December 27, 2014_____

Compatibility Determination

<u>Use:</u>   Wildlife Observation and Photography

<u>Refuge Names:</u> Oxbow National Wildlife Refuge

<u>Establishing Authority:</u> Oxbow National Wildlife Refuge (NWR) was established in 1974 under an Act Authorizing the Transfer of Certain Real Property for Wildlife, or Other Purposes. (16 U.S.C. 667b).

<u>Refuge Purpose:</u> Oxbow NWR's purpose is its "...particular value in carrying out the national migratory bird management program." (16 U.S.C. 667b-d, as amended)

<u>National Wildlife Refuge System Mission:</u> To administer a national network of lands and waters for the conservation, management, and where appropriate, restoration of the fish, wildlife, and plant resources and their habitats within the United States for the benefit of present and future generations of Americans.

<u>Description of Use:</u> Oxbow NWR has 2.5 miles of trails, one canoe launch and a parking area. Access to the refuge for this activity is achieved through walking, snowshoeing or cross-country skiing. Wildlife observation and photography include walking on open and established trails to observe and/or photograph the natural environment.

In addition, future management of Oxbow NWR includes opening five to six miles of trails on the portion of the Refuge North of Route 2. Two additional canoe launches and landing areas are also proposed along with parking areas off Jackson Road and north of Shirley Road. A viewing platform and other public use programs are proposed as well.

<u>Availability of Resources:</u> Wildlife observation and photography occur through the use of existing staff, resources, and facilities. Existing resources for wildlife observation include trails. The amount and character of these opportunities will be a direct reflection of the refuge's staff and funding levels. The following components of a wildlife observation and photography program will need to be developed to fully implement the program outlined in the Comprehensive Conservation Plan. Additional components may be developed at a later date. Specific costs will be determined as implementation of the program occurs. Some of these projects are either underway or have been completed. Projects completed in part or in whole by volunteers require less fiscal resources.

- Construct, Improve and Maintain Visitor Trails, Wildlife Viewing Platforms, Photography Blinds
- Design and Construct Accessible Interpretive Trail
- Develop and maintain parking areas and canoe launches

The CCP proposes hiring additional law enforcement staff that would be assisting with monitoring these programs.

<u>Anticipated Impacts on Refuge Purpose:</u> We predict that the impacts of wildlife observation and photography uses will be minimal. Possible impacts include disturbing wildlife, removing or

trampling of plants, littering, vandalism and entrance into closed areas. There will be some removal of vegetation to place the observation platforms and photo blinds and to establish new trails. In the event of persistent disturbance to habitat or wildlife the activity will be restricted or discontinued. Little energy will be expended by wildlife leaving areas of disturbance.

Public Review and Comment: The compatibility determination was included in the Draft CCP/EA. The Draft CCP/EA was available for comment from July 20 through September 3, 2003. Refuge staff held four public meetings to collect public comments, written and verbal, on the draft CCP/EA, including all compatibility determinations.

Determination:
Use is not compatible ___.
Use is Compatible with the following stipulations _X_.

The following stipulations are required to ensure compatibility:
Law enforcement patrol of public use areas should minimize the above-mentioned types of violations. The current "Refuge open ½ hour before sunrise to ½ hour after sunset" regulation restricts entry after daylight hours, and should be maintained along with "Public Use Restricted to Trails Only".

Special use permits are required for organizations conducting wildlife observation and photography activities on the refuge. A fee may be charged for the special use permit. The areas used by such tours will be closely monitored to evaluate the impacts on the resource. If adverse impacts appear, the activity will be moved to secondary locations or curtailed entirely. Specific conditions may apply depending upon the requested activity and will be addressed through the special use permit.

Commercial photography is subject to a special use permit and commercial photographers will be charged a fee. The fee is dependent on size, scope and impact of the proposed activity.

Periodic evaluations will be done on trails to assess visitor impacts on the habitat. If evidence of unacceptable adverse impacts appears, these uses will be curtailed, relocated or discontinued. Refuge regulations will be posted and enforced. Closed areas will be established, posted and enforced. The known presence of any threatened or endangered species likely to be disturbed by trail activity will preclude use of that site as a trail.

All photographers must follow refuge regulations. Photographers in closed areas must follow the conditions outlined in the special use permit which normally include notification of refuge personnel each time any activities occur in closed areas. Use of a closed area should be restricted to inside blinds to reduce disturbance to wildlife. No baits or scents may be used. At the end of each session, the blind must be removed. All litter will be removed daily.

Justification: The National Wildlife Refuge System Improvement Act of 1997 (P.L. 105-57) identifies six legitimate and appropriate uses of wildlife refuges: wildlife observation and wildlife photography, environmental education, interpretation, hunting, and fishing. These priority public uses are dependent upon healthy wildlife populations. Where these uses are determined to be compatible, they are to receive enhanced consideration over other uses in planning and management.

The majority of visitors to the refuge are there to view the wildlife and upland, wetland, and grassland habitat areas. Some visit to develop an understanding of natural or cultural history. This visitation is in accordance with a wildlife-oriented activity and is an acceptable secondary use. There will be some visitor impacts from this activity, such as trampling vegetation (Kuss and Hall, 1991) and disturbance to wildlife near trails (Klein, 1993 and Burger, 1981), but the knowledge, appreciation and understanding of management gained by visitors will provide support for the Service. The long-term benefits gained through wildlife observation and photography activities outweigh the impacts listed above.

These activities will not materially interfere with or detract from the mission of the National Wildlife Refuge System or the purposes for which the refuge was established.

Literature Cited:

Burger, J. 1981. The Effect of Human Activity on Birds at a Coastal Bay. Biol. Conserv. 21:231-241.

Klein, M.L. 1993. Waterbird Behavioral Response to Human Disturbances. Wildl. Soc. Bull. 21:31-39.

Kuss, F.R. and C.N. Hall. 1991. Ground Flora Trampling Studies: Five Years After Closure. Environ. Manage. 15(5):715-727.

Signature - Refuge Manager: _____ /s/ Elizabeth A. Herland 12/21/2004
                                          (Signature and Date)

Concurrence - Regional Chief: _____ /s/ Anthony D. Léger 12/27/2004
                                          (Signature and Date)

Mandatory 15-year Reevaluation Date: _____ December 27, 2019

(This page intentionally left blank)

Appendix H: Draft Water Quality Report

NASHUA RIVER BASIN
1998 WATER QUALITY ASSESSMENT REPORT

North Nashua River at the Route 31 Bridge, Fitchburg, MA

COMMONWEALTH OF MASSACHUSETTS
EXECUTIVE OFFICE OF ENVIRONMENTAL AFFAIRS
BOB DURAND, SECRETARY
MASSACHUSETTS DEPARTMENT OF ENVIRONMENTAL PROTECTION
LAUREN A. LISS, COMMISSIONER
BUREAU OF RESOURCE PROTECTION
GLENN HAAS, ACTING ASSISTANT COMMISSIONER
DIVISION OF WATERSHED MANAGEMENT
DAVID TERRY, ACTING DIRECTOR

NASHUA RIVER BASIN

1998 WATER QUALITY ASSESSMENT REPORT

Prepared by:

Mollie J. Weinstein, Laurie E. Kennedy and Jane Colonna-Romano

Department of Environmental Protection
Division of Watershed Management

Report Number:

81-AC-3

DWM Control Number:

46.0

Massachusetts Department of Environmental Protection
Division of Watershed Management
Worcester, Massachusetts

January 2001

ACKNOWLEDGEMENTS

Coordination of local, state and federal agencies and private organizations is fundamental to the success of the Massachusetts Watershed Initiative. We would like to thank Jo Anne Carr, Executive Office of Environmental Affairs and the Nashua River Watershed Team. Data and information used in this report was provided in part by the following agencies and organizations:

State
- Department of Environmental Protection (DEP):
  - Bureau of Strategic Policy and Technology's Wall Experiment Station
  - Bureau of Resource Protection
  - Bureau of Waste Prevention
  - Bureau of Waste Site Cleanup
- Massachusetts Metropolitan District Commission (MDC)
- Massachusetts Department of Public Health (MA DPH)
- Department of Fisheries, Wildlife, and Environmental Law Enforcement (DFWELE)
  - Division of Fisheries and Wildlife
  - Riverways Program
- Department of Environmental Management (DEM)

Federal
- Environmental Protection Agency (EPA)
  - New England Regional Laboratory
- United States Geological Survey (USGS)
  - Water Resources Division

Regional
- Nashua River Watershed Association (NRWA)
- Nashua River Watershed Stream Teams
  - Catacunemaug Brook Stream Team
  - Phillips Brook Stream Team
  - North Nashua River Fitchburg Stream Team
  - Nashua River Clinton Stream Team
  - Unkety Brook Stream Team
  - Nissitissit River (Squan-A-Tissit Chapter of Trout Unlimited)
  - Nashua River Pepperell Stream Team
  A Monoosnuc Brook Greenway Project and a shoreline survey along Willard Brook was also conducted.

Appreciation is also extended to several DEP employees for their contributions: Tom Dallaire, Juliet Mathers, Rick McVoy, Ph.D., Elaine Hartman, Warren Kimball, Arthur Screpetis, Paul Hogan, Matt Klansek, Katie O'Brien, and Craig Paradis.

It is impossible to thank everyone who contributed to the assessment report process: field, laboratory, data management, writing, editing, and graphics, as well as meetings, phone calls, and many e-mails. All of these contributions are very much appreciated.

Cover photo credit: Warren Kimball, Regional Watershed Manager, DEP Central Regional Office

NASHUA RIVER BASIN – RIVER SEGMENT ASSESSMENTS

The following segments in the Nashua River Basin are included in this report:

INTRODUCTION

The Massachusetts Watershed Initiative is a collaborative effort between state and federal environmental agencies, municipal agencies, citizens, non-profit groups, businesses and industries in the watershed. The mission is to improve water quality conditions and to provide a framework under which the restoration and/or protection of the basin's natural resources can be achieved. Implementation of this initiative is underway in a process known as the "Watershed Approach". The "Five-year Cycle" of the "Watershed Approach", as illustrated in Figure 5, provides the management structure to carry out the mission. Information researched and developed in the first three years of the "Five-year Cycle" was utilized by the Massachusetts Department of Environmental Protection (MA DEP) to report on water quality conditions in the Massachusetts portion of the Nashua River Basin. This report fulfills part of MA DEP's mandate under the Clean Water Act (CWA).

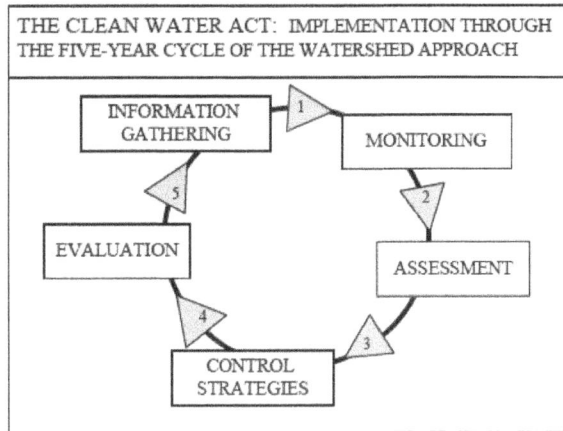

THE CLEAN WATER ACT: IMPLEMENTATION THROUGH THE FIVE-YEAR CYCLE OF THE WATERSHED APPROACH

Figure 5. Clean Water Act Implementation Cycle

The objective of the CWA is to restore and maintain the chemical, physical, and biological integrity of the Nation's waters (Environmental Law Reporter 1988). To meet this goal, the CWA requires states to develop information on the quality of the Nation's water resources and report this information to the U.S. Environmental Protection Agency (EPA), the U.S. Congress, and the public. EPA and the states are responsible for implementation of the CWA mandates. Under Section 305(b) of the CWA, MA DEP must submit a statewide report every two years to the EPA, which summarizes the status of water quality in the Commonwealth. The most recent 305(b) Report is the *Commonwealth of Massachusetts Summary of Water Quality 2000* (MA DEP 2000a). The statewide 305(b) Report is based on the compilation of current assessment information for the Commonwealth's 27 watersheds. Assessments made for 305(b) reporting utilize data from a variety of sources. The 305(b) Report provides an evaluation of water quality, progress made towards maintaining and restoring water quality, and the extent to which problems remain at the statewide level.

The Nashua River Basin 1998 Water Quality Assessment Report has been developed by MA DEP's Division of Watershed Management (DWM) to provide data and detailed assessment information for selected segments (a specifically defined reach of river or an individual lake) in the Nashua River Basin. This assessment information is maintained by MA DEP in the Water Body System (WBS) database, which is updated every two years and used to generate the state's 305(b) Report. The assessments contained in this report will be submitted to EPA in the 2002 305(b) Report. Described in the following section (Assessment Methodology) are the standardized assessment methodologies for the interpretation of instream biological, habitat, physical/chemical, toxicity, and other data.

ASSESSMENT METHODOLOGY

WATER QUALITY CLASSIFICATION

The Massachusetts Surface Water Quality Standards designate the most sensitive uses for which the surface waters of the Commonwealth shall be enhanced, maintained and protected; prescribe minimum water quality criteria required to sustain the designated uses; and include provisions for the prohibition of discharges (MA DEP 1996). These regulations undergo public review every three years. These surface waters are segmented and each segment is assigned to one of the six classes described below:

Inland Water Classes

1. **Class A** – *These waters are designated as a source of public water supply. To the extent compatible with this use they shall be an excellent habitat for fish, other aquatic life and wildlife, and suitable for primary and secondary contact recreation. These waters shall have excellent aesthetic value. These waters are designated for protection as Outstanding Resource Waters (ORW's) under 314 CMR 4.04(3).*

2. **Class B** – *These waters are designated as a habitat for fish, other aquatic life, and wildlife, and for primary and secondary contact recreation. Where designated they shall be suitable as a source of water supply with appropriate treatment. They shall be suitable for irrigation and other agricultural uses and for compatible industrial cooling and process uses. These waters shall have consistently good aesthetic value.*

3. **Class C** – *These waters are designated as a habitat for fish, other aquatic life and wildlife, and for secondary contact recreation. These waters shall be suitable for the irrigation of crops used for consumption after cooking and for compatible industrial cooling and process uses. These waters shall have good aesthetic value.*

Coastal and Marine Classes

4. **Class SA** – *These waters are designated as an excellent habitat for fish, other aquatic life and wildlife and for primary and secondary recreation. In approved areas they shall be suitable for shellfish harvesting without depuration (Open Shellfishing Areas). These waters shall have excellent aesthetic value.*

5. **Class SB** – *These waters are designated as a habitat for fish, other aquatic life and wildlife and for primary and secondary contact recreation. In approved areas they shall be suitable for shellfish harvesting with depuration (Restricted Shellfishing Areas). These waters shall have consistently good aesthetic value.*

6. **Class SC** – *These waters are designated as a habitat for fish, other aquatic life, and wildlife and for secondary contact recreation. They shall also be suitable for certain industrial cooling and process uses. These waters shall have good aesthetic value.*

The CWA Section 305(b) water quality reporting process is an essential aspect of the Nation's water pollution control effort. It is the principal means by which EPA, Congress, and the public evaluate existing water quality, assess progress made in maintaining and restoring water quality, and determine the extent of remaining problems. In so doing, the States report on waterbodies within the context of meeting their designated uses (described above in each class). Each class is identified by the most sensitive, and therefore governing, water uses to be achieved and protected. These uses include: *Aquatic Life, Fish Consumption, Drinking Water, Primary* and *Secondary Contact Recreation, Shellfishing* and *Aesthetics*. Three subclasses of Aquatic Life are also designated in the standards: Cold Water Fishery (capable of sustaining a year-round population of cold water aquatic life such as trout), Warm Water Fishery (waters which are not capable of sustaining a year-round population of cold water aquatic life), and Marine Fishery (suitable for sustaining marine flora and fauna).

A summary of the state water quality standards (Table 3) prescribes minimum water quality criteria to sustain the designated uses. Furthermore these standards describe the hydrological conditions at which water quality criteria must be met (MA DEP 1996). In rivers and streams, the lowest flow conditions at and above which criteria must be met is the lowest mean flow for seven consecutive days to be expected once in ten years (7Q10). In artificially regulated waters, the lowest flow conditions at which criteria must be met is the flow equal or exceeded 99% of the time on a yearly basis or another equivalent flow which has been agreed upon. In coastal and marine waters and for lakes and ponds the most severe hydrological condition is determined by MA DEP on a case by case basis.

The availability of appropriate and reliable scientific data and technical information is fundamental to the 305(b) reporting process. It is EPA policy (EPA Order 5360.1 CHG 1) that any organization performing work for or on behalf of EPA establish a Quality System to support the development, review, approval, implementation, and assessment of data collection operations. To this end, MA DEP describes its Quality System in an EPA-approved Quality Management Plan to ensure that environmental data collected or compiled by the Agency are of known and documented quality and are suitable for their intended use. For external sources of information, MA DEP requires the following: 1) an appropriate *Quality Assurance Project Plan* including a QA/QC plan, 2) use of a state certified lab (certified in the applicable analysis), 3) data management QA/QC be described, and 4) the information be documented in a citable report.

EPA provides guidelines to the states for making their use support determinations (EPA 1997). The determination of whether or not a waterbody can be assessed to determine if it supports each of its designated uses is a function of the type(s), quality and quantity of available current information. Although data/information older than five years are usually considered "historical" and used for descriptive purposes, they can be utilized in the use support determination providing they are known to reflect the current conditions. While the water quality standards (Table 3) prescribe minimum water quality criteria to sustain the designated uses, numerical criteria are not available for every indicator of pollution. Best available guidance in the literature may be applied in lieu of actual numerical criteria (e.g., freshwater sediment data may be compared to *Guidelines for the Protection* and *Management of Aquatic Sediment Quality in Ontario* 1993 by D. Persaud, R. Jaagumagi and A. Hayton).

Each designated use within a given segment is individually assessed as 1*) support*, 2) *partial support*, or 3) *non- support*. The term *threatened* is used when the use is fully supported but may not support the use within two years because of adverse pollution trends or anticipated sources of pollution. When too little current data/information exists or no reliable data are available the use is *not assessed*. In this report, however, if there is some indication that water quality impairment may exist based on any given variable, it is identified with an "Alert Status". It is important to note, however, that not all waters are assessed. Many small and/or unnamed lakes, rivers and estuaries are currently *unassessed*; the status of their designated uses has never been reported to EPA in the state's 305(b) Report nor is information on these waters maintained in the WBS database.

Table 3. Summary of Massachusetts Surface Water Quality Standards (MA DEP 1996). *Note: Italics are direct quotations.*

Dissolved Oxygen	Class A, BCWF*, SA : ≥ 6.0 mg/L and ≥ 75% saturation unless background conditions are lower Class BWWF**, SB: ≥ 5.0 mg/L and ≥ 60% saturation unless background conditions are lower Class C: Not ≤ 5.0 mg/L for more than 16 of any 24 –hour period and not ≤ 3.0 mg/L anytime unless background conditions are lower; levels cannot be lowered below 50% saturation due to a discharge Class SC: Not ≤ 5.0 mg/L for more than 16 of any 24 –hour period and not ≤ 4.0 mg/L anytime unless background conditions are lower; and 50% saturation; levels cannot be lowered below 50% saturation due to a discharge
Temperature	Class A: < 68°F (20°C) and Δ 1.5°F (0.8°C) for Cold Water and ≤ 83°F (28.3°C) and Δ 1.5°F (0.8°C) for Warm Water Class BCWF: ≤ 68°F (20°C) and Δ3°F (1.7°C) due to a discharge Class BWWF: ≤ 83°F (28.3°C) and Δ3°F (1.7°C) in lakes, Δ5°F (2.8°C) in rivers Class C, SC: ≤85°F (29.4°C) nor Δ5°F (2.8°C) due to a discharge Class SA: ≤85°F (29.4°C) nor a maximum daily mean of 80°F (26.7°C) and Δ1.5°F (0.8°C) Class SB: ≤85°F (29.4°C) nor a maximum daily mean of 80°F (26.7°C) and Δ1.5°F (0.8°C) between July through September and Δ 4.0°F (2.2°C) between October through June
pH	Class A, BCWF, BWWF: 6.5 – 8.3 and Δ0.5 outside the background range. Class C: 6.5 – 9.0 and Δ1.0 outside the naturally occurring range. Class SA, SB: 6.5 – 8.5 and Δ0.2 outside the normally occurring range. Class SC: 6.5 – 9.0 and Δ0.5 outside the naturally occurring range.
Fecal Coliform Bacteria	Class A: an arithmetic mean of < 20 organisms /100 ml in any representative set of samples and < 10% of the samples > 100 organisms/100 ml. Class B: a geometric mean of < 200 organisms /100 ml in any representative set of samples and < 10% of the samples > 400 organisms /100 ml. (This criterion can be applied on a seasonal basis at the discretion of the MA DEP.) Class C: a geometric mean of < 1000 organisms /100ml, and < 10% of the samples > 2000 organisms/100 ml. Class SA: approved Open Shellfish Areas: a geometric mean (MPN method) of < 14 organisms/100 ml and < 10% of the samples > 43 organisms/100 ml (MPN method). Waters not designated for shellfishing: < a geometric mean of 200 organisms in any representative set of samples, and < 10% of the samples > 400 organisms /100 ml. (This criterion can be applied on a seasonal basis at the discretion of the DEP.) Class SB: approved Restricted Shellfish Areas: < a fecal coliform median or geometric mean (MPN method) of 88 organisms/100 ml and < 10% of the samples > 260 organisms /100 ml (MPN method). Waters not designated for shellfishing: < a geometric mean of 200 organisms in any representative set of samples, and < 10% of the samples > 400 organisms /100 ml. (This criterion can be applied on a seasonal basis at the discretion of the MA DEP.) Class SC: < a geometric mean of 1000 organisms/100 ml and < 10% of the samples > 2000 organisms/100ml.
Solids	All Classes: *These waters shall be free from floating, suspended, and settleable solids in concentrations or combinations that would impair any use assigned to each class, that would cause aesthetically objectionable conditions, or that would impair the benthic biota or degrade the chemical composition of the bottom.*
Color and Turbidity	All Classes: *These waters shall be free from color and turbidity in concentrations or combinations that are aesthetically objectionable or would impair any use.*
Oil & Grease	Class A, SA: *Waters shall be free from oil and grease, petrochemicals and other volatile or synthetic organic pollutants.* Class SA: *Waters shall be free from oil and grease and petrochemicals.* Class B, C,SB, SC: *Waters shall be free from oil and grease, petrochemicals that produce a visible film on the surface of the water, impart an oily taste to the water or an oily or other undesirable taste to the edible portions of aquatic life, coat the banks or bottom of the water course or are deleterious or become toxic to aquatic life.*
Taste and Odor	Class A, SA: *None other than of natural origin.* Class B, C,SB, SC: *None in such concentrations or combinations that are aesthetically objectionable, that would impair any use assigned to each class, or that would cause tainting or undesirable flavors in the edible portions of aquatic life.*
Aesthetics	All Classes: *All surface waters shall be free from pollutants in concentrations or combinations that settle to form objectionable deposits; float as debris, scum or other matter to form nuisances; produce objectionable odor, color, taste or turbidity; or produce undesirable or nuisance species of aquatic life.*
Toxic Pollutants ~	All Classes: *All surface waters shall be free from pollutants in concentrations or combinations that are toxic to humans, aquatic life or wildlife… The division shall use the recommended limit published by EPA pursuant to 33 USC 1251, 304(a) as the allowable receiving water concentrations for the affected waters unless a site-specific limit is established.*
Nutrients	*Shall not exceed the site-specific limits necessary to control accelerated or cultural eutrophication.*

*Class BCWF = Class B Cold Water Fishery, ** Class BWWF = Class B Warm Water Fishery, Δ criterion (referring to a change from ambient) is applied to the effects of a permitted discharge. ~ USEPA. 19 November 1999. Federal Register Document. [Online]. United States Environmental Protection Agency. http://www.epa.gov/fedrgstr/EPA-WATER/1998/December/Day-10/w30272.htm.

DESIGNATED USES

The Massachusetts Surface Water Quality Standards designate the most sensitive uses for which the surface waters of the Commonwealth shall be enhanced, maintained and protected. Each of these uses is briefly described below (MA DEP 1996):

- AQUATIC LIFE - suitable habitat for sustaining a native, naturally diverse, community of aquatic flora and fauna. Three subclasses of aquatic life are also designated in the standards for freshwater bodies; *Cold Water Fishery* - capable of sustaining a year-round population of cold water aquatic life such as trout, *Warm Water Fishery* - waters which are not capable of sustaining a year-round population of cold water aquatic life, and *Marine Fishery* - suitable for sustaining marine flora and fauna.

- FISH CONSUMPTION - pollutants shall not result in unacceptable concentrations in edible portions of marketable fish or shellfish or for the recreational use of fish, shellfish, other aquatic life or wildlife for human consumption.

- DRINKING WATER - used to denote those waters used as a source of public drinking water. They may be subject to more stringent regulation in accordance with the Massachusetts Drinking Water Regulations (310 CMR 22.00). These waters are designated for protection as Outstanding Resource Waters under 314 CMR 4.04(3).

- PRIMARY CONTACT RECREATION - suitable for any recreation or other water use in which there is prolonged and intimate contact with the water with a significant risk of ingestion of water. These include, but are not limited to, wading, swimming, diving, surfing and water skiing.

- SECONDARY CONTACT RECREATION - suitable for any recreation or other water use in which contact with the water is either incidental or accidental. These include, but are not limited to, fishing, boating and limited contact incident to shoreline activities.

- AESTHETICS - all surface waters shall be free from pollutants in concentrations or combinations that settle to form objectionable deposits; float as debris, scum or other matter to form nuisances; produce objectionable odor, color, taste or turbidity; or produce undesirable or nuisance species of aquatic life.

- AGRICULTURAL AND INDUSTRIAL - suitable for irrigation or other agricultural process water and for compatible industrial cooling and process water.

Other restrictions which denote specific subcategories of use assigned to the segment that may affect the application of criteria or specific antidegradation provision of 314 CMR 4.00, which are specified along segments of the Connecticut River, include:

- CSO – These waters are identified as impacted by the discharge of combined sewer overflows in the classification tables in 314 CMR 4.06(3). Overflow events may be allowed by the permitting authority without a variance or partial use designation where the provisions 314 CMR 4.06(1)(d)10 are met. The waterbody may be subject to short-term impairment of swimming or other recreational uses, but support these uses through most of their annual period of use; and the aquatic life community may suffer some adverse impact yet is still generally viable).

[Note: The State Water Quality Standards (SWQS) have "CSO" listed where CSO impacts occur. However, this is only a notation and <u>does not</u> have regulatory significance unless all of the provisions of 314 CMR 4.06 (1) (d) 10. have been met (Facilities Plan Approval, Use Attainability Analysis, etc.) and MA DEP makes a formal administrative determination after a public hearing and MEPA filing that a B(CSO) designation is supported and appropriate (Brander 2000).]

The guidance used to assess the *Aquatic Life, Fish Consumption, Drinking Water, Primary* and *Secondary Contact Recreation* and *Aesthetics* uses follows.

AQUATIC LIFE USE

This use is suitable for sustaining a native, naturally diverse, community of aquatic flora and fauna. The results of biological (and habitat), toxicological, and chemical data are integrated to assess this use. The nature, frequency, and precision of the MA DEP's data collection techniques dictate that a weight of evidence be used to make the assessment, with biosurvey results used as the final arbiter of borderline cases. The following chart provides an overview of the guidance used to assess the status (support, partial support, non-support) of the *Aquatic Life Use*:

Variable (# indicates reference)	Support—Data available clearly indicates support. Minor excursions from chemical criteria (Table 3) may be tolerated if the biosurvey results demonstrate support.	Partial Support – Uncertainty about support in the chemical or toxicity testing data, or there is some minor modification of the biological community. Excursions not frequent or prolonged.	Non-Support – There are frequent or severe violations of chemical criteria, presence of acute toxicity, or a moderate or severe modification of the biological community.
BIOLOGY			
Rapid Bioassessment Protocol (RBP) II or III (4)	Non-Impaired	Slightly Impaired	Moderately or Severely Impaired
Fish Community (4)	Best Professional Judgement (BPJ)	BPJ	BPJ
Habitat and Flow (4)	BPJ	BPJ	Dewatered Streambed due to artificial regulation or channel alteration
Macrophytes (4)	BPJ	Non-native plant species present, but not dominant, BPJ	Non-native plant species dominant, BPJ
Plankton/ Periphyton (4)	No algal blooms	Occasional algal blooms	Persistent algal blooms
TOXICITY TESTS			
Water Column (4)	>75% survival either 48 hr or 7-day exposure	>50 - ≤75% survival either 48 hr or 7-day exposure	≤50% survival either 48 hr or 7-day exposure
Effluent (4)	Meets permit limits	(NOTE: if limit is not met, the stream is listed as threatened for 1.0 river mile downstream from the discharge.)	
Sediment (4)	>75% survival	>50 - <75% survival	<50% survival
CHEMISTRY- WATER			
DO (3, 6)	Criteria (Table 3)	Criteria exceed in 11-25% of measurements.	Criteria exceeded >25% of measurements.
pH (3, 6)	Criteria (Table 3)	Criteria exceed in 11-25% of measurements.	Criteria exceeded >25% of measurements.
Temperature (3, 6) [1]	Criteria (Table 3), [1]	Criteria exceed in 11-25% of measurements.	Criteria exceeded >25% of measurements.
Turbidity (4)	Δ 5 NTU due to a discharge	BPJ	BPJ
Suspended Solids (4)	25 mg/L max., Δ10 mg/L due to a discharge	BPJ	BPJ
Nutrients (3) Total Phosphorus(4)	Table 3, (Site-Specific Criteria; Maintain Balanced Biocommunity, no pH/DO violations)	BPJ	BPJ
Toxic Pollutants (3, 6) Ammonia-N (3, 4) Chlorine (3, 6)	Criteria (Table 3) 0.254 mg/L NH_3-N [2] 0.011 mg/L TRC	BPJ	Criterion is exceed in > 10% of samples.
CHEMISTRY – SEDIMENT			
Toxic Pollutants (5)	≤ L-EL [3], Low Effect Level	One pollutant between L-EL and S-EL	One pollutant ≥ S-EL (severe)
Nutrients (5)	≤ L-EL	between L-EL and S-EL	≥ S-EL
Metal Normalization to Al or Fe (4)	Enrichment Ratio ≤ 1	Enrichment Ratio >1 but ≤10	Enrichment Ratio ≥10
CHEMISTRY- EFFLUENT			
Compliance with permit limits (4)	In-compliance with all limits	NOTE: If the facility is not in compliance with their permit limits, the information is used to threaten one river mile downstream from the discharge.	
CHEMISTRY-TISSUE			
PCB – whole fish (1)	≤500 µg/kg wet weight	BPJ	BPJ
DDT (2)	≤14.0 µg/kg wet weight	BPJ	BPJ
PCB in aquatic tissue (2)	≤0.79 ng TEQ/kg wet weight	BPJ	BPJ

[1] maximum daily mean T in a month (min 6 measurements evenly distributed over 24-hours) <criterion, [2] Ammonia levels for pH of 9.0, actual "criterion" varies with pH and is evaluated case-by-case. [3] For the purpose of this report, the S-EL for total PCB in sediment (which varies with TOC content) with 1% TOC is 5.3 PPM while a sediment sample with 10% TOC is 53ppm.

Note: The National Academy of Sciences/National Academy of Engineering (NAS/NAE) guideline for maximum organochlorine concentrations (i.e., total PCB) in fish tissue for the protection of fish-eating wildlife is 500µg/kg wet weight (PPB, not lipid-normalized). PCB data (tissue) in this report are presented in µg/kg wet weight (PPB) and are not lipid-normalized to allow for direct comparison to the NAS/NAE guideline.

FISH CONSUMPTION USE

Pollutants shall not result in unacceptable concentrations in edible portions of marketable fish or shellfish or for the recreational use of fish, shellfish, other aquatic life or wildlife for human consumption. The assessment of this use is made using the most recent list of Fish Consumption Advisories issued by the Massachusetts Executive Office of Health and Human Services, Department of Public Health (DPH), Bureau of Environmental Health Assessment (MA DPH 1999). The DPH list identifies waterbodies where elevated levels of a specified contaminant in edible portions of freshwater species poses a health risk for human consumption; hence the *Fish Consumption Use* is assessed as non-support in these waters. In 1994, DPH also issued a statewide "Interim Freshwater Fish Consumption Advisory" for mercury (MA DPH 1994). The interim advisory states that "pregnant women should be advised of the possible health risk from eating fish from Massachusetts freshwater bodies in order to prevent exposure of developing fetuses to mercury". This precautionary measure was aimed at pregnant women only; the general public was not considered to be at risk from fish consumption. MA DPH's interim advisory does not include fish stocked by the state Division of Fisheries and Wildlife or farm-raised fish sold commercially. Because of the statewide interim advisory, however, no fresh waters can be assessed as supporting the *Fish Consumption Use*. The following is an overview of the guidance used to assess the status (support, partial support, non-support) of the *Fish Consumption Use*.

Variable (# indicates reference)	Support —No restrictions or bans in effect	Partial Support – A "restricted consumption" fish advisory is in effect for the general population or a sub-population that could be at potentially greater risk (e.g., pregnant women, and children	Non-Support – A "no consumption" advisory or ban in effect for the general population or a sub-population for one or more fish species; or there is a commercial fishing ban in effect
DPH Fish Consumption Advisory List (8)	Not applicable, precluded by statewide advisory (Hg)	Not applicable	Waterbody on DPH Fish Consumption Advisory List *

DRINKING WATER USE

The Drinking Water Use denotes those waters used as a source of public drinking water. These waters may be subject to more stringent regulation in accordance with the Massachusetts Drinking Water Regulations (310 CMR 22.00). They are designated for protection as Outstanding Resource Waters in 314 CMR 4.04(3). This use is assessed by MA DEP's Drinking Water Program (DWP). Below is EPA's guidance used to assess the status (support, partial support, non-support) of the drinking water use.

Variable (# indicates reference)	Support-- No closures or advisories (no contaminants with confirmed exceedences of MCLs, conventional treatment is adequate to maintain the supply).	Partial Support – Is one or more advisories or more than conventional treatment is required	Non-Support – One or more contamination-based closures of the water supply
Drinking Water Program (DWP) Evaluation	Reported by DWP	Reported by DWP	Reported by DWP

PRIMARY CONTACT RECREATIONAL USE

This use is suitable for any recreational or other water use in which there is prolonged and intimate contact with the water with a significant risk of ingestion of water (1 April to 15 October). These include, but are not limited to, wading, swimming, diving, surfing and water skiing. The chart below provides an overview of the guidance used to assess the status (support, partial support, non-support) of the *Primary Contact Use*.

Variable (# indicates reference)	Support-- Criteria are met, no aesthetic conditions that preclude the use	Partial Support –Criteria exceeded intermittently (neither frequent nor prolonged), marginal aesthetic violations	Non-Support –Frequent or prolonged violations of criteria, formal bathing area closures, or severe aesthetic conditions that preclude the use
Fecal Coliform Bacteria (3, 9) *	Criteria met OR <u>Dry Weather Guidance</u> <5 samples--<400/100 ml maximum <u>Wet Weather Guidance</u> Dry weather samples meet and wet samples ≤2000/100 ml	Guidance exceeded in 11-25% of the samples OR <u>Wet Weather</u> Dry weather samples meet and wet samples >2000/100 ml	Guidance exceeded in > 25% of the samples
pH (3, 6)	Criteria exceeded in ≤10 % of the measurements	Criteria exceeded in 11-25% of the measurements	Criteria exceeded in >25% of the measurements
Temperature (3)	Criteria met	Criteria exceeded 11-25% of the time	Criteria exceeded 25% of the time
Color and Turbidity (3, 6)	Δ 5 NTU (due to a discharge) exceeded in <10 % of the measurements	Guidance exceeded in 11-25% of the measurements	Guidance exceeded in >25% of the measurements
Secchi disk depth (10) **	Lakes - ≥1.2 meters (≥ 4')	Infrequent excursions from the guidance	Frequent and/or prolonged excursions from the guidance
Oil & Grease (3)	Criteria met	Criteria exceeded 11-25% of the time	Criteria exceeded >25% of the time
Aesthetics (3) Biocommunity (4)**	No nuisance organisms that render the water aesthetically objectionable or unusable; Lakes – cover of macrophytes < 50% of lake area at maximum extent of growth.	Lakes – cover of macrophytes 50-75% of lake area at their maximum extent of growth.	Lakes – cover of macrophytes >75% of lake area at their maximum extent of growth.

Note: Excursions from criteria due to natural conditions are not considered impairment of use. The *Primary Contact Recreational Use* status cannot be rated higher than either the *Secondary Contact Recreational* or the *Aesthetics Use* status.

* Fecal Coliform bacteria interpretations require additional information in order to apply this use assessment guidance. Bacteria data results (fecal coliform) are interpreted according to whether they represent dry weather or wet weather (storm water runoff) conditions. Accordingly, it is important to interpret the amount of precipitation received in the study region immediately prior to sampling and streamflow conditions.

** Lakes exhibiting impairment of the primary contact recreation use (swimmable) because of macrophyte cover and/or transparency (Secchi disk depth) are assessed as either *partial* or *non-support*. If no fecal coliform bacteria data are available and the lake (entirely or in part) met the transparency (Secchi disk depth) and aesthetics guidance this use is *not assessed*.

SECONDARY CONTACT RECREATIONAL USE

This use is suitable for any recreation or other water use in which contact with the water is either incidental or accidental. These include, but are not limited to, fishing, boating and limited contact incident to shoreline activities. Following is an overview of the guidance used to assess the status (support, partial support, non-support) of the *Secondary Contact Use*.

Variable (# indicates reference)	Support-- Criteria are met, no aesthetic conditions that preclude the use	Partial Support –Criteria exceeded intermittently (neither frequent nor prolonged), marginal aesthetic violations	Non-Support –Frequent or prolonged violations of criteria, or severe aesthetic conditions that preclude the use
Fecal Coliform Bacteria (4) *	<u>Dry Weather Guidance</u> <5 samples--≤2000/100 ml maximum >5 samples--≤1000/100 ml geometric mean ≤ 10% samples ≥2000/100 ml <u>Wet Weather Guidance</u> Dry weather samples meet and wet samples ≤4000/100 ml	<u>Wet Weather Guidance</u> Dry weather samples meet and wet samples >4000/100 ml	Criteria exceeded in dry weather
Oil & Grease (3)	Criteria met	Criteria exceeded 11-25% of the time	Criteria exceeded >25% of the time
Aesthetics (3) Biocommunity (4) **	No nuisance organisms that render the water aesthetically objectionable or unusable; Lakes – cover of macrophytes < 50% of lake area at their maximum extent of growth.	Macrophyte cover is between 50 – 75%	Macrophyte cover exceeds 75% of the lake area.

Note: Excursions from criteria due to natural conditions are not considered impairment of use. The *Secondary Contact Recreational Use* status cannot be rated higher than the *Aesthetics Use* status.

* Fecal Coliform bacteria interpretations require additional information in order to apply this use assessment guidance. Bacteria data results (fecal coliform) are interpreted according to whether they represent dry weather or wet weather (storm water runoff) conditions. Accordingly it is important to interpret the amount of precipitation received in the subject region immediately prior to sampling and streamflow conditions.

** In lakes if no fecal coliform data are available, macrophyte cover is the only criterion used to assess the *Secondary Contact Recreational Use*.

For the *Primary* and *Secondary Contact Recreational* uses the following steps are taken to interpret the fecal coliform bacteria results:
1. Identify the range of fecal coliform bacteria results,
2. Calculate the geometric mean (monthly, seasonally, or on dataset), (Note: the geometric mean is only calculated on datasets with >5 samples collected within a 30-day period.)
3. Calculate the % of sample results exceeding 400 cfu/100 mLs,
4. Determine if the samples were collected during wet or dry weather conditions (review precipitation and streamflow data),
   Dry weather can be defined as: No/trace antecedent (to the sampling event) precipitation that causes more than a slight increase in streamflow.
   Wet weather can be defined as: Precipitation antecedent to the sampling event that results in a marked increase in streamflow.
5. Apply the following to interpret dry weather data:
   ≤10% of the samples exceed criteria (step 2 and 3, above) assessed as Support,
   11-25% of the samples exceed criteria (step 2 and 3, above) assessed as Partial Support,
   >25% of the samples exceed criteria (step 2 and 3, above) assessed as Non-Support.

AESTHETICS USE

All surface waters shall be free from pollutants in concentrations or combinations that settle to form objectionable deposits; float as debris, scum or other matter to form nuisances; produce objectionable odor, color, taste or turbidity; or produce undesirable or nuisance species of aquatic life. The aesthetic use is closely tied to the public health aspects of the recreational uses (swimming and boating). Below is an overview of the guidance used to assess the status (support, partial support, non-support) of the *Aesthetics Use*.

Variable (# indicates reference)	Support – 1. No objectionable bottom deposits, floating debris, scum, or nuisances; 2. objectionable odor, color, taste or turbidity, or nuisance aquatic life	Partial Support - Objectionable conditions neither frequent nor prolonged	Non-Support – Objectionable conditions frequent and/or prolonged
Aesthetics (3)* Visual observation (4)	Criteria met	BPJ (spatial and temporal extent of degradation)	BPJ (extent of spatial and temporal degradation)

* For lakes, the aesthetic use category is generally assessed at the same level of impairment as the more severely impaired recreational use category (*Primary* or *Secondary Contact*).

References

1. Coles, J.C. 1998. *Organochlorine Compounds in Fish Tissue from the Connecticut, Housatonic and Thames River Basins Study Unit, 1992-94*. National Water-Quality Assessment Program. U.S. Department of the Interior, U.S. Geological Survey. Marlborough, MA.
2. Environment Canada. 04 November 1999. Canadian Environmental Quality Guidelines. [Online]. Environment Canada. http://www.ec.gc.ca/ceqg-rcqe/tistbl_e.doc [28 September 1998].
3. MA DEP. 1996. (Revision of 1995 report). *Massachusetts surface water quality standards*. Massachusetts Department of Environmental Protection, Division of Water Pollution Control, Technical Services Branch. Westborough, MA (Revision of 314 CMR 4.00, effective June 23, 1996).
4. MA DEP. 1999. Open File. *Department of Watershed Management 305(b) Assessment Guidance*. Massachusetts Department of Environmental Protection, Division of Watershed Management. Worcester, MA
5. Persaud, D., R. Jaagumagi, and A. Hayton. 1993. *Guidelines for the protection and management of aquatic sediment quality in Ontario*. Water Resources Branch, Ontario Ministry of the Environment. Queen's Printer for Ontario. Canada.
6. USEPA. 1997. Guidelines for Preparation of the Comprehensive State Water Quality Assessments (305(b) Reports) and Electronic Updates: Supplement. Assessment and Watershed Protection Division (4503F), Office of Wetlands, Oceans and Watersheds, Office of Water, U.S. Environmental Protection Agency. Washington, DC.
7. USEPA. 19 November 1999. Federal Register Document. [Online]. United States Environmental Protection Agency. http://www.epa.gov/fedrgstr/EPA-WATER/1998/December/Day-10/w30272.htm.
8. MA DPH. 1999. *Freshwater Fish Consumption Advisory List*. The Commonwealth of Massachusetts, Bureau of Environmental Health Assessment. Boston, MA.
9. Kimball, W.A., 1996. Memorandum to 305(b) Committee. *Re: Small data sets/ wet weather data*. Massachusetts Department of Environmental Protection, Office of Watershed Management. Grafton, MA.
10. MA DPH. 1969. *Article 7 Regulation 10.2B of the State Sanitary Code*. Commonwealth of Massachusetts. Department of Public Health. Boston, MA.
11. Churchill, N. 1999. Personal Communication. *Shellfish Project Classification Area Information as of 1 January 1999*. Department of Fisheries, Wildlife, and Environmental Law Enforcement, Division of Marine Fisheries. Pocasset, MA.

NASHUA RIVER BASIN DESCRIPTION AND CLASSIFICATION

DESCRIPTION

The Nashua River is a tributary of the Merrimack River, one of several New England rivers draining to the Atlantic Ocean. The Nashua River's 530 square-mile total drainage area lies primarily within Worcester and Middlesex counties in Massachusetts, and a small area of Hillsborough County, New Hampshire. The Nashua River Basin is located in north central Massachusetts and southern New Hampshire. Although the Nashua River flows northeast to the Merrimack River, its major tributaries flow in a southeast direction. The area drained by the major tributaries lies to the west of the Nashua River.

In Massachusetts the Nashua River Basin is bordered to the west by the Millers and Chicopee river basins, to the south by the Blackstone River Basin and to the east by the Merrimack and Concord river basins (Figure 6). The communities of Ashburnham, Ashby, Ayer, Bolton, Boylston, Clinton, Dunstable, Fitchburg, Gardner, Groton, Harvard, Holden, Lancaster, Leominster, Lunenburg, Paxton, Pepperell, Princeton, Rutland, Shirley, Sterling, Townsend,

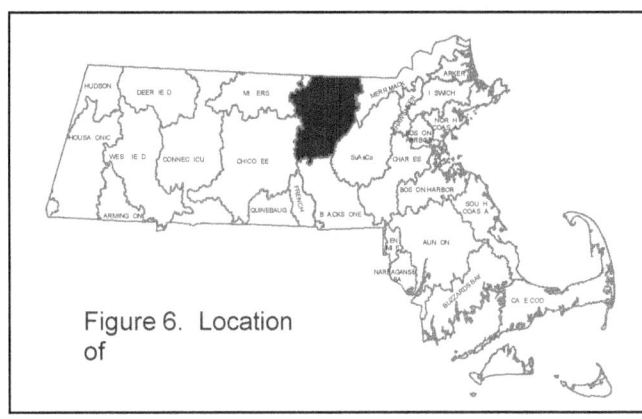

Figure 6. Location of

West Boylston, and Westminster lie wholly or in part within the basin boundaries in Massachusetts. The Nashua River Basin has a land-use pattern typical of rural areas in Massachusetts and New Hampshire; concentrated settlements and strip development with much of the basin underdeveloped and containing large areas of privately owned open spaces (Kimball 1998). Paper production has been the prominent industry in Fitchburg and Leominster in the Nashua River Basin since the early 19th century. Although these cities continue to be the population and economic centers, the industrial community now includes plastics, fabricated metal products, machinery, and chemical manufacturing.

For the purpose of this report, the Nashua River begins at the outlet of Lancaster Millpond in Clinton and flows in a northerly direction to its confluence with the North Nashua River in Lancaster. This portion of the river is commonly referred to as the "South Branch" Nashua River. The North Nashua River, from its headwaters in Fitchburg at the confluence of the Whitman River and Flag Brook, flows in a southeasterly direction for a distance of approximately 19 miles. The North Nashua River has an elevation drop of 360 feet. Downstream of the confluence with the North Nashua River, the mainstem falls another 110 feet along its remaining 37-mile northeasterly course to its confluence with the Merrimack River in Nashua, New Hampshire. Two major tributaries, the Squannacook and Nissitissit rivers join the mainstem Nashua River in Massachusetts. In Massachusetts there are 105 named streams in the Nashua River Basin that have been assigned SARIS (Stream and River Information System) code numbers (Halliwell *et al.* 1982). These streams and rivers flow an estimated 321 miles.

The topography of the Nashua River Basin is characterized by rolling hills with numerous lakes, ponds and reservoirs that provide temporary storage for high runoff during storm events. The valleys of the Nashua River Basin contain glacial sediments overlying bedrock the depths of which range from 0 to 200 feet. The valleys along the mainstem of the Nashua River contain mostly glaciofluvial sands and gravels. The sediment underlying the tributary valleys is composed of coarser sand and gravels, with the exception of the North Nashua River which is underlain by finer grained glaciolacustrine sediments (MA DEM 1989).

The "South Branch" Nashua River was dammed in 1906 to form Wachusett Reservoir. Massachusetts Metropolitan District Commission (MDC) owns and operates this reservoir, which is required by Massachusetts General Laws (1896) to release 12 million gallons per week (an average of 1.8 MGD) to the "South Branch" Nashua River (CDM 1975). [Note: MDC/MWRA is allowed to withdraw 126 MGD from the reservoir for public water supply purposes. The majority of this water is transferred out of the Nashua River Basin.] Water released from Wachusett Reservoir to the river is only one-fifth of the river's natural flow (de Lima 1991). In a hydrological sense, the Wachusett Reservoir effectively isolates 115 square-miles of the watershed.

The average discharge of the North Nashua River near Fitchburg is 122 cfs and in Leominster is approximately 200 cfs (Socolow *et al.* 2000). The discharge of the North Nashua River under extreme low flow conditions (7-day, 10-year) is estimated to be 8.8 and 32.8 cfs at Fitchburg and Leominster, respectively (USGS 1998).

The average discharge of the mainstem Nashua River downstream of Pepperell Pond is 584 cfs. Although Pepperell Paper Company is required to maintain a minimum flow of 60 cfs in the Nashua River downstream of the dam (unless the natural flow into Pepperell Pond is lower), streamflow fluctuation due to hydropower generation make estimates of low flow difficult. The estimated 7-day, 10-year low flow in the Nashua River at the USGS gage in Pepperell is 46 cfs (USGS 1998).

A total of 158 lakes, ponds or impoundments (the term "lakes" will hereafter be used to include all) have been identified and assigned Pond and Lake Information System (PALIS) code numbers in the Nashua River Basin (Ackerman 1989 and MA DEP 2000d). The total surface area of the Nashua River Basin lakes is 10,629.8 acres.

The Massachusetts Water Resource Authority's (MWRA) Wachusett Reservoir receives more than 50% of its annual inflow from the Quabbin Reservoir; inflows from Wachusett tributaries account for another 30% of its annual inflow. Wachusett Reservoir's elongated shape and large size result in long detention times, and significant dilution and settling of tributary inflows. Almost 90% of the total annual inflow to Wachusett Reservoir enters the reservoir at or above Thomas Basin, a narrow basin of the reservoir bounded on its lower end by the Route 12 bridge. The constriction at the Route 12 bridge narrows the reservoir from approximately 1,000 feet to 50 feet, and makes Thomas Basin an effective detention and sedimentation basin which helps to maintain the high quality of water in the main body of the reservoir (MDC 2000).

Additionally, the Nashua River Basin includes the Oxbow National Wildlife Refuge and the former "Fort Devens Reservation" ordered closed by Congress in 1991. The Nashua River and many of its tributaries run directly through the former base, with wetlands located along its banks. The Oxbow National Wildlife Refuge was established in 1974 and encompasses 711 acres of riparian woodland and adjacent wetlands on the floodplain of the Nashua River bordering the "Fort Devens Reservation" (USFWS 1993). The reservation is a 9,400-acre former U.S. Army base that lies between the towns of Ayer and Shirley in Middlesex County, and Lancaster and Harvard in Worcester County. The Fort Devens installation is comprised of three primary areas, the Main Post, North Post, and South Post (EPA 2000). There are approximately 4,830 acres in the South Post of Devens that provide a large area of unfragmented natural habitat that is adjacent to the Oxbow National Wildlife Refuge. The four communities (Ayer, Harvard, Lancaster and Shirley) linked by the Nashua River and Devens share the common interests of protecting and enhancing the Nashua River and its watershed and mitigating the impacts generated by Devens redevelopment or *ReUse Plan* (NRWA 1999).

CLASSIFICATION

Consistent with the National Goal Uses of "fishable and swimmable waters", the classification of waters in the Nashua River Basin according to the SWQS, include the following (MA DEP 1996):

Class A Public Water Supplies in the Nashua River Basin:

- Ashby Reservoir, source to outlet in Ashby and those tributaries thereto
- Lovell Reservoir, source to outlet in Fitchburg and those tributaries thereto
- Scott Reservoir, source to outlet in Fitchburg and those tributaries thereto
- Wachusett Lake, source to outlet in Westminster and those tributaries thereto
- Overlook Reservoir, source to outlet in Fitchburg and those tributaries thereto
- Falulah Reservoir, source to outlet in Fitchburg and those tributaries thereto
- Muschopauge Pond, source to outlet in Rutland and those tributaries thereto
- Notown Reservoir, source to outlet in Leominster and those tributaries thereto

- Simonds Pond, source to outlet in Leominster and those tributaries thereto
- Goodfellow Pond, source to outlet in Leominster and those tributaries thereto
- Haynes Reservoir, source to outlet in Leominster and those tributaries thereto
- Morse Reservoir, source to outlet in Leominster and those tributaries thereto
- Distributing Reservoir, source to outlet in Leominster and those tributaries thereto
- Fall Brook Reservoir, source to outlet in Leominster and those tributaries thereto
- Meetinghouse Pond, source to outlet in Westminster and those tributaries thereto
- Asnebumskit Pond, source to outlet in Paxton and those tributaries thereto
- Fitchburg Reservoir, source to outlet in Ashby and those tributaries thereto
- Kendall Reservoir, source to outlet in Holden and those tributaries thereto
- Pine Hill Reservoir, source to outlet in Holden and those tributaries thereto
- Quinapoxet Reservoir, source to outlet in Holden and those tributaries thereto
- Wachusett Reservoir, source to outlet in Clinton and those tributaries thereto
- Shattuck Reservoir, source to outlet in Fitchburg and those tributaries thereto

All Class A waters are designated as ORWs (Rojko *et al.* 1995). In the Nashua River Basin sections of two Class B waters (Squannacook and Nissitissit Rivers) are also designated as ORWs. The designation of ORW is applied to those waters with exceptional socio-economic, recreational, ecological and/or aesthetic values. ORWs have more stringent requirements than other waters because the existing use is so exceptional or the perceived risk of harm is such that no lowering of water quality is permissible. Generally, new or increased discharges of pollutants are prohibited for wastewater and storm water. Also, there are more stringent criteria for the discharge of dredge or fill material to wetlands in ORWs. ORWs also include certified vernal pools, and may include surface waters found in National Parks, State Forests and Parks, Areas of Critical Environmental Concern (ACEC) and those protected by special legislation (MA DEM 21 November 2000). Wetlands that border ORWs are designated as ORWs to the boundary of the defined area.

The Central Nashua River Valley Area of Critical Environmental Concern (ACEC), designated in January 1996 by the Massachusetts Secretary of Environmental Affairs, is approximately 12,900 acres in size and is located in Bolton (700 acres), Harvard (1,850 acres), Lancaster (10,100 acres) and Leominster (250 acres). The heart of this ACEC is the 20-mile riparian corridor of the North Nashua and Nashua Rivers situated south of Route 2 in Leominster, Lancaster, Bolton and Harvard. Associated with this corridor are extensive surface waters, wetlands, floodplains and aquifers, as well as interrelated riparian and upland wildlife and rare species habitat, forest, farmlands, and publicly and privately owned open space. Approximately 61% (7,900 acres) of the ACEC is open space (Oxbow National Wildlife Refuge, Bolton Flats Wildlife Management Area, and over 1,000 acres of other state, municipal and privately owned conservation and recreation lands. Another 4,830 acres of the South Post of Fort Devens are not open to the public) (MA DEM 21 November 2000).

Class B Cold Water Fisheries in the Nashua River Basin:

- Squannacook River, from its source to Hollingsworth and Vose (paper company Groton/Shirley)
- Nissitissit River, from the Massachusetts/ New Hampshire state line to its confluence with the Nashua River in Pepperell

Class B Warm Water Fisheries in the Nashua River Basin:

- Nashua River, from its source to the New Hampshire State Line
- North Nashua River, from its source to the Leominster POTW (CSO)
- North Nashua River, from the Leominster POTW to the confluence with the Nashua River
- Phillips Brook, from Fitchburg to the confluence with the North Nashua River (CSO)
- South Nashua River, from the outlet at Wachusett Reservoir to the confluence with the North Nashua River
- Squannacook River, from Hollingsworth and Vose (paper company Groton/Shirley)to its confluence with the Nashua River

Unlisted waters not otherwise designated in the SWQS are designated *Class B, High Quality Water.* According to the SWQS, where fisheries designations are necessary, they shall be made on a case-by-case basis.

SUMMARY OF EXISTING CONDITIONS AND PERCEIVED PROBLEMS

The Nashua River has a long history of water quality degradation. In the 1960's and early 1970's, paper manufacturing facilities in Fitchburg and Pepperell, inadequately treated municipal wastewater in Fitchburg, Leominster, Clinton and Ayer, and combined sewer overflows (CSO) in Fitchburg and Leominster caused severe pollution impacts in the North Branch and mainstem Nashua Rivers (Johnson *et al.* 1990). While the water quality in the mainstem and North Branch Nashua River has improved considerably with implementation of advanced wastewater treatment, impacts on stream biota and elevated bacteria levels remain problematic.

The Clean Water Act section 303(d) requires states to identify those waterbodies that are not meeting Surface Water Quality Standards (SWQS). Table 4 identifies waterbodies in the Nashua River Basin in Massachusetts that are on the 1998 Section 303(d) list of waters (MA DEP 1999a). It should be noted that in 1994, MA DPH issued a statewide *Interim Freshwater Fish Consumption Advisory* for mercury (MA DPH 1994). This precautionary measure was aimed at pregnant women only; the general public was not considered to be at risk from fish consumption. Because the advisory encompasses all freshwaters in Massachusetts, the *Fish Consumption Use* can not be assessed as support. Therefore, all freshwaters in Massachusetts are technically (by default) listed as 303(d) waters with mercury as the associated stressor/pollutant. Furthermore the 1998 303(d) list contains an attachment (#3) of the MA DPH fish consumption advisories (MA DEP 1999a).

Table 4. 1998 303(d) list of impaired waters, Nashua River Basin.

1998 303(d) Listed Waterbody		Cause of Impairment
North Nashua River	Fitchburg West WWTP to Fitchburg Paper Company Dam #1, Fitchburg	Other habitat alterations and Pathogens (fecal coliform bacteria)
	Fitchburg Paper Company Dam #1 to Fitchburg East WWTP, Fitchburg	Fecal coliform bacteria
	Fitchburg East WWTP, Fitchburg, to Leominster WWTP, Leominster	Fecal coliform bacteria
Nashua River	Outlet Lancaster Mill Pond to Clinton WWTP, Clinton	Unknown toxicity
Nashua River *	Confluence with the Squannacook River, Shirley/Groton/Ayer to Pepperell Dam, Pepperell	Organic Enrichment/ Low DO
Bare Hill Pond	Harvard	Noxious aquatic plants
Fort Pond	Lancaster	Nutrients
Grove Pond	Ayer	Metals
Harbor Pond	Townsend	Noxious aquatic plants
Mirror Lake	Harvard	Metals
Pierce Pond	Leominster	Noxious aquatic plants
Plow Shop Pond	Ayer	Metals
Flannagan Pond *	Ayer	Noxious aquatic plants
Barrett Pond *	Leominster	Noxious aquatic plants

*needs confirmation (additional data collection is necessary to confirm the presence of impairment)

The MA DPH Fish Consumption List includes five waterbodies in the Nashua River Basin; Wachusett Reservoir, Pepperell Pond, Grove Pond, Plow Shop Pond, and Mirror Lake because of elevated levels of mercury in fish tissue. The advisories recommend the following (MA DPH 1999):

Wachusett Reservoir, Boylston/West Boylston/Clinton/Sterling (Advisory issued by MA DPH June 1989):
- Children under 12, pregnant women and nursing mothers should not consume fish except for lake trout (less than 24 inches long) and salmon.
- All other people should not eat smallmouth bass, largemouth bass, or lake trout (greater than 24 inches long); May eat unlimited amounts of salmon and lake trout (less than 24 inches long); and should limit consumption of all other Wachusett Reservoir fish to one five-ounce meal per week.

Pepperell Pond, Pepperell/Groton (Advisory issued by MA DPH June 1994):
- Children under 12, pregnant women and nursing mothers should refrain from consuming any fish from Pepperell Pond in order to prevent exposure of developing fetuses and young children to mercury.
- The general public should refrain from consumption of largemouth bass caught from Pepperell Pond.
- The general public should limit consumption of all other Pepperell Pond fish to two meals per month.

Mirror Lake, Ft. Devens, Harvard (Advisory issued MA DPH May 1996):
- Children under 12, pregnant women and nursing mothers should refrain from consuming any largemouth bass from Mirror Lake in order to prevent exposure of developing fetuses and young children to mercury.
- The general public should limit consumption of largemouth bass caught from Mirror Lake to two meals per month.

Plow Shop Pond, Ft. Devens, Ayer (Advisory issued by US Army):
- The general public should not consume any fish from this waterbody.

Grove Pond, Ft. Devens, Ayer (Advisory issued by town of Ayer):
- The general public should not consume any fish from this waterbody.

Another major issue in the Nashua River Basin is the redevelopment of the Fort Devens base. The following information provides a description of the base's historical use and on going restoration, redevelopment and remediation activities (EPA 17 November 2000).

> The Army established Fort Devens in 1917 as a temporary training camp for soldiers during World War I. In 1931, the camp became a permanent installation and operated for over 60 years serving a variety of military purposes. In 1991, the Fort Devens base was targeted for realignment and closure and by 1996, the base was closed and the transformation of the site for public and private use began.
>
> The Fort Devens installation primarily comprises three primary areas, the Main Post, North Post, and South Post. The Main Post provided all base housing, community services, administrative buildings, training facilities, ammunition storage and an 8.8-acre vehicle maintenance yard. The Main Post also is the site of an 84-acre municipal landfill that existed before the base was established, and was used by the Army. The North Post was primarily a military airfield, but was also used to train troops. In addition, it contains a wastewater treatment plant. The South Post contained areas for troop training, firing range activities, and an air drop zone.
>
> The numerous operations at the Fort Devens base have resulted in the possible contamination of over 80 areas of the installation. Three of these areas were of particular concern to the Superfund program: the maintenance yard and municipal landfill located on the Main Post, and the airfield located on the North Post. The maintenance yard consisted of an unpaved parking area where military vehicles leaked fuel and oil onto the ground. Additionally, underground storage tanks located at the maintenance yard had released waste oil, resulting in contamination of the surrounding soil with polyaromatic hydrocarbons, which are carcinogenic. The municipal landfill had deteriorated to a point where there was a significant threat of arsenic contamination to the groundwater under the site. Groundwater also is contaminated at the North Post, where a plume of polychloroethylene was detected under the airfield. Polychloroethylene is a solvent that was used extensively by the Army to clean parachutes at the airfield. Many other contaminated areas of the Fort Devens site are being addressed under authorities other than Superfund.
>
> At its peak, over 15,000 military personnel and their families lived on the Fort Devens base. The current land use around the site is primarily rural and residential, with an estimated 3,500 households located within two miles of the Fort Devens boundary. In addition, the Nashua River and many of its tributaries run directly through the site, with wetlands located along its banks. The Oxbow National Wildlife Refuge is located just below the southern boundary of the Main Post.
>
> The closure of Fort Devens and the remedies chosen to clean up the site were key factors in its redevelopment. As an Army base, Fort Devens had extensive infrastructure in place and was being

used for a variety of operations. At the time of the base's closure, studies indicated that approximately 5.6 million square feet of land and over 2 million square feet of existing buildings and facilities had potential reuse because of their location and access to major highways and rail service. Several public and private sector employers have taken advantage of this redevelopment potential and have located, or are planning to locate, at the site. The redevelopment of Fort Devens is expected to revitalize the local economy impacted by the base's closure.

As part of the redevelopment of the Fort Devens site, the Department of Defense (DoD) transferred large portions of the site to other Federal departments and the State to provide public services and attract private businesses. DoD retained control of 5,000 acres of land, including all of the South Post and portions of the Main and North Posts, for construction of a new Army Reserve enclave and training area. DoD transferred the remainder of the site to the Department of Labor (DOL), the Department of Justice (DOJ), and a State-designated developer for public and private development. DoD transferred approximately 22 acres of land to DOL, which is building a Jobs Corp Center; 222 acres to the DOJ, where a Federal Bureau of Prisons Hospital is being built; and approximately 836 acres along the Nashua River to the Fish and Wildlife Service (FWS) for an extension to the Oxbow National Wildlife Refuge. The remainder of the Main and North Posts was transferred to the Massachusetts Government Land Bank to promote and oversee private redevelopment.

SOURCES OF INFORMATION

Multiple local, state and federal agencies provided information used in the water quality assessment of the Nashua River Basin. Within the Department of Environmental Protection (DEP) information was obtained from three programmatic bureaus: Bureau of Resource Protection (BRP, see below), Bureau of Waste Prevention (industrial wastewater discharge information) and the Bureau of Waste Site Cleanup (hazardous waste site cleanup information). Specifically, water quality, habitat assessment, and biological data, toxics in fish flesh data, and lake synoptic survey data were provided by DEP BRP Division of Watershed Management (DWM) Watershed Planning Program. The DEP Central Regional Office Nashua River Watershed Team and the DWM Watershed Permitting Program provided water withdrawal and wastewater discharge permit information (Water Management Act, and National Pollutant Discharge Elimination System). [Note: The BRP DWM Drinking Water Program evaluates the status of the *Drinking Water Use* and this information is therefore not provided in this assessment report.] Projects funded through various DEP grant and loan programs also provide valuable information that may be used in the water quality assessment report (MA DEP 2000c). A summary of these projects for the Nashua River Basin is provided in Appendix E.

Other state agencies contributing information to this report include: the Metropolitan District Commission (MDC), the Massachusetts Department of Public Health (MA DPH), the Department of Fisheries, Wildlife, and Environmental Law Enforcement (DFWELE) Division of Fisheries and Wildlife and its Riverways Program, and the Department of Environmental Management (DEM).

The MDC's Division of Watershed Management (MDC DWM) is responsible for securing and maintaining an adequate supply of high quality drinking water to meet the demands of the 46 communities served by the Massachusetts Water Resources Authority (MWRA). Water quality sampling and watershed monitoring are an integral part of their mission. The Environmental Quality Section staff at Wachusett Reservoir conduct the sampling activities. Their routine water quality sampling data, conducted at 20 stations on 15 tributaries, includes weekly sampling for fecal coliform bacteria, temperature, dissolved oxygen (DO) and pH measurements and monthly nutrient sampling. Samples were almost always collected between 7:30 and 11:00 in the morning, generally on Tuesday or Wednesday (Pistrang 2000). Additional sampling during storm events and special studies are also summarized in their annual water quality reports for Wachusett Reservoir and Watershed (Getman *et al.* 1996, Pistrang *et al.* 1997 and 1998). Their water quality monitoring data from 1995 to 1999 is summarized in this assessment report. The MDC also conducts benthic macroinvertebrate sampling in the Wachusett Watershed and has used a modified RBP III evaluation for their analysis (Pistrang 2000). Most organisms were identified to genus or species if keys were available with the exception of the chironomids. For purposes of determining total number of taxa, chironomids were separated into general groupings based on overall physical appearance. Benthic macroinvertebrates were sampled at a total of 14 stations in the Wachusett Reservoir Watershed by MDC in 1996.

Federal agencies contributing to the information used in this report include the EPA and United States Geological Survey (USGS). The EPA provided compliance monitoring evaluations at five NPDES facilities during August 1998 (Fitchburg East and West, Leominster, Clinton, and Ayer WWTPs) (Kundarauskas 1998). *In-situ* meters were also deployed by EPA to obtain diurnal dissolved oxygen data at four locations between 16 and 24 July and 10 – 13 August 1998 (inlet and outlet of Pepperell Pond, Groton School and the Ice House Dam) (MA DEP 1998). EPA also collected sediment quality data. This monitoring included sediment oxygen demand (SOD) measurements at eight locations during November 1998. Sediments for toxicity testing were collected at five of the locations using the test organisms *Chironomus tentans* and *Hyallela azteca* as well as physicochemical analysis in March 1999 (McDonald 1999):

- grain size
- Total Organic Carbon (TOC)
- Simultaneously extracted metals/acid volatile sulfides (SEM/AVS)
- Cyanide (Cn)
- total metals: silver (Ag), arsenic (As), barium (Ba), beryllium (Be), cadmium (Cd), cobalt (Co), chromium (Cr), copper (Cu), nickel (Ni), lead (Pb), antimony (Sb), selenium (Se), thallium (Tl), vanadium (V), zinc (Zn), and mercury (Hg)

Sediment sampling station locations in the Nashua River included:

- NR1 upstream of the "Tank Bridge" and railroad tracks,
- NR2 downstream of the "Tank Bridge" across from the boat landing in the Oxbow National Wildlife Refuge,
- NR3 approximately 30m upstream of the Ice House Dam,
- NR4 adjacent to the abandoned Devens air strip, and
- NR5 just upstream of the Pepperell Dam.

Hydrological data was obtained from USGS at five stations: North Nashua River in Fitchburg, North Nashua River in Leominster, the Stillwater River in Sterling, the Squannacook River in West Groton and the mainstem Nashua River in East Pepperell (Socolow *et al.* 1998 and Socolow *et al.* 1999).

A directed study of fish in lakes in northeastern Massachusetts (MA) was performed by the DEP Office of Research and Standards (ORS) during 1999 in order to examine possible spatial patterns in the occurrence of higher fish mercury concentrations and to compare the fish contamination situation in this localized geographical region to state-wide and regional data (MA DEP 2000b). Northeastern Massachusetts has an important history of industrialization dating back into the nineteenth century with the extensive burgeoning of mills along the Merrimack River. Most of this industry is now gone and the infrastructure for the mills is now slowly being converted to non-manufacturing uses. Many of the older, larger towns are relatively densely populated areas, yet surrounding lands are relatively undeveloped. This region was recently identified through the use of an air deposition model as having the highest predicted annual levels of recent wet and dry atmospheric deposition of mercury in the state. The area has the state's largest concentration of point sources of atmospheric mercury emissions: three municipal solid waste incinerators and a medical waste incinerator. Zones downwind from major point sources may be subject to increased deposition of a variety of contaminants (e.g., smelters, tailings piles and power stations). While historic records do not exist of atmospheric mercury deposition in this area, past widespread burning of coal for domestic heat and industrial boilers in the late nineteenth and first half of the twentieth centuries probably contributed to a relatively high background mercury signature in the environment of this part of the state. The objectives of the study were to:

1) sample fish from as many lakes in northeastern MA where fishing takes place as possible in order to determine if fish consumption advisories are needed for those lakes;
2) determine whether the frequency of advisories is greater in this area than across the state as a whole;
3) determine if there are any spatial patterns in fish mercury concentrations within the study area related to the locations of the major point sources of mercury emissions;
4) determine how well measured mercury concentrations match those predicted by a fish tissue mercury prediction model developed by MA DEP;
5) compare mercury concentrations in fish from the region with those from other parts of Massachusetts.

The lakes sampled in this study were chosen on the basis of the following: size of lake (4 hectares minimum size); availability of fish species; fishing pressure; access; and proximity to other lakes. Three lakes in the Nashua River Basin were selected for inclusion in this study: Fort Pond (Lancaster), Hickory Hills Lake (also known as Dickinson Reservoir, Lunenburg), and Bare Hill Pond (Harvard) (MA DEP 2000b).

Historical Fish Toxics Monitoring in the Nashua River
In the summer of 1985 white sucker (*Catostomus commersoni*) were collected by DEP at nine sites (five on the North Branch Nashua River, including Snows Millpond, two on the "South Branch", and two on the mainstem Nashua River) as part of the Massachusetts Fish Toxics Monitoring Program. White suckers ingest large volumes of sediment while feeding, thus increasing the probability of absorbing contaminants through the gut. Ten suckers were collected, processed as a composite sample and subsequently analyzed for heavy metals from each site (Johnson *et al.* 1990). The data were submitted to MA DPH. No specific fish consumption advisories were issued.

In addition to state and federal agencies, regional, local, and citizen monitoring groups provide data/information for the watershed management process which may be used to indicate areas of both high and degraded water quality, as well as causes and sources of contamination. The Nashua River Watershed Association (NRWA), founded in 1969, is a nonprofit organization dedicated to educating and advocating for the protection of the watershed's natural resources. Since 1993, the NRWA has also organized and conducted a volunteer water quality monitoring program (NRWA 1999). The NRWA, with support of the DFWELE Riverways Program, have also organized Stream Teams in various subwatersheds since 1995 to establish stewardship of streams by local citizens, schools, businesses and civic groups. These include: Catacunemaug Brook Stream Team, Phillips Brook Stream Team, North Nashua River Fitchburg Stream Team, Nashua River Clinton Stream Team, Unkety Brook Stream Team, Nissitissit River (Squan-A-Tissit Chapter of Trout Unlimited), and the Nashua River Pepperell Stream Team. A Monoosnuc Brook Greenway Project and a shoreline survey along Willard Brook was also conducted. The NRWA, with input from the watershed communities and many groups, agencies, and individuals, created a 2020 Vision Plan for the Nashua River watershed: *Dedicated to a healthy ecosystem with clean water and open spaces for human and wildlife communities, where people work together to sustain mutual economic and environmental well being intended as a guide for growth, conservation, and resource protection* (NRWA 1 December 2000b).

Site specific evaluations of other water quality issues in the Nashua River Basin related to either wastewater discharges and/or water withdrawals were conducted either through field investigations (where resources could be allocated) or through the review of discharge monitoring reports (DMRs) and annual water withdrawal reports submitted by the permittees. Water withdrawal and wastewater discharge permit information was provided by the DEP Central Regional Office Nashua River Watershed Team and the DWM Watershed Permitting Program (Water Management Act - WMA and National Pollutant Discharge Elimination System –NPDES).

The Nashua River Basin has facilities that discharge to the mainstem of the river and to several of its tributaries (Appendix F, Table F1). The following types of NPDES discharges occur in the watershed (Hogan 2000):
- *Municipal wastewater treatment plants (WWTPs):* these facilities treat wastewater from domestic and industrial sources within the WWTP service area. They range in size from the Town of Pepperell WWTP that has a capacity of 0.705 MGD and treats only municipal, sanitary wastewater to the Fitchburg East facility with a treatment capacity of 12.4 MGD. A significant number of combined sewer overflows (CSOs) in the City of Fitchburg and combined manholes in the City of Leominster also discharge into the North Branch and mainstem Nashua rivers. Elevated bacteria levels, common after rain and snow melt events, cause short-term violations of the MA Water Quality Standards, and result in short-terms limitations of the primary and secondary contact recreational uses.
- *Industrial WWTPs and non-process discharges:* the majority of industrial process wastewaters are treated at the municipal WWTPs under conditions of their industrial pre-treatment program (IPP). The IPP is controlled by the municipality and is a condition of the municipal WWTP NPDES permit. Significant industrial WWTPs include two paper processing plants in the watershed, the Hollingsworth and Vose Company and the Pepperell

Paper Company. Several industries also have general permits issued to the facilities by USEPA for the discharge of non-contact cooling water and storm water. While these discharges are authorized and controlled under general permits, the associated impacts from these facilities are minimum and do not get significant environmental review from DEP.

- *Other.* Power plants include Pinetree Power (Fitchburg), Pepperell Paper Company Power Plant, Fitchburg Paper Mill Dam #4 (FERC #11058) (FERC 12 December 2000).

All six municipal wastewater treatment plants in the Nashua River Basin submit toxicity testing reports to EPA and DEP as required by their NPDES permits. Data from these toxicity reports are maintained by DWM in a database entitled "Toxicity Testing Data - TOXTD". Information from the reports includes: survival of test organisms exposed to ambient river water (used as dilution water), physicochemical analysis (e.g., hardness, alkalinity, pH, total suspended solids) of the dilution water, and the whole effluent toxicity test results. Data from January 1996 to April 2000 were reviewed and summarized (ranges) for use in the assessment of current water quality conditions in the Nashua River Basin. These include:

- Ayer WWTP MA0100013
- Fitchburg East WWTP MA0100986
- Leominster WWTF MA0100617
- MWRA Clinton MA0100404
- Pepperell WWTF MA0100064
- West Fitchburg WWTP MA0101281

Two institutional NPDES discharges also conduct toxicity testing of their effluents (MCI Shirley MA0033824 completed tie-in to the Devens WWTP in January 1999). These include:

- Groton School WWTP MA0033324
- River Terrace Healthcare MA0025763

Four industrial NPDES discharges also conduct toxicity testing of their effluents. These include:

- Hollingsworth and Vose MA0004561
- Indeck Pepperell Power MA0032034
- Pepperell Paper Company MA0005185
- Simonds Industries Inc. MA0022896

Two non-contact cooling water (NCCW) NPDES discharges and one water treatment plant (WTP) also conduct toxicity testing of their effluents. These include:

- B.F. Goodrich MAG250864 NCCW
- Holden Trap Rock Company MA0020320 NCCW
- Rutland WTP MAG640033

Note: The following minor NPDES facilities have also conducted toxicity testing but do not discharge into streams assessed in this report. These facilities include:

- Kelly Company, Clinton MA0027448 (Counterpane Brook) no longer discharges
- NOVACOR Chemicals, Leominster MA0000442 (Wass Brook) no longer discharges
- Suprenant Cable Corp., Clinton MA0001783 (Counterpane Brook) no longer discharges
- P.J. Keating Co., Fitchburg MA0003689 (tributary to Lake Shirley) (Appendix F, Table F1)

One additional institutional NPDES facility (MA0028444 St. Benedict Center, Harvard – a retreat center and bakery) discharges into an unnamed tributary of the Nashua River (Appendix F, Table F1) not assessed in this report. Cushing Academy, Ashburnham (MA0101958) a former discharge in the Nashua River Basin, was connected to the Ashburnham sewer system in 1996. Their wastewater is treated at the Gardner WWTP in the Millers River Basin (Moylan 2000).

A list of registered and permitted ~~water~~ Water Management Act (WMA) withdrawals (both public water suppliers and other industrial users) is provided in Appendix F, Table F2 (LeVangie 2000). In cases where water withdrawal information was available, it was included in the segment assessment. In order to determine where stream segments might be affected by water withdrawal activities, a review of the WMA files is necessary.

TOTAL MAXIMUM DAILY LOADS (TMDL)

As part of the Federal Clean Water Act, states are required to develop Total Maximum Daily Load (TMDL) Reports for lakes, rivers and coastal waters not meeting the states water quality standards as indicated by the states 303d list of impaired waters. A TMDL is the greatest amount of a pollutant that a waterbody can accept and still meet standards. Further information on the 303d list and the TMDL program are available on the DEP website at: http://www.state.ma.us/dep/brp/wm/wmpubs.htm.

RIVERS
EPA has contracted Tetra Tech, Inc. and Numeric Environmental Services (NES) to develop a set of computer models and GIS tools which will be used by the agencies for detailed water quality analysis and development of a TMDL on the mainstem of the Nashua River (Hartman 2000). Although the models and TMDL will target the 8.8 mile reach of the Nashua River between the confluence with the Squannacook River and the Pepperell Dam (MA81-06) (which is on the 1998 303d list for organic enrichment/low dissolved oxygen), the tools will be available for further evaluation of other constituents (e.g., suspended solids) and for other sections of the mainstem and tributaries. TetraTech has completed the first step of model development: a calibrated hydrologic model, GIS soils and land use mapping, and an NPSM model for total nitrogen and total phosphorus within the BASINS environment (EPA 2000). NES is continuing development of the NPSM model to include nutrient cycling, to add in the mainstem reaches portion of the model, and to integrate the subwatershed component as part of a larger model outside of BASINS (NES 2000). NES is also developing a wasteload allocation QUAL2 model for low flow, steady state conditions. The models will assist the agencies in determining NPS and point source contributions through development of scenarios for baseline, present and future watershed conditions. The models will also help to determine NPS remediation actions if necessary, and provide information for WWTF NPDES permitting.

LAKES
Of the nine lakes in the Nashua River Basin on the 1998 303d list, only Bare Hill Pond has a final EPA approved TMDL for Total Phosphorus which includes options for aquatic plant management (see publication on the website above) (Mattson 2000 and MA DEP 1999b). Total Phosphorus TMDLs for Fort Pond, Harbor Pond, Pierce Pond, Flannagan Pond and Barrett Pond are scheduled to be developed on the Five-year watershed cycle in years 2004 and 2009. Plow Shop Pond and Grove Pond, which are listed for metals on the 303d list, are part of a cleanup memorandum of understanding between the Army, DEP and the EPA dated 17 September 17 1998. In a Decision of the Army dated 18 April 1997, the Army determined that "No Further Action" for cleanup of Mirror Lake is required. The lake will however, probably remain on the 303d list for mercury contamination in fish and a therefore TMDLs will have to be developed for *all three* of these lakes as well.

OBJECTIVES

This report summarizes information generated in the Nashua River Basin through *Year 1* (information gathering in 1997) and *Year 2* (environmental monitoring in 1998) activities established in the "Five-Year Cycle" of the Watershed Initiative. Data collected by DWM in 1998, in accordance with the draft Nashua River Monitoring Plan (Kimball 1998), are provided in Appendices A, B, C and D (QA/QC, data tables, a technical memorandum; Biological Assessment of Streams in the Nashua River Watershed from 1998 Data, and a technical memorandum: Nashua River 1998 Chlorophyll *a*, Phytoplankton and Periphyton Sampling). Together with other sources of information (identified in each segment assessment), the status of water quality conditions of lakes and streams in the Nashua River Basin was assessed in accordance with EPA's and DEP's use assessment methods. Not all waters in the Nashua River Basin are included in the DEP/EPA Water Body System (WBS) database or this report.

The objectives of this water quality assessment report are to:

1. Evaluate whether or not surface waters in the Nashua River Basin, defined as segments in the WBS database, currently support their designated uses (i.e., meet water quality standards),
2. identify water withdrawals (habitat quality/water quantity) and/or major point (wastewater discharges) and nonpoint (land-use practices, storm water discharges, etc.) sources of pollution that may impair water quality conditions,
3. identify the presence or absence of any non-native macrophytes in lakes,
4. identify waters (or segments) of concern that require additional data to fully assess water quality conditions,
5. recommend additional monitoring needs and/or remediation actions in order to better determine the level of impairment or to improve/restore water quality, and
6. provide information to the Nashua River Watershed Team for use in its annual and 5-year watershed action plans.

SEGMENT REPORT FORMAT

The segment order in this assessment report follows the Massachusetts Stream Classification Program (Halliwell *et al.* 1982) hierarchy. Stream segments are organized hydrologically (from most upstream to downstream). Tributary summaries follow the segment into which they discharge. Lakes segment summaries are presented after the stream segments. Each stream segment summary is formatted as follows:

SEGMENT IDENTIFICATION

Name, water body identification number (WBID), location, length/size, classification.

Sources of information: coding system (waterbody identification number e.g., MA34-01) used by DEP to reference the stream segment in databases such as 305(b) and 303(d), the Massachusetts SWQS (MA DEP 1996), and other descriptive information.

SEGMENT DESCRIPTION

Major land-use estimates (the top three uses for the subwatershed) and other descriptive information.

Sources of information: descriptive information from USGS topographical maps, base geographic data from MassGIS, land use statistics from a GIS analysis using the MassGIS land use coverage developed at a scale of 1:25,000 and based on aerial photographs taken in 1985,1990,1992, and 1997 as shown below (EOEA 1999a):

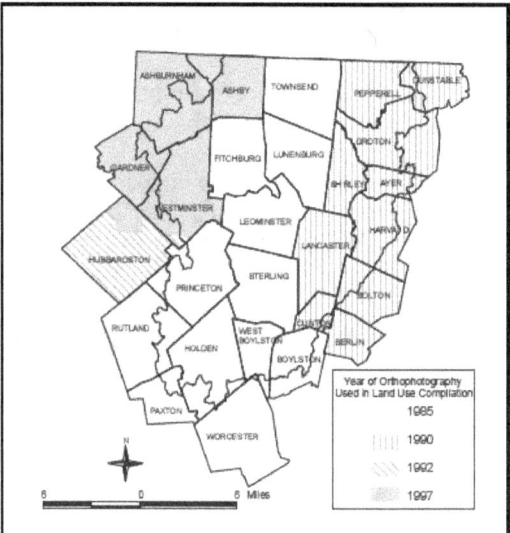

SEGMENT LOCATOR MAP

Subbasin map, major river location, segment origin and termination points, and segment drainage area (gray shaded).

Sources of information: MassGIS (EOEA 1999b) data layers (stream/lake segments, and quadrangle maps).

WATER WITHDRAWALS AND WASTEWATER DISCHARGE PERMIT INFORMATION

Water withdrawal, NPDES wastewater discharge.

Sources of information: WMA Database Printout (LeVangie 2000); open permit files located in Worcester DEP Office (MA DEP 2000e and f, Kimball 2000 and Hogan 2000).

USE ASSESSMENT

Aquatic Life, Fish Consumption, Drinking Water (where applicable), Primary Contact, Secondary Contact, and Aesthetics.

Sources of information include: DWM 1998 Survey data (Appendix B and Appendix C); USGS streamflow data (Socolow *et al.* 1998 and Socolow *et al.* 1999); EPA sediment quality information (McDonald 1999); MDC water quality data (Getman *et al.* 1996, Pistrang *et al.* 1997 and 1998, and Pistrang 2000); DEP DWM Toxicity Testing Database "TOXTD"; NRWA and Stream Team reports. The MA DPH Freshwater Fish Consumption Advisory List (MA DPH 1999) was used to assess the *Fish Consumption Use*. The DEP Drinking Water Program maintains current drinking water supply data. Where other sources of information were used to assess designated uses, citations are included.

SUMMARY

Use summary table (uses, status, causes and sources of impairment).

RECOMMENDATIONS

Additional monitoring and implementation needs.

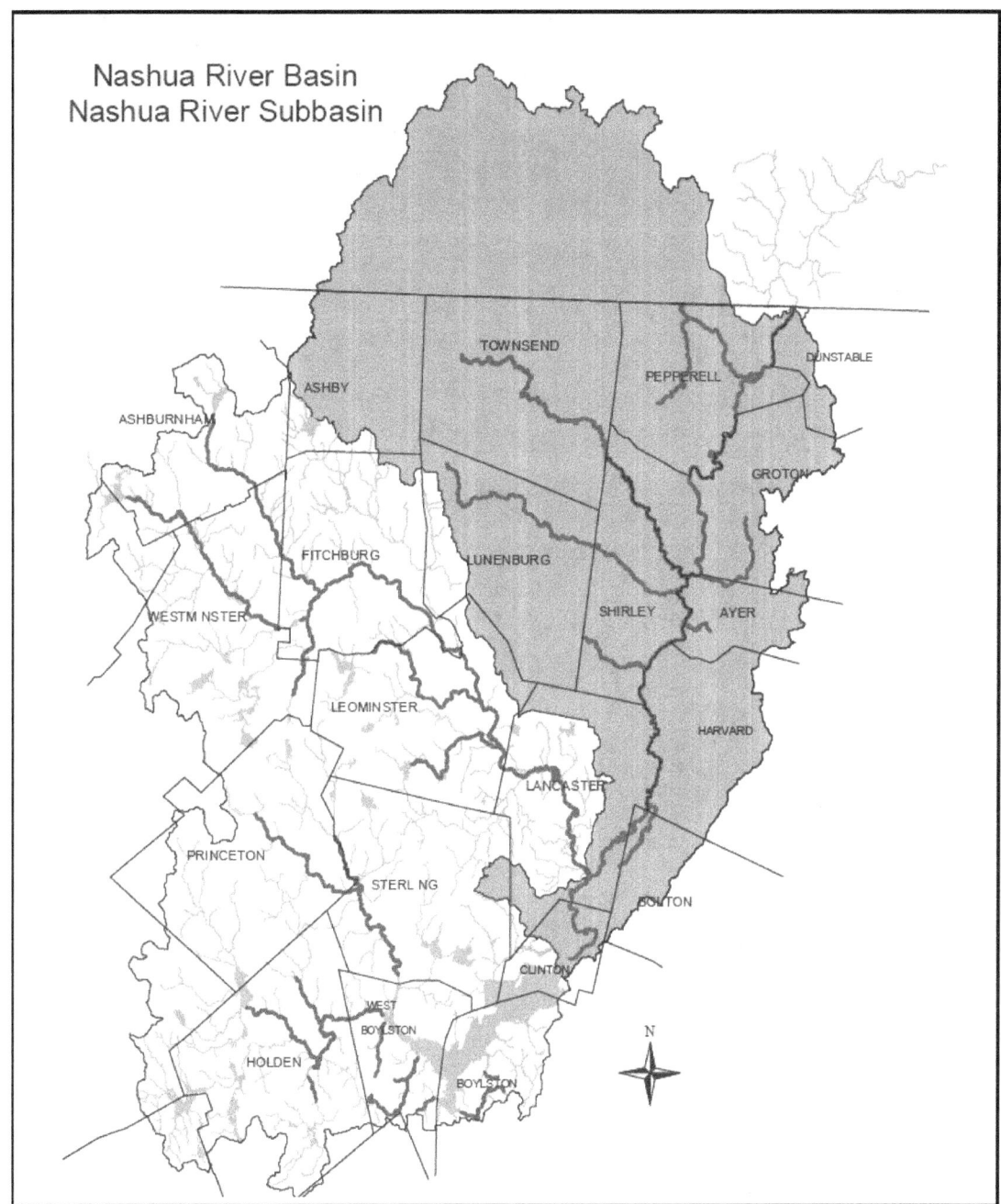

Figure 11. Mainstem Nashua River Subbasin.

NASHUA RIVER (SEGMENT MA81-05)

Location: Confluence with North Nashua River, Lancaster to confluence with Squannacook River, Shirley/Groton/Ayer.
Segment Length: 13.5 miles.
Classification: Class B, Warm Water Fishery.

Land-use estimates for the subwatershed (map inset, gray shaded area):

Forest	63%
Residential	13%
Agriculture	7%

NRWA conducted water quality monitoring in 1996 at five stations and one station in 1997 on this segment of the Nashua River. Fecal coliform bacteria, pH or DO samples were collected on multiple occasions during 1996 (NRWA 1997 and 11 January 2000).

WITHDRAWALS AND DISCHARGES

NPDES:
MA0033824 MCI Shirley. The facility was discharging to the mainstem Nashua River during the 1998 survey. MCI Shirley began its connection to the Devens WWTP in August 1998 and completed its connection in January 1999 (Kimball 2000).

MA0100013 Ayer is permitted (permit issued July 2000) to discharge treated effluent via outfall #001 to the Nashua River. The facility's permitted average monthly flow is 1.79 MGD. The permit limit for whole effluent toxicity is $LC_{50} \geq 100\%$. In August 1998 EPA conducted a compliance inspection of this facility. They noted that the total phosphorus concentration in the Ayer effluent was 25.8 mg/L (Kundarauskas 1998). The recently issued permit includes an average monthly TP limit of 1.0 mg/L. Ammonia nitrogen concentrations ranged between BDL and 11.6 mg/L while TRC ranged from BDL to 0.32 mg/L (TOXTD database).

USE ASSESSMENT

AQUATIC LIFE
Biology

The 1998 DWM RBP III survey was conducted downstream from McPhearson Road railroad bridge, Ayer/Shirley (station NM23B, Appendix C). This sampling station was located at the downstream end of this segment. The benthic macroinvertebrate data were found to be 48% comparable to the regional reference station (SL00) which is located on the Stillwater River (sampled upstream from Crowley Rod, West Boylston). This degree of comparability indicates moderate impairment.

The DWM phytoplankton sample analysis revealed the presence of some *Ulothix* sp. as well as a lot of bacteria (Appendix D). Sewage fungus was found at Ice House Dam Pond along with *Euglena* sp. and *Scenedesmus* sp. These genera are commonly found in areas of organic enrichment. Some fibers that looked like paper waste were also present in the sample.

Habitat and flow

Flow was measured by DWM at two stations (NM21, and NM25) between May and October 1998 (Appendix B, Table B3). Flow ranged from 36.3 to 92.5 cfs at the upstream station (NM21) and from 74.5 to an estimated high of 349 cfs at NM25.

Toxicity

Ambient

Ayer WWTP collects Nashua River water (where railroad tracks cross the Nashua River at McPhearson Road) for use as dilution water in their whole effluent toxicity tests. Between March 1996 and March 2000, survival of *C. dubia* exposed (48-hour) to the river water was not less than 80%.

Effluent

Ayer WWTP also conducted 16 effluent toxicity tests on *C. dubia* between March 1996 and March 2000. The LC_{50}'s were all $\geq$ 100% effluent.

Sediment

EPA conducted a Nashua River acute sediment toxicity study in the spring of 1999 (McDonald 1999). Four stations were sampled in the segment of the Nashua River (NR1-upstream of railroad bridge, Harvard/Lancaster; NR2-downstream boat landing in the Oxbow National Wildlife Refuge; NR3-upstream of Ice House Dam; NR4-adjacent to Devens abandoned airstrip) on 16 March 1999, soon after ice-out. Eight ten-organism replicate toxicity tests (10-day exposure) were run on both *Hyallela azteca* and, *Chironomus tentans* (Table 6). Artificial sediment was utilized as the control.

Table 6. EPA sediment toxicity data, Nashua River (segment MA81-05).

Station Name	Survival *H. azteca* (average)	Survival *C. tentans* (average)
Control	83%	94%
NR1	75%	78%
NR2	66%	88%
NR3	89%	81%
NR4	98%	71%

Chemistry – water

Dissolved oxygen, temperature, pH, turbidity, suspended solids, ammonia-nitrogen, phosphates, were measured by DWM once per month at four stations (NM21, NM21A, ICEHSEDM, and NM25/A) and on six occasions between May and October 1998 (Appendix B, Table B1). Ayer WWTP collects dilution water for their whole effluent toxicity where railroad tracks cross the Nashua River at McPhearson Road and conducted on 12 occasions. Results from both the DWM survey (Appendix B, Table B5 and B6) and the TOXTD database are summarized below. EPA deployed a YSI 6000 meter between 10 and 13 August 1998 in the Nashua River upstream of the Ice House Dam (MA DEP 1998).

DO

DWM DO readings were $\geq$ 6.3 mg/L and 67% saturation at all four stations, although these data do not represent worse case (pre-dawn) conditions (Appendix B, Table B5). The minimum diurnal DO was 6.1 mg/L (MA DEP 1998).

Temperature

The maximum temperature measured by DWM was 23.5°C (Appendix B, Table B5). NRWA temperature measurements were within the same range as the DWM survey data (NRWA 1997).

pH

Instream pH measurements by DWM ranged from 6.3 to 7.2 SU. Out of the 24 measurements, three were below 6.5 SU representing wet weather conditions. Measurements of pH reported in the Ayer WWTP toxicity testing reports were within the same range as DWM survey data as were the NRWA data (NRWA 1997).

Turbidity
   Laboratory turbidity measurements collected by DWM ranged from 1.6 to 3.1NTU. Hydrolab measurements when taken were higher, ranging from 4 to 12 NTU.

Suspended Solids
   DWM suspended solid concentrations did not exceed 8.8 mg/L. Measurements of suspended solids reported in the Ayer WWTP toxicity testing reports were all BDL with one exception (14 mg/L).

Ammonia-Nitrogen
   DWM suspended ammonia-nitrogen concentrations did not exceed 0.11 mg/ L with the highest concentrations at the most upstream station. Ammonia (as N) from the Ayer WWTP toxicity testing reports ranged between BDL and 0.55 mg/L.

Phosphorus
   DWM total phosphorus concentrations did not exceed 0.25 mg/L. The highest concentrations were at the most upstream station.

Total Residual Chlorine
   The Ayer WWTP toxicity testing reports indicated that TRC was BDL.

Hardness
   DWM hardness measurements ranged from 17 to 62 mg/L. Measurements of hardness reported in the Ayer WWTP toxicity testing reports were in the same range.

Chemistry – sediment
   Sediment quality data were also reported in the EPA sediment toxicity study - spring of 1999 (McDonald 1999). Sediment samples were analyzed for grain size, TOC, simultaneously extracted metals-SEM, acid volatile solids-AVS, cyanide and total metals. When the bulk sediment concentrations were compared to guidance in Persaud *et al.* (1993), no exceedances of the S-EL occurred at stations NR1, NR2 and NR4 although the concentrations of Cd, Cr, Cu, Pb, Zn, and Hg exceeded the L-ELs. At station NR3, however, the concentration of Ni exceeded the L-EL and Cd, Cr, Cu, Pb, Zn, and Hg exceeded their S-ELs. Cyanide was not detected in any of the samples.

   The bioavailability of certain divalent metals is a function of the binding capacity of the sediment. The analysis of SEM-AVS was conducted to evaluate bioavailability and therefore potential toxicity of the sediments. It should be noted that even though station NR3 had the highest divalent metal concentration, it also showed strongly negative values for SEM-AVS, indicating a large binding capacity and low potential for toxicity.

Based on a moderately impacted benthic community, degraded sediment quality, sediment toxicity, and slightly elevated nutrients (phosphorus), the *Aquatic Life Use* in this segment of the Nashua River is assessed as non-support.

PRIMARY CONTACT AND SECONDARY CONTACT
   Fecal coliform bacteria samples were collected by DWM at the same stations and dates as described above with the exception of the ICEHSEDM site (Chemistry-water section). Upstream of the MCI Shirley discharge (stations NM21 and NM21A) fecal coliform bacteria counts were ≤200 cfu/100mL under dry weather sampling conditions. During wet weather sampling, the fecal coliform bacteria counts were higher (maximum of 3,500 cfu/100mL) (Appendix B, Table B7). Samples collected downstream from the Ayer WWTP discharge (NM25/A) ranged from 49 to 2,000 cfu/100mLs, the highest during wet weather, although one dry weather sample exceeded 400 cfu/100mLs (1,200 cfu/100mLs on 22 July 1998). NRWA fecal coliform bacteria levels were generally low (NRWA 1997).

Based on the fecal coliform bacteria data and best professional judgement, both the *Primary* and *Secondary Contact Recreational* uses are assessed as support in the upper 10.6 mile reach of this segment. Aesthetic quality degradation (objectionable turbidity and sewage odors), including and downstream from the Ice House Dam Impoundment, and elevated fecal coliform bacteria counts (dry weather conditions) result in both recreational uses being assessed as non-support in the lower 2.9 mile reach.

AESTHETICS

Observations of the river upstream of the Ice House Dam Impoundment indicated high aesthetic quality. This reach of the mainstem Nashua River includes the Oxbow National Wildlife Refuge. However, the aesthetics quality of the "Ice House Dam impoundment" was described as having objectionable turbidity (Kimball 2000). DWM's habitat assessment also noted a sewage odor and instream turbidity near the McPhearson Road railroad bridge.

Upstream of the Ice House Dam Impoundment the *Aesthetics Use* is assessed as support. Based on the objectionable instream turbidity in the impoundment and turbidity and sewage odors downstream of the impoundment, the *Aesthetics Use* is assessed as non-support for the lower 2.9 mile reach.

Nashua River (MA81-05) Use Summary Table

Designated Uses		Status	Causes		Sources	
			Known	Suspected	Known	Suspected
Aquatic Life		NON-SUPPORT	metals, unknown toxicity, nutrients		municipal point sources, contaminated sediments	
Fish Consumption		NOT ASSESSED				
Primary Contact		SUPPORT 10.6 miles NON-SUPPORT 2.9 miles	pathogens, turbidity, odor		municipal point source, urban runoff	
Secondary Contact		SUPPORT 10.6 miles NON-SUPPORT 2.9 miles	turbidity, odor		municipal point source	
Aesthetics		SUPPORT 10.6 miles NON-SUPPORT 2.9 miles	turbidity, odor		municipal point source	

RECOMMENDATIONS - NASHUA RIVER (MA81-05)

- Identify WMA withdrawals in this segment of the Nashua River's subwatershed. Evaluate compliance with registration and/or permit limits. Determine potential impacts of withdrawals on streamflow/habitat

- Since MCI Shirley connected to the Devens WWTP, fecal coliform bacteria sampling should be conducted in this segment of the Nashua River to reevaluate the status of the *Primary Contact Recreational Use*.

- The Town of Ayer is under enforcement orders to update its wastewater management plan (Kimball 2000). An industrial pretreatment program will be needed because of a number of food processing industries that discharge to the town's WWTF. The town is considering an upgrade of the plant with a groundwater discharge as well as the possibility of regionalization with Devens. The Devens Group has contracted for a new 3.0 MGD WWTF that discharges to the groundwater. The facility will be expandable by an additional 4.0 MGD which will discharge to the Nashua River and will service parts of Shirley (including the MCI facility) and possibly Ayer.

- Continue to monitor nutrient concentrations in this segment of the Nashua River and evaluate NPDES facility's compliance with their effluent TP limit (1.0 mg/L). Evaluate the results of the water quality models and reports being developed for the Nashua River Basin TMDL. Utilize these tools to evaluate present and/or future conditions under different scenarios, the need for additional monitoring (e.g., nutrient, suspended solids) and subsequent control strategies (point source and/or non-point source) (Hartman 2000).

- Because of the evidence of benthic community impairment in the Nashua River, additional monitoring should be conducted to evaluate causes and sources of impairment. This investigation should include biological monitoring (benthic macroinvertebrate and fish), sediment quality characterization (physico/chemical and toxicity testing), instream toxicity testing, fecal coliform bacteria monitoring (wet/dry) and water quality monitoring to include site specific contaminants of concern.

- Work with the NRWA to implement their Future Actions (NRWA 1997).

STILL RIVER (SEGMENT MA81-15)

Location: Headwaters, Lancaster to confluence with Nashua River, Harvard, Leominster
Segment Length: 3.1 miles.
Classification: Class B.

No land-use estimates were available for the Still River subwatershed.

NRWA conducted water quality monitoring in 1996 at one station on this segment of the Still River. Fecal coliform bacteria, pH or DO samples were collected on multiple occasions during 1996 (NRWA 1997).

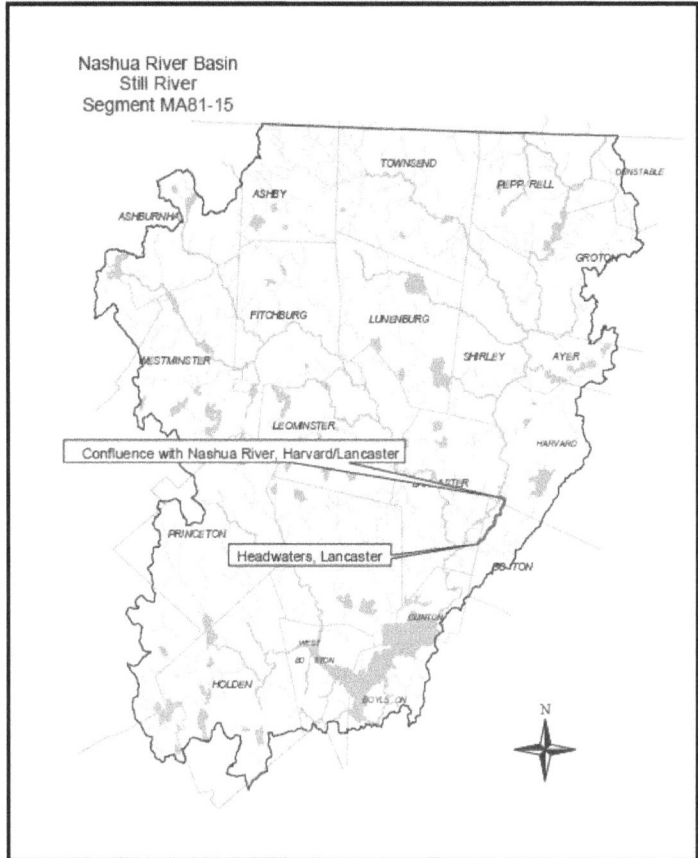

Nashua River Basin
Still River
Segment MA81-15

Confluence with Nashua River, Harvard/Lancaster

Headwaters, Lancaster

USE ASSESSMENT

Not enough quality assured sampling has been conducted and limited current final data/information was available, therefore all uses for Still Brook (Segment MA81-15) are currently not assessed.

Still River (Segment MA81-15) Use Summary Table

Aquatic Life	Fish Consumption	Primary Contact	Secondary Contact	Aesthetics

RECOMMENDATIONS - STILL BROOK (SEGMENT MA81-15)

- Identify WMA withdrawals in the Still Brook subwatershed. Evaluate compliance with registration and/or permit limits. Determine potential impacts of withdrawals on streamflow/habitat

CATACOONAMUG BROOK (SEGMENT MA81-16)

Location: Outlet Lake Shirley, Lunenburg to confluence with Nashua River, Shirley/Ayer.
Segment Length: 2.5 miles.
Classification: Class B.

Land-use estimates for the subwatershed (map inset, gray shaded area):

Forest	54%
Residential	15%
Agriculture	11%

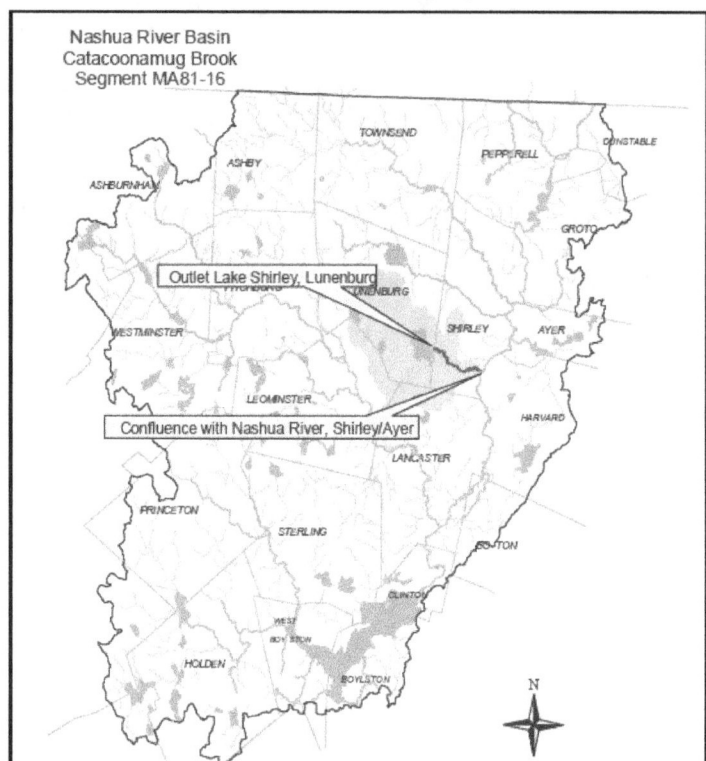

Nashua River Basin
Catacoonamug Brook
Segment MA81-16

A shoreline survey of Catacoonamug Brook from Route 2a to Flat Hills Rd was conducted by the Catacunemaug Brook Stream Team in June 1999. Their shoreline survey indicated that the overall condition of the brook was good. According to the stream team, the brook is a wonderful resource for the town of Lunenburg and provides excellent riparian, wildlife and aquatic habitat. Threats to the brook include, storm drain discharges, road runoff, agricultural practices, and construction activities (Catacunemaug Brook Stream Team 1999).

NRWA conducted water quality monitoring in 1996 and 1997 at five stations on Catacoonamug Brook. Fecal coliform bacteria, pH or DO samples were collected on multiple occasions during both years (NRWA 1997 and 11 January 2000).

WITHDRAWALS AND DISCHARGES
WMA:
The Shirley Water District is permitted (9P221127001) to withdraw 0.3 MGD of groundwater from Catacoonamug and Patterson wells (Appendix F, Table F2). Their actual withdrawals averaged 0.3 MGD in 1998 (Kimball 2000).

USE ASSESSMENT

Not enough quality assured sampling has been conducted and limited current final data/information was available, therefore all uses for Catacoonamug Brook (Segment MA81-16) are currently not assessed.

Catacoonamug Brook (Segment MA81-16) Use Summary Table

Aquatic Life	Fish Consumption	Primary Contact	Secondary Contact	Aesthetics

RECOMMENDATIONS - CATACOONAMUG BROOK (SEGMENT MA81-16)
- Identify other WMA withdrawals in the Catacoonamug Brook subwatershed. Continue to evaluate compliance with registration and/or permit limits. Determine potential impacts of withdrawals on streamflow/habitat.

- Work with the Catacunemaug Brook Stream Team to implement their short/long-term project plans.

NONACOICUS BROOK (SEGMENT MA81-17)

Location: Outlet Plow Shop Pond, Ayer to confluence with Nashua River, Ayer/Shirley.
Segment Length: 1.5 miles.
Classification: Class B.

Land-use estimates for the subwatershed (map inset, gray shaded area):

Forest	50%
Open Land	16%
Residential	15%

NRWA conducted water quality monitoring in 1997 and 1998 at one station each year on this segment of the Nonacoicus Brook. Fecal coliform bacteria, pH or DO samples were collected on multiple occasions during both years (NRWA 11 January 2000).

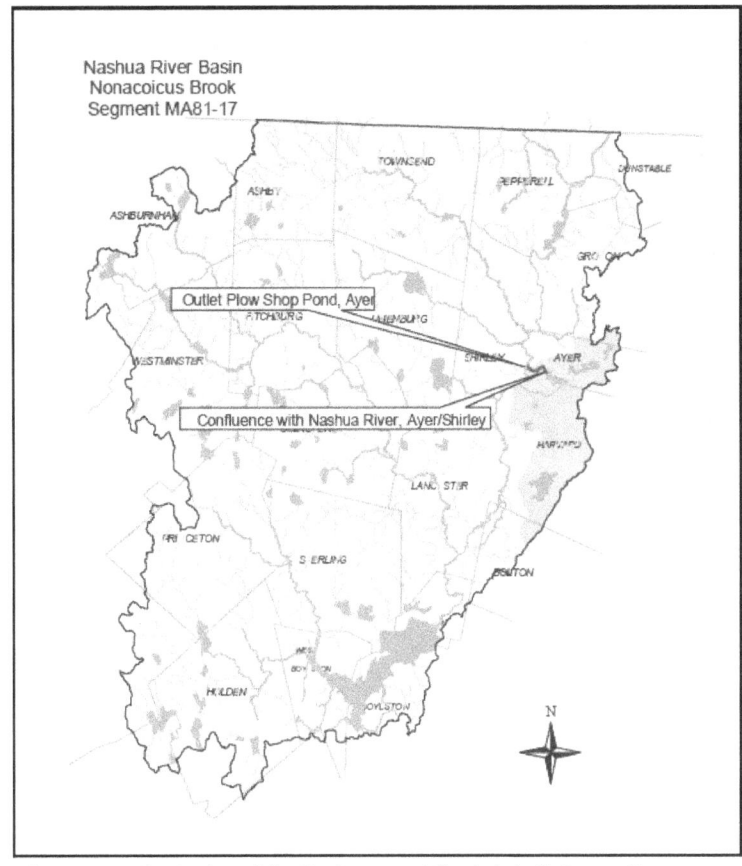

Nashua River Basin
Nonacoicus Brook
Segment MA81-17

Outlet Plow Shop Pond, Ayer

Confluence with Nashua River, Ayer/Shirley

USE ASSESSMENT

Not enough quality assured sampling has been conducted and limited current final data/information was available, therefore all uses for Nonacoicus Brook (Segment MA81-17) are currently not assessed.

Nonacoicus Brook (Segment MA81-17) Use Summary Table

Aquatic Life	Fish Consumption	Primary Contact	Secondary Contact	Aesthetics

RECOMMENDATIONS - NONACOICUS BROOK (SEGMENT MA81-17)

- Identify WMA withdrawals in the Nonacoicus Brook subwatershed. Evaluate compliance with registration and/or permit limits. Determine potential impacts of withdrawals on streamflow/habitat.

MULPUS BROOK (SEGMENT MA81-22)

Location: Headwaters, Lunenburg to confluence with Nashua River, Shirley/Ayer
Segment Length: 11.85 miles.
Classification: Class B.

Land-use estimates for the subwatershed (map inset, gray shaded area):

Forest	68%
Residential	12%
Agriculture	8%

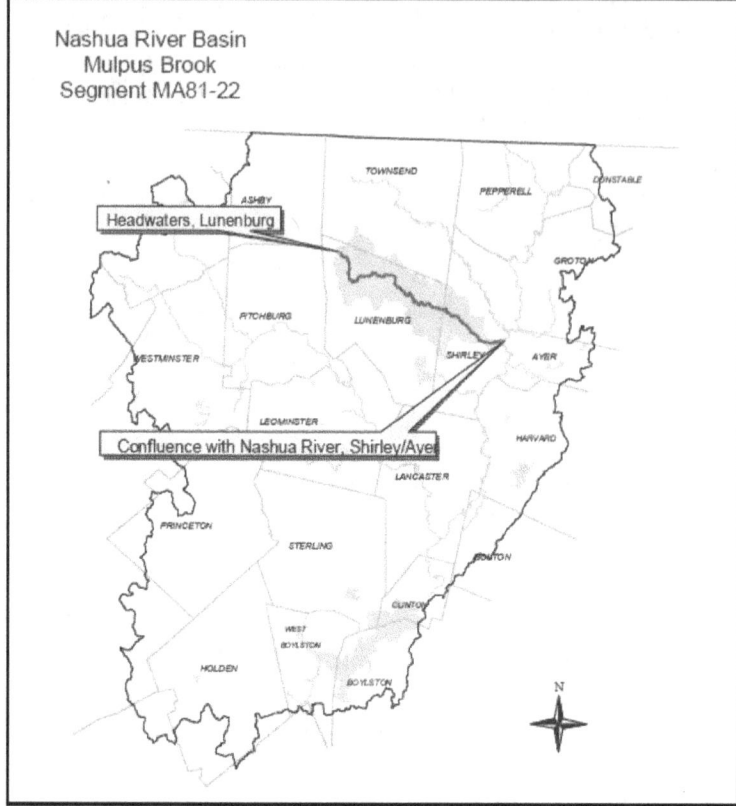

Nashua River Basin
Mulpus Brook
Segment MA81-22

USE ASSESSMENT

No sampling has been conducted and no current data/information was available, therefore all uses for Mulpus Brook (Segment MA81-22) are currently not assessed.

Mulpus Brook (Segment MA81-22) Use Summary Table

Aquatic Life	Fish Consumption	Primary Contact	Secondary Contact	Aesthetics

RECOMMENDATIONS - MULPUS BROOK (SEGMENT MA81-22)
- Identify WMA withdrawals in the Mulpus Brook subwatershed. Evaluate compliance with registration and/or permit limits. Determine potential impacts of withdrawals on streamflow/habitat.